PRAISE FOR *POLICING BLACK LIVES:*

"Robyn Maynard's meticulously-researched and compelling analysis of state violence challenges prevailing narratives of Canadian multiculturalism and inclusion by examining how structures of racism and ideologies of gender are complexly anchored in global histories of colonization and slavery. This book should be read not only by those who have a specific interest in Canadian histories and social justice movements but by anyone interested in the abolitionist and revolutionary potential of the Black Lives Matters movement more broadly."

— Angela Y. Davis, Distinguished Professor Emerita in the History of
Consciousness and Feminist Studies, University of California, Santa Cruz

"In this eye-opening and timely book, Robyn Maynard deftly and conclusively pulls back the veil on anti-Black racism in Canada, exploding the myth of multiculturalism through an emphatically and unapologetically intersectional lens. In compelling and accessible prose, Maynard provides a sweeping overview of Canadian state violence from colonial times to the present, seamlessly articulating the relationship - and distinctions - between settler colonialism and anti-Blackness, and centering Black women, trans and gender nonconforming people within the broader narrative. Through an analysis squarely situated in the global socioeconomic context, *Policing Black Lives* explores parallels between state violence in Canada and its neighbor to the South, as well as the unique legal, social and historical forces informing criminalization through segregation, surveillance, "stop and frisk"/carding/street checks, the war on drugs, gang policing, the school to prison pipeline, welfare "fraud" and child welfare enforcement, and the conflation of immigration and criminality. The result is both eye-opening and chilling, firmly pointing to shared fronts of struggle across borders. *Policing Black Lives* is a critical read for all in Canada and the United States who #SayHerName and assert that #BlackLivesMatter, and essential to movements for Black liberation on Turtle Island."

— Andrea J. Ritchie, author *Invisible No More:*
Police Violence Against Black Women and Women of Color

"A crucial work in chronicling Black experiences in Canada. If you only read one book this year, make it this one. *Policing Black Lives* is a comprehensive and necessary book for anyone who cares about the past, present and future of Black life in this country. Brilliant work!"

— Black Lives Matter Toronto

"We are all taught that Canada is a racial haven. Literally given permission to believe that racism doesn't exist in the other America. But Robyn Maynard's *Policing Black Lives* tells us a very different story. One that is hidden and forgotten by a country that prides itself on being progressive, tolerant, and inclusive. If you ever believed Canada would be the country you fled to, Maynard's work will have you think otherwise. Anti-Black racism is a global phenomenon and we must understand its impact in places outside of the U.S. context. Thanks Maynard for opening all of our eyes to a scary history and frightening present for Black Canada."

— Patrisse Cullors-Khan, co-founder of the Black Lives Matter Global Network

"Robyn Maynard has given us a singular, well-researched book on the lived experiences of African Canadians with the police and justice systems throughout Canada. It is an essential primer for Canadians to fully understand why Black people across Canada are asserting that Black Lives really do matter, and why anti-Black racism continues to destroy lives and families."

— Sylvia D. Hamilton, filmmaker, writer and professor of journalism at the University of King's College.

"Black Canadians are over-represented in arrest and incarceration statistics, have a 60% drop-out/push-out rate in high schools in places like Halifax, Toronto, and Montreal; Black children are more likely to be seized by child welfare agencies, and twice as likely than White children to be living below the poverty line. Black Canadians have poorer health outcomes, experience higher rates of diabetes, hypertension, and AIDS/HIV. Disproportionate rates of incarceration (especially for Black men) have been flagged as the causes of several diseases such as AIDS/HIV, Hepatitis B, and numerous mental health issues. Researchers have now named racial violence and trauma as being a leading factor affecting the health and well-being of African Canadians.

The fact of the matter is that in Canada, and the rest of the world, a stringent anti-Blackness is the norm. Robyn Maynard's book is thus timely, urgent, and cogent as it brilliantly elucidates the grotesque anti-Black racist practices coming from the state, and other institutions imbued with power over Black people's lives.

In naming this great offence, and in speaking truth to power, Maynard's work has the power to mobilize Black people and all persons of conscience to resist, rebel, and revolt against the forces that rob Black people of their dignity, humanity, and their lives."

— Afua Cooper is the James R. Johnston Chair of Black Canadian Studies in the Faculty of Arts and Social Sciences, Dalhousie University.

"Grounded in an impressive and expansive treatment of Black Canadian history, Maynard has written a powerful account of state anti-Black violence in Canada. Empirically rich and theoretically nimble, this work is an outstanding contribution to Black Canadian Studies."

— Barrington Walker, associate professor, history, Queen's University

"Robyn Maynard brilliantly and eloquently shows the multiple ways state violence has targeted, marginalized, and oppressed African-descended men, women, and children in Canada from slavery to the present. She offers powerful lessons for making anti-blackness in Canada legible to activists, scholars, policy makers, and community members committed to building a future nation — and world — free of racism, heteropatriarchy, xenophobia, and exploitation."

— Erik S. McDuffie, author of *Sojourning for Freedom: Black Women, American Communism, and the Making of Black Left Feminism*

POLICING BLACK LIVES

POLICING BLACK LIVES

STATE VIOLENCE IN CANADA FROM SLAVERY TO THE PRESENT

ROBYN MAYNARD

FERNWOOD PUBLISHING

HALIFAX & WINNIPEG

Editing: Fazeela Jiwa
Cover design: Tania Craan
Printed and bound in Canada

Published by Fernwood Publishing
32 Oceanvista Lane, Black Point, Nova Scotia, B0J 1B0
and 748 Broadway Avenue, Winnipeg, Manitoba, R3G 0X3
www.fernwoodpublishing.ca

Fernwood Publishing Company Limited gratefully acknowledges the financial support of the Government of Canada, the Manitoba Department of Culture, Heritage and Tourism under the Manitoba Publishers Marketing Assistance Program and the Province of Manitoba, through the Book Publishing Tax Credit, for our publishing program. We are pleased to work in partnership with the Province of Nova Scotia to develop and promote our creative industries for the benefit of all Nova Scotians. We acknowledge the support of the Canada Council for the Arts, which last year invested $153 million to bring the arts to Canadians throughout the country.

Canada Canada Council Conseil des arts NOVA SCOTIA Manitoba
for the Arts du Canada

Library and Archives Canada Cataloguing in Publication

Maynard, Robyn, 1987–, author
Policing Black lives: state violence in Canada from slavery to the present / Robyn Maynard.
Includes bibliographical references and index.
Issued in print and electronic formats.
ISBN 978-1-55266-979-2 (softcover).—ISBN 978-1-55266-980-8 (EPUB).
—ISBN 978-1-55266-981-5 (Kindle).

1. Blacks—Canada—History. 2. Blacks—Canada—Social conditions.
3. Race discrimination—Canada—History. 4. Canada—Race relations—History. I. Title.

FC106.B6M39 2017
305.896'071
C2017-903099-X
C2017-903100-7

Contents

Acknowledgements

WRITING *POLICING BLACK LIVES* WAS A community affair — born out of move-ment work, it is geared toward nourishing those same movements that have given me life over the last years. The book could not have been completed if I had not been able to lean on those friends, family and community organizers that I'm lucky enough to have around me. Most of the writing of what became this book was accomplished during the first two years of my son's life. Because getting anything done with a small child takes an enormous amount of work, I extend my sincerest gratitude to my loving and generous partner, Brennan Luchsinger, and to Leta and Jay Luchsinger for caring for their grandson when I required time, outside of Lamar's naps, for reflection and writing.

I will be forever indebted to Ted Rutland for his dedication to supporting me throughout the revision process and, in particular, for attentively reading the manuscript and helping me clarify and organize my thoughts. Rachel Zellars and Délice Mugabo provided detailed and nuanced support for several parts of the book. Rachel's in-depth knowledge of slavery in Canada was invaluable to the development of the first chapter and helped to shape the framework for the entire work. I extend my thanks, as well, for the thorough feedback of Nora Butler Burke, Liam Michaud and Graham Latham on earlier versions of various chapters. My anonymous reviewers contributed enormously toward the development of the ideas and arguments presented in this work. Additionally, Harsha Walia and Syed Hussan generously shared their body of knowledge on Canadian immigration policy. The careful reading of Rochelle Ross was a lifesaver at the end of revisions and, along with Frédérique Chabot, she was of enormous assistance during the proofing of my first draft, as well as Juniper Belshaw, Hannah Harris-Sutro and Asam Ahmad. Any omissions or errors, however, are solely my responsibility.

I have a disability which affects the use of my arms, so many practical aspects of this book could not have come together in a timely way without the gener-osity of Nora Butler Burke and Graham Latham, who assisted with practical writing support, helped me figure out dictation software and supported me with day-to-day physical tasks that allowed me to find time to get writing done. As well, Fred Burrill, Chris Dixon, Jaggi Singh, Macho Philpovic, Shirene Eslami, Chloe Menetrier, Tyler Megarry, Kerre King, Derek Broad, LeRoi Newbold, Anna Mathen, Judy Grant, Anna Leventhal and Anita Shoepp have provided support, for which I will always be grateful. As well, I am greatly indebted to the patience of my editor, Candida Hadley, through numerous delays in the creation of earlier incarnations of this project. I thank Angela Y. Davis, Erik McDuffie, Barrington Walker, Sylvia Hamilton, Afua Cooper, Patrisse Cullors-Khan, BLM-TO and Andrea J. Ritchie for generously providing blurbs for the book.

The ideas found in the following pages of this book are not solely my own, but are deeply inspired by the Black creative, political and intellectual movements of our time. I have been lucky to organize against anti-Black racism and police violence in Montréal alongside my sisters Marlihan Lopez, Nydia Dauphin, Gabriella Kinté and many other fierce Black feminists who have greatly inspired me to both keep writing and keep fighting. More broadly, I must extend my gratitude to Patrisse Cullors-Khan, Opal Tometi and Alicia Garza, the founders of Black Lives Matter, for starting both a hashtag and the movement that changed my life. Similarly, I am deeply indebted to the unapologetic words and actions of Black Lives Matter Toronto for putting their bodies on the line for queer Black folks everywhere and helping to make space for a widening framework of racial and gendered oppression across these lands.

Finally, I'd like to extend love and gratitude to my mother, father and sister — Noreen, Frank and Victoria Maynard — for the years of love and support.

ON STATE VIOLENCE
AND BLACK LIVES

> African Canadians have always been in a relationship of social subordination in dealing with the state. It is irrelevant whether the relationship is with the government, the judicial system, the education or social-welfare systems, or any other state-controlled or state-influenced institution. (Carty 1999: 197)

BEFORE THIS BOOK WAS A COHESIVE idea, it was germinating in my mind for years. I've spent much of the last decade doing paid and unpaid outreach, advocacy and organizing work with marginalized and criminalized people. Working with racialized youth in state care and in street-based economies, as well as with adult street-based sex workers, I have been constantly and painfully aware of the gross racial and economic injustices at the fault lines of Canadian society. Though I have not worked exclusively with Black communities, I've regularly witnessed enormous and disproportionate levels of what can only be called state-sanctioned violence and concerted neglect of Black people.

I remember speaking with a Black teenager who was being regularly followed and harassed by a police officer on his way home from school. The officer would call his name, sometimes search him for drugs (which were never found) and intimidate and humiliate him. He suffered this abuse largely in silence, as he did not want his parents to be disappointed in him. Another notable memory is the experience shared with me by a Black transgender woman in her fifties or sixties, who had fled violence in her country of origin and did not have Canadian citizenship. To support several family members, she worked as a sex worker. She was frequently harassed and sometimes threatened by the police, who would call her "nigger" and "tranny" while she was working. Because she was afraid of being arrested, deported and separated from her family, she soon began to try to avoid the police by working on streets and alleys in extremely isolated, unlit areas instead of bars frequented by her clients, friends and community — in effect, sacrificing physical safety out of fear of arrest. In addition, I have witnessed the often hostile treatment and heightened surveillance that Black women receive at the hands of their social workers, the suffering felt by both youth and their families when Black children are seized by child welfare and the shame that many Black youth are made to feel by teachers in their schools just because they are Black.

The past few years that I have spent writing this book, I've found myself organizing and attending far too many vigils and marches on the subject of Black death. Bony Jean-Pierre, an unarmed Haitian man in his forties, was killed in Montréal North, shot multiple times with rubber bullets at close range. His death occurred in the context of a drug raid that uncovered cannabis — a substance on the brink of legalization and smoked openly by white citizens across the city — as well as two rocks of crack and assorted paraphernalia (S. Michaud 2016). Later that same year, the police in Ottawa beat to death Abdirahman Abdi, an unarmed Black Somali man living with mental health issues. They had been called in because he was allegedly harassing customers at a coffee shop. However, witnesses saw the police subject him to repeated blows to the face and neck, kneel on his head and then leave him unconscious in a pool of his own blood, handcuffed, without medical attention (Cole 2016b). He died a few days later in the hospital. Further, highly publicized police killings in the United States in recent years, including the police murders of Alton Sterling, Philando Castile, Korryn Gaines and hundreds of other Black men and women, have served as all-too-frequent reminders of both how little value is placed on Black life and the seemingly limitless level of hostility directed at Black individuals and communities.

In combing through the world of research for something that would describe the realities that I was seeing, I realized that there was still far too little literature addressing, in one place, the specificities of how criminal and immigration laws, inequitable access to work and housing and other state policies and institutions interact to shape the conditions of Black life in this country. It has become increasingly clear that none of these incidents are isolated; they are part of a larger pattern of the devaluation of Black life across Canada.

I felt compelled to write this book because anti-Blackness, particularly anti-Blackness at the hands of the state, is widely ignored by most Canadians. This book is intended to be a humble addition to a wealth of brilliant, if under-recognized, Black Canadian scholarship from both inside and outside the academy that has meticulously intervened in Canada's national mythology of benevolence and tolerance: Agnes Calliste, Barrington Walker, Charmaine A. Nelson, Rachel Zellars, Afua Cooper, Dionne Brand, Esmerelda Thornhill, Rinaldo Walcott, Cecil Foster, El Jones, Desmond Cole, Katherine McKittrick, Awad Ibrahim, Grace-Edward Galabuzi, George J. Sefa Dei, Tamari Kitossa, Wanda Thomas Bernard, Malinda Smith, Njoke Wane, Akua Benjamin, Carl James, Délice Mugabo, Akwasi Owusu-Bempah, Makeda Silvera, Dorothy Williams, Harvey Amani Whitfield, Sylvia Hamilton, Linda Carty, Adrienne Shadd, Peggy Bristow, Anthony Morgan, the African Canadian Legal Clinic and others whom I am surely missing.

Despite the brilliant work of the Black scholars cited above, state violence against Black persons in Canada has, by and large, remained insulated by a wall of silence and gone largely unrecognized by much of the public, outside of brief media flashpoints. Anti-Blackness in Canada often goes unspoken. When acknowledged, it is assumed to exist, perhaps, but in another time (centuries ago), or in another place (the United States). Many Canadians are attuned to the growing discontent surrounding racial relations across the United States, but distance themselves from the realities surrounding racial disparities at home. Most know, for example, the names Trayvon Martin and Michael Brown as victims of anti-Black police violence, but could not name those Black Canadians cited above or recite the names of Andrew Loku, Jermaine Carby or Quilem Registre.[1] A generalized erasure of the Black experience in Canada from the public realm, including primary, secondary and post-secondary education, combined with a Canadian proclivity for ignoring racial disparities, continues to affect mainstream perceptions of Black realities throughout the nation. In addition, unlike in the United States, systematic collection of publicly available race-based data is rare at the national, provincial or municipal level and at most universities. Together, these factors have led to a discernable lack of awareness surrounding the widespread anti-Blackness that continues to hide in plain sight, obscured behind a nominal commitment to liberalism, multiculturalism and equality. My goal in the writing of this book is to make anti-Blackness, as it has evolved in Canada, legible for activists, policymakers, students and concerned community members.

Anti-Blackness has not always been obscured. During the period of slavery, many slave owners demonstrated no shame in owning Black and Indigenous people as property. For instance, throughout the eighteenth century, it was common for slave owners to place their names on runaway slave notices in

Canada. After slavery's abolition in 1834, though, anti-Black racism in Canada has been continually reconfigured to adhere to national myths of racial toler-ance. By 1865, textbooks bore little allusion to any Black presence in Canada, erased two centuries of slavery, included no mention of segregated schools (an ongoing practice at the time) and alluded to the issue of racial discord only in the United States (Winks 1997: 363). During much of the first half of the twentieth century, despite segregated schooling in many provinces, discrimina-tion in employment and housing and significant Ku Klux Klan membership, Canadian newspapers and politicians nonetheless continuously framed the so-called "Negro problem" as an American issue (Mathieu 2010). The exist-ence of anti-Blackness remains widely unspeakable in many avenues to this day. For instance, in 2016, shortly following the above-mentioned police killing of Abdirahman Abdi, Matt Skof, the president of the Ottawa Police Association, told the press that it was "unfortunate" and that he was "worried" that Canadians would assume race could play a factor in Canadian policing, arguing that those issues were only pertinent in United States (Nease 2016). The long history of anti-Blackness in Canada has, for the most part, occurred alongside the disa-vowal of its existence. Black individuals and communities remain "an absented presence always under erasure" (Walcott 2003: 27).

Canada, in the eyes of many of its citizens, as well as those living elsewhere, is imagined as a beacon of tolerance and diversity. Seen as an exemplar of human rights, Canada's national and international reputation rests, in part, on its historical role as the safe haven for the enslaved Black Americans who had fled the United States through the Underground Railroad. Today, it is well known, locally and internationally, as the land of multiculturalism and relative racial harmony.

Invisibility, however, has not protected Black communities in Canada. For centuries, Black lives in Canada have been exposed to a structural violence that has been tacitly or explicitly condoned by multiple state or state-funded institutions. Few who do not study Black Canadian history are aware that dominant narratives linking crime and Blackness date back at least to the era of the transatlantic slave trade, and that Black persons were disproportionately subject to arrest for violence, drugs and prostitution-related offences through-out Canada as early as the nineteenth and early twentieth centuries. The history of nearly a hundred years of separate and unequal schooling in many provinces (separating Black from white students), which lasted until 1983, is not taught to Canadian youth (Hamilton 2011). A history that goes unacknowledged is too often a history that is doomed to be repeated.

The structural conditions affecting Black communities in the present go similarly under-recognized. In 2016, to little media fanfare, the United Nations' Committee on Economic, Social and Cultural Rights (CESCR) confirmed that anti-Black racism in Canada is systemic. The committee highlighted enormous racial inequities with respect to income, housing, child welfare rates, access to quality education and healthcare and the application of drug laws (U.N. CESCR 2016). Many Canadians do not know that, despite being around 3 percent of the Canadian population, Black persons in some parts of the country make up around one-third of those killed by police (Wortley 2006). It is not yet common knowledge that African Canadians are incarcerated in federal prisons at a rate three times higher than the number of Blacks in the Canadian population, a rate comparable to the United States and the United Kingdom (Owusu-Bempah and Wortley 2014). Fewer still are aware that that in many provincial jails, the rate is even more disproportionate than it is at the federal level (Owusu-Bempah and Wortley 2014).

In addition to being more heavily targeted for arrest, because so much of Canada's Black population was born elsewhere, significant numbers of those eventually released will be punished again by deportation to countries they sometimes barely know, often for minor offences that frequently go unpunished when committed by whites (Sapers 2013; African Canadian Legal Clinic [ACLC] 2001; ACLC n.d.). Black migrants, too, are disproportionately affected by punitive immigration policies like immigration detention and deportation, in part due to the heightened surveillance of Black migrant communities (Barnes 2002; Burt et al. 2016). Black children and youth are vastly over-represented in state and foster care (Pon, Gosine and Phillips 2011), and are far more likely to be expelled or pushed out of high schools across the country (Rankin and Contenta 2009a; Commission des droits de la personne et des droits de la jeunesse [CDPDJ] 2011). Black communities are, after Indigenous communities, among the poorest racial groups in Canada (ACLC n.d.). These facts, along with their history and context, point to an untold story of Black subjection in Canada.

Though anti-Blackness permeates all aspects of Canadian society, *Policing Black Lives* focuses primarily on state or state-sanctioned violence (though, at times, this is complemented with an enlarged scope in instances when anti-Black state practices were buttressed by populist hostility, the media or civil society). The reason for this focus is simple: the state possesses an enormous, unparalleled level of power and authority over the lives of its subjects. State agencies are endowed with the power to privilege, punish, confine or expel at will. This book traces the role that the state has played in producing the demonization, dehumanization and subjection of Black life across a multiplicity of institutions. I use the word "state" throughout this text to include federal and provincial governments, government-funded programs such as schools, social and child services, and the enforcement wings of state institutions such as the municipal, provincial and national police.

The framework of "state violence" throughout this book is used to draw attention to the complex array of harms experienced by marginalized social groups that are caused by government (or government-funded) policies, actions and inaction. This use of the term state violence follows in the traditions of Black feminist activist-intellectuals such as Angela Y. Davis (1998), Joy James (1996), Beth Richie (2012), Andrea Ritchie (2006), Ruth Wilson Gilmore (2007) and others who have contributed enormously to studying anti-Black state violence while also actively organizing against it.

The state is imagined by many to be the protector of its national subjects. But this belief is a fiction — one that can be maintained only if we ignore the enormous harms that have been directly or indirectly caused by state actions. "Valorizing the state as the natural prosecutor of and protector from violence," writes Joy James, "requires ignoring its instrumental role in fomenting racial and sexual violence" (1996: 148). It is more accurate to say that the state protects some at the expense of others. The purpose of state violence is to maintain the order that is "in part defined in terms of particular systems of stratification that determine the distribution of resources and power" (Iadicola and Schupe 2003: 310). In a society like Canada that remains stratified by race, gender, class and citizenship, state violence acts to defend and maintain inequitable social, racial and economic divisions. As such, the victims of this violence have been the dispossessed: primarily but not exclusively people who are Indigenous, Black, of colour, particularly those who are poor, women, lacking Canadian citizenship, living with mental illness or disabilities, sexual minorities and other marginalized populations. Often legally and culturally sanctioned as legitimate, the harms inflicted by state actors are rarely prosecuted as criminal, even when the actions involve extreme violence, theft and loss of life (Ritchie, Mogul and Whitlock 2011). Grave injustices — including slavery, segregation and, more recently, decades of disproportionate police killings of unarmed Black civilians — have all been accomplished within, not outside of, the scope of Canadian law (Kitossa 2016). Not only is state violence rarely prosecuted as criminal, it is not commonly perceived *as violence*. Because the state is granted the moral and legal authority over those who fall under its jurisdiction, it is granted a monopoly over the use of violence in society, so the use of violence is generally seen as legitimate.

When state violence is mentioned, images of police brutality are often the first that come to mind. However, state violence can be administered by other institutions outside of the criminal justice system, including institutions regarded by most as administrative, such as immigration and child welfare departments, social services, schools and medical institutions. These institutions nonetheless expose marginalized persons to social control, surveillance and punishment, or what Canadian criminologist Gillian Balfour calls "non-legal forms of governmentality" (2006: 170). These bureaucratic agencies, too, have the repressive powers generally presumed to belong only to law enforcement. They can police — that is, surveil, confine, control and punish — the behaviour of state subjects. Policing, indeed, describes not only cops on their beat, but also the past and present surveillance of Black women by social assistance agents, the over-disciplining and racially targeted expulsion of Black children and youth in schools, and the acute surveillance and detention of Black migrants by border control agencies. Many poor Black mothers, for example, have experienced child welfare agents entering and searching their homes with neither warrant nor warning — in some instances seizing their children — as a result of an anonymous phone call. Further, state violence can occur without an individual directly harming or even interacting with another. It can be, in short, structured into societal institutions (Galtung 1969).

This expansive understanding of state violence allows us, throughout the following chapters, to examine the seemingly disconnected state and state-funded institutions that continue to act, in concert, to cause Black suffering and subjugation. State violence is not evenly distributed across populations, but deeply infused along the lines of race, class and gender. These factors play a significant role in the likelihood of one's exposure to either direct or structural forms of state violence. State violence has historically impacted and targeted different groups of people throughout history to different degrees, according to shifting notions of race, ethnicity, class and ability — or willingness to subscribe to social norms. In the present, it continues to impact differently marginalized groups of individuals. But it is not arbitrary that Black communities are subject to state violence at such disproportionate rates. Black subjection in Canada cannot be fully understood, and therefore cannot be fully redressed or countered, without placing it in its historical context. The endemic anti-Blackness found within state agencies has global and historical roots and can be traced back to the transatlantic slave trade.

RACE AND RACIAL SUBJUGATION

Blackness, like all racial categories, is not a biological fact but has been historically and socially constructed (Haney-Lopez 1994). Across time, the meanings assigned to race have shifted. Cedric Robinson (1983) shows that the use of constructed categories of race — and varying levels of worth assigned these races — existed in ancient Europe within its own boundaries long before the creation of Blackness. Blackness, he argues, was invented by Europeans at the advent of the transatlantic slave trade. To create "the Negro," meaning, in effect, the African slave, Europeans had to erase and repress the hundreds of years of contact between the ancient West and North Africa, undertaking "immense expenditures of psychic and intellectual energies" (1983: 3). The construction of the African as a subhuman and bestial life form justified the commodification of Black life and labour that would enrich the nations of Europe for centuries to come (Wynter 2003). Subsequently, Black life was reduced to "dumb, animal labor, the benighted recipient of the benefits of slavery" (Robinson 1983: 4).

During the transatlantic slave trade, Black men, women and children were thought not to be full human beings but interchangeable commodities (Hartman 1997: 21). Enslaved Black people were seen as lacking sentience, possessing a limited ability to feel pain and were represented as animalistic, hypersexual and dangerous (Hartman 1997; James 1996). In recent decades, writers including Saidiya Hartman (1997), Rinaldo Walcott (2014), Lewis R. Gordon (1995 and 1997) and Sylvia Wynter (2003) have documented how, despite the abolition of the slave trade worldwide, the transition from slavery to freedom did not substantially change the meanings that had become inextricably associated with Blackness. Those marked as Black — a category demarcated by anatomical and physiological attributes, as well as skin colour and hair — were not seen as individual human beings. In *Black Skin, White Masks,* Frantz Fanon states that people with African features had their very existence reduced to pathology, assigned the same meaning across the colonial and slave-holding world. He writes, "I am given no chance. I am overdetermined from without. I am the slave not of the 'idea' that others have of me but of my own appearance" (2008: 87).

Long after the formal emancipation of enslaved Black populations and the formal decolonization of the Global South, anti-Blackness remains a global condition and continues to have enormous impacts on Black individuals and communities. It is "our existence as human beings," writes Rinaldo Walcott, that "remains constantly in question and mostly outside the category *of a life*" (2014: 93, emphasis in original). Despite the end of slavery as a legal form of controlling Black movement and curtailing Black freedom, the enduring association of Blackness with danger and criminality was further consolidated, and new forms of policing Black people's lives emerged. Under slavery, the policing of everyday Black life was the standard. "[A] violent regulation of black mobilities" was required for slave owners to maintain the institution (S. Browne 2015: 53). Emancipation required new, or at least modified, expressions of racial logics; people designated Black have been homogenously rendered as menacing across much of the world, and surveilled and policed accordingly.

Throughout the late nineteenth and early twentieth centuries, criminality, danger and deviance became more fully assigned to Blackness. In the United States, almost immediately after emancipation, newly freed Black men and women were targeted with arrest, imprisoned and forced to perform free labour under the jurisdiction of the Thirteenth Amendment (Davis 2003; Haley 2016). In the mid-twentieth century, Frantz Fanon demonstrated how shared beliefs about the criminal proclivities of Black peoples existed throughout the French Empire, the Southern United States, South Africa and West Africa (2008: 82–88). In 1970s Britain, Black cultural theorist Stuart Hall critiqued the links between Blackness and violence in the panic surrounding "young Black muggers" that resulted in a significant increase in law enforcement agencies policing Black communities in Britain (Hall et al. 2013). Today, Black men and women in the United States remain unduly targeted by criminal justice, in a system of mass incarceration unknown throughout much of the world (Alexander 2012; Davis 2003). In other parts of the world where chattel slavery flourished, such as Brazil, racial profiling and Black incarceration is also endemic (Alves and Vargas 2015).

Given the "global anti-Black condition" (Walcott 2014: 93), it should come as no surprise that the associations between Blackness, crime and danger continue to have enormous power in Canada nearly two centuries after the British abolished slavery in all their colonies. Black and white Canadians appear to commit relatively equal levels of most crimes, yet the Black population, viewed as dangerous, continues to bear the burden of the "criminal" stigma. Canadian politicians, police and newspapers have, for centuries, linked Blackness or Black "cultures" to criminality and danger. They have been treated as menaces to be kept out, locked up or removed. From ordinances attempting to ban Blacks from Canadian cities in 1911 (Shepard 1997) and the discovery that the Montréal police used pictures of young Black men as targets for their shooting practice throughout the 1980s (Henry and Tator 2006: 78) to the targeted deportation of nearly a thousand Jamaicans in the mid- to late-1990s (Barnes 2002), the encoding of Black persons as criminal, dangerous and unwanted holds enormous power across Canadian institutions.

Black subjection has changed forms in important ways in a society that purports to be colourblind. Today, the denigration of Blackness is sometimes difficult to pinpoint. Explicit hatred of Black persons, for example the use of a racial epithet or a violent hate crime, is no longer culturally acceptable. Most Canadians of any political persuasion would largely reject any politic based on open hatred, and would be unlikely to support an open call to bring back "whites only" immigration policies or to re-segregate education and ban Black youth from schools. This form of racism — while being reinvigorated in some segments of society amid an upswing of white supremacist movements — has largely fallen out of mainstream political favour in an era where formal equality prevails in Canadian law (Fleras 2014).

Liberal democracies like Canada continue to practise significant racial discrimination, yet they now do so while proclaiming a formal commitment to equality. It is, after all, "the wedding of equality and exclusion in the liberal state" that distinguishes modern state racism from the previous forms of racism found under slavery (Hartman 1997: 10). Racism has merely become more difficult to both detect and contest. While many Black people in twenty-first century Canada officially have rights equal to those of other national subjects, "official" equality means little when it is the state that is both perpetrating and neglecting to act in the face of racial subjugation, neglect and other forms of violence.

Because many forms of *overt* racism are not tolerated, state-sanctioned violence relies on the blameworthiness of those whom it harms. Anti-Blackness, which attaches Blackness to criminality and danger, rationalizes state violence against Black communities because Black people are presumed to be "guilty in advance" — as always and already blameworthy (Gordon 1997: 22). Indeed, state-mandated violence and subjugation are conceived of, often, as rational responses to a threat — the threat of Blackness. Hate speech masquerades as protectionism, and the violence perpetuated upon Canada's Black population, when visible, becomes "justice served." Joy James, Black American racial theorist and activist, reminds us that racism helps to invert our perceptions of who is causing harm and who is on its receiving end. She observes, "Anti-black racism has played a critical, historical role in rationalizing (and inverting) hierarchies of oppressor and oppressed" (1996: 27). Though anti-Black racism has justified centuries of racial violence, with lasting impacts on the dignity, health and well-being of Black peoples, Black communities themselves are blamed for the state violence that they have been continually subjected to.

The state violence that targets Black populations makes visible that Canada's Black population has been excluded from those seen as "national subjects" (Thobani 2007) and denied many of the accompanying protections and rights. Further, Black persons are represented not only as other-than-national subjects, but are constituted historically and presently as a threat to "real" Canadians. Accordingly, state violence against Black communities often takes place in the name of protecting "us" from "them," rendering anti-Blackness and, indeed, Black suffering invisible.

In Canada, then, as elsewhere, the legacy of Black enslavement lives on, and the associations of Blackness with pathology, though modified in some ways, continue to have significant impacts on Black life. To use the words of Black slavery scholar Saidiya Hartman, "Black lives are still imperilled and devalued by a racial calculus and a political arithmetic that were entrenched centuries ago" (2007: 6). To be Black in Canada is to live in slavery's "afterlife" and to have one's existence demarcated by "skewed life chances, limited access to health and education, premature death, incarceration, and impoverishment" (2007: 6). *Policing Black Lives* traces the role of the state in slavery and its afterlives, following the intensive policing of Black life in Canada that originated on slave ships and persists into the present, spanning the criminal justice, immigration, education, social service and child welfare systems.

Though *Policing Black Lives* tells the story of anti-Blackness in Canada, any study of institutional anti-Blackness must necessarily be informed by the reality that Canada is a settler colony founded on colonization and genocide. In settler colonies like Canada and the United States, Black and Indigenous oppression are historically and currently connected. Indeed, recent writings by Black and Indigenous studies scholar Tiffany King (2013, 2014) argue that we cannot truly understand the conditions of Black life in settler societies without examining the relationship of anti-Blackness and slavery to settler colonialism and genocide. These were not, she argues, isolated historical processes. Instead, there was a relationship between the genocidal settlement project that tried to annihilate Indigenous peoples and take their land and the brutal logics of enslavement that attempted to reduce Black men, women and children into non-human things (King 2013; Sium 2013).

Though there is a relationship, the racial logic of slavery and settler colonialism take different forms and are not reducible to one another; anti-Blackness and settler colonialism rest on somewhat different foundations. Indigenous peoples are seen as "in the way," and laws and policies are used toward destroying Indigenous communities to secure unfettered access to Indigenous land (Sium

2013; Tuck and Yang 2012: 6; see also Wolfe 2007). The overarching goal of white settler colonialism is to eradicate Indigenous peoples, either through assimilation or genocide — to turn them into "ghosts" (Tuck and Yang 2012: 6). The reserve system, the imposition of residential schools intended to "kill the Indian in the child," forced sterilization of Indigenous women, ongoing resource extraction and pipelines extending across Indigenous territory are only a few examples that demonstrate a unique logic of genocide and theft targeting Indigenous peoples (Palmater 2011). Contrastingly, in the logic of Black enslavement, it is Black *personhood* that is under attack: "the slave" is a useful commodity, but "the person underneath is imprisonable, punishable, and murderable" (Tuck and Yang 2012: 6). By the logic of slave societies, Black chattel are things, but Black *people* are "monsters" (Tuck and Yang 2012: 6). Despite differing racial logics, the living legacy of slavery and the ongoing practice of settler colonialism at times result in similar forms of repression. Black and Indigenous peoples experience grossly disproportionate incarceration, susceptibility to police violence, poverty and targeted child welfare removal.

We create an incomplete history of anti-Blackness without addressing settler colonialism; acknowledging the relationship between Black and Indigenous oppression is of fundamental importance in any intellectual or political movement geared toward racial justice. Due to scope, *Policing Black Lives* does not undertake a comprehensive analysis of the relationship between settler colonialism and slavery/anti-Blackness. Where relevant, though, I attempt to draw parallels or distinctions between the ways that state violence has targeted both Indigenous and Black peoples. The examples I provide are not exhaustive and should not stand in for the important work of Indigenous scholars and activists such as Sarah Hunt, Cindy Blackstock, Colleen Cardinal, Bridget Tolley, Lee Maracle, Leanne Betasamosake Simpson, Pamela Palmater, Eve Tuck, Naomi Sayers, Emma LaRocque, Chelsea Vowel, Bonita Lawrence, Arthur Manuel, Audra Simpson, Howard Adams and Lina Sunseri, to name only a few.

IN DEFENCE OF ALL BLACK LIVES

All Black people are not demonized equally or identically. Gender, sexual orientation, (dis)ability, mental health and place of birth also mediate the way that anti-Blackness is experienced. Black feminist scholarship and activism has forced a necessary re-examination of what and whom we imagine when we speak of violence against the Black body. It is common in discussions surrounding anti-Black racism to focus on the Black male body as the state's primary target. Most literature and research focuses on the means by which young Black heterosexual males have been demonized by popular culture and the criminal justice system. This has frequently allowed state violence against Black individuals who are not young Black men to go unseen and unchallenged. Kimberlé Crenshaw and Andrea J. Ritchie, legal scholars and the authors of *Say Her Name: Resisting Police Brutality Against Black Women* (2015), insist that we expand our gaze to see how the demonization of Black bodies extends to Black women and sexual minorities across the gender spectrum.[2] Though it is obviously important that these pages address how law enforcement interacts with young Black males, it is equally important to make visible, for example, how Black sexual minorities and Black students with disabilities may face particular scrutiny and hostility in schools, or the unique realities faced by Black trans women on city streets. To use the words of Crenshaw and Ritchie: "No analysis of state violence against Black bodies can be complete without including *all Black bodies* within its frame" (2015: 26, emphasis added). To correct past oversights, whenever data is available, particular attention is paid in each of these chapters to Black women, sexual minorities across the gender spectrum and people with disabilities and/or mental illnesses.

Continuing in this direction, a considerable number of Black persons are harassed, arrested, expelled and suspended or placed in state care solely because of their Blackness, despite having committed no crime. Law enforcement violence against an innocent Black woman is an obvious manifestation of racial injustice. Yet, it is my intention that this work also challenges widely held dichotomies of who is innocent/guilty and how this affects our perception of who is undeserving/deserving of state violence or protection. It should not be seen as *less violent* when the police harm a Black youth who is, in technical terms, "criminal," or as *more violent* when the police harm an innocent Black youth with no previous infractions.

Black communities experience significant societal pressure to appeal to white middle-class norms and to defend our communities on the pretext that we, too, are upstanding, law-abiding and virtuous citizens — that this proves us worthy of the human dignity that we are denied. This is called the "politics of respectability" (Alexander 2012: 227). But as Black communities continue to learn, appeals to respectability are insufficient as a long-term strategy because "our very blackness places us all beyond the bounds of respectability" (Roberts 1994: 180–181). Additionally, to focus solely on the protection of those Black folks perceived as good or innocent is to abandon those who have been designated as "bad" by the law or by Euro-Christian morality. This leaves "bad" Black people undefended: those community members stigmatized by real or imagined involvement in illicit economies, those youth or adults who have used or sold illegal drugs, those whose gender presentations or sexualities have been deemed deviant, sex workers, undocumented migrants and incarcerated persons. Stigmatized and rendered disposable, these Black persons are most vulnerable to state abuse, exploitation, confinement and even death with little or no outcry. The horrible conditions experienced by many Black youth in state care, and those who reside in Canada's provincial jails or immigration centres are testaments to this fact. To counter this abandonment, I centre these historically expendable lives in this book whenever possible.

I wish to contribute to a framework for racial justice in which we perceive the injustices levelled at all Black lives. I would like, of course, to value the life of Viola Desmond, known unofficially as "Canada's Rosa Parks," a Black woman of upstanding status who famously refused to sit in the "Blacks only"[3] section of a theatre in Nova Scotia in 1946 and challenged segregation. In addition, I wish to honour the full value of the life of Chevranna Abdi, a Black transgender woman and drug user living with HIV who died in 2003 after being dragged down several flights of stairs, face down, by police officers in Hamilton, Ontario. Even in death, Abdi was ridiculed by the media and ignored by the larger LGBTQI*[4] and Black communities. In short, it is urgent that all Black lives are seen as valuable and all Black suffering is acknowledged.

It is dangerous to fail to recognize the ways that anti-Blackness has shaped, and continues to shape, the contours and possibilities of Black freedom. Yet, we risk presenting narratives of Black dehumanization as totalizing: "at stake is not recognizing anti-Blackness as total climate," but also at stake is "not recognizing an insistent Black visualsonic resistance to that imposition of non/being," explains Christina Sharpe (2016: 21). By insisting on the persistent devaluation of Black life, it is not my intention to eclipse the very real realities of Black refusal, subversion, resistance and creativity that have flourished, despite centuries of systematic hostility and oppression. Though it is not the primary focus of this book, there exist extraordinary histories of resilience, many documented and more still unwritten, that are a testament to a politics of sustained Black cultural, intellectual and spiritual creative practices, despite policies intended to extinguish these acts. These histories span centuries. In 1734, an enslaved Black woman named Marie-Joseph Angélique attempted to flee her white mistress. She faced enormous consequences for her insistence on independence and agency. Accused of burning down Montréal, she was arrested, tortured and publicly hanged (Cooper 2006). In the nineteenth century, hundreds of free Black men and women in Southwest Ontario risked state and populist repression by forming vigilance committees that resisted white American slave catchers' attempts to re-enslave Blacks who had escaped their bondage and had fled to Canada (Bristow 1999: 17). Black communities in the Prairies fought against the impunity granted to the Ku Klux Klan in the early twentieth century (Backhouse 1999). The resilience needed to survive everyday life amid structural and populist violence is not always credited, and there is a tendency to overlook "the subversive tactics of ordinary people" and focus only on the "spectacular feats such as those carried out by freedom fighters, demonstrators, or rioters" (Roberts 1994: 183). Less glorified, but just as significant, are the everyday acts of resilience and survival undertaken by Black individuals faced with institutional racism and deprivation, documented, for example, by Makeda Silvera (1989), Dionne Brand (1991) and Sylvia Hamilton (1999).

Worldwide, we are currently in the midst of a revitalization of Black resistance, and by no means has Canada been exempt. Growing out of and building upon the community organizing traditions in the late 1980s of groups like the Black Action Defence Committee, protests by Black communities have erupted across Canadian cities in recent years.[5] In addition to the everyday bravery of Black survival and care, there has been new life breathed into the Black radical imagination, spurring new forms of activism, art, intellectual work and resistance. This resurgence is taking place not only in the United States, but also in regions less well known for their Black populations, including solidarity actions in Palestine and Black organizing in numerous nations across Latin America.[6] Conversations across Black communities around the world are rendering it clear that anti-Blackness knows no borders: few, if any, places in the world have been untouched by the legacies of European colonization and slavery, or the racist worldviews left in their wake. Contemporary movements for the dignity of Black life are underway throughout the African diaspora, many, but certainly not all, under the banner of #BlackLivesMatter. At the same time, the unique realities of anti-Black racism as it has evolved locally across different regions are also being widely shared and disseminated.

Due to limitations of space and scope, the following pages are not a thorough history of Black activism, and this work does not describe all of the brilliant feats accomplished by Black communities against racial discrimination in Canada. But as a Black activist and writer, I situate myself and my writing within the growing movement that fights for Black lives and against state violence. This book describes, in sometimes painstaking detail, the structural conditions that mandate ongoing Black suffering in Canada, as it is my hope that in recognizing our conditions, we will be better placed to challenge them. For that reason, though this book is for everyone with an interest in Black lives in Canada, it is written most particularly for those who are committed to working toward an affirmation of Black resilience, Black life and Black humanity.

CHAPTER ONE

DEVALUING BLACK LIFE, DEMONIZING BLACK BODIES

Anti-Blackness from slavery to segregation

The more I see of Canada, the more I am convinced of a deep-rooted hatred of the Negro here. (William Wells Brown, American Black activist, after a visit of Canada in 1861 in Yee 1997: 10)

The historical relationship between Black peoples in Canada and "mainstream" society has been one of subordination, which doubtlessly taints a historical record often written by, spoken about and interpreted by those who hold power within the relationship. (Dionne Brand 1991: 31)

ANY BOOK ON THE POLICING OF Black lives must start when the global devaluation of the Black body began: 1444. This year, during which the first African was captured and stolen from African shores by European raiders, marks the beginning of a violent reorganization of the inhabitants of our world and the commencement of large-scale exploitation of Black lives and their labour under the transatlantic slave trade (Cooper 2006). As well, this moment was the beginning of new and lasting meanings that would come to define what it was to be Black. Between 1444 and the 1880s, approximately fifteen million Africans were bound, chained, piled like things and forced to leave the African continent against their will (Rodney 1982; Thompson 1987). Many Africans died while being marched to the West African shores before the sea journey had even begun. The holding trunks that were packed full of captured Africans who had not yet boarded the ships had a mortality rate of over 20 percent. On the Middle Passage, the mortality rate of enslaved Africans on the ships was significant. Rebellion was so "incessant" — in the form of hunger strikes, jumping overboard or attempted insurrection — that the enslaved were chained right hand to right leg, left hand to left leg (James 1989: 8–9). The ships, as described by Black cultural historian C.L.R. James, were sites of abject misery, such that "no place on earth concentrated so much misery as the hold of a slave-ship" (1989: 8). The captured Africans who did survive the journey were sold into slavery. Thus began, as well, the racial logic underpinning slavery that positioned Black peoples' lives and bodies as inferior, usable, disposable chattel, and the institutionalized belief that Black movement itself needed to be carefully controlled and contained. This dehumanization of Blackness enabled the settlement of the lands now called the Americas, in parallel with the large-scale genocide of its Indigenous inhabitants. In 1492, Christopher Columbus's arrival in the Americas ushered in the "new world order," setting the stage for historically unprecedented genocide and ensuing global colonialism that would destroy over 90 percent of Indigenous populations in some areas (many of which, in the Caribbean, would be repopulated with newly enslaved Africans) (Beckles 2013; Wynter 1995). Slavery, pillaging, wealth expropriation and genocide — this barbarism, termed "European civilization," that went global in the late fifteenth century was only the beginning of hundreds of years of state-sanctioned racist violence waged against Black life worldwide, including in Canada.

Slavery was practised in Canada for over two hundred years. Yet, the realities of Canadian slavery and the hostility enacted upon Black populations in Canada are not taught in most Canadian schools. Slavery in Canada is a topic that remains under-taught and under-researched, and there is a telltale absence of Black Studies departments in most Canadian universities (besides one minor concentration in Black and African Diaspora Studies at Dalhousie University, launched in 2016). As such, too few historians have critically addressed the issue of slavery as it existed in Canada, and few Canadians are familiar with this part of their history. When mentioned at all, slavery is often described as benign and short-lived.

It is a myth that enslavement can be benign. The domination and subjugation of one group of humans by another is always predicated on violence, or the threat of violence. This violence is legible in many forms. The act of capture and the means used to initially enslave Black bodies is a foundational violence upon which the ensuing enslavement rests. The process of "holding" a human being in bondage necessitates social and material deprivation, surveillance and corporal punishment (Nelson 2016a). Further, many forms of violence are quite visceral. For example, acclaimed African Nova Scotian historian, poet and filmmaker Sylvia Hamilton tells the story of Lydia Jackson, a young, free Black woman in eighteenth-century Nova Scotia who was captured, enslaved and sold to a master and his wife. Following her capture and enslavement, Jackson was regularly beaten in the head and face with tongs, sticks and ropes; in one instance, she was stomped upon as she lay on the ground, while she was nine months pregnant. This violence was sanctioned by the state — the court rejected her complaint of abuse (1999: 28).

Discussing a similar instance of the torture of a female slave named Hetty (as described in the slave narrative of Mary Prince, an enslaved Black woman in Bermuda), Canadian slavery historian Charmaine A. Nelson points out that the motivation for this form of abuse is clearly not intended to modify behaviour. Rather, the corporal punishment that enslavement relied upon demonstrates that beyond slavery's economic functions, an underlying and virulent dehumanization of Blackness underscored the institution. The torture of both Hetty and Lydia Jackson shows that the practice of slavery embodied not only economic exploitation but also a visceral "hatred of blacks" and the slave owners' "inability to see their slaves as humans," leading to "barbaric punishments that actually damage their own economic interests" (2016c: 106). Yet, even in the absence of explicit, physical violence against the enslaved, the very situation that causes the enslaved to comply with his or her condition, knowing that violence awaits any attempt to change it is itself a continual form of violence, re-enacted at every moment of acquiescence. Enslavement is a form of racial terror based in the attempt toward a total psychological, physical and economic submission of one human being to another (Hartman 1997). Black Canadian legal scholar Esmerelda Thornhill argues that, as a general matter of practice, Black enslaved people in Canada were "objects to be used, misused, abused, enjoyed, damaged or destroyed ... all at the whims of a white owner" (2008: 325).

It is the practice of slavery that set the stage for the subsequent centuries of dehumanization of Black life across Canada. Social amnesia about slavery, as is common in Canada, makes it impossible to understand anti-Black policing in the current epoch. It is only in recovering this original brutality by engaging with the *making* of the perceived relationship between Black bodies, inferiority and pathology that we may more thoroughly understand the contemporary disenfranchisement of Black life through policing and other state institutions.

BLACK BONDAGE

All major European empires — Portuguese, British, French, Spanish and Dutch
...on the brutality of subjugating captured African men, women
...t, there were particular articulations of domination inflicted by
...untry and colony. The practice of slavery itself differed
...s and national custom, as well as geographically
spec... ources, original inhabitants, etc. Cana... n slavery
itself... ace, as pre-1867 Canada was made...
in cha... ns under British and French rule, each of...
a diffe... slavery. Yet, one quality uniting these pracu...
Indige... ould come to be called Canada is that slavery nev...
took t... e large-scale plantations found in the American South, the
Caribbean or South America. Plantations, though their establishment was
desired by some colonists, were found to be incompatible with Canada's climate
and short growing season (Mackey 2010). As a result, the number of enslaved
people in Canada was always lower, and the economy less reliant on slave labour
than other parts of the Americas and the Caribbean. These distinctions have
underpinned the assumption in some existing scholarship that enslavement in
Canada was relatively benign. Yet, the absence of slave plantation economies
does not negate the brutality of the centuries-long, state-supported practice
of slavery. White individuals and white settler society profited from owning
unfree Black (and Indigenous) people and their labour for hundreds of years
while exposing them to physical and psychological brutality, and the inferiority
ascribed to Blackness in this era would affect the treatment of Black persons
living in Canada for centuries to come.

The first non-Indigenous settlements of pre-Confederation Canada began as
the French settler colonies of New France, Île Royale (now Cape Breton Island)
and the Atlantic Provinces. When the first Black enslaved person, Olivier Le
Jeune, landed on the shores of what is now Québec in 1628, Indigenous people, called the "Panis," were already being enslaved by the French (Rushforth
2014). In New France, the buying and selling of Black men, women and children and the non-consensual unpaid labour extracted from approximately four
thousand Indigenous and Black enslaved people helped build infrastructure
and wealth for white settlers during the seventeenth and eighteenth centuries
(Trudel 1960: 137–156). New France's colonists supported slavery for many
reasons: to make up for lagging profits in the fur trade, to try to replicate the
wealth they had seen in the slave economies of the West Indies and as a means
of obtaining free labour for domestic and agricultural work (Rushforth 2014:

138). The holding of enslaved people, already practised for several decades, received official approval on May 1, 1689, when King Louis XIV provided royal assent in response to the petitions of the colonists (Winks 1997: 4–5). Though slavery was not practised in all households, it was nonetheless seen as a normal, natural facet of settler colonial society, spanning wide differences in social class and occupation. Slave ownership was practised in cities and rural areas. Its practitioners included leading gov___ ___nt officials, judges, members of the Executive Council, busin__ ___rds, notaries, doctors, high ranking military officer, ___ ___en hospitals (Trudel 1960: 137–156). As part of th ___ ___rance, it was not uncommon for Black and Indigenous p_ __ _e sold side-by-side with livestock, at slave auctions and in the newspapers (Riddell 1920).

The defining racial logic governing slavery in much of the world at that time held that Indigenous persons were ill-suited for slavery and that the enslavement of Black people was "natural" (Rushforth 2014: 170–179). The plantations of the West Indies, the United States and South America dealt largely, but not exclusively, in enslaved Blacks. In New France, though, Indigenous persons made up two-thirds of the slave population. The settler colonists eagerly embraced the slavery of Indigenous persons as "spoils of war" during their territorial warfare and expansion throughout the continent and largely preferred Indigenous to Black slaves.

Regardless of race, the life conditions of slaves held by the French settlers were markedly inhumane. Iroquois and African "galley slaves" in New France were beaten with chains and rods as a form of punishment or reprisal (Rushforth 2014: 149). Due to their brutal life conditions, many enslaved people died before reaching twenty years of age (Trudel 1960: 160). Like elsewhere in slave-holding societies, sexual violence was a feature of French-controlled slavery. Though little published data on sexual violence in New France exists, Ken Donovan's (2014) research on the French-owned colony of Île Royale found that white slave owners frequently raped and otherwise sexually coerced and exploited their Black female slaves. Enslaved Black women were sexually victimized on Île Royale, he states, as "part of a shared culture of abuse throughout the French Atlantic World" that originated in the slave ships, where rape was a defining feature (Donovan 2014: 148). Black enslaved women, cast throughout the Americas as sexually depraved, were largely considered un-rapeable (Hartman 1997). It was almost inconceivable for white settlers to recognize the rape of a Black woman as rape and deal with it as such, since they were, first and foremost, chattel. Black men, too, were subject to sexual violence under

American slavery (Foster 2011), and likely were not immune to rape and sexual assault under the French and British iterations of enslavement and abuse.

Black Canadian historian, Afua Cooper, expands the analysis of the sexual violence experienced by many enslaved women toward what she calls reproductive violence. Beginning at conception, enslaved women's children were not their own, but the property of their white masters, regardless of paternity (Cooper 2006: 90). Indeed, under slavery even Black women's wombs were not safe from the reach of their white masters or from the violence of being reduced to property. The psychological violence enacted by legally denying the right to one's own infant is enormous and contradicts any suggestion of slavery's benevolence. In Île Royale, slave owners appear to have fathered numerous illegitimate children who would become their slaves (Donovan 2014: 148). The enslavement of these Black children suggests that they were descendants of enslaved women and were therefore likely to be the products of coerced sexual relations in the context of a rigid racial hierarchy. Further demonstrating the reproductive violence of enslavement in New France, Black feminist and slavery scholar Délice Mugabo has found evidence that Black women in New France often gave birth to "mullato" (mixed Black and white) babies, who upon birth were removed from their mothers and sent away (to the "regions"). The mixed ancestry of the babies and the separation of Black women from their children right after birth demonstrates, she says, the intense dehumanization and gendered violence that Black women, children, families and communities were subjected to (Mugabo 2015). Indigenous women were surely not exempt from this practice and were also subject to multiple other forms of sexual and reproductive violence throughout the colonization of the Americas (Smith 2005). The violence of enslavement, then, was not only racialized but also gendered, and the institution at times impacted enslaved Black men and women in different ways.

After France's defeat in the Seven Years War with Britain in 1763, the Treaty of Paris surrendered French control of its Canadian colonies to Britain. For enslaved Black people, this did not signify any liberation. Slave ownership was given official approval by England and all existing owners retained the rights to their human chattel. Additional enslaved Black men, women and children, moreover, were soon brought into the colony. A British and, later, American preference for enslaved Black people over Indigenous ones, along with American-British territorial conflicts, led to multiple influxes of enslaved Black people brought into the pre-Confederate Canadian colonies. As such, the practice of Black enslavement was expanded and consolidated under

British rule. The power of anti-Black racial logic to determine human worth saw a similar consolidation in law as well as in custom. As each wave of Black lives faced their own particular experience of anti-Blackness throughout the eighteenth and nineteenth centuries, the conflation of Blackness with inferiority and danger solidified its hold in the white settler imaginary.

The British, of course, had ample experience with slavery in pre-Confederate Canada prior to the conquest of New France — an experience that included the British colony that was to later become Nova Scotia. Alongside enslavement, land dispossession and brutal violence underwrote much of their policy toward Indigenous peoples. Prior to the 1752 Peace and Friendship Treaty between the British Crown and the Mi'kmaq people, the British waged ongoing military assaults on the Mi'kmaq people of the Atlantic Coast. As well, they traded blankets infected with disease and introduced a scalping policy that spanned decades (Lawrence 2005: 35).

Like in New France, slave owners in eighteenth century Nova Scotia were not only elite settlers but were found in all ranks of white society (Whitfield 2010: 33). Enslaved Black men, women and children were largely forced to perform domestic and agricultural work. Agricultural work was extremely physically arduous. Contesting assertions made by some Canadian slavery scholars that domestic slavery was "mild" as compared to plantation economies, Atlantic Canadian slavery scholar Harvey Amani Whitfield has written that domestic slavery engendered its own dimensions of brutality and involved being on-call twenty-four hours a day and performing gruelling labour (2010: 30). In this era, it was not uncommon for young children to be bought and sold, separately from their parents, for the use of their domestic labour (29–30). Further challenging assumptions that domestic servitude in the British-controlled colonies of New France and Nova Scotia was benign, Nelson notes that the comparably small holdings of slavers in pre-Confederation Canada resulted in particularly acute isolation from a larger community of slaves. The enslaved, she argues, were routinely separated across massive distances from their kin (2016c: 62). Additionally, the smaller size of the enslaved population meant a level of white surveillance that was possibly more extreme than in plantation societies. This visibility and constant scrutiny made it far more difficult for the enslaved to successfully escape; for example, unlike in Caribbean plantation societies, there were no self-sustaining Maroon communities to be reached (Nelson 2016c: 81).

Whitfield notes that archiving in this era in Nova Scotia evinces repressed information on rape and paternity, so one cannot empirically verify the scope of sexual violence. Regardless, he shows that there are signs of possible sexual violence against Black enslaved women. Citing suspicious examples of slave owners owning one enslaved woman and very young children, Whitfield quotes Graham Russel Hodges who notes that "black girls worked and lived in close proximity to white masters" and the result was often an "exploitative sexual relationship" (Hodges 1997: 50–51 in Whitfield 2006: 70). Buttressing these claims, Cooper draws clear links between domestic slavery and sexual violence. For Cooper, there existed intrinsic sexual and physical risks in domestic servitude, due to the dual factors of constant nearness to one's "master" and having no ownership over one's own body (2006: 90). As in French-controlled New France, the lack of bodily autonomy was embodied in reproductive violence that reduced the women's unborn children to property. Enslaved Black women were highly valued because they could increase their masters' wealth by "breeding" more slaves. This fact was acknowledged by John Wentworth, the soon-to-be governor of Nova Scotia who, in 1784, wrote a note accompanying nineteen slaves sent to his cousin in Dutch Guiana that stated, "The women are stout and able and promise well to increase their numbers" (in Hamilton 1999: 15). The British conquest of France also, then, expanded the territory upon which the British practised slavery in what we call Canada, and expanded, too, the institutionalized racial violence that reigned over Black peoples' lives.

Beyond New France and Nova Scotia, the practice of slavery extended across other colonies that later became Canada. English-speaking Upper Canada, which existed from 1791 to 1841 (in present-day Southern Ontario), was also a slave-holding colony. In fact, "the best people in the capital [of Upper Canada] owned Negroes" (Riddell 1920: 67). The creation of French-speaking Lower Canada, a small part of the former colony of New France and territorial precursor to present-day Québec, carried forward the French authorization of slavery, which was practised for fifty years.

Though the Canadian colonies' economies were not entirely based on slavery, the economic value of centuries of unpaid Black labour was nevertheless significant: "slaves did not pay so well in Canada as in Georgia, but they *paid*" (Riddell 1920: 115). In addition to the benefits that slave owners gained from unfree labour, the white settlers of pre-Confederation Canada both participated in and profited from the global Atlantic slave trade (Nelson 2016a, 2016c). The settlements of Québec City, Montréal and Halifax were "transatlantic network ports" that frequently received ships containing enslaved Black men and women arriving from the Caribbean. Further, white settlers in these colonies were deeply economically implicated in the trade of commodities produced by enslaved people, including sugar, rum and molasses (Nelson 2016a, 2016c).

Unpaid and non-consensual Black labour was critical for the economic growth of Ontario, Québec and the Atlantic provinces (Abdi 2005: 51), and enslaved Blacks were a source of wealth that were often passed down from parent to child in wills (Riddell 1920: 71). But in addition to their economic value, the subjection of Black men and women was a status symbol. In Montréal, enslaved Black women were "particularly fashionable and noteworthy possessions" (Nelson 2016c: 75). It is enormously significant that the logic of Black subjection played such an important role in white social status. That "fashion" included the day-to-day violence and domination inherent in enslaving a human being demonstrates the economically *and* culturally significant role that Black confinement and dehumanization played for white settlers.

Enslaved Black people, of course, contested their designation as objects in multiple ways. For example, in the early nineteenth century in what is now Ontario, an enslaved woman named Peggy refused to be subordinated by the white couple that owned her. She had been described by her white mistress as "insolent," "pilfering" and "lying," and though her master intended to sell or imprison her, she eventually escaped them.[1] This "disobedient" behaviour is one of many forms of resistance that the enslaved used to contest their designation as property, described by Saidiya Hartman as part of the "everyday" ways in which enslaved people "interrupted, re-elaborated, and defied the constraints of everyday life under slavery" (1997: 51). Despite the logistical difficulties of running away that life within largely white settlements presented, as well as the likelihood of being caught, punished and re-enslaved, Black fugitivity was common all over the British-run colonies. Fugitive slave advertisements are important archival evidence attesting to the frequency of escape attempts, and such notices frequently appeared in newspapers (see Riddell 1920: 67–70; Nelson 2016a, 2016b). This fact testifies to both the ignoble condition of living in bondage and the courage and ingenuity of enslaved Black people. For the enslaved to attempt escape, they would often have to track their masters' movements and schedules, change their appearance and clothing and stave off the constant white surveillance that defined pre-Confederation Canadian cities (Nelson 2016a, 2016b). Attempting to flee bondage came with enormous risks. When caught, these runaways — more appropriately termed "freedom seekers" (Nelson 2016a) — were frequently beaten, taken to court, held for extended periods in colonial jails or a mix of the three (Cooper 2006: 99; Nelson 2016a). In Truro, Nova Scotia, for example, a recaptured enslaved person (of unknown gender) was punished by having a hole punctured in their ear, and a knotted whiplash laced through the hole was used to drag them to death

(Winks 1997: 51). Escaping a life of bondage is itself an act of great courage, a "refusal to stay in spaces of dispossession, disposability, and lived objecthood" (S. Browne 2015: 70).

"FREE" BLACK LIFE: ELUSIVE EMANCIPATION, FREEDOM RUNNERS AND THE UNDERGROUND RAILROAD

Many narratives of the eighteenth and nineteenth centuries whitewash the practice of Black bondage in Canada. Often, popular and official histories focus on a simplistic liberation narrative based on the freedom granted to some enslaved American Blacks during the American Revolutionary War of 1775–1783 and the War of 1812. Actually, this era was much more ambiguous, characterized by both the migration of newly emancipated Black communities and the migration of significant populations of enslaved Black men, women and children into Canada as the property of their white owners. During the 1775–1783 War, the British promised to grant land and full equality to anyone who would pledge loyalty to the king and fight on the British side of the conflict. The Black American enslaved people who accepted this bargain are commonly referred to as the Black Loyalists. Represented simplistically as a British liberation of Black enslaved people, this act is widely celebrated as a demonstration of early British-Canadian tolerance and benevolence, particularly as compared to the United States. For example, Citizenship and Immigration Canada's timeline of Black history mentions the existence of slavery, but minimizes its prevalence. Instead, it focuses largely on nineteenth-century Canada's historic role as a "safe haven" for runaway slaves, celebrating British liberation of the Black Loyalists and Canada's role in the Underground Railroad in a manner that underscores Canadian tolerance and benevolence (Government of Canada "Key Events in Black Canadian History" n.d.).

Further scrutiny of the Loyalist migration uncovers a much less emancipatory narrative. Even the terminology "Black Loyalists" has been contested. Historian Barry Cahill has pointed out that, in many cases, it was likely not loyalty to the British crown, but the desire to be free from enslavement and institutionalized racial terror that motivated and united most enslaved Blacks who escaped their masters and agreed to fight for the British (Cahill 1999). Similarly, he argues, the British did not liberate Black enslaved people out of benevolence, but as a political manoeuvre designed to steal rebel "property" and help win the war (Cahill 1999). The notion that the British were motivated by benevolence or opposition to slavery is also contradicted by the fact that, though thousands of freed Blacks migrated to pre-Confederation Canada after the Revolutionary War, thousands more enslaved Blacks arrived into Nova Scotia as the property of white Loyalist slaveholders and settlers. The aftermath of the Revolutionary War, in fact, greatly expanded the practice of slavery in pre-Confederation Canada. Over twelve hundred enslaved Black people were brought across the border as the property of their white Loyalist masters, who soon acquired elite places in society. These slave owners imported not only Black people, but also ideas of the value of Black lives and the role of Black persons in a white settler society (Whitfield 2004: 105–106). In short, along with importing the Black men, women and children that they held as property, the white Loyalists imported the logic of Black subordination and confinement as natural and normal (Whitfield 2010: 26). Some enslaved Black peoples actually escaped pre-Confederation Canada to seek freedom in the Northern states in the late eighteenth and early nineteenth centuries, in a migration that has been called the "reverse Underground Railroad" (Thomson 1979). As well, in the same period, many free Black persons were caught and re-enslaved (Whitfield 2010: 26). In short, pre-Confederation Canada was, by no means, solely a "sanctuary" for enslaved Black Americans at this time. Even upon the arrival of newly emancipated peoples, the state-sanctioned ownership of Black bodies and lives persisted, as did the institutionalized subjection of the first "free" Black communities.

If the history of Black enslavement in pre-Confederation Canada is an important site of examination, and one required to trace the deep roots of anti-Blackness in Canada, it is just as crucial to examine the life conditions of non-enslaved Black peoples, both before and after the abolition of slavery. Before the arrival of the Black Loyalists, some free Black peoples already lived in Canada. Later, waves of arrivals of formerly enslaved — and some free — American Blacks greatly expanded the free Black population. Looking at the experience of early non-enslaved Black people, as well as the freed Black refugees from the United States, provides additional insights about early Canadian attitudes toward Blackness. These histories allow us to see that Black freedom remained elusive even in the absence of formal bondage. Whether formally bonded or emancipated, Black life in Canada was subject to intensive economic, political and social devaluation. Indeed, it is the treatment of so-called emancipated Black life that shows us the persistence of state-sanctioned and popular anti-Blackness that prevailed under the banner of white benevolence.

During the height of slavery as it was practised in Canada, not all Black people were enslaved. Black lives were, however, presumed inferior to white ones, and the material realities of non-enslaved Blacks often bore more similarities than differences to those of legally enslaved Blacks. In 1783, 3,500 freed Blacks — the Black Loyalists — were evacuated from New York City to Nova Scotia. They were bestowed with a nominal equality in their new home, but their life conditions did not resemble the freedom that was allotted to white settlers. Few freed Blacks received the land that they had been promised by the British Crown, and those who did received one-quarter of that allotted to white Loyalists arriving at the same time — an amount of land that was too little for subsistence. Denied the land and provisions they were promised, many freed Blacks were forced to become cheap labourers for white farmers or white business owners in towns and cities (J.S.G. Walker 2008: 57). Their freedom, then, nonetheless resulted in the reproduction of an economy of Black servitude.

This structurally mandated Black impoverishment led, paradoxically, to widespread white hostility. The cheapness of this Black labour, though it was no fault of the Black workers, led to Canada's first race riot in 1784. The riot was caused by white workers in the town of Shelburne, Nova Scotia, who were angered at the low wages accepted by local Black workers. These white workers, intent on destroying Black property and attempting to force Black people to leave permanently, formed a mob and attacked the Black areas in Shelburne and nearby Birchtown (Tulloch 1975: 80). The harsh conditions faced by Black communities demonstrated how profoundly anti-Blackness had penetrated society, even in conditions of freedom from bondage. Indeed, twelve hundred of the Black Loyalists were so disillusioned by the realities of racial inequity that, in 1792, they opted to embark on yet another migration — an arduous sea journey to Sierra Leone in search of true emancipation (Walker 1980 in Bolaria and Li 1988: 191).

Another wave of "free" Black migration to Nova Scotia occurred after the War of 1812. Between 1813 and 1816, again, enslaved Africans who managed to escape their masters (and a small number of free Blacks) were promised land in return for their loyal military service to the British Crown. Yet again, the freed Blacks — having just escaped slavery — received a substantively more hostile reception than whites, along with institutionalized discrimination at every level of society. Some Black refugees were denied land entirely. In cases where they did receive land, the amount was too little to survive on and was often known by the Nova Scotia government to be infertile. Around the time of the 1813–1816 migration, the Nova Scotia government attempted to ban further Black migration, using the purportedly non-racist claim that Black persons were climatically unsuitable (Whitfield 2004: 108–109). The material conditions of the freed Blacks in Nova Scotia show that anti-Black racism affected more than just the enslaved. Carrying on in the Black radical tradition, non-enslaved Black men and women remained deeply involved in the social, educational, cultural and religious life of the Black community (Hamilton 1999). But regardless, "the legal freedom of people of African descent [in Nova Scotia] usually went hand-in-hand with social and economic marginality so acute that it almost represented a surrogate for slavery" (Whitfield 2004: 109). Black people fleeing institutionalized racial violence would only encounter it again, in another form, making clear the brutal realities behind the false veneer provided by Canadian mythology.

After the abolition of slavery in Canada, the United States remained a deeply divided violent slave society until the American Civil War (1861–1865). Enslaved Blacks attempted to escape to Canada in the early 1800s by means of the Underground Railroad, with the help of famed escaped-slave-turned-abolitionist Harriet Tubman. Often referred to as Black fugitives at the time and by many historians, those escaping slavery have been renamed as "Freedom Seekers" (Hill 1981), and later, "Freedom Runners" (Hamilton 2014) by those wishing to convey more accurately the dignity and courage required to flee violence and dispossession at great personal risk. The latter name emphasizes the groups' bravery and humanity, rather than the criminality implied in the term "fugitive" (Hamilton 2014). The thousands of enslaved who fled north in the 1800s inevitably risked their lives to escape their horrific circumstances. The *Fugitive Slave Act* of 1850, for example, was a brutal law that mandated American law enforcement officials and citizens to track down Black enslaved people who had escaped to the so-called "free states" of the North. One of its effects was to increase the urgency that led many enslaved men and women to cross into Canada to find refuge. The period between the passing of the *Fugitive Slave Act* and the end of the Civil War saw the largest number of freedom runners entering Canada seeking reprieve from subjugation, bondage and brutal racist violence (Bolaria and Li 1988). Free Black men and women in Ontario played important roles fighting anti-Blackness on both sides of the border. Mary Ann Shadd Cary, the first Black woman to run a newspaper, ran the *Provincial Freeman*, where she advocated for abolition and wrote editorials denouncing sexual violence against Black women by white men (Bristow 1999: 110). Shadd Cary was also the assistant secretary of the Chatham vigilance committee, one of many vigilance committees established to protect newly freed Black people from being re-enslaved by American slave catchers. In 1858, armed with clubs, hundreds of Black men and women and some white male supporters rescued an enslaved Black ten-year-old child named Sylvanus Damarest from a train in

Chaffin, Ontario. For this "crime," five committee members were arrested and some committee members were charged with starting a riot (Bristow 1999: 116–18). This era of Black resistance (and the state repression that accompanied it) can be counted among the earliest Black struggles against forced removals in Canada, and as foregrounding the anti-deportation struggles of later years.

The Underground Railroad is perhaps the most well-known and widely celebrated part of Canada's history of race relations, seeming to set Canadians apart from the brutal and damning anti-Blackness of their American neighbours. The formal appearance of racial tolerance — a major part of Canada's identity today — played an important role in Canada's acceptance of these Black freedom runners. Analyzing Canadian media at this time, historian Jason Silverman found that newspapers lauded Canada's abolition of slavery, stating that "White Canadians were willing to tolerate black refugees in order to prove their eminence over American civil liberties, and they self-righteously chided the United States for perpetuating the institution of slavery" (Silverman 1985: 35). Yet, despite Canadians' apparent pride in their tolerance, freedom from formal bondage did not protect the Black freedom runners from the violence of racist hostility or formal and informal segregation in post-abolition Canada. In many ways, they faced similar conditions to the emancipated Blacks that had arrived before them.

The racism faced by Black persons entering Canada was recognized in this period by American Black abolitionist leaders like Mary Ann Shadd Cary. After denouncing racial segregation in some white churches and public schools to no avail, Shadd Cary distanced herself from Canadian anti-slavery efforts (Yee 1997: 10). In the abolitionist journal *Voice of the Fugitive*, Shadd Cary neatly summed up the Canadian contradiction, calling the white Canadian an "anti-slavery Negro hater" (November 4, 1852 in Silverman 1985: 158). Indeed, freedom runners often experienced the same anti-Black racism north of the border that they had sought to flee in the U.S. For example, in 1891, in Chatham, a town where many of the freedom runners had settled, a band of armed whites tried to force an elderly Black couple from their land (though they were fought off by gunfire) (Winks 1997: 327). Black lives, whether recent Black Americans or Canadian-born, while nominally free, were relegated to a separate and unequal status in all realms of society.

The freedom runners, free Black migrants and Canadian-born Black people could escape neither the reality of the devaluation, nor the state-sanctioned and popular hostility which was enacted on all Black lives in Canada. Regardless of legal status, Canada was far from the land of Black liberation, or even basic tolerance. Black lives in Canada were accorded far less value than those of white settlers, and Black unfreedom prevailed in various forms. The image of Canada as a safe haven from racial intolerance was then, as it remains today, complex, multilayered, ambivalent and equivocal. All Black life in Canada, regardless of origin, was subjected to segregation, vilification and criminalization lasting deep into the twentieth century.

FOLLOW THE COLOUR LINE: SEGREGATION IN CANADA'S JIM CROW ERA

> How does one tell the story of an elusive emancipation and a travestied freedom? (Hartman 1997: 10)

Slavery was officially abolished across the British Empire in 1834. In the preceding decades, the practice had been declining, as numerous judicial decisions slowly stripped it of its legality — for example, no new enslaved people could be brought into some parts of Canada after 1793. In congruence with other slave-holding nations, no reparations were granted to the formerly enslaved or their descendants to account for the centuries of abuse and stolen wealth. Though formalized Black bondage was officially over, the meaning of Blackness had been consolidated under slavery and remained intact in the post-abolition period. In the end, slavery had accomplished more than an economic subjugation, it had created particular meanings of what it meant to be Black — meanings that were attached to Black people's bodies. The fact of Black enslavement altered the signification of Black skin and features, regardless of the legal status of freedom or unfreedom. As historian James S.G. Walker points out, "black enslavement made a powerful impression on whites" and, following abolition, "it was possible to witness the transfer of status from a legal condition to a biological characteristic, from 'slave' to 'black'" (1994 in Walker 2010: 25). The attributes that had been attached to Blackness — subservience, criminality, lack of intelligence and dangerousness — set a road map for treatment of Black life throughout the nineteenth and twentieth centuries. Despite the end of formal bondage, Black people's lives would continue to be devalued and their movements subject to surveillance and containment. White settlers and their governments would proactively enforce a racially divided society in which Black lives were worth less.

The British colonies of North America were consolidated into the independent nation of Canada in 1867, and the following hundred years would bring a massive population influx to secure the settlement and build the nation-state.

Though many describe this process as immigration, the accurate term is colonization. After all, it was not the settlement of empty land, but the theft of *peopled*
lands. With formal policies like the *Indian Act* (1876), Canadian state policies
forced Indigenous peoples onto reserves, instituted patriarchal governance
and destroyed cultural practices while legislating the annexation of territory
(Smith 2005). European migration was, fundamentally, a tactic employed to
secure the dominion of white settlers over stolen land and resources. To use
the words of Indigenous feminist and academic Audra Simpson, "settling thus
is not innocent — it is dispossession, the taking of Indigenous lands" and it is
both "gendered and murderous" (2016b: 2).

The process of peopling stolen lands was not haphazard, but purposeful; so
was the parallel process of structuring settler society according to racial and
gender hierarchies. Canada's history as a white-dominated, Anglo-Saxon state
was not a natural evolution but required careful, indeed brutal, engineering.
Canada's colonization was premised upon an explicitly white supremacist racial
hierarchy, whereby white male settlers were seen as the rightful inheritors of
Canadian lands, wealth and social and political rights. After his re-election
in 1878, Prime Minister John A. Macdonald orchestrated a state-sanctioned
famine for Indigenous communities in the Prairies. The hunger, sickness and
death that followed this planned starvation allowed for a forced relocation onto
and confinement within reserves. In one instance, in the spring of 1883, the
government withheld food from nearly five thousand Indigenous people, who
were then forcibly marched hundreds of kilometres to reserves in Battleford,
Saskatchewan. This violent "clearing" of the land largely vacated it for white
settlement and enabled the construction of the railroads (Daschuk 2013).

Whiteness, of course, was a politically and socially constructed category,
subject to change over time. For example, Italian and Irish people were not
yet considered to be white; as such, they experienced different forms of racial/
ethnic discrimination throughout the early to mid-twentieth century. European
and American settlers, though, were brought into the country and systematically allotted enormous rights and privileges over Indigenous persons' lands
and resources, alongside a proactive subordination of women, people of colour,
Indigenous persons and, of course, Black populations.

To ensure Black subjugation after slavery's end, widespread segregation
practices were enacted across all facets of society. Yet, Black resilience meant
that Black men, women and children survived inside the nation despite being
a largely unwanted population. Both white supremacy and the outer appearance of racial tolerance were integral to the nation-building process and the

creation of Canadian national identity. Racial segregation — a form of violence in and of itself — entails the enforced (rather than voluntary) confinement of racialized populations to particular spaces (e.g., certain neighbourhoods, schools, public spaces and businesses). The segregation of Black communities — which, like slavery, was a form of controlling Black movement and institutionalizing subordination — was based on the idea that Black people were both inferior and dangerous to whites. Formally and informally, segregation was one of Canada's foremost strategies for maintaining white dominance across all aspects of society after slavery's end. In the United States, Jim Crow referred to the *de jure* segregation of Black from white in the public facilities of the former Confederate states. Canada had its own iteration of practices that separated Black from white in what some historians call "Canada's Jim Crow." Canadians produced "their own distinct language and rationalizations" when "propping up white supremacist ideology and practices" (Mathieu 2010: 6). Segregation in the post-abolition period cut across all aspects of society. Public education, immigration, employment and housing were all subject to a veiled Jim Crow-style segregation that either formally or informally kept Black persons in social, economic and political subjugation (Mathieu 2010).

Publicly funded education has long been a site of social advancement for white Canadians. By the same coin, the disinvestment in Black schooling attempted to confine Black communities to a subjugated role in society. Nova Scotia's "Africans' schools" existed from 1816 to the 1850s and were intended to instill the values of obedience and submission in the Black populace so they might better accept their role as menial labourers (Black Learners Advisory Committee [BLAC] 1994). In Canada West, segregation was justified by the need to protect white children from the perceived dangers of proximity to Black children. Formalized less than a decade after slavery's abolition, the *Act of Union* of 1840 legally endorsed the concept of separate schooling. This endorsement informally blocked Black children's access to schools in Canada West. Segregation was soon given a more official sanction by the *Common Schools Act* of 1850, which formally reinforced and entrenched the practice (Silverman 1985: 129, 134). Both of these Acts were premised on the association between Blackness and danger. Black children, it was believed, would have a morally corrupting influence on white children (K. McLaren 2008: 7). Yet, the uniquely Canadian iteration of segregation took the form of outwardly expressed benevolence. Canadian officials denied the presence of any racial discrimination even as Black students were segregated. But Ontario Member of Parliament Malcolm Cameron championed the practice of segregation even as he publicly bragged about "a Christian and moral education to be provided to all Canadians without discrimination" (in McLaren 2004: 31).

For the next hundred years, segregated education was common in many parts of the country. It was practised in Ontario, Alberta and Nova Scotia, with some areas excluding Black children entirely from public schools (Hamilton 2011; BLAC 1994; Shepard 1997). Segregated Black schools were not just spatially separated from white schools, but also intended to provide an inferior education. They were both underfunded and unequally resourced. Some Black schools were not just underfunded, but were entirely abandoned by the state. By the mid-1850s, many Black schools in Nova Scotia and Ontario were closing because they did not receive any government funds (Silverman 1985: 137). Throughout over a century of segregation in Nova Scotia, Black children faced intentional discrimination. They were placed in dilapidated, unheated buildings, taught by poorly trained teachers and faced significant underfunding compared to the resources dedicated to the education of white youth (BLAC 1994).

Where segregation was not formally granted legal protection, whites, regardless, barred Black students from going to school in many areas. In one instance in Campsie, Alberta, in the early twentieth century, a school physically locked the doors to prevent a Black child's entry. Despite parental complaints, the provincial authorities would not act (Shepard 1997: 106). In Halifax County in the 1940s, the Black population was not large enough to justify segregated schools, so Black children were told that they "had not the ability to learn" to keep them from attending school with white children (BLAC 1994). Despite little to no financial support or resources, many Black parents and broader Black communities struggled for Black children to receive adequate education. Black teacher Mary Bibb even opened a school for Black children in nineteenth-century Canada West (Cooper 1999).

The last segregated school in Canada closed in 1983 (James et al. 2010: 46). The history of segregating Black children in many provinces makes visible that not only were Black youth less valued, but they were also represented as a threat to white Canadians. State policies acted, or failed to act, to confine and contain Black youth and children. The attempt to restrict Black access to quality education also had the effect of keeping Black peoples in positions of economic subordination to Canada's white population.

Alongside education, immigration policy was also based around white supremacy in the first half of the twentieth century, and a hostile anti-Blackness prevailed. The Canadian government invested significant resources into seeking out white European and American migrants. The plains, following the genocidal removal of significant numbers of Indigenous populations, were intended to be white. As of 1896, salaried immigration agents were employed to court would-be migrants from the United States and Europe, and white settlers in Canada were offered 160 acres of free farmlands (Mathieu 2010: 27). While white settlers were proactively courted, the Canadian Department of Immigration invested significant government resources into proactively preventing Black migration. Officially, for diplomatic purposes, the government repeatedly denied that they would exclude any person on the basis of their race, but the reality on the ground was quite different. In the early twentieth century, would-be Black migrants who were fleeing racial terror inflicted by the Ku Klux Klan were subjected to unnecessary and unwarranted medical examinations to deter them at the border. Further, medical examiners were paid a government bonus for each Black migrant that they turned away at the U.S.–Canada border (Shepard 1997; Mathieu 2010: 42). The Department of Immigration also paid for advertisements that dissuaded Black Americans from migrating. The department went as far as paying Black American doctors to go to Oklahoma and Kansas to convince would-be Black migrants that the Canadian climate was dangerous (Mathieu 2010: 42) and that "they might die of cold in northern climes" (Valverde 2008: 180). One such doctor was instructed to go to the United States and tell African-American men that their wives and daughters would be "stripped of their clothes" and "examined by boards of men" — invoking the horrors of the slave auction with the explicit goal of preventing their migration (Shepard 1997: 97).

The racist motivations behind demographic selection were seldom expressed in official documents, but lay hidden behind polite euphemisms, carefully crafted to avoid the outward appearance of racism. The official, publicized government position did not explicitly prohibit Black migration; it tended to focus on "climate." Climatic unsuitability was a quality attributed to Black peoples due to their connection to Africa despite their having already worked as slaves and free persons for hundreds of years in Canada. Accordingly, section 38 of the 1910 *Immigration Act* empowered the Governor in Council to prohibit entry of immigrants belonging to "any race deemed unsuited to the climate or requirements of Canada" (in Calliste 1993: 133). Similar conceptions of "climatic unsuitability" appeared in Canadian immigration policies until the 1960s.

American Black people were not the only unwanted ones. Immigration agents informed steamship companies that they were not to sell tickets to African-Caribbean peoples. If they disobeyed this order, they would be held financially responsible for the cost of a Black migrant's refusal at the border for up to three years afterward, including the migrant's possible detention and deportation (Calliste 1993: 137). The restriction of Black American and Black Caribbean migrants had concrete effects on the demographics of the country. Racist exclusion remained on this trajectory deep into the mid-twentieth century. Chinese, Japanese and Indian migrants were also restricted or banned for extended periods due to white supremacist sentiments, and those who entered were subjected to exploitative labour practices (B. Walker 2008).

Ironically, whites-only migration policies were also seen as ways to avoid the racism found south of the border. A major justification for the functional ban on Black migration in the late nineteenth and early twentieth centuries was to avoid the "Negro problem" that existed in the United States (Mathieu 2010: 23). Racism, this suggests, was represented as an American problem that was foreign to Canada (Silverman 1985: 35). In a similar vein, a historical analysis of media and public opinion at the time found that Canadians were staunchly opposed to Black migration, yet refused to think this racist. It was believed, in fact, that racism could be avoided to the extent that Black people were kept out of the country entirely (Mathieu 2010).

That anti-Blackness was couched in the language of climatic unsuitability and an importable "Negro problem" allowed the Department of Immigration to represent the *de facto* ban on most Black migration as humanitarian. William D. Scott, superintendent of immigration from 1903 to 1924, justified denying entry to Black Caribbean labourers by claiming that, through "years of experience," the state "decided not only in the interest of Canada, but also in the interest of coloured people themselves, not to encourage their settlement in this country" (in Calliste 1993: 136). While immigration agents were given directives to disguise the anti-Black migration policies as non-racist, in private correspondence Scott more bluntly stated official policy: "Africans, no matter where they come from are not among the races sought, and, hence, Africans no matter what country they come from are in common with the uninvited races, not admitted to Canada" (in Calliste 1993: 135–136). Informal but institutionally sanctioned exclusions of Black populations were effective, and Black migration remained minimal. Between 1896 and 1914, three million immigrants, mostly white settlers, came to Canada (Palmer 1975 in McLaren 1990). In that same period, Black American and Caribbean migrants made up only approximately five thousand arrivals from the last decades of the twentieth century until 1920 (Mathieu 2010).

Anti-Blackness, articulated in the guise of benevolence, continued into immigration policy in the mid-twentieth century. In 1955, for example, the federal director of immigration (unsuccessfully) fought the entry of Black Caribbean domestics, stating that they would "vegetate to a low standard of living" and that allowing their migration would be "an act of misguided generosity since it would not have the effect of bringing about a worthwhile solution to the problem of coloured people and would quite likely intensify our own social and economic problems" (in Calliste 1993: 133). Canada was intended to be white. Black migration was to be prevented at all costs, with few exceptions under the particularly Canadian veneer of humanitarianism.

When the migration of people of colour could not be prevented, state and non-state measures continued to ensure that white settlers would receive benefits systematically denied to Black and other racially marginalized populations. Housing and land were two major forms of economic advancement withheld to Black Canadians in many cities and towns. Many white companies and landowners steadfastly refused to sell or lease land to those with African features, including the Canada Land Company, which systematically refused to sell land to Black would-be landowners in Canada West (Silverman 1985: 152). In Winnipeg and Hamilton between the two world wars, Black communities were often restricted into segregated housing (Mathieu 2010: 211), and in Toronto in 1959 over 60 percent of landlords surveyed stated they would not be comfortable renting to Blacks (Mosher 1998: 95–98 in Mathieu 2010: 211). Even orphans were housed separately. In Nova Scotia, Black orphans were placed in a separate home for "coloured" children until the 1960s (Bernard and Bernard 2002). Segregation that barred Black families from housing played an important role in preventing Black economic mobility.

Segregated residentially, Black populations also faced restrictions beyond the home. Subject to practices of containment, Black presence itself was heavily surveilled and restricted. The 1920s through the end of the Second World War saw an expanded focus on restricting Black presence in public space. Black movement in some areas was commonly restricted through "sundown laws," curfews or bylaws that meant that Black people had to be indoors or out of town by a particular time of the evening (Walker 2010: 3). For example, in the 1940s, June Robbins, a Black woman who lived in Chatham and worked in Wallaceburg, described travelling thirty-four miles a day to and from work because Black people were not allowed to stay in Wallaceburg after dark (Brand 1991: 151). Similar informal but widely enforced segregation policies restricted Indigenous peoples' movements from 1885 to the mid-twentieth century under the "pass system." Indigenous people living on reserves could not leave unless they obtained written permission from Indian agents. The pass system was brought in as an emergency measure after the Northwest Resistance of 1885 and was enforced until 1941, though the practice was never officially brought before Parliament (Williams 2015).

Canadian hotels and hospitals often refused to serve Black patrons (Walker 1997: 130–132 in Mathieu 2010: 169). Black Canadians were also confined to separate battalions during both world wars, and in many parts of Canada were banned from restaurants and cemeteries (Thornhill 2008: 330, 333). Policing could be called upon to enforce the colour line when restrictions were challenged, which they frequently were. The Black community protested with placards to condemn the anti-Black practices of a roller-skating rink on Yonge Street in Toronto that had refused to admit a young Black boy in 1940 (Brand 1991: 206). Viola Desmond, a Black woman in Nova Scotia, was arrested in November 1946 for the crime of not sitting in the upstairs area set aside for Blacks in the theatre (Thornhill 2008: 333). In Québec, the Supreme Court repeatedly ruled in favour of segregation whenever it was legally challenged by Blacks who had the courage to contest their social position (Walker 1997: 144–151 in Mathieu 2010: 169–170).

A white supremacist colour line also segregated labour, relegating Black labourers to odious working conditions, exploitatively low pay and often degrading positions. Formal and informal segregation in the labour market trapped Black workers in jobs that allowed for their survival but little else, keeping them "in their place" relative to white settlers. In 1916, the Dominion Iron and Steel Company in Nova Scotia was given permission to import a thousand Caribbean labourers due to lack of available labour. These men were relegated to the lowest-paying, most dangerous work directly next to the ovens and furnaces (Calliste 1996 in McCalla and Satzewich 2002: 38). The norms of Black people serving white people — established under slavery — continued unabashedly on the railroads. Canadian railroad companies were formally segregated. White men had the title and corresponding pay of "conductors" and Black men performing many similar functions (with additional demeaning forms of labour) were given the low-paying, lower-status title of "porters." Sleeping car porters were Black men who shined shoes, took care of white passengers' children and answered to passengers' whims. All were called "George" while on the job (Mathieu 2010: 11), which demonstrates both the importance of public displays of Black submission as well as the fact that Blacks were not seen as human beings, but believed to be closer to interchangeable objects. Indeed, the Pullman Car Company explicitly designed (and enforced) the role of the Black deferential porter because of the racial significance of Black submission that it reproduced for white passengers (Mathieu 2010). In the words of acclaimed Black porter and union activist Stanley Grizzle, "this was a job where, every day, you were made to feel that you were beneath the passengers. You were a servant, the epitome of a white man's stereotype of the Black man" (1998: 67). Further, Black porters had to submit to racially degrading practices, such as specialized IQ tests, that were not applied to white employees (Grizzle 1998: 71). Still, due to widespread segregation, this was one of the only employments available to Black men, and for that reason it was a significant site for Black activism in cities across the country. In Halifax, Winnipeg, Toronto, Edmonton, Calgary and Vancouver porters and their wives — who organized themselves as "Ladies Auxiliaries" — were heavily active in organizing for labour rights, as well as public education and Black history weeks, food cooperatives and healthcare (Brand 1991; Grizzle 1998). In 1945, the first collective agreement of a Black union was signed between Black porters and the Canada Pacific Railway (Grizzle 1998: 7). Despite significant labour organizing on the part of the porters, the Canada Pacific Railway managed to maintain segregated job descriptions until 1978 (Calliste 1995: 312).

The legacy of slavery meant that Black women, too, remained captive within the same forms of labour they had performed under bondage. Until the Second World War, one of the only employments available to Canadian-born Black women was that of domestic service, a role which consisted of nearly twenty-four hours a day of submission and deference. In the words of former domestic worker Bee Allen, "The mistress didn't want any of your life to keep you from getting up early and getting her breakfast" (in Brand 1991: 117). Despite structurally enforced gendered and racial subjection, in the early 1900s, some Canadian-born Black domestic workers were actively engaged in organizing with the United Negro Improvement Association, and some of the very few that made it into factory work also attempted to organize unions (Brand 1991). Despite Black resistance, anti-Black labour segmentation was persistent. In 1941, 80 percent of Black adult females in Montréal were employed as domestic servants, facing isolation in hostile white households, working sixteen-hour workdays with no time off and sometimes being paid clothing in lieu of wages (Walker 1981: 132 in Brand 2008: 243). After the end of the Second World War, many Black women attempted to escape domestic work and were increasingly able to access industrial and clerical work, albeit under difficult conditions. However, this shift led the government to import Black female labour from elsewhere (Brand 1991).

As Black labour was mandated to subservience, white supremacy in the organization of labour continued long after the formal abolition of Black slavery. All of these forms of segregation functioned to maintain a separate and unequal role for Black persons in Canada. No longer considered commodities, the ongoing subjugation of now nominally free Black people was justified by linking them to drugs, hypersexuality, danger and criminality. This association had significant impacts on Black freedom and Black mobility, which were substantially curtailed by law enforcement, the courts and immigration officials. The policing of Black bodies was the policing of an anti-Black social order.

FROM CHATTEL TO CRIMINAL: EVOLVING PRACTICES OF POLICING AND CONFINEMENT

The formal abolition of slavery marked significant changes in popular and state representations of Blackness. Though Blackness continued to be imagined as pathological, it is possible to witness a shift that transitions its articulation from chattel to criminal. But the association between Blackness and criminality, though it took root firmly in the late nineteenth and twentieth centuries, can actually be traced back even further to fugitive slave advertisements. The etymology linking Blackness to crime in the popular imaginary stems from the representation of Black freedom seekers who had escaped bondage, in the form of runaway slave advertisements. Seeking freedom, indeed, is one of the first crimes publicly associated with Blackness (Nelson 2016a, 2016b). Fugitive advertisements, placed largely by white slave owners, facilitated the dehumanization of the enslaved, who were regarded as both property and criminal for daring to steal themselves from their owners, committing the contradictory crime of "self-theft" (Wood 2000).

Fugitive slave advertisements are also important in the etymology of policing Black life in Canada. One of the only representations of Black enslaved people, these notices linked Blackness to crime in the public realm (Extian-Babiuk 2006; Nelson 2016a). Their height, weight and style of dress were included, and it was not uncommon for the enslaved in these advertisements to be labelled "cunning and idle" (Nelson 2016a). Further, they allowed for a concerted surveillance of Blackness in the public sphere by white slave owners as well as law enforcement (Nelson 2016a). Born out of fugitive slave ads and expanded greatly after abolition, the practice of publicly associating Black life and Black independence with crime and danger has an enduring legacy that continues to impact Black mobility.

Underlying the racism disguised as benign by citing medical or climatic concerns, or the fear of importing America's race problems, laid a more naked fear and hatred of Black people in Canada. Resonating loudly into the present, the ever-unsubstantiated association of Blackness with immorality, depraved sexuality and criminality was firmly entrenched. In a post-slavery era, these tropes were used to justify the ongoing surveillance of Black communities and the restriction of Black movement. This was accomplished in part by municipal, provincial and national policies, and buttressed by media representations. Though no disproportionate Black-on-white harm was ever recorded, an imagined relationship between Blackness and criminality was enormously effective as a means of justifying and maintaining Black subjection.

Black men and women were presumed to possess a pathological sexuality that threatened to contaminate Canada's white settlers. The Black-male-as-rapist trope proved quite powerful in Canada, and the anti-Black hysteria linking Blackness to sexual danger that permeated the media and public opinion had a foothold within the highest levels of government. In 1868, just over three decades after the abolition of slavery, Prime Minister John A. Macdonald evoked both the "Black rapist" myth and the threat of lynch mobs to justify keeping rape a capital offence. He justified the need for the death penalty because of the "frequency of rape committed by Negroes," whom he argued were "very prone to felonious assaults on white women; if the sentence and imprisonment were not very severe, there would be a great dread of people taking the law into their own hands" (Backhouse 2005: 115; Walker 2010). While enormously politically effective, this trope was based on fears that were not substantiated by reality. In examining one hundred years of court records in Ontario, legal historian Barrington Walker found the incidences of Black men raping white women to be statistically insignificant (Walker 2010: 116). Yet, this reality did not affect popular opinion; Black men were widely portrayed as "oversexed and hence as probably rapists" (Valverde 2008: 180). The safety of white women was widely invoked as a reason to exclude Black men from settlement within civil society. An influential women's group, the Imperial Order Daughters of the Empire, petitioned to the federal government in 1911 for Black men to be excluded from Canadian society: "We do not wish that the fair name of Western Canada should be sullied with the shadow of lynch law, but we have no guarantee that our women will be safer in their scattered homesteads than women in other countries with a Negro population" (Palmer 1938: 36 in Valverde 2008: 180).

Despite wanting to avoid the *appearance* of American-style racism, state officials and powerful white settler groups mobilized around the image of Black

men as dangerous sexual predators. Besides invoking fear in the white population to support anti-Black legal and immigration policies, these statements
must also be seen as a means of terrorizing Black communities. The fact that
important political figures invoked the threat of possible lynching and made
only lightly veiled threats geared toward Black men likely did not go unnoticed
by the Black population. This form of statement, particularly when heard by
Black men who had fled lynching in the United States, served to threaten
Black communities into continued submission. If lynchings did not function
to terrorize and subordinate Black communities in Canada, as they did in the
American South, *the threat* of lynching achieved a similar effect.

One case that embodies the sexualized hysteria surrounding Black males,
criminality and Black "foreigners" is the case of Hazel Huff in Edmonton. In
April 1911, white teenager Hazel Huff accused a Black man of breaking into
her home, stealing a diamond ring and drugging and assaulting her. A widely
reported frenzy ensued and the purported assault was immediately blamed on
the recent influx of Black migrants who had fled from the Klan in Oklahoma
(Shepard 1997: 78). Newspapers played an important role in linking the presence of Black men to danger and crime, using terms such as "black rapist beast"
and headlines including "The Black peril" and "A Negro Atrocity — White Girl
Flogged and Assaulted by Late Arrivals at Edmonton" (Shepard 1997: 79).
Though shortly afterward, Huff confessed to the police that she had made the
story up, the authorities kept the admission secret, and the resounding hysteria
surrounding the dangers of Black male lust nearly resulted in the lynching of
an innocent Black man named Witsue (Mathieu 2010: 53). This same year,
Edmonton passed a resolution completely banning Blacks from the city (Boyko
1991: 155 in Abdi 2005: 53). This corresponded to other prairie cities, as
Calgary and Winnipeg also called to stop Black migration entirely between
1910 and 1911 due to widespread (and unsubstantiated) fears of Black crime
(Abdi 2005: 53). Hatred and fear of Blackness were thus used by all levels of
government — buttressed by the police and the white settler population —
to fuel further anti-Black policies and reinforce the perception that Blackness
equalled criminality.

The racial terror enacted by the state and citizenry alike continued well
into the twentieth century. The Ku Klux Klan and other white nationalists
were active forces in Canada that acted in tandem with the state processes that
criminalized Blacks and discouraged their migration. By 1922, there were Klan
members in Saskatchewan, Alberta, British Columbia, Ontario and Québec
(Mathieu 2010: 171) and their membership continued to increase. By the late

1920s, the Klan's western wing had signed up 25,000 members (Backhouse 1999: 189). In June 1927, an estimated ten thousand people gathered in Moose Jaw, Saskatchewan, as Klansmen burned a sixty-foot cross and proclaimed, "one flag, one language, one race, one religion, race purity, and moral rectitude" (Backhouse 1999: 189). In 1920 in St. Catharines, Ontario, several newspapers reported that a white mob had set the town hall on fire and attempted to lynch a Black ex-soldier (Mathieu 2010: 171).

Importantly, Klan activities cannot be dismissed as marginal to Canadian society. The research of William Calderwood demonstrates that it was common for Protestant ministers in Saskatchewan to be active in the Klan, and that their congregations were aware of this and untroubled (Calderwood 1972 in Valverde 2008: 80). Moose Jaw's Ku Klux Klan financially supported a wing of a hospital, which boasted a plaque celebrating "Law and Order, Separation of Church and State, Freedom of Speech and Press, [and] White Supremacy" (Mathieu 2010: 169). Even racist threats and cross burnings, used widely in the United States as means of instilling fear in Blacks and maintaining white supremacy, were tacitly allowed by Canadian state powers. On February 28, 1930, seventy-five men in white hoods staged a march through Oakville, Ontario, and planted and burned a cross in the centre of town. Then, they forcibly separated an interracial couple, Ira Johnson and Isabel Jones, and brought Jones to the home of her white relatives. They then kidnapped the terrified Ira Johnson, also finding and kidnapping his elderly aunt and uncle, then returned them to Johnson's house where they were forced to stand in the front yard as the Klan burned a large cross to the ground. This was met with state and citizen acquiescence, and it was reported that a police officer shook the perpetrators' hands, and made no arrest or complaint. Subsequently, the Oakville mayor was quoted in the *Globe* as stating that the Klan had acted "quite properly" (Backhouse 1999: 173–175). Only after significant Black activism and the support of a Black lawyer came a highly rare and quite mild condemnation: four men were charged with having their faces masked and disguised by night (Backhouse 1999: 193). As seen in this case and others like it, though far more harm was committed against Black persons by white Canadians than the other way around, the Black population was nonetheless treated as a source of danger.

Historically, appealing to the need to protect white womanhood has justified anti-Black state practices and the criminalization of Black men. The intensive focus on rape in this era cannot be understood outside of its racial context and should not be mistaken for a genuine societal attempt to end sexual violence against white women (or any women). The protection of white women, in this context, was mobilized as a protection of white settler society: the (possible) rape of a white woman by a Black man was treated as an affront against the property of white men. The moral outrage surrounding rape was, after all, highly selective: working-class white women who were raped by white men and white women who were raped by family members often received little in the form of legal protection or popular support and were subject to both scrutiny and hostility (Crenshaw 1995). The politicization of rape was far less about protecting white women than it was about justifying the oppression of Black men. White women, however, were not passive or blameless. The Imperial Order Daughters of the Empire, the Woman's Christian Temperance Union and numerous other white women's organizations across Canada proactively mobilized the protection of "white's women's virtue" toward racist ends, to forward anti-Asian and anti-Black sentiment (Backhouse 1999). Further, the elevated status of white women in this context makes visible the degraded exclusion of Black women from the category of womanhood, as it erased the widespread, ongoing reality of white men's sexual victimization and rape of Black women.

Just as pathological representations of the nature of Black males justified their ongoing subjection, shared beliefs about Black women's sexual deviance served, under slavery, to justify their rape, often at the hands of white men. After slavery's abolition, while the mere suggestion of the rape of a white woman by a Black man led to widespread outcry and political action, the rape of a Black woman elicited no public outrage. If white womanhood represented the idealized female subject, then Black women were cast outside of this formulation entirely, as less than women and, indeed, less than human (Haley 2016). The racial logic underlying rape was made clear in the courts. In an analysis of one hundred years of trials between 1858 and 1958 in Ontario, Barrington Walker found that the courts heavily sanctioned the rape of white women by Black men, in the rare instances that it occurred. In comparison, white men who sexually assaulted Black women were granted considerable leniency (Walker 2010: 141). In 1900, Sarah Dorsey, a thirty-eight-year-old Black woman, was subject to a brutal sexual attack by six white men in Glencoe, Ontario. Despite strong evidence to the contrary, all six men were found innocent and told by the judge "to behave themselves" (Walker 2010: 162–164).

The 1867 trial of Jonathan George, a Black man, demonstrates the means by which gender acted in concert with race to normalize sexual violence against Black women. George, accused of raping a Black woman named Hannah Brown, was found guilty of the crime and sentenced to hang. Yet, white elites, including the county clerk of the peace, mobilized to have George released in a rare moment of interracial solidarity. They circulated a petition demanding a reduced sentence that was signed by four hundred Windsor residents. These actions were not based on any claim to George's innocence, but rather on the relative triviality of the crime. For them, the rape of a Black woman was of little significance. The white elites continually raised the idea of Black women's inherent sexual depravity, the implication being that George's crime was less serious because of Hannah Brown's status as a Black woman, as well as what they suspected to be a history of sexual immorality and possible prostitution (Walker 2010: 93–97). Though Black women were no longer the property of white men, their lives were nonetheless accorded little value and even less protection by the state. Legal *inaction* could allow for as much harm as legal action.

The purportedly "natural" depravity of Black women did more than degrade their social status and value in the eyes of white society. It not only made them "rapeable" in the eyes of the law, but it rendered them criminal as well. Black women's sexuality was represented as a threat, and those deemed to be exercising their sexuality outside of established social norms were deemed criminal. Though selling sexual services for money resulted in no measurable harm and likely complemented Black women's income in an era of extreme economic deprivation, involvement in the sex trade was widely regarded as a public danger, purportedly responsible for the degradation of society. While any women associated with sexual immorality were highly stigmatized, Black women were vilified by moral reformers in the early twentieth century as being particularly prone to promiscuity — police and court workers feared Black women would seduce and corrupt white settler society (Murphy 1923 and Pon 1996 in Sangster 2002: 52). The Edmonton Police used these stereotypes in a push to bar Black migration, claiming that upon three years of their arrival "20 percent of them [African Americans] were undesirables, either prostitutes or men living upon the avails of prostitution" (Edmonton Police Department 1911 in Mathieu 2010: 24). In examining arrest records, we see that this stereotype appears to have resonated across the country.

Prostitution laws were widely used in the late nineteenth century. Indeed, legal historian Constance Backhouse notes that possible prostitution offences constituted the majority of women's recorded crimes. Much of the enforcement of these laws was directed at those society deemed undesirable, a category which was always based on race, ethnic origin and class. Prostitution laws were weaponized to arrest and imprison Black and Indigenous women, along with poor and working-class Irish women, who were, at the time, considered less ideal settlers than other white Europeans (Backhouse 1985). Naomi Sayers notes that prostitution laws were added to the federal *Indian Act*, amended in 1879, which had the result of allowing law enforcement officers increased access to Indigenous women's homes, as well as increasing the capacity to surveil their movements in public space (Sayers 2013).

Across the country, Black women were arrested and incarcerated for purported prostitution offences at vastly disproportionate rates. Between 1864 and 1873, Black women were 3 percent of the population in Halifax but made up 40 percent of incarcerated women, and a large percentage of these were likely to be serving prostitution-related sentences (Fingard 1984 in Backhouse 1985: 401). In Vancouver, 28.5 percent of women arrested on morality charges between 1912 and 1917 were Black, though their proportion of the city's overall population was exponentially smaller (Marquis 1995). In Calgary and Toronto, Black women thought to be sex workers faced disproportionate arrest rates in the early twentieth century (Bedford 1981 in Backhouse 1985: 401), and Hamilton also saw large numbers of arrests of "Afro-American prostitutes" (Weaver 1995 in Mosher 1998: 44). Black women charged with these offences were widely represented as subhuman and bestial. In one example from 1892, a Black woman named Fanny Young was charged for vagrancy and sentenced to serve two years as punishment. She was described animalistically in the *Free Press* as a "misshapen colored woman [who] has lived like a wild beast on the outskirts of the city" (in Mosher 1998: 174).

It is difficult to gauge Black women's actual rates of involvement in prostitution given the wide scope of prostitution laws. The wording of the laws, in fact, appears to criminalize women's independent movement and sexuality as much as their possible occupation. Prostitution laws, at one point, allowed for the arrest of "all common prostitutes *or night-walkers* wandering in fields, public streets or highway and not giving a satisfactory account of themselves" (Backhouse 1985: 389, emphasis added). Maintained in some form for over a century afterward, this law encapsulated not only the selling of sexual services but women's presence in public space more largely. Black women, already widely assumed to be criminally sexual, were therefore easy targets for prostitution laws.

Prostitution laws constituted a range of dangers for Black women. A prostitution charge could mean months to years of hard labour, or a prison or reformatory sentence (Backhouse 1985: 403). Meanwhile, Black women's portrayal as criminally promiscuous meant that their involvement or perceived involvement in prostitution made them easy targets for any person inclined toward sexual assault. Nineteenth-century rape laws meant that "sexual coercion by physical contact [was] tolerated" against those deemed prostitutes (Backhouse 1985: 413). In Canada sexual violence remained a looming threat over large numbers of Black women, as they were some of the main targets of prostitution laws.

Pathological understandings of Black women's sexuality also allowed for significant scrutiny and hostility to be directed at Black women who were migrants. Upon their arrival to Montréal in 1911, fifty-eight Black women who had recently arrived from the Caribbean were met with populist racism made visible in the media. The *Montreal Herald*, for example, warned of an influx of "dark-skinned" women who were deemed "unfit" mothers due to stereotypes about Black female immorality and sexual pathology (in Calliste 1993: 140–141). Later that year, on the grounds that Caribbean women were both morally and physically unfit, immigration officers closed their entry to Québec entirely (Calliste 1993: 134).

While Black women's sexuality and access to public space was policed using prostitution laws, Black men became some of the targets for Canada's drug laws. Drug laws were, since their inception, a mechanism of legally mandated, racially motivated surveillance, harassment and incarceration for racialized persons. Canada's *Indian Act* in 1886 prohibited "status Indians" from buying or consuming alcohol, a measure not repealed until 1985. This resulted in thousands of arrests (Maracle 1993 in Boyd 2006: 132). Meanwhile, Canada's first laws concerning opium, enacted in 1908, were explicitly crafted to target Chinese labourers rather than to address pharmacological evidence of harm (Boyd 2006; Gordon 2006). The perceived threat of drugs was highly sexualized, attached to fears of racial mixing and the dangers of non-white migration more largely.

Black men were soon added to the list of perceived drug criminals. In 1922, Edmonton Juvenile Court judge and moral reformer Emily Murphy wrote a highly influential text entitled *The Black Candle*, which was instrumental in the creation of subsequent federal drug laws (Palmer 1982). The text, which linked drugs to the destruction of the white race, targeted Chinese men, Mexicans and Greeks, but a significant portion of the photos exhibited in the text feature Black men and women and the text singled out Black men who worked as porters (Murphy 1973: 36). One image depicts a white woman lying next to a Black man above a caption that reads "When she acquires a habit, she does not know what lies before her; later she does not care" (Murphy 1973: 31). Murphy and others saw drugs as a racial and sexual danger to white purity and evoked tropes of Black men as traffickers who would enslave white women (Boyd 2006: 135). These portrayals had real effects on Black lives. Between

1908 and 1930, Chinese and Black men were frequently singled out by the police for arrests under opium laws (Boyd 2006: 133). Opium was not the only racially motivated target. The eventual criminalization of cocaine and cannabis was related to exerting control over Caribbean immigrants, who were tied in the public imaginary to fabricated dangers surrounding drug use (Giffen, Endicott and Lambert 1991 in Gordon 2006).

After slavery, associations between race and crime, and particularly between Blackness and crime, took hold as an important means of legitimating the ongoing state surveillance and control over Black people's lives. Beyond prostitution and drug laws, the creation and application of criminal laws in general were used by the Canadian government to manage deep-seated fears and anxieties about Blackness. Tracing the lineage of racism in Canada's legal system from the 1700s to the present day, Black Canadian legal scholar Esmerelda Thornhill concludes that "the law has colluded — and continues to collude — with race in ways that accommodate and foster ongoing … anti-Black racism" (2008: 332). The data supports this claim. Examinations of court records between the years of 1890 to 1920 found open racism in the sentencing of Black offenders by many magistrates (Denison 1920 and Mosher 1998 in Mosher and Akins 2015: 335). From 1908 to 1960, Blacks convicted of violent offences would receive far more severe sentences (Mosher and Akins 2015: 339). The result of these court decisions was a consistently disproportionate rate of incarceration for Black people. In 1911, Black males were incarcerated at a rate eighteen times higher than that of white males, while in 1931 they were incarcerated at a rate ten times higher than whites (Mosher 1998 in Mosher and Akins 2015: 339). Incarceration had replaced enslavement as a legal means to literally strip people of their freedom, as well as separate families and inhibit future employment opportunities. Black incarceration was thus highly effective in maintaining Black disenfranchisement and subjugation in post-abolition Canada. The association of Blackness with danger allowed for the policing of Black peoples' lives by white settler society, law enforcement and immigration agencies — Black emancipation had not yet been actualized.

CONCLUSION

Slavery was maintained by surveillance, confinement and control over Black movement. However, these practices continued far beyond the period of formalized bondage in Canada — separate and unequal access to economy, education and housing as well as a heightened exposure to police surveillance and incarceration maintained state control over Black peoples lives. The representations of Blackness that were consolidated between the era of chattel slavery through to the mid-twentieth century had important effects across all major state institutions. Yet, after the Second World War both old and revamped iterations of casting Blackness as pathology would remain close to the surface as Canada ushered in the era of multiculturalism.

CHAPTER TWO

THE BLACK SIDE
OF THE MOSAIC

Slavery, racial capitalism
and the making of
contemporary Black poverty

We often tend to think of racism as attitudinal. We think about it as
explicit — we don't necessarily also think about it as being embedded
in social, economic and political structures. (Davis 2015: n.p.)

The adoption of multiculturalism helped stabilize white supremacy by
transforming its mode of articulation in a decolonizing era. (Thobani
2007: 146)

THE REALITIES OF BLACK LIFE IN contemporary Canada remain shrouded
behind a carefully curated national mythology of racial equality. According to
this national myth, the late 1960s and early 1970s began the dawn of a new era
in Canada, characterized by a commitment to human rights and racial equality.
As the story goes, after loosening highly selective racial restrictions throughout
the 1960s, state officials proudly embraced Canada's newly minted status as a
"multicultural" nation, a status formally adopted in 1971. A significant investment in crafting a national identity based in racial and cultural harmony and
inclusion was underway. This represented, to many, a turning point in Canadian
history. Shortly before his election as prime minister of Canada, Liberal leader
Justin Trudeau voiced, in no uncertain terms, that Canada's success as a nation
is based in its racial inclusivity. On the forty-fourth anniversary of official state
multiculturalism, he stated, "Canada's success is rooted in its unique approach

to liberty through inclusive diversity" (Liberal Party of Canada 2015). Diversity, arguably, has been achieved — racialized persons from around the globe, each arriving with vibrant, unique and distinct cultures, now coexist alongside long-standing communities of formerly enslaved and free Black persons who have existed in Canada for three or more generations. On the surface, an official multiculturalism policy enshrined in law, along with the *Charter of Rights and Freedoms*, appears to counter past forms of state-based discrimination. This appearance of equality, however, relies on the erasure of the conditions of Black life in Canada's recent past, as well as its present. For most Black people residing in Canada, neither racial equity, nor "inclusion" or "liberty," to use Trudeau's words, have been achieved. Instead, the realities of ongoing Black subjection only remain more hidden from view. Economic, social and political subjuga-tion remain a definitive facet of Black life in Canada. This reality, too frequently rendered invisible by the rhetoric of Canada as a welcoming mosaic, was neither natural nor accidental, but constructed by people. Multiculturalism is better understood as part of a historically continuous practice of outward tolerance, of trying to "contain blackness through discourses of Canadian benevolence" (Walcott 2003: 44). Its uncritical and ubiquitous adoption into Canadian identity has served to disguise and insulate Canada's racial hierarchies, and has obscured the state's role in failing to address — even proactively re-creating — the material conditions of Black suffering.

It is more accurate to say, perhaps, that Canada has been remarkably effective at hiding the persistent anti-Blackness that has spanned four centuries of Black life. During the early settlement and colonization of Canada, Black persons in Canada did not arbitrarily find themselves in a lower social and economic status than white Canadians. Rather, first slavery, then segregationist state policies regarding immigration, labour and education put them there and kept them there, despite both organized and everyday acts of resistance. Changes to the global and domestic economy in the second half of the twentieth century did not substantially change the fact of Black economic subjugation.

Despite and alongside an embrace of multiculturalism, processes of extracting Black wealth remain structured into society long after the aboli-tion of slavery, both domestically and internationally. Black Canadians are among the poorest populations in Canada, and continue to face discrimin-ation in access to employment, housing, education, wages and positions in the public service (United Nations Committee on the Elimination of Racial Discrimination 2012: 7). Structurally mandated poverty persists, defines and constrains the lives of a significant proportion of Canada's Black population, regardless of whether they were born in Canada or abroad, and regardless of level of education.

Because discussions around contemporary anti-Black racism are often centred on police violence, many forms of structural violence that cause widespread suffering often remain invisible. In 1967, Black power activists Stokely Carmichael and Charles V. Hamilton famously insisted that the racist violence directed at Black Americans extends beyond flagrant and straightforward acts of racial violence by white citizens or the state. They pointed out that, while much of the general public was quick to denounce a church bombing, most were unwilling to speak out when hundreds or thousands of Black lives were "destroyed and maimed physically, emotionally and intellectually" because of conditions of poverty (1967: 4). In Canada, too, immense harms have been enacted on Black populations because of the stress of poverty and economic and racial discrimination. Some of these harms are measurable: racial discrimination against Black communities has been found to have effects on physical and mental health including addiction, HIV/AIDS, diabetes, cardiovascular disease, higher infant mortality, depression, renal damage, asthma, pain and other chronic conditions (James et al. 2010; ACLC 2012; Toronto Public Health 2013). Poor racialized people, often women, increasingly suffer from the negative health effects of economic disadvantage. Since poverty inflicts harm on communities, deliberate or unaddressed state policies that disadvantage racialized groups must be conceived of as state-sanctioned economic violence (James 1996).

But neither descriptions of the harms of Black poverty nor statistics that exemplify the depth of Black poverty shed light on its structural nature. On the contrary, to many they are evidence of Black pathology and cultural inferiority — Black people, to some, are assumed to be poor because of deficiencies intrinsic to Black culture. It's important, then, to examine the shifting state discourses surrounding Canadian race politics, as well as to retrieve and expound the state processes that have, in the background, relegated Black communities to economic vulnerability and the corresponding political and social subjugation that accompanies poverty.

SHIFTING LANGUAGES OF DOMINATION: BLACK SUBJUGATION AS MULTICULTURALISM

Significant changes at the global and national levels were underway in the years following the Second World War. Worldwide, Black and brown organizing posed enormous challenges to white supremacy and the hierarchical racial organization of the world's peoples. A multiplicity of Third World liberation movements challenged the legitimacy of worldwide white supremacy, and railed against the racist logics that had allowed European nations to profit from the unfettered pillage and plunder that was colonization. Civil rights and Black liberation movements overturned Jim Crow–style racism in Canada and the United States, while Third World decolonization movements in African and Caribbean nations successfully fought against and ended the colonization of much of the Global South.

In Canada, popular support was waning for many of the eugenic and climatic justifications that had protected racial discrimination and racial hierarchies from sanction. This shift came as a result of concerted and tireless organizing by racialized populations. Black organizing, in particular, played a prominent role in challenging the racist hostility that predominated the first half of the twentieth century. In Ontario, for example, Black community members undertook campaigns to put a stop to the still-popular blackface minstrel shows, which featured in church fundraising efforts until the 1960s. A successful legal battle in Dresden, Ontario, was mounted against local businesses that refused to serve Black patrons in 1955. Further, Black organizing in this decade was integral to the creation of Ontario's Human Rights Commission (Grizzle 1998: 97). As well, mass meetings throughout the 1950s protested discriminatory policies targeting Caribbean migrants and saw some success by the early 1960s (Carty 1999: 215).

As a result of this hard-won shift, in tune with racial justice movements worldwide, many of the previous articulations of racism and xenophobia on which Canada had previously relied were blunted. Between 1947 and 1965, each province enacted anti-discrimination legislation that outlawed out-dated Jim Crow–style racism that had segregated Black and other racialized groups from white society. Indeed, many visible forms of discrimination were outlawed at this time. In 1958, Canada signed the international *Convention concerning Discrimination in Respect of Employment and Occupation*. By the 1960s, all Canadian provinces had anti-discrimination legislation outlawing the most blatant displays of racism in housing, labour and public space, and federal immigration legislation no longer openly promoted white supremacist ideals (Mathieu 2010: 211). Still, though the era of "whites only" signs was over, the underlying racialism that structured both the global and national economies remained in many ways unchanged, and the second half of the twentieth century saw a reconsolidation of many old racial hierarchies under a new name.

Recent decades have seen a major transformation in the demographic makeup of Canada. By 1961, 95 percent of Canada's settler population were whites of European heritage (Galabuzi 2006: 62). This was the result of the genocidal and assimilationist policies geared toward Indigenous populations, as well as explicitly racist immigration policies that, for much of the nineteenth and early twentieth centuries, barred or heavily controlled the migration of Black, Japanese, Chinese and Indian and other racialized people. But since the post-war economic boom in Europe, fewer and fewer white Europeans were emigrating to settle Canada (Galabuzi 2006: 81). By the later twentieth century, however, due to the nature of capitalist expansion, the Canadian economy required population growth and reproduction of the labour force to prevent economic stagnancy (Bolaria and Li 1988: 207). By the 1960s, the economy required an influx of highly skilled professional workers. For Canada to become an advanced industrial nation, new source countries were required.

As the previous chapter noted, the state's twentieth-century goal of creating a "white Canada" had always been both illusory and hypocritical. Canada, after all, was built on stolen Indigenous lands with profits, in part, from goods produced by slave plantations elsewhere and was economically reliant on the slave labour of Black people and the "coolie labour" of Chinese, Japanese and South Asian persons. But the near-total exclusion of Black and other people of colour from the benefits of Canadian citizenship came to an end in the 1960s. Canada's 1962 *Immigration Act* removed all references to race, ethnicity or geographical areas in the determination of those eligible for citizenship, officially ending nearly one hundred years of racial segregation by the federal Department of Immigration. This trend continued with the introduction of the points-based system in 1967, in which migrants were said to be evaluated for their potential economic contribution to the country based on factors such as education level, age and language capacity, rather than race or country of origin. When the *Immigration Act* of 1976 passed into law in 1978, it remained nominally race-neutral while expanding the ease with which professionals from around the world could enter Canada to become citizens. These changes to the *Immigration Act* resulted in a massive influx of highly skilled and educated migrants from Africa, the Middle East, Asia, South America and the Caribbean, who mostly arrived in Montréal, Toronto and Vancouver. Critics point out that despite official rhetoric, white European nations were still preferred as source countries and white settlers continued to be prioritized over racialized people (Choudry et al. 2009: 16; Thobani 2007). Some have pointed out that bureaucratic mechanisms were used to favour white immigrants and that in non-white nations, immigration officers were more difficult to access and applications were less clear than in predominantly white countries (Symons 1998 in Tettey and Puplampu 2005: 33). Further, the distribution of immigration offices worldwide has been described as racist, with far more offices in white European-based nations than in nations populated by people of colour (Law Union of Ontario 1981: 46 in Bolaria and Li 1988: 175). Even so, economic necessity put an end to the state's early goal of creating a solely white, European-descended Canada.

Demographic changes were accompanied by a shift in official discourse surrounding race. Complementing the changes to immigration selection processes, "multiculturalism" was officially adopted as a policy in 1971 by Prime Minister Pierre Elliott Trudeau. Beyond guaranteeing English and French linguistic rights, the widely acclaimed policy declared that Canada may not discriminate on the basis of race, gender or other factors. Further, it declared that all are guaranteed equality before the law and equal opportunities, including employment and freedom to preserve one's cultural heritage. Theorized as a mosaic, the philosophy of multiculturalism proclaims that no culture, race or ethnicity is above any other, and racial and ethnic minorities are encouraged to maintain their cultural identities upon arriving in Canada.

Alongside a new flag in 1967 and a new national anthem in 1970, multiculturalism was part of Canadian branding (Sharma 2001). Following its introduction, Canadian multiculturalism was championed domestically and internationally through broadly disseminated documentation and highly mediatized governmental speeches. It was excellent publicity for Canada, and allowed Canadians to feel proud of the Canadian identity as one of tolerance (Sharma 2001). Yet, the earnest promotion of Canada as a beacon of tolerance at the advent of multiculturalism served to disguise Canada's brutal and violent history of slavery and colonization, as well as its continuing abuses of Indigenous, Black and other racialized communities. The words of Conservative MP Heath Macquarrie in the House of Commons in 1970 demonstrate this era's distortion of history: "The great moment in Canadian history, one which reflects its unique character among nations, is surely that it has achieved nationhood by peaceful means, by the *getting together* of different communities" (*Hansard* February 17, 1970: 3702, emphasis added, in Sharma 2001: 429).

This optimism obscured a far less equitable reality. Himani Bannerji has argued compellingly that the formal equalities guaranteed in the *Multiculturalism Act* did not translate into material reality (2000). She points out that the existence of racial stratifications is not evidence of the failure of multiculturalism. Instead, she argues that multiculturalism was itself a stand-in for what could have been meaningful change. While "difference" was celebrated on a surface level, white (male) supremacy and the subjugation of many racialized groups remained intact. Bannerji has argued that the preservation of "culture" takes the place of enacting meaningful policies to materially combat racism and discrimination, allowing for the ongoing economic subjugation of non-white migrant groups (2000).

Behind the rhetoric of multiculturalism lies a more naked erasure of the ongoing violence experienced by racialized populations. In particular, it elides the unique realities of state violence as it is experienced by Indigenous and Black peoples living in Canada. According to acclaimed Indigenous (Dene) scholar Glen Sean Coulthard, the 1960s were characterized by a shifting language toward Indigenous communities by state officials, toward recognition for "Aboriginal 'cultural rights' within legal and political state frameworks" (2014: 2–5). This shift, he argues, came in response to the political challenges posed by Red Power movements, as a means to stifle dissent and the appearance of conflict. This began with the 1969 "White Paper," continued with the 1973 *Calder v. British Columbia (AG)* decision and, most notably, was exemplified by the state's formal recognition of Indigenous treaty rights in section 35(1) of the *Constitution Act* of 1982 (Coulthard 2014: 4-6). Rather than representing a major shift away from colonial governance, he argues, these acts of recognition merely used new language to describe the same colonial relationship of dispossession, land theft and violence. Multiculturalism has played an integral role in the process of advancing an ever-evolving settler colonialism. Indigenous (Mohawk) scholar Audra Simpson has written that official state multiculturalism serves to mask a settler strategy of dispossession. To Simpson, "where there is a language and a commitment to multiculturalism, as the protection, preservation and perhaps even celebration of one's cultural difference," there is also "a simultaneous commitment to the taking of territory" (2016a: 3) that remains part of the capitalist accumulation of the settler state. She notes that, while Indigenous cultures are formally recognized under multicultural rhetoric, Indigenous peoples and lands continue to be destroyed in the name of profit. In Attawapiskat, for example, peopled lands continue to be flooded and contaminated by the DeBeers diamond mine only miles away from the community. As a result, the Attawapiskat communities live in portable housing in sub-zero temperatures, all with the full knowledge and sanction of the Canadian government (Simpson 2016a: 4). Multiculturalism, in this case, serves only to disguise the government's ongoing politic of resource and land extraction.

Additionally, official multiculturalism has effaced the state's ongoing anti-Blackness. Rinaldo Walcott (2003: 14) has argued that Canada's official multiculturalism has fostered the ongoing invisibility of Black life in Canada, obscuring both the history of slavery and contemporary Black presence. Indeed, multiculturalism has masked the ongoing policy of Black subjection that has undergirded official and unofficial state policies, regardless of language centred on formal equality and rights to cultural retention. When multiculturalism was introduced, Black migrants and Black Canadians were largely living and working in conditions of extreme exploitation, or else excluded from high paying labour and facing high unemployment rates — in other words, Black Canadians were nowhere near equal with white Canadians (Bolaria and Li 1988: 185–205). These conditions have remained largely unchanged. Multiculturalism did not address the life and labour conditions of Black persons in Canada, and it was not intended to. Anti-Black racism across Canadian institutions persisted in spite of, and alongside, a federally mandated multiculturalism.

The second half of the twentieth century and into the present has seen both the substantive growth of Canada's Black population as well as its relegation into one of the lowest paid, least secure segments of the Canadian workforce, marked by high vulnerability to unemployment, underemployment and poverty. To understand the state processes that economically subjugated Black migrants (and long-standing Black Canadian communities), it is necessary to first address the larger global context of postcolonial displacement across Africa and the Caribbean — the root causes of Black migration.

FROM STOLEN PEOPLE TO STOLEN RESOURCES: THE ORIGINS OF BLACK DISPLACEMENT

According to commonly accepted reasoning, racialized and Black migrants and refugees from the Global South seek refuge in countries like Canada because of the economic opportunities that are available. Within this understanding, Canada generously and benevolently allows sanctuary and opportunity to the disadvantaged, racialized peoples of this world. This portrait of global migration is, however, incomplete and misleading; it invisibilizes Canada's role in supporting the root causes of Black (and brown) displacement.

The condition of Black migrants — in Canada and worldwide — has been the result of what Cedric J. Robinson (1983) has called racial capitalism. Robinson (1983) has argued that capitalism, like the global systems of inequality that preceded it, relies on the use of race and racial hierarchies to justify unequal power relationships and make them appear natural. To Robinson, the history of slavery and colonization are inseparable from the development of modern capitalism. The enormous wealth disparities that persist along racial lines in contemporary society appear "normal," writes Robinson, because of dehumanizing racial logics set in place long ago. The concept of racial capitalism allows us to understand the ongoing economic subjugation of the Global South to the Global North long after decolonization, as well as the enormous wealth divisions that persist between white and racialized or Black peoples in the Global North. Indeed, as Robinson has argued, the profit motivations of capital combined with the long-standing pathologization of Blackness can together help decipher the conditions that continue to be imposed by European, Canadian and American governments upon Black nations worldwide. To fully understand the reasons for Black migration to countries like Canada, it's necessary to look at Canada's participation in global economic processes — notably, neocolonialism and neoliberalism — that have caused the massive displacement of African and Caribbean communities from their homelands in the second half of the twentieth century to the present.

Following highly organized, courageous and resilient nineteenth-century Black liberation movements that contributed to the abolition of slavery, as well as the mid-twentieth-century Third World liberation movements which contributed to a near worldwide decolonization, Black and other people of colour the world over were made to pay dearly for their audacity to fight for their independence. White European nations and European-descended white settler colonies, now accustomed to relying on the stolen lands, resources and labour of the darker nations, were not easily dissuaded. Worldwide, beginning in the fifteenth century, the economic relationship between African peoples and people of European descent has been one of unidirectional and un-ending wealth extraction. This has continued into the present, largely unchanged by either abolition or decolonization. To use the words of Robin D.G. Kelley, "we are hardly in a 'postcolonial' moment" — though the official and formalized aspects of colonization have ended, "the political, economic, and cultural links established by colonial domination still remain with some alterations" (2000: 27)

That the entirety of the slave trade and colonization of Africa created enormous wealth for Europeans (and for former British colonies like Canada and the United States) is a matter of historical fact (Rodney 1982; Beckles 2013). Following the abolition of slavery, no reparations were granted to formerly enslaved Black persons anywhere in the diaspora to make amends for the millions of Black lives lost, or for the genocide that decimated the Indigenous populations of the Caribbean islands. Further, there were no reparations granted for the millions of dollars in labourpower and resources stolen, which had played a fundamental role in the economic development of European nations, including Europe's white settler colonies (Beckles 2013). The British Empire did not compensate the much-wronged African peoples, but they did compensate former slave owners: British slave owners were paid twenty million pounds in 1838 as reparations for the loss of their slaves from the colonies (Beckles 2013). Following the Haitian revolution, which achieved Haitian independence in 1804, France used the threat of military involvement to extract a so-called independence debt from the Haitian peoples. As a result, billions of dollars, including interest, were transferred to France from the Haitian peoples between independence and 1947, leaving the Haitian economy destitute (Bryan 1984).

White European-descended nations profited enormously from colonization, and they would continue to profit from the global economic system that followed the independence of many former colonies. Decolonized African and Caribbean nations were not, like Haiti, formally charged an independence debt. However, an informal independence debt would nonetheless be extracted by coercion through the development of international development and "aid" organizations. This continued a centuries-long wealth transfer from Black to white, and more largely, from the Global South to the Global North. Unlike colonization, this wealth transfer was brokered not by individual nations, but by the International Monetary Fund (IMF), which by the early 1980s became the new "supervisor of African treasuries" with significant power to make political choices in countries which were said to be independent (Birmingham 2008). This paternalism followed a familiar racial logic, echoing resoundingly with a belief widely held since slavery: African peoples were not able to care for themselves, but required benevolent white leadership (Smith 2006). Instead of reparations for the centuries of stolen resources, the IMF imposed a large-scale privatization of resources — a sell-off of African public assets to northern investors — and imposed trade deals that favoured the Global North. As a result, newly independent nations gained little wealth from their now privatized precious metals, minerals and other valuable raw materials. In addition, due to the economic controls put in place by the IMF and the World Bank, African nations often continued to rely, as they had under imperialism, on mineral extraction rather than food production. States were prevented from subsidizing agricultural production and forced to rely on American food imports, which significantly undermined self-sufficiency in global agriculture and led to widespread hunger in sub-Saharan Africa (Federici 2012; Leech 2012). Indeed, this economic restructuring of the world, which affected not only African but also Asian, Caribbean, South and Central American nations, is frequently and accurately referred to as neocolonialism, since it replicated the geography and inequality of the unidirectional resource transfer from the now nominally independent countries to their former rulers.

African peoples almost everywhere had become formally free from both slavery and colonization, yet remained shackled by poverty and debt. The neocolonial structural adjustment policies imposed by the IMF and the World Bank (led by the United States and Europe, and supported by Canada) led to debt, deteriorated social conditions, currency devaluations, land privatization and an end to communally held properties, cuts to health, education and social services, and a transfer of economic planning from African governments to the World Bank and other non-governmental organizations (Federici 2012; Smith 2006). This global economic reorganization, falling under the label "neoliberalism," accelerated in the 1990s, expanding privatization and free market ideals over more of the planet than ever before.

Despite vocal anti-globalization movements all over the Global South in the 1990s, the rubric of "development" and "free trade" allowed workers around the purportedly decolonized world to be subjected to far-below-minimum wages and deplorable working conditions, and they were punished for attempting to fight for better wages. Labour-intensive production was much more profitable in the "underdeveloped regions," and reliance on cheap labour in the Global South, including much of the Caribbean and Africa, became the norm in the global economy (Kazemipur and Halli 2001). As production was globalized, corporations increasingly circumvented workplace gains in the North by moving their production "offshore" to benefit from the unregulated, and thus cheapened, labour of the Global South. The so-called global assembly lines of sweatshops worldwide were fed by the work of young Black and brown women, who were also disproportionately harmed by the gutting of social services and the push toward cash crops over subsistence farming, as both had traditionally been women's employment (Federici 2012: 87).

By the late 1990s, Western-imposed "development" had resulted in $500 billion being transferred from the Global South to the Global North annually, leading to the further impoverishment of people of colour across the world (Shiva 1997: 11). By this time, the grave effects of these policies — displacement, poverty, starvation and conflict — were felt all over the Global South, particularly by women (Federici 2012). In particular, the impact of neoliberalism on Africans has been grossly disproportionate (Leech 2012). Unlike in the previous generation of imperialists, when the responsibility for massacres of dark-skinned peoples could be attributed to governments and their militaries, "today, millions of Africans are dying every year but no one is held responsible for it" (Federici 2001: 84). Though technically not military warfare against African peoples, this form of imperialism disguised as an economic program has nonetheless created similar results (Federici 2012: 76–77). The pathologization of Blackness has continued to mask the nature of this large-scale structural violence. The modern crisis faced by Africans — the consequence of neoliberalism — is instead still commonly attributed to "the perverse nature of African politics," an inherent flaw that is seen to stem from the inferiority of African peoples and cultures, and from a view that "tragedy is Africa's destiny" (Smith 2006: 6).

Canada has not merely been a passive economic support for policies aimed at undermining African and Caribbean independence and economic self-sustainability. Though Canadian activities in the continent of Africa do not have the influence of, for example, the United States or China, Canada has proactively participated in forcing African nations to accept neoliberal policies of trade and governance. The influence of IMF and World Bank policies on Canadian foreign policy to Africa "cannot be overemphasized" — for example, the Canadian International Development Agency (CIDA) brokered $590 million in African debt relief in 2005, but support was conditional on the acceptance of policies created by the IMF and the World Bank, policies that continue to be known for destroying lives and livelihoods and causing socioeconomic hardships with long-standing effects (Akuffo 2012). Similar market-based policies have been imposed by CIDA toward Burkina Faso, Ghana, Senegal and Mozambique (Akuffo 2012). Canadian governments and governmental agencies have successively pushed African nations toward cutting public expenditures, privatizing public assets and gearing national economies toward export production (Akuffo 2012).

In addition to economic forms of domination imposed by the government, the presence of Canadian forces in African and Caribbean nations has also demonstrated a more naked aggression. Despite Canada's reputation as a "peacekeeping" nation, the Canadian government has been opposed to anti-colonial struggles and has had a contentious role in many conflicts including the struggle in Somalia (Engler 2015). The research of critical race feminist Sherene Razack has explored how Canadian "peacekeeping" in Black-dominated nations has been largely a colonial practice in which violence toward Black communities abroad has been rationalized as "both normal and necessary" (2004: 8). Further, she brings to light the brutalities inflicted by Canadian peacekeeping troops on Somalis throughout the 1990s, including now-infamous incidents: in one example, Canadian troops photographed the 1993 torture of a Black Somali man, Shidane Abukar Arone, and in another example, a Black soldier was smeared in feces with the words "I love the KKK" in 1995 by a member of Canada's Airborne Regiment (2004: 4–5). Canada's role in perpetuating displacement and even racial terror upon the world's racialized populations is rarely discussed in public conversations on immigration control.

Canada also has a direct role in the displacement of Haitian peoples. Many have now detailed the Canadian government's role in the 2004 *coup d'état* against Haiti's first democratically elected government in three decades, overthrowing Haiti's democratically elected President Jean-Bertrand Aristide. Canada's Royal Canadian Mounted Police (RCMP) joined United Nations (U.N.) troops in this mission and both are seen by many Haitians as occupiers (Engler and Fenton: 2005). Canada provides continued support for the ongoing presence of the U.N. Stabilization Mission in Haiti with $15 million a year, as well as with Canadian forces and police officers (Government of Canada n.d.). As well, the U.N. has finally admitted responsibility for its role in Haiti's cholera epidemic, which has so far resulted in at least ten thousand deaths and hundreds of thousands rendered ill (Katz 2016), and its soldiers have also faced multiple allegations of sexual assault and abuse of minors (Charbonneau and Osterman 2012). However, discussions in Canadian politics surrounding Haitian migrants and refugees rarely acknowledge Canadian complicity in this displacement.

Canadian private interests have also played an important role in the dispossession of Black-dominated countries. In the wider Caribbean, Canadian banks have a long history of imperialism. Though banks are private institutions of capital, they have been allowed to act as "national" institutions abroad that forward Canadian national interests (Hudson 2010). Throughout the twentieth century, anti-colonial activists regularly took aim at the Royal Bank of Canada in Trinidad and Jamaica. In the 1970s, C.L.R James and Black Caribbean students living in Canada decried the fact that Canadian banks owned the majority of commercial and retail banking across the Commonwealth Caribbean, at a rate estimated by *Maclean's* magazine to be ranging between 60 and 90 percent at the time (Hudson 2010). Other private interests, provided with state sanction, contribute to forcing people out of their homes and homelands: Canadian-owned gold companies continue to cause large-scale displacement of African and Caribbean populations, as well as Indigenous communities in Latin America (Gordon and Webber 2008).

Global push factors such as northward capital and resource flows, in which

Canada has knowingly participated, have forced legions of Black and other racialized persons to leave their homes to face uncertainty, possible incarceration, labour exploitation, poverty and humiliation in industrialized countries, as they have followed the flow of capital and resources from South to North. The pillaging of resources brokered by international organizations has resulted in widespread hunger, sparked ethnic conflict and created large numbers of refugees fleeing hunger and violence. Many of these displaced people, including millions of continental Africans, have sought refuge in the United States, Europe, Australia, New Zealand and Canada — the very countries that implement, support and profit from these harmful policies. To escape the conditions imposed by neocolonization and attempt to procure means of survival, Caribbean and African migrants and refugees have found ways to enter Canada and other white-dominated nations. If colonialism and slavery reorganized the earth and its inhabitants in a historically unprecedented way, neocolonialism constitutes yet another massive forced migration of Black peoples out of their homelands.

In Canada, the subjugation of the formerly enslaved and colonized African populations has occurred concurrently with the ever-expanding settler colonial encroachment onto Indigenous territories. The logics of settler colonial capitalist expansion and the Black subjugation that occurred in the second half of the twentieth century, though not identical, are linked (King 2013). Economic marginalization has been a devastating reality inflicted by the state upon Canada's Indigenous population — who, indeed, are the poorest demographic in Canada (ACLC n.d.). The economic marginalization of Canada's Indigenous population has occurred by different means than has Black subjugation: the state has undercut "Indigenous political economies and relations to and with land" and accomplished "the near wholesale dispossession of Indigenous peoples' territories and modes of traditional governance" (Coulthard 2014). While Canada has forced Indigenous peoples onto reserves that represent a tiny fraction of Indigenous peoples' historic territories (Manuel and Derrickson 2015), the state has simultaneously underfunded on-reserve education and child welfare, and has failed to address ongoing minimal access to clean water, adequate housing and healthcare. Together, these measures have been geared toward destroying Indigenous peoples' ways of life (Coulthard 2014). As Black populations have been continuously displaced to a nation built on stolen lands, the meanings still ascribed to Blackness in Canada mean that most Black migrants were not and are not afforded the privileges granted to white settlers and some racialized migrants.

Black displacement to Canada has often been met with further violence: later chapters will explore the lengths the Canadian government has undertaken to prevent, deter and deport increasingly large numbers of racialized migrants by means of border regulation. Here, however, I examine how Black displaced people who arrived in Canada were met with state-sanctioned economic violence, including labour exploitation or wholesale abandonment. They were confined and constrained into the bottom of the labour market, treated as disposable, expendable and unwanted, channelled into subservient and menial labour and otherwise put "in their place" despite official proclamations of multiculturalism. For this reason, the realities of Black migrants are integral to any discussions about the promise of multiculturalism, or of Black poverty and economic precarity in Canada.

LEGACIES OF UNFREE BLACK LABOUR: TEMPORARY WORK PROGRAMS AND UNDOCUMENTED WORKERS

Black communities in Canada are not, and have never been, monolithic. Canada's history of Black bondage has left an important legacy across Canadian society, one that impacts different communities in different ways. Continental Africans, Caribbean and Canadian-born Black populations whose families went back generations all share the experience of economic violence — though this was often accomplished by entirely different state processes. In particular, looking at the history of Canada's temporary work program clearly demonstrates that state processes directing Black migrant labour were strongly influenced by ideas of Blackness that had been developed under slavery.

One of the most flagrant examples of the still-powerful meanings that had been attached to Blackness is Canada's reorganization of racialized migrant labour after the Second World War, when the government introduced the Caribbean Domestic Scheme and the Caribbean Seasonal Agricultural Workers Program. Though the widespread segregation of the early twentieth century had faced legal defeats across the country, the Canadian economy continued to rely on the subjugation of disposable Black labourers with few rights. This was accomplished through newly instituted temporary migrant worker programs. Through the Caribbean Domestic Scheme and the Caribbean Seasonal Agricultural Workers Program, Black subjugation was merely transformed and rebranded for a multicultural era. While race could no longer be openly used to deny labour rights to non-white workers, immigration status would serve the same purpose. Canada's temporary work programs provided an updated means of enforcing Black economic precarity and the exploitation of Black labourers in a way that closely mirrored the conditions of Black enslavement.

After the Second World War, as white women were being liberated from their relegation to unwaged domestic labour, Black migrant women were used to fill the subjugated place that white women had just vacated. Beginning officially in 1955, the Caribbean Domestic Scheme allowed Canadians to sponsor single, childless women from Jamaica, Trinidad and Barbados to labour in Canada as domestic workers (after they had undergone invasive gynecological examinations) (Macklin 1992: 689). Many Caribbean women who were fleeing the intensive poverty of neocolonialism in the Caribbean islands attempted to immigrate to Canada, but most had few legal options outside of the Caribbean Domestic Scheme. This was due to the structure of Canada's immigration laws: even though by the 1960s, country and race specific immigration controls had been replaced by a purportedly race-neutral selection processes, the selection of migrants remained highly determined by sex, race and class — most racialized migrant women were unable to enter the country as independent immigrants (Thobani 2007). From the inception of the program, domestic work permits had been one of the only legal pathways to immigration for racialized women who did not possess considerable funds to invest (Oxman-Martinez, Hanley et al. 2004: 4–5). Black women, even those trained as nurses and teachers, were only able to enter the country as domestics (Bolaria and Li 1998: 201).

Though the Caribbean Domestic Scheme provided some needed opportunities for Black women to earn wages and live in Canada, the structure relied on the same representations of Black women that began under slavery and re-created many of the same exploitative practices. Black women were believed to be naturally suited to be the domestic servants of white families, just as they had been in the centuries before. Notions of Black women's docility and subservience and Canada's long history of having Black "girls" tend house extended to the notion that Caribbean women were "good island girls" (Crawford 2003).

While Caribbean women could live and work in Canada under this program, it nonetheless reproduced Black women's economic, political and social subordination in Canadian society. Economic precarity and vulnerability to abuse was structured into the program itself: because the workers' immigration status was tied directly to their employers, their ability to work and live in Canada was entirely in the hands of their bosses. Domestic workers had to give one year of service before they could apply for permanent residence status. This granted the employers enormous powers over their fate — domestic workers could be, and were, deported for resisting workplace abuse or exploitation, or refusing dangerous working conditions (Silvera 1989; Bakan and Stasiulis 1997: 37). Black domestic workers were often paid far less than minimum wage, subjected to long hours and forced to work while ill, as well as enduring racial slurs and other forms of harassment (Silvera 1989). Continuing the long-standing history of state-sanctioned sexual violence toward Black women, Black domestic workers faced high rates of sexual abuse in the homes they worked and lived in, and had little recourse for fear of deportation (Law Union of Ontario 1981 in Bolaria and Li 1988: 203; Silvera 1989). Often, this abuse was reinforced rather than kept in check by immigration officers, who, having the power to deport Black women, were generally regarded as punitive rather than supportive in instances of workplace abuse (Silvera 1989). It is undeniable that race was a factor in the conditions faced by Caribbean domestic workers: European domestics were largely able to arrive as landed immigrants, which meant that they were free to change employers or otherwise challenge abusive situations, and they were granted the more respected status of "nannies" (Bakan and Stasiulis 2008).

Not only was the very structure of the program economically exploitative, but it was highly carceral and punitive — the conditions of the work allowed for a continuation of surveillance practices that were instituted under slavery. The uninterrupted scrutiny of enslaved domestics by white households was, after all, one of the earliest forms of racialized surveillance (S. Browne 2015; Collins 1990). Domestic work entailed "techniques of surveillance" that included "close scrutiny, sexual harassment, assault, violence, or the threat thereof" that were directly reproduced in the conditions of "free" Black domestic workers (Collins 1998: 20–21 in S. Browne 2015: 57). Interviews of Caribbean domestics, conducted by Makeda Silvera, bring to life the intimate control that white households had over even the most minute movements and actions of the Black women who worked in their homes (1989). One worker reported that even the way that she used her hand as she picked up a dirty cup was subject to the control of her employers (1989). Indeed, beyond the economic exploitation and physical and sexual abuse, the banal and everyday humiliation of having one's movements constantly monitored was itself a form of violence that was indicative of Black women's subordinated role in society.

Despite the extremely hostile and precarious conditions they faced, African-Caribbean women could and did fight back in large and small ways (Silvera 1989). Domestic workers tried to report abuse to immigration officials despite the risk, and would sometimes leave abusive employers even though it could mean their eventual deportation. A twenty-one-year-old Antiguan woman named Julie refused her deportation and went public about the abuse she faced (though she was eventually deported) (Silvera 1989: 25). Black women organized more formally with the Jamaican Canadian Association of Domestic Workers, and some Caribbean women bravely attempted legal challenges. Most famous is the case of the "seven Jamaican mothers" who faced deportation in 1975 for having omitted mentioning that they had dependent children when they applied to work as domestics. With the support of the advocacy group INTERCEDE, they mounted a successful and highly public legal challenge with the Canadian Human Rights Commission (Burman 2007; Silvera 1989). The workers were involved in picketing, flyers and large rallies about the patriarchal and racist nature of these targeted deportations, and were aware of and vocal about the facts that no non-Black women were harassed or deported during that period and Caribbean men were never asked about children. They eventually received popular support and were victorious in overturning their deportations (Silvera 1989).

This organizing, though successful in overturning the deportation orders, was able to effect only cursory changes to the program. In 1981, the program underwent minor changes and was renamed the Foreign Domestic Movement program (and later renamed the Live-in Caregiver Program) but the underlying exploitation remained endemic (Hsiung and Nichol 2010: 770). Further, after the successful mobilizations of Caribbean women in the 1970s, who had shown themselves to be far less subservient than was believed, over the next decades the Canadian government began to prioritize Filipina workers instead (though Caribbean women and some Black African women were still employed through the Live-in Caregiver Program in smaller numbers) (Hodge 2006). In effect, Caribbean women were punished for not ascribing to societal representations of Black women's docility. This removed a legal, albeit still exploitative, way for Black women to enter and work with temporary status and funnelled them instead into "illegality," exposing them to lower wages and even more exploitative conditions (Bakan and Stasiulis 2008: 264; Daenzer 1997: 922). In the 1990s, a set of interviews conducted with Caribbean domestic workers in Ontario found that significant numbers of Black Caribbean workers in Toronto were working without status as domestics in exploitative conditions (Bakan and Stasiulis 2008).

Today, despite decades of organizing for the labour rights granted to Canadian citizens, the Live-in Caregiver Program's workers remain continually vulnerable to physical and sexual abuse under fear of deportation, and continue to report working long hours without overtime pay as well as being forced to perform tasks outside their contracts (Stiell and England 1997; Hodge 2006;

CUPE 2015). A fairly recent survey of both English-speaking Caribbean and Filipina domestic workers in Toronto found that some workers received as low as $2.14 per hour (Bakan and Stasiulis 2008: 272). It is clear that anti-Blackness and sexism, complemented by other forms of racism and xenophobia, continue to constrict the lives of poor racialized and Black women employed by temporary work programs.

Black men from the Caribbean, too, were streamlined into highly exploitative labour by temporary work programs — this, too, occurred just as Canada began to outwardly embrace its multicultural approach to racial equality. The Caribbean Seasonal Agricultural Workers Program (SAWP) was initiated in 1966 between the Canadian government and those of Jamaica, Barbados and Trinidad and Tobago. It was later extended to Mexico and the eastern Caribbean islands. The program admitted Caribbean workers for temporary jobs, for limited amounts of time, without any path to citizenship. These workers filled Canadian labour needs in agriculture, a structural necessity of the Canadian economy (Bolaria and Li 1988: 198). Yet, temporary workers have always faced some of the worst working conditions in Canada, and are barred from the labour protections that protect Canadian citizens. A 1973 Task Force Report for the Department of Manpower and Immigration found deplorable working conditions for the migrant agricultural workers. It outlined non-existent health facilities and evidence of malnutrition, with the report's authors stating that they were "shocked, alarmed, and sickened" at some of the arrangements for migrant workers (Department of Manpower and Immigration Canada 1973: 17–18 in Bolaria and Li 1988: 199). Through the Non-Immigrant Employment Authorization Program (NIEAP), which replaced the SAWP in 1973, approximately three thousand to seven thousand temporary agricultural workers arrived in Canada each year between 1973 and 1984, mostly from the Caribbean but also from Mexico (Bolaria and Li 1988: 197). Official multiculturalism did not change the fact that vulnerable citizenship status functioned with racial discrimination to create unequal types of workers, with Black migrants receiving fewer rights, lower wages and poorer working conditions.

Today, the program is called the Seasonal Agricultural Worker Program and remains rife with abuse. Still employing mostly men from the Caribbean and Mexico, the workers remain prohibited from joining unions, and reports continue to note that workers are paid exploitatively low wages, often work twelve- to fifteen-hour days and are placed in substandard housing. Further, though few women are allowed through this program, those that do are subject to particularly punitive surveillance and control by their employers (Justicia for

Migrant Workers n.d.). Abuse is rampant and well documented in the Seasonal Agricultural Worker Program (SAWP); workers are regularly held captive in situations of coercion by employers who seize their identification (Brem 2006). SAWP workers may be subject to deportation and blacklisting for attempting to organize for better and safer working conditions (Otero and Preibisch 2015).

While the commercial agricultural business, and the Canadian economy more largely, reap enormous profits from the cheapened labour of Black and brown workers, the workers are afforded none of the protections of Canadian labourers (Choudry and Smith 2016). Agricultural work is characterized by very low wages and is a highly dangerous occupation (Orkin et al. 2014). Although temporary workers pay taxes, they often do not have access to health or unemployment benefits. Temporary agricultural workers are denied Canadian medical care when they are ill or injured on the job. Instead, they frequently have their contracts terminated and are deported. Labour policy indicates that in case of illness or injury, "the employer, after consultation with the [worker's] government agent, shall be entitled for non-compliance, refusal to work, or any other sufficient reason, to terminate the worker's employment … and so cause the worker to be repatriated" (Employment and Social Development Canada 2013 in Orkin et al. 2014: 193). A study published in the *Canadian Medical Association Journal* has documented that between 2001 and 2011, 787 SAWP workers were deported due to injury, largely for medical-surgical reasons or poisoning (Orkin et al. 2014: 193). Though migrants are technically entitled to care in Canada, it is a relatively common practice for migrants hired within the SAWP to be deported without receiving medical treatment when injured (McLaughlin and Hennebry in Orkin et al. 2014: 193). Despite the significant profits derived from the labour of Black and brown agricultural and domestic workers, they remain a wholly separate class of workers whose exploitability is continually maintained by the looming threat of deportation.

Temporary labour programs make clear how racial capitalism has normalized the subjugation and exploitation of Black and brown workers, both supported and structured by state policies. Further, the very inception of these work programs was informed by the devaluation of Black life and labour under slavery. The state-mandated treatment of Black Caribbean workers demonstrates how, at the advent of a widely celebrated multiculturalism, virulent anti-Black policies overshadowed Canada's "mosaic." Indeed, the Caribbean temporary work programs can rightly be seen as an extension and consolidation of Jim Crow-style labour practices in Canada.

Today, wealthy countries worldwide increasingly rely upon temporary, unfree labour to cut domestic labour costs (Walia 2013). In Canada, the amount of family-class immigrants continues to drop substantively due to increasingly restrictive immigration policies (Walia and Chu 2015), and the Canadian economy now relies more than ever on temporary racialized workers who have, *de facto,* fewer rights. After remaining steady throughout the nineties, the number of agricultural workers almost doubled in 2004, growing to nearly forty thousand in 2013. Although many workers return to Canada year after year, subsidizing the agricultural economy and the food eaten by the Canadian population, they remain unwanted as national subjects. Out of the forty thousand migrant agricultural workers in 2013, only 173 were able to become permanent residents of Canada. The number of domestic workers — who do have a path to Canadian citizenship — has remained more stable, at just over twenty thousand in 2013 (Citizenship and Immigration Canada 2014). More than ever, multicultural Canada relies economically on unfree labour, which follows the exclusionary logics of slavery to create a class of people who can be used for physical labour but from whom are withheld the basic rights accorded to Canadian-born labourers. Though not counted in statistics about racialized or Black poverty, these workers clearly constitute what Bolaria and Li call an economic class defined by "super-exploitation" (1988: 205). It is rare that migrant justice and Black organizing in Canada present temporary work programs as a Black issue. But because the devaluation of Black life by the Canadian state played a substantive role in the creation of Canada's temporary work programs, and continues to impact thousands of Black workers, it is important that this reality not fall under the radar.

Undocumented Black workers, too, are subject to extreme levels of economic exploitation and vulnerability. Canada benefits enormously from the presence of "illegal" migrant labour, due to savings in wages and social benefits (Bolaria and Li 1998: 232–234). Because of the clandestine nature of undocumented work, the poverty levels of Black undocumented migrants have not so far been measurable. Still, undocumented workers generally work in the most dangerous occupations, and because they live and work under constant threat of detention and deportation, they remain highly vulnerable to wage exploitation and workplace abuse, with no access to recourse or benefits of any kind. An open letter delivered to Prime Minister Justin Trudeau from the Non-Status Women's Collective of Montreal states their condition clearly:

> We clean your homes, serve you in restaurants, work on assembly lines, produce the food you eat. We pay taxes. However, we are excluded from all social programmes: education, healthcare, child

benefits, daycare, and unemployment insurance. We are among the most exploited people in society: we work long hours in very difficult conditions, we do not get minimum wage, we do not have job protection, we are not unionized. (Non-Status Women's Collective 2015)

The precarity faced by undocumented Black workers is an important and often-overlooked facet of the conditions of highly vulnerable Black labourers in Canada. Considering the legacy of slavery and racist dehumanization, economic justice for undocumented workers is not only an immigration issue, but also a racial justice issue. In the words of an editorial entitled "Amnesty for Black Women Workers" published in *Our Lives: Canada's First Black Women's Newspaper,* "[Black undocumented women] deserve to be legal in this country and to enjoy the benefits of our labour" (1986: 1).

The structural segregation of the economy based on citizenship maintains several layers of a disposable and rights-less migrant workforce. Both temporary and undocumented workers live and labour in conditions of unfreedom — arbitrary punishment, deprivation of wages, vulnerability to the whims and abuses of their employers — in a form of near-bondage that is not dissimilar from the conditions of enslavement. To use the words of migrant justice advocate Chris Ramsaroop, "It's no coincidence that the same black and brown people that underwent slavery and indentureship are also going through this today" (in Cole 2016a). This connection is frequently made by migrant workers, activists and scholars (Cole 2016a; Bolaria and Li 1988: 185–205). However, the lingering legacy of slavery that manifests in state labour policies has not been confined only to temporary and undocumented workers — all Black communities have been impacted by the devaluation of Black life and labour.

ORGANIZED ABANDONMENT: THE STATE'S ROLE IN IMPOVERISHING BLACK COMMUNITIES

The protections of Canadian citizenship (or permanent resident status) have not protected Canada's African diaspora from an economic subjugation. The often-abject economic conditions of African, Caribbean and Canadian Black populations demonstrate that, regardless of citizenship or place of birth, structural racism continues to foster significant wealth disparities. Migrant Caribbean and African populations have also been streamed into un/underemployment, poverty, low wages and highly gendered work. These same conditions of poverty and precarity define the lives of Canada's long-standing African Canadian population — in particular, African Nova

Scotians. In short, it is *Blackness* that is the determinant of poverty and economic vulnerability.

Ruth Wilson Gilmore (2007, 2015) has described how under modern (racial) capitalism, racialized populations have been subject to an "organized abandonment." Black and other racialized populations, she argues, have been largely deemed expendable since the welfare state transitioned into a more neoliberal economy. These communities have been subjected to discriminatory employment and labour practices while receiving little state support, and relegated to low-wage work or unemployment, all further accentuated by an increased reliance on offshore labour. In short, they have been abandoned into economic precarity and poverty. Indeed, while cutbacks in social spending and increased reliance on offshore production have created larger wealth gaps between the rich and poor in Canada, the wealth gap has been racialized, as it has been in the United Kingdom and the United States as well. To borrow the words of Stuart Hall, "Race is the modality in which class is lived" (Hall et al. 2013: 394). In Canada, both Black populations born elsewhere and African Canadians have been subject to distinct state processes of abandonment, which have cemented the economic subjugation of Black communities.

After the end of formal colonialism, racial capitalism and neoliberalism went beyond the displacement of Black and brown populations living in the Global South. Those same displaced populations faced acute economic inequalities, along racial lines, upon arrival to Canada and other European-descended nations. Though neocolonialism was a push factor that forced millions of formerly enslaved and colonized African and Caribbean populations out of their homelands, their arrival in the Global North did not protect them from highly racialized wealth disparities — just the opposite. Though in the 1960s, racialized migrants briefly began to come closer to equity with the earnings of white Canadians, this was short-lived. In the ensuing decades, many racialized migrants fared far worse than white migrants who arrived either previously or simultaneously, even when education and language proficiency is considered (Galabuzi 2006: 9). This can be explained by the unequal societal distribution of poverty and opportunity that was exacerbated by neoliberalism.

Since the beginning of the 1980s, poverty levels in Canada and across the Global North have been steadily rising (Kazemipur and Halli 2001: 218). Margaret Thatcher, Brian Mulroney and Ronald Reagan all pushed for large-scale reform, such as massively diminishing the welfare state. Calls for neoliberal policies — the balancing of budgets and deficit reductions — translated into significant cuts to social services, equity initiatives and supports for low-income families. Wealth, according to proponents, would supposedly "trickle down" to the less affluent. Instead, the opposite occurred. A significant income gap widened between the rich and the poor within Canada, one that would become increasingly stark with each passing decade. Growing wealth gaps did not impact all communities in Canada equally, but followed a colour line — the income of most racialized migrants was no longer comparable with that of other immigrants or of white Canadians (Galabuzi 2006: 11; Bolaria and Li 1988). The effects of what many have called a "war on the poor" were felt, in particular, by women and trans peoples, those with disabilities, racialized youth and especially by Black and Indigenous communities (see Federici 2012: 91–114; Mirchandani and Chan 2005). This racialized wealth gap did not occur haphazardly: a comparative statistical analysis of the economic conditions of racialized and white permanent residents and citizens in Canada demonstrates a history of racial discrimination in wage, working conditions and employment (Galabuzi 2006).

Though preservation of ethnic and racial "culture" was purportedly prioritized as multiculturalism was strengthened — recognized in section 27 of the *Charter of Rights and Freedoms* in 1982, then passed into law in 1988 — neoliberal policies consistently impoverished Canada's racial minorities, pushing Black people deeper into the margins of society. Black poverty, whether Canadian-born, Caribbean or African, began to climb in earnest. The wealth gap has been both racialized and gendered: in 1981, 70 percent of Blacks earned less than $16,000 and 85 percent of Black women earned less than that amount. Of those women, half earned less than $8,000 (1981 Census of Canada in Bolaria and Li 1988: 195). By the end of the 1980s, Black women earned less than other immigrant populations, and 27 percent less than other women (Calliste 1991 in Yesufu 2005: 135). Black migrants, permanent residents and Black Canadians all received lower income for doing the same work as white Canadians, and faced significant discrimination in employment and promotion, even though many migrant Black populations had comparatively higher levels of education than white Canadians at this time (Bolaria and Li 1988). African Nova Scotians working in the civil service experienced systemic discrimination across all levels of employment, which extended to their ability to access housing and social services (Report of the Special Committee on Visible Minorities 1984, Report of the Royal Commission on Equality in Employment 1984 and Head 1975 in Bolaria and Li 1988: 195). Streamed into the lower echelons of the economy, Black women remained over-represented in low-end manufacturing and service sectors in comparison to Canadian born, non-Black women (Leah 1991, Boyd 1986 and Ng 1988 in Yesufu 2005: 134).

Throughout the 1990s, multiculturalism was increasingly promoted as part of Canadian identity through political and electoral discourse (Bannerji 2000: 8), though it served only to mask the intensifying social and racial inequalities born of the 1980s. Even when accounting for education and language, income inequality expanded significantly in this decade regardless of birthplace and citizenship (Galabuzi 2006). The celebration and preservation of cultures intrinsic to Canada's multiculturalism policy continued to function as a smokescreen, standing in for meaningful change or the implementation of anti-racist policies that could have challenged the status quo (Bannerji 2000). This growing racial wealth gap was partly the effect of ongoing neoliberal restructuring: in the early 1990s, the Canadian federal government, following the example of the United States, eliminated the Canada Assistance Plan, which had included the provision of Canadian standards of social, medical and education resources. This led to more cuts in public spending on welfare and social programs by provincial governments, leading to an increase in poverty (Neve and Pate 2004). Until now, Black and other racialized people continue to be relegated to low-wage, non-unionized work. Some forms of racial discrimination have been structural: the lack of recognition of foreign credentials and experience, for example, and arbitrary requirements for "Canadian experience." But these have been compounded and complemented by more outright discrimination (Ontario Human Rights Commission 2013).

Along with discriminatory employment practices, government-designed resettlement programs in the 1990s and 2000s have been documented as playing an important role in impoverishing Black and other racialized migrants. Since the 1990s, the government defunded and narrowed immigrant employment programs, refocusing their efforts on pushing skilled racialized immigrants to take any job (frequently temporary, contractual, low end and low earning), rather than channelling them into their skilled fields. Immigration resettlement programs have been found to funnel racialized migrants into the lowest echelons of the labour market, with men being funnelled into low-paid manual labour and women into the service sector (Creese and Wiebe 2009: 59). Focus groups on highly educated sub-Saharan Black migrants in Vancouver found that two-thirds of participants had been in Vancouver over five years, but regardless of this "Canadian experience," most men worked in manual labour and most women worked in low-skilled or manual labour for basic survival income (Creese and Wiebe 2009: 61). Black migrant poverty and economic subordination, then, has not occurred as a "natural" outcome of Black migration or as a result of cultural pathology, but was created and/or supported by state forces.

Black women, as always, have been disproportionately impacted by purportedly "neutral" state policies. Black African and Caribbean women's poverty in Canada is a direct outcome of both government action and inaction over the years. Yet, their work today remains highly undervalued, and this has been accomplished in part by state immigration and resettlement practices. The points-based system and Canada's family class policies, while widely believed to be neutral and merit driven, promote both gender inequality and women's subordination to men. This form of immigration selection continues to favour men, and tends to categorize women as men's "dependents." This, in turn, affects migrant women's ability to access services geared toward employment and placement, and reinforces the role of women as the primary and, importantly, un-waged family caregivers (Creese and Wiebe 2009: 59; Thobani 2007: 134–136). Black and other racialized migrant women, often highly educated, are not only channelled into low-wage work, but they are also continually channelled by immigration settlement agencies into retraining programs geared toward "women's work" — that is, widely underpaid forms of labour in caregiving or service provision (Creese and Wiebe 2009: 59–62). A focus group by Adenike O. Yesufu on recently migrated African women in Edmonton in the early twenty-first century found that 80 percent of respondents had post-secondary education, over 50 percent had acquired their higher education in Canada, and yet many made under $15,000 per year, while the rest of the group made under $30,000. The sample included women trained as lawyers, accountants, computer programmers, high school teachers, secretaries and engineers, most of whom were working as housekeepers, nannies and other menial, low-paying jobs (Yesufu 2005: 136–137). This focus group is indicative of a larger reality facing African and Caribbean women: race and gender determine social and economic position far more than education background and experience. Nearly 60 percent of all African migrants living in Alberta have a post-secondary education, yet more than 40 percent of African women in Alberta work in the service sector, and more than one in ten work in processing and manufacturing (Lamba, Mulder and Wilkinson 2000 in Okeke-Iherjirika and Spitzer 2005: 211). I include these facts not to suggest that those who are designated as "unskilled" due to lack of education are more deserving of poverty, but to demonstrate the *power* that race and gender still have to transcend so-called objective measures of personal worth. No matter what their background or education, Black women continue to be seen as "the help."

That Black migrant communities were systematically de-skilled upon their arrival is an often-overlooked facet of understanding Black poverty in Canada today. Indeed, it represents the power of anti-Blackness to transcend even economic interests: even in moments when Canada required highly educated professionals, Black migrants meeting those exact criteria were nonetheless largely streamlined into low-skilled work and relative powerlessness. Challenging popular misconceptions that all "newcomers" face economic barriers, a comparative analysis between whites and racialized first generation migrants found that, even when accounting for education and age, the racialized men made less than 70 percent of the earnings of first generation white men, and racialized women earned less than 50 percent of the earnings of first generation white men, making clear that "a colour code" and a gendered hierarchy are ongoing realities of today's labour market (Block and Galabuzi 2011: 3).

Canada's acceptance of Somali refugees has also demonstrated the role state policies have played in creating poverty and precarity for people of African descent who arrive in Canada. While this will be addressed in more detail later, it is important here to note that Somali refugees arriving in the 1990s and 2000s faced distinct barriers and uniquely discriminatory treatment that relegated them into extreme economic vulnerability. Because of barriers to permanent resident status, it was difficult for Somalis to access legal and stable work, which relegated Somali families to poverty and unstable, dilapidated housing (Pegg 2004; Ontario Council of Agencies Serving Immigrants [OCASI] 2016).

The material conditions of Black life in Canada make clear that "diversity" — that is, the increased presence of Black communities — is not a triumph of racial egalitarianism and multiculturalism. Demographic shifts toward larger Black and racialized populations in the country should not stand in for evidence of a lack of racism. Indeed, Canada's Black population has grown substantially in recent decades. Despite immigration measures that have rendered Black migration comparatively more difficult than that of many other populations, over half of Canada's Black population (53 percent) was born elsewhere (Statistics Canada 2011). Over sixty thousand Africans arrived in Canada in during the 1980s and this number had reached 282,600 by 2001, including refugees and asylum seekers (Statistics Canada 2003 in Tettey and Puplampu 2005: 26). Statistics Canada reported in 2007 that there were 82,000 Haitians living in Canada, mostly in Québec (2007a). Between 2006 and 2011, 145,700 people arrived from Africa (Statistics Canada 2013). In 2011, just under 945,700 persons self-identified as Black, making up approximately 3 percent of Canada's population and Canada's third-largest visible minority. Almost one-quarter of Canada's Black population is Jamaican (22.8 percent), followed by Haitians (13.9 percent), people from the British islands, (10 percent), Somalians (4.4

percent) and Trinidadian/Tobagonian (3.7 percent). Almost half (42 percent) of Canada's Black population lives in Toronto and nearly a quarter (24 percent) in Montréal (Statistics Canada 2011). Despite Canada's growing Black population, Black poverty persists across nationality, regardless of place of birth.

While some may be tempted to blame xenophobia or fear of Black "newcomers" — instead of anti-Blackness — for the material deprivation of Canada's Black communities, the conditions of Canada's most long-standing Black communities refute this explanation. Almost 10 percent of Black Canadians, largely African Nova Scotians, have ancestry in Canada dating back three generations or more (Statistics Canada 2011). Since the abolition of slavery, Black Canadians have been relegated to extreme poverty and have been subject to discrimination in wages, education, housing and social services (Bolaria and Li 1998: 194–196). After surviving centuries of hardship, Canada's oldest Black communities in Nova Scotia were subject to economic neglect. In the 1960s, nearly 80 percent of Black Nova Scotians lived in "conditions of utter poverty" (BLAC 1994: 27). Caribbean-born women as well as Black women with citizenship were largely relegated to domestic work (Bolaria and Li 1998: 201). Reportedly, young Black girls in Nova Scotia often had to stay out of school to tend to their families, because their families' poverty meant that their mothers were required to work as domestics (BLAC 1994). Many Black women in Halifax were relegated to domestic work well into the 1990s (Brand 1999).

Perhaps the most famous example of the devaluation of one of Canada's most long-standing Black populations is Africville, a centuries-old Black community that had been deliberately underserviced, impoverished and used as a dump by the city of Halifax. Before it was destroyed by the Halifax government in the 1960s, its Black residents were forcibly removed or relocated. The last building in Africville was, in fact, bulldozed in 1967 (Clairmont and Magill 1999: 257). In addition to Africville, hundreds of other Black Haligonians were displaced throughout the 1960s (Rutland forthcoming; Jones and Walker 2016). A housing survey conducted in 1973 in Halifax revealed that 69 percent of Black homes lacked running water and indoor plumbing, 50 percent lacked central heating, most homes required major repairs, and public transportation and garbage collection was nearly nonexistent (in Rutland *forthcoming*). This carries forward the tradition of feigned benevolence masking anti-Black practices: just as "climatic" reasons were used to discourage Black migration, the forced displacement of poor Black families was undertaken, supposedly, "for their own benefit." While a newly minted multiculturalism policy would soon claim to preserve ethnic communities, the forcibly relocated Black residents of Halifax were largely abandoned by the municipal and federal governments to poverty and loss of culture and community. Today, Nova Scotia's Black communities continue to face ongoing racial discrimination in employment, compounded by discrimination in education and housing, and remain subject to grossly disproportionate rates of poverty.

Indeed, statistics on Black poverty and unemployment today demonstrate a remarkable consistency between markedly heterogeneous Black populations. The economic hardships faced by those with African features cross national-ity, as well as time spent in Canada. Though new migrants often fare worse, Black communities that have lived in Canada for centuries are also subjected to the ills of poverty. Recent Black migrants, second generation Caribbean and African migrants, and Canada's oldest Black populations all face exceedingly high rates of poverty. For example, persons with Haitian ancestry average an income of less than $20,000 per year, with women earning even less than Haitian men, and these numbers are nearly identical for people of continental African ancestry (Statistics Canada 2007a, 2007b). Black Nova Scotian women, whose ancestry in Canada can be traced up to four generations back, also live in extreme poverty compared to white Canadians; 57 percent of unattached Black Nova Scotian women lived below the low income cut-off rate in 2006, regardless of their education background, compared to 13 percent of other Nova Scotians, pointing to systemic issues in hiring and pay (Statistics Canada 2006 in MacEwen and Saulnier 2010: 11). In 2011, both Black Nova Scotian men and women earned significantly less than white Nova Scotians, and had higher unemployment rates than the rest of the province, as well as anywhere else in Canada (Bombay and Hewitt 2015: 32). The 2011 National Household Survey found that over one-third of African Nova Scotians (34.8 percent) earned low incomes, compared to less than one in five (16.5 percent) non-African Nova Scotians (in African Nova Scotian Affairs 2014).

Across Canada, the rate of Black unemployment is 73 percent higher than the rate of unemployment held by white Canadians (Block and Galabuzi 2011). As well, periods of economic growth do not extend to Black popula-tions — during 2000 and 2005, the earnings of white Canadians went up by 2.7 percent, while lowering by 0.7 percent for Black populations. Black people, regardless of their qualifications and skills, are among the poorest persons living in Canada, and Black women are especially so. Black women earn 88 percent of the earnings of white women, 79 percent the earnings of Black men, and a jar-ring 57 percent of the earnings of white Canadian men (Canadian Association of Social Workers 2005: 2; Block and Galabuzi 2011). Recent statistics have shown that approximately two-thirds of Black children live in poverty nationally (ACLC n.d.). Additionally, in 2000, over one-third of Black women in families (34.5 percent) were poor and over half (52.7 percent) of single Black women lived in poverty, compared to 13.7 percent for all women in families and 41.9 percent for all single Canadian women (ACLC n.d.: 17). In Montréal, Black communities experience the highest poverty rate of all racialized groups in the city, with almost half of the city's Black population being categorized as low-income earners, compared to a rate of 65 percent for newer immigrants (Caldas and Sylvain 2009 in ACLC n.d.: 3). In Toronto, 2012 data from the Toronto District School Board found that 48 percent of Black children lived in families with incomes of less than $30,000 a year, compared to 9 percent of white children — a rate five times higher. As well, almost 40 percent of white children in grades seven to twelve had parents in management positions, a rate almost four times higher than that of Black children at 12 percent (Toronto District School Board 2012 in Polyani et al. 2014).

Black poverty, unemployment and precarity have been the result of high rates of employment and exclusion from highly paid jobs. Deliberate state policies *created* a low-paid, underemployed workforce with low job security. This has been accompanied by neglect, which the African Canadian Legal Clinic addresses as "a failure to implement equitable policies to address disparities in employment, economics, and education" (2012: 6). Indeed, though the rate of poverty for all racialized migrants has increased, numerous factors — including persistent anti-Black discrimination in the labour force, lower wages, higher unemployment rates, and insecure employment — have led to "the most striking" earnings gap for Black Canadians, regardless of their immigration status or level of education (Samuel and Basavarajappa 2006 in ACLC 2012: 13).

Racism is not the only factor that impacts the vastly unequal wealth distribution in Canadian society; anti-Blackness intersects in important ways with other forms of oppression. The combined forces of neoliberalism and multiple articulations of state-level anti-Black racism have pushed nearly all Black bodies to the margins of society. Yet, institutional violence through the form of economic discrimination is particularly acute for those Black lives that are marginalized even within the Black community. Black people are not marginalized identically, and economic disenfranchisement is not identically experienced. The material conditions of Black people with disabilities and Black sexual minorities has been largely invisibilized in data collection in Canada and remains largely ignored by policy makers, academics and local, provincial and national government agencies. It is important not to cast aside the realities of these communities due to the demonstrable lack of concerted data. By considering only the already well-documented forms of Black economic subjugation, we risk missing, yet again, a moment to interrupt the erasure of Black persons who live at the intersection of multiple oppressions, whose stories are complex and often go untold.

The discrimination faced by Black people with disabilities persists across the diaspora. In recent years, Black Americans and Canadians have begun organizing politically around the issue of Black disability, including the formation of a Black Disability Coalition and a recently published book entitled *Disability Incarcerated: Imprisonment and Disability in the United States and Canada* by Liat Ben-Moshe, Allison C. Carey and Chris Chapman (2014). Despite a lack of Canadian-specific studies on poverty specific to Black persons with disabilities, there is much to infer from the information available that makes clear the lived effects of ableism. In 2000, over a quarter of all women over fifteen years old with disabilities lived in poverty, with an average income of $17,200, while men in the same demographic averaged $26,900 (Statistics Canada 2006: 297 in Public Health Agency of Canada 2008). Neoliberalism and cuts to social services has had important effects on people living with cognitive disabilities. Efforts of deinstitutionalization have been undercut by the lack of psychiatric and mental health resources, which has led to people with cognitive and mental disabilities being "literally dumped into the streets," impoverished and without housing (Neve and Pate 2004: 28). As a group, since Black communities are already subject to extremely high rates of poverty and unemployment across Canada and experience discrimination in accessing social and health services (Toronto Public Health 2013), the further economic marginalization likely experienced by Black people with disabilities, especially women, must not be ignored.

The societal hostility faced by anyone with African features becomes, as well, infinitely more extreme when that person also falls outside of gender or sexual norms. There is little information on income inequality specific to Black sexual minorities in Canada, but American research tells us that people of colour who are sexual minorities often face conditions of devastating poverty due to the combined factors of state racism and massive discrimination in terms of jobs, housing and social services (Movement Advancement Project [MAP] and Centre for American Progress 2015). In Canada, Black people of any gender experience widespread discrimination in hiring processes and are largely restricted from high-paying jobs. Many trans people, particularly those who are racialized, face particularly acute discrimination in employment, leading to grossly inequitable access to employment, health, housing and income, and as a result, they experience extremely high rates of poverty (Namaste 2005; Spade 2011).

The poverty of Black trans people results from multiple and intersecting forms of marginalization. Structural barriers in securing employment and housing include racism, lack of family and community support, significant financial barriers in coverage for gender transition surgery and difficulty in procuring legal identification (which can "out" trans people to their employers or health or social service providers). These barriers can cause not only poverty, but extreme isolation and marginalization (Action Santé Travesti(e)s et Transsexuel(le)s du Québec [ASTT(e)Q] 2011). A survey of four hundred transgender persons in Ontario found a median income of $15,000 per year and noted that, due to employment discrimination, only 37 percent were employed full-time (Bauer et al. 2011). Because the lives of trans women of colour are often demarcated by poverty, many earn a living through the sex trade, a criminalized form of labour that is therefore marked by an absence of labour rights or income security (Namaste 2005: 70; Fletcher 2013). Homophobic or transphobic discrimination also impacts the way that poverty is experienced by Black sexual minorities, because it can limit access to emergency and support resources intended for impoverished people. Transphobia, homophobia and racism within service provision means that accessing even last-resort resources such as food banks, shelters and social workers is fraught with peril. Despite racialized trans folks being one of the most precarious populations, many social services are not adapted to their needs or realities, sometimes even refusing them services (Kidd 2003; ASTT(e)Q 2011; Abramovich 2012). Yet, youth who are racial and sexual minorities experience high rates of homelessness and are often among those most needing shelter (Abramovich 2012). Homophobic and/or transphobic stigma and discrimination, combined with high rates of abject poverty and social isolation, endanger the very lives of Black sexual minorities (Grant et al. 2011). The economic realities of Black sexual minorities are too often invisible, and are essential for any study or advocacy around Black poverty. Ableism, homophobia and transphobia compound the experience of state-sanctioned economic violence that is directed at the African diaspora in Canada.

CONCLUSION

Anti-Blackness serves an economic function, as it has since the practice of chattel slavery and later systems of Black subjugation. The devaluation of Black life has widely justified a worldwide and national devaluation of Black labour, which serves the interest of capital. The making of contemporary Black poverty and precarity did not occur by one simple process, but is the result of numerous state policies and agencies that have acted in concert on heterogeneous and diverse Black populations. This has resulted, too, in enormous profits for the Canadian economy (Bolaria and Li 1988; Galabuzi 2006).

Multiculturalism has served a role similar to that of the Underground Railroad, allowing Canadian state officials and the general public to congratulate themselves on Canada's comparative benevolence, while rendering invisible the acute economic and material deprivation currently facing many Black communities. Despite the promises of a widely celebrated multicultural policy, the reality of the state's treatment of Black lives in Canada since the Second World War make visible not only the ongoing devaluation of Black labour, but the ongoing devaluation of Black life itself. While economic violence has played an important role toward this end, it does not, by far, encapsulate the full extent of Black dehumanization in Canada.

In Canada, as in the United Kingdom and United States, the racialized poverty that resulted from the slashing of social services and supports was attributed to pathological individual or cultural failures of the poor, rather than being a result of economic policies. Racialized poor people, in particular, were represented as lazy and idle (stereotypes that had also been attributed to Blackness under slavery).

This important shift in public discourse did more than cast disenfranchised populations as unsympathetic. Throughout the advance of neoliberalism in the past several decades, the victims of harsh economic policies were increasingly represented as victimizers. Black and other racialized persons, migrants, single mothers and others abandoned by a diminishing welfare state were scapegoated as freeloaders and possible criminals. Indeed, at the same time as neoliberal states have scaled back investment in social services and supports, a significant investment of public funds has turned toward policing and incarceration (Gilmore 2015). In Canada, state abandonment in the mid- to late twentieth century was accompanied by a renewed investment in state surveillance and repression in Black communities. As the following pages explore, Black communities were scapegoated for all kinds of social and economic ills, and were made to be the targets of state violence that included intensive policing and confinement.

CHAPTER THREE

ARRESTED (IN)JUSTICE

From the streets to the prison

> I am crime. I have known this is my first encounter with the police
> ... what can I think when police officers pursue me because they
> see me, when what I have supposedly done is determined by police
> officers after I've been stopped — what can I think but that they lie
> in wait, confident that there is a problem with my very existence that
> will emerge and provide them with what they already know, and that
> problem ... is that I exist? (Gordon 1997: 21)

WHILE SLAVERY WAS OFFICIALLY ABOLISHED ALMOST two centuries ago,
Canada's legacy of exerting control over Black bodies was reconsolidated,
perhaps most strongly, in the criminal justice system. Today, law enforcement
officials, jails and prisons, as well as the courts and parole boards, play an
increasingly significant role in the "managing" of Black populations in Canada
that have, as elsewhere, been made disposable. Black people in Canada are
subject to invasive police surveillance that makes it difficult to exist in public
space. Black folks, as well as being more likely to be stopped and questioned,
are more likely than the general population to be charged, severely sentenced
and incarcerated in jails or prisons, and are less likely to be granted parole.
The economic subordination and abandonment of Black communities has
acted in parallel with expanding the scope of racialized surveillance and punishment across the criminal justice system. As well, the policing of Black life,
while serving an economic function — that is, the repression of marginalized

populations — also engenders forms of violence that exceed the economic (Wilderson 2010; King 2014). The attribution of danger to Black bodies has been so successful that the policing of Black people extends quickly into bodily harm. To be Black is not only to be targeted for questioning or arrest, it is also to be "proximate to death" (Sharpe 2016: 16) — that is, to live with an accentuated vulnerability to being violently beaten by police or by prison guards, to being placed in long-term solitary confinement for months that a time, or to being killed by the police. In the case of Abdirahman Abdi, to be Black meant not only to be violently assaulted by a law enforcement officer but also to be left, bleeding, for an extended period before emergency services were even contacted (Cole 2016b). Black life has been so effectively stigmatized that even highly spectacular forms of state violence are largely unrecognized as such, and go uncontested by much of mainstream society.

The demonization of Black communities that has been continually reinforced by the criminal justice system has been largely accomplished by age-old associations between Blackness and criminality. While earlier pages explored how this trope dates back centuries, in recent decades, it has been increasingly the case that, to use the words of Angela Y. Davis, "fear of Black *people*, whether economically or sexually grounded, is ... being grounded in a fear of crime" (1998: 65, emphasis added). In the name of public safety, Canada has excluded ever-increasing rates of Black populations from state protections — and from participation in social, economic and political life — and has undertaken a renewed investment in targeting Black communities, which are widely regarded as "criminal."

THE RACIALIZATION OF CRIME

Defenders of the status quo have argued that Blacks are not unjustly profiled, policed and incarcerated because of their race, but because they are, in fact, more likely to break the law than whites. With an ahistorical lens, one could look at the enormous racial disparities across the criminal justice system as evidence not of racism, but as proof of the prevalence of Black criminality. In this view, the high rates of Black prisoners are seen as just, if perhaps unfortunate. This seemingly commonsensical understanding of the high rates of Black incarceration dates back four centuries in Canada.

The genealogy of modern incarceration and policing starts in the era of slavery and colonization. Indeed, the slave ships, which embodied captivity at its most extreme, served to foreshadow Black incarceration today (S. Browne 2015; Rodriguez 2007). Racialized surveillance, too, stems from centuries prior.

As explored earlier, public associations between Blackness and crime can be traced back to runaway slave advertisements dating back to the seventeenth century, in which self-liberated Blacks were portrayed as thieves and criminals. All free and enslaved people were subject to the surveillance of a larger white community and law enforcement officials, who together scrutinized the presence of Black bodies in public space as possibly criminal "runaways" (Kitossa 2005; Nelson 2016a, 2016c). After slavery's abolition, the associations between Blackness and crime served important political, social, economic and cultural functions in maintaining the racial order, and the ongoing surveillance and policing of Blackness — and the corresponding wildly disproportionate arrest and incarceration rates — were quintessential in the late nineteenth and early twentieth centuries in Canada. These associations with Blackness, today, while articulated through a slightly different language (thugs, gansgsters or, in Québec, "les yos"), remain markedly unchanged.

The history of racialized surveillance, policing and incarceration in Canada was also profoundly shaped by, and geared toward, the aims of settler colonialism. The imposition of forcing Indigenous persons onto reserves and then, beginning in 1846, residential schools, were the initial modes of confinement levelled at Indigenous persons, confining Indigenous populations onto tiny portions of land and attempting to destroy political sovereignty and traditional relationships to land, to clear the way for settler societies and resource extraction (Hunt 2013). Canada's first policing body, the North-West Mounted Police (now the Royal Canadian Mounted Police [RCMP]), created in 1873, played an important role in the Canadian government's arsenal toward quelling Indigenous rebellion and protecting the economic interests of white settlers (Comack 2012). In recent years, though, the criminal justice system, particularly law enforcement, jails and prisons, has become a primary means of settler violence over Indigenous bodies; "criminal control" remains an integral part of conquest (Nichols 2014: 448). Indigenous persons now make up a substantial proportion of those held captive in Canada's jails and prisons: while representing around 5 percent of Canadian society, they make up almost one-quarter of the current total inmate population Canada-wide (Sapers 2015). This is a rate of incarceration even higher than that of Canada's Black population. Policing remains a site of colonial dispossession of Indigenous peoples and their resources. This adversarial role was seen as recently as the Oka "crisis" of 1990, and in 2007–2008 in the response to road blockades and land occupations in Tyendinaga Mohawk Territory, where the Ontario Provincial Police deployed hundreds of armed police officers, including snipers. The RCMP continues an ongoing surveillance of Indigenous land defenders (Amnesty International 2012). This makes clear that policing remains, as well, integral to the project of settler colonialism in Canada. Both historically and in the present, policing Blackness occurs alongside and as a part of the policing of Canada's Indigenous communities.

In the present, fear of Blackness is euphemistically articulated through a fear of crime, and treated as such by the state. The contemporary association between Blackness and crime is frequently reflected in national discourse. In 1990s Ontario, popular associations between Black migrants and crime were commonly made by politicians and the police (Henry 1994). Former mayor of Toronto June Rowlands stated in numerous campaign speeches that Black youth are responsible for the crime rates and commit more crimes than whites. This has also been repeated by senior police officers, including senior police officer Chief McCormack, who stated, "there is a real problem in the Black community" (Henry 1994: 220). This association touches the very fabric of law enforcement. In 2014, a *Journal de Montréal* writer discovered that the course material for the first year of police college in one Montréal institution taught students that Blacks commit more crimes than whites and are more prone to violence, theft and sexual assault (Berthomet 2014). The Canadian population continues to associate race — and Blackness in particular — with criminality (Owusu-Bempah and Wortley 2011). High-profile media outlets and persons in power continue to support this notion. *Globe and Mail* columnist Margaret Wente defended the practice of racially focused policing, arguing that police are correct to assume that "Blacks persons, and particularly Jamaicans, are more prone to criminality" (2002).

Still, policing is presented as a race-neutral practice. To use the words of former Toronto police deputy chief Peter Sloly, police "go where crime occurs. We go where the community calls us to go" (in Mascarenhas 2015). Assertions of racial profiling or systemic racism continue to be vehemently denied by most police leaders (Tanovich 2004). Confronted with data demonstrating enormous disproportions in police stops, president of the Toronto Police Association Mike McCormack nonetheless argued in a *Toronto Star* op-ed that it is "irresponsible" to suggest that race plays a role in policing (McCormack 2015). However, racial profiling has played an important role in creating criminals.

"Crime" itself is not a neutral category. So-called criminal behaviour is widespread, and overall, activities deemed criminal are both common and evenly distributed across race and class (Commission on Systemic Racism in the

Ontario Criminal Justice System 1995, henceforth csr Report 1995). Almost 40 percent of all youth report having committed an act of violence, selling drugs or destroying property in their lifetime (Public Safety Canada 2012: 4–5), but 40 percent of youth are not in juvenile detention. Most people who commit crimes do not go to jail. It is not, after all, breaking the law which renders one a criminal — it is being caught, arrested and convicted (Davis 2003).

The enormous discretion granted to law enforcement in where to seek out crime and to determine who *seems* suspicious plays a significant role in who becomes a criminal offender. Racial profiling — surveillance or police encounters that occur because of stereotypes regarding race, ethnicity or religion — serves an important role in determining policing practices. The assumption, then, that Black people are likely to be criminals results in more Black people being watched, caught, charged and incarcerated. It is Black people who will be *made* into criminals by the very policing strategies that target them. In other words: "Profiling is a self-fulfilling prophecy. The more that a group is targeted, the greater the likelihood that criminality will be discovered — particularly for those offences that are prevalent in society" (Tanovich 2004: 916). This self-fulfilling prophecy is reflected in a Montréal study that found that over-surveillance, not Black proclivity for crime, is the leading factor in the disproportionate arrest of Black youth. Black youth experienced far more surveillance by police and security guards than white youth, and this over-surveillance may have accounted for almost 60 percent of their over-representation in the criminal justice system. This effect snowballs into further criminalization: "each new arrest contains the risk of a new charge, resulting in a worsening of the criminal record (if the charge is proved) and the probability of a longer sentence and more restrictive conditions than the previous time" (Bernard and McAll 2008: 12 in cdpdj 2011: 35). The enormous discrepancy of Black youth in jail — a rate four times higher than white youth in Ontario — stands as a testament to the power of profiling to create criminals (Rankin and Winsa 2013). Black people are not "more criminal"; they are placed behind bars for crimes that, had they been white, would have been far more likely to have gone unseen and unpunished.

Racial profiling is also disguised and justified by falsely making crime an issue of immigration. The profiling of Black communities is frequently blamed not on racism, but is instead justified by the assertion that some (Black) *nationalities* are more prone to criminality. Much of the focus of police and commentators in Montréal and Toronto is on Black communities *as migrants* (Mosher 1998: 7–10). One study of police practices found that street gangs were represented as an immigration issue, and cites an anonymous police officer stating: "Here [in Québec] our kids are born with a hockey puck in their hand, but there [a country of immigrant origin] they come into the world with a grenade in their hands" (Symons 2002: 118; see also Wente 2002; Charest 2009). Jamaicans and Somalis, too, face enormous scrutiny (Foster 1996; Pratt and Valverde 2002). Statistics released by Public Safety Canada (2012) contradict the association between immigration and criminality; it was found that foreign-born youth had lower rates of so-called "delinquent behaviour" than Canadian-born youth. Despite perceptions buttressed by certain journals and politicians, the immigration-crime relationship is not based on objective proof (Mosher 1998: 10–11). Further, the documented intensive racial profiling and the high levels of Black people incarcerated in provincial jails in Nova Scotia — where the Black population is largely Canadian-born — makes clear that linking (Black) immigrant communities with criminality is a mere smokescreen for anti-Black sentiment.

There do appear to be some racial discrepancies in the committing of particular crimes: white men are more likely to be sex offenders and drug dealers, while Black youth may be over-represented in youth gang membership (despite white youth still being the large majority of gang members) (Owusu-Bempah and Wortley 2014). Regardless of minute differences, it is racially disproportionate policing, rather than racially disproportionate crime, that has resulted in the enormous levels of Black people behind bars in Canada today (Khenti 2014). Indeed, the decisions taken on which crimes to focus on and where to look for them are deeply informed by race (Roberts 1993).

NO FREEDOM TO CIRCULATE: POLICE PROFILING AND THE RESTRICTION OF BLACK MOVEMENT

Profiling is itself a form of violence, because it infringes on Black people's ability to move freely and without fear in public space. Taken-for-granted associations between Blackness and criminality have granted police largely unchecked authority over Black communities, giving them access to quasi-legal (or illegal) identity checks, searches, seizures and car stops, at a rate unimaginable to most non-racialized Canadians. Black existence in public space is itself seen as criminal and thus subject to scrutiny, surveillance, frequent interruption and police intervention.

In the early 1990s, social anthropologist Frances Henry interviewed 134 Caribbean people living in Toronto and found that every single person interviewed could relate a story of police harassment. Respondents highlighted that

Black Caribbean people were unable to gather in groups without drawing police presence (Henry 1994: 203, 216). Similarly, the 2011 report on racial profiling of youth found that many Black and brown respondents felt that they did not have the right to circulate or socialize in public without being subject to police scrutiny, including having their photos taken by police without explanation (CDPDJ 2011: 25). Black teenagers in Québec reported that they experienced police harassment in metro stations, and were frequently forced to "disperse" once two or more of them were together (CDPDJ 2011: 31). Young Black people in Toronto reported being stopped, documented and then told to leave neighbourhoods in which they did not reside (Rankin and Winsa 2012). A 2003 study of students found that more than one-third of Black students who were not engaged in criminal behaviour had been stopped by police, compared with less than one-tenth (4 percent) of white students; almost a quarter (23 percent) of these Black students had been searched, compared to 5 percent of white students (Wortley and Tanner 2003). While the ability to walk freely in public space is something that is taken for granted by most white Canadians, the same cannot be said for people of African descent.

Being stopped by police, however, often encompasses more than being asked a few questions or being forced to move. The Toronto Police Service has steadily amassed the names, personal information and movements of millions of people using "contact card" stops from largely non-criminal encounters. This practice, known widely as "carding," has been used to create a massive "known to police" database of the citizenry, which is not subject to outside oversight or any regulation on the purging of information. The *Toronto Star,* by means of Access to Information and Privacy requests, discovered that between 2008 and mid-2011, 1.25 million contact cards were filled out, and nearly one-quarter of those documented were Black. Young Black males in particular were carded at a rate of 3.4 times that of their population in the city, and these rates were even higher for Black people stopped in predominantly white neighbourhoods. Some data appears to suggest that every Black man has been documented in certain neighbourhoods (Rankin and Winsa 2012). Carding was widely defended by the mayor and the police union, but widespread outrage in the Black community led to a reduction in carding by 75 percent in 2013. Despite this reduction in overall documentation, the proportion of Black people who were carded actually *increased* (Rankin and Winsa 2014). The practice is currently being debated but the massive database of Black lives remains in the hands of the Toronto Police Service, despite continued contestation by the Black community.

Similar findings can be seen in Kingston, Halifax and Montréal, where, instead of carding, the same practice is referred to as "street checks." A report commissioned by the police chief in Kingston, Ontario, found that people of African descent were three times more likely than whites to be stopped, and that both Black men and Black women faced far higher individual stop rates than white men and women (Wortley and Marshall 2005 in Khenti 2014). Between 2006 and 2016, Black people living in Halifax were stopped by both the Halifax Regional Police and the RCMP for street checks at a rate that was three times higher than the general population (Previl 2017a and 2017b).

Most disturbingly, police profiling often targets Black *youth*, a form of state violence that is particularly chilling. Black youth are, after all, at the intersections of powerlessness: they experience the powerlessness inherent to childhood and adolescence combined with that of being a subordinated racial group. The resources allotted to policing Black and other racialized youth in public spaces has little to do with an existing public danger. In particular, the fears of dangerous young immigrant gangs, perpetuated by the Montréal police, are largely unfounded. In the last twenty years, the Montréal police have repeatedly named racialized youth in street gangs to be a high organizational priority and have allocated their resources accordingly. In 1996, the Montréal police force declared that approximately 1,300 teenagers between the ages of fifteen and nineteen were an organizational priority, and specifically named Jamaican, Haitian, "Asiatic," Latino and "extreme right" youth as the targets (Symons 2002: 117). Gladys Symons, in conducting twenty-eight interviews with the Service de Police de la Ville de Montréal (SPVM) from 1997 to 1998, found that officers frequently identified the issue of youth and street gangs as a problem stemming from immigration (Symons 2002: 118–119). Yet, the priority is one *chosen* by law enforcement officials, not based on the realities of crimes in Montréal. *Le Devoir* reported in 2010 that the SPVM found that criminal activity by street gangs was only 1.6 percent of reported crime in 2009. When questioned by journalists on why they continued to focus so many resources on fighting this relatively insignificant issue, they stated that it was based on the public *perception* of the prevalence of street gang activity, unfounded though it was (*Le Devoir* 2010 in Bernard and McAll 2010: 13). The assumption that Black youth are dangerous and criminal is indeed the justification for targeting them with highly punitive policing practices.

The Montréal police's focus on the largely fabricated street gang crisis served as a justification for a massive spike in street checks that had a significant impact on Montréal's Black communities and Black youth in particular. "Anti-street gang" squads had been deployed between 2001 and 2007, a period that saw an increase of 60 percent in "random" identity checks on Black communities, purportedly to battle the crisis of youth of colour involved in dangerous gangs (Charest 2009). Included in that growth, the number of "random" stops had particularly militarized Black neighbourhoods: the stops had risen by 91 percent and 126 percent respectively in the largely Black neighbourhoods of St. Michel and Montréal-Nord. Though Black communities were already disproportionately affected by street checks in 2001, in 2006–2007, in some neighbourhoods nearly half (40 percent) of young Black males were stopped and carded compared with just over 5 percent of whites. An average of 721 Black people were stopped per month. The author of the investigation notes that only a minority of these checks could be seen as justified, as a very small minority resulted in arrests and the rest were largely malicious in intent (Charest 2009). Here, the fabricated profile of young Black people as possible dangerous gang members allowed for entire Black neighbourhoods to be militarized by near constant police surveillance. After the 2008 police killing of an unarmed Latino teenager, Fredy Villanueva, and the police shooting of two other teenagers, a small uprising occurred in the neighbourhood. Racialized youth accused the police of extreme levels of harassment and profiling that was impacting their day-to-day lives. Afterward, an internal police study of the SPVM, which was leaked to the newspaper *La Presse*, found that the perceptions of racialized youth were accurate (Charest 2009). Other forms, too, of controlling Black people's movements are practised by law enforcement. For example, in 2004, the police announced a crackdown on what are called "incivilities," creating more than two dozen new categories of acts which are said to disturb the peace, including prostitution, spitting, loitering and noise. These have reportedly dispropor-tionately targeted Black, Latino and South Asian youth (Tanovich 2006: 84).

The ongoing scrutiny of Black life practised by law enforcement — and the cataloguing the Black population into massive law enforcement databases — has significant impacts on the psychological well-being of Black communities. It must be seen, and addressed, as a form of state violence. Even profiling that does not result in arrest or violence is itself harmful: the American Psychological Association has found that it can cause post-traumatic stress disorder and other stress-related disorders, as well as alienation (in Ontario Human Rights Commission [OHRC] 2003: 17). These effects touch entire families. One mother cited in the 2003 OHRC report, *Paying the Price: The Human Cost of Racial Profiling*, said, "Now I feel very afraid for my two boys. I'm afraid for them to go out. I can't sleep when they go out. I'm scared when they go out with Black friends. They're like a magnet. It's not fair that four Black kids can't walk around"

(OHRC 2003: 25). The hostile and scary imposition into of the lives of Black communities is experienced as a form of violence and intimidation, in which the act of leaving one's house is fraught with danger and anxiety for fear of harassment by police (Henry 1994). In particular, young people who are just learning how society functions were found to experience the most harms from racial profiling, harms that often last long into their adulthood (OHRC 2003: 18). Black activists, as well as legal experts such as Justice Harry Laforme and criminologist Akwasi Owusu-Bempah, have compared the concerted surveillance of Black bodies in public spaces to apartheid-era South Africa's pass laws (under which Black movement was subjected to heavy surveillance and Black people could not circulate outside of designated zones) (in Rankin and Winsa 2012). Over-surveillance creates for Black subjects a reality in which merely existing is treated as suspect. This reality is wholly unimaginable to white citizens, who are free from "the feeling of dread" that is inflicted by profiling (Martinot and Sexton 2003: 176). The harm regularly inflicted on communities and especially youth who are subject to constant scrutiny, daily fears of harassment and continual interference in day-to-day life cannot be fully quantified, as the effects of being regularly and systematically dehumanized cannot be captured by statistics. The intensive targeting of Black folks in public space demonstrates a fundamental disregard for the dignity of Black life.

CANADA'S "WAR ON DRUGS": DRUG PROHIBITION, BLACK INCARCERATION

Background

While profiling can be understood as a ritualistic low-level violence inflicted on Black communities, it is the "War on Drugs" that has been instrumental in placing so many Black communities in captivity within jails and prisons today. The profiling and surveillance of Black life, of course, pre-exists and exceeds the War on Drugs. Nonetheless, in the past three decades ideologies and practices of drug law enforcement have consolidated, and have given new breadth and scope toward, the criminalization of Blackness.

As explored in an earlier chapter, since the early twentieth century, the criminalization of drugs was related not to the pharmacological or social harms engendered by drugs, but was a result of anti-Black and anti-Chinese sentiment. The criminalization of drugs was used as a tool in the repression of these communities (Gordon 2006). In line with similar processes in the United States, a new period of moral panic linking danger and drugs to the Black population took hold in the 1980s, even as the use of marijuana, heroin and cocaine had been lowering at a stable rate since peaking in 1979 (Adlaf, Smart and Canale 1991 in Khenti 2014: 191). Prime Minister Brian Mulroney announced the War on Drugs, following the lead of President Ronald Reagan in the United States. Drugs, it was argued, represented an emergent threat to the security and safety of "the public." As a result, despite a total void of scientific evidence, the so-called "war" was purportedly waged to combat the harms of illegal substances that were said to be ravaging communities. A "national drug strategy," made up of legislation between 1988 and 1999, significantly strengthened the power of law enforcement officers to seize the assets of drug offenders, and provided other forms of heightened policing powers (Khenti 2014: 191). Media reports and policing efforts followed suit, and in the coming years, Blackness was baselessly but inextricably linked to dangerous drug crime — both in the public perception and in law enforcement practices (Khenti 2014; Nunn 2002).

This manufactured "crisis" did not emerge out of nowhere. The War on Drugs declared in the 1980s had political utility amid the substantive rollback of state supports and social welfare undertaken by Brian Mulroney. In Canada, like in the United States and the United Kingdom, the past three decades have seen the mobilization of a fear of crime to gain popular support for "law and order" platforms geared toward so-called public safety. This was part of a larger political strategy aimed at making sense of the chaos stemming from the economic and social fallout of colonialism. Amid growing racial and economic disparities, fear-based policies allowed states to exert control over their disenfranchised populations and to quell discontent under the banner of "security." Indeed, the anti-crime focus of the last several decades has been, in part, a reactionary response to racial and social justice movements (Gordon 2006; Sudbury 2004a; Gilmore 2007; Hall et al. 2013).

In Canada, as elsewhere, racial and wealth disparities had never been passively accepted by Black communities. In the 1960s and 1970s, acclaimed Black activists Rocky Jones and the Black United Front in Halifax played an influential role in challenging the racism that caused Black poverty, displacement and disenfranchisement in Nova Scotia (Rutland *forthcoming*). Discrimination against Black communities in Montréal led to a two-week-long university campus occupation and uprising in 1969 that culminated in the burning of the computer labs of Sir George Williams University in Montréal, and led to a violent police response (Austin 2013). In the 1980s, Haitian taxi drivers took up important and highly visible struggles against racist hiring and pay practices in Montréal (Mills 2016). This Black activism, like elsewhere across the country, was subject to intensive police surveillance and was seen as a criminal threat to Canada's national security (Austin 2013). Black activists were viewed as a threat — the RCMP, for example, had been spying on Black activists in Halifax throughout the 1960s and 1970s (*Canadian Press* July 20, 1994). One article in the *Toronto Star* wrote of the Sir George Williams student protesters, "you can call 'em militants if you like. In this corner it comes out hoodlums" (1969 in Williams 1971: 119). Wider society, student and labour movements, too, were pushing for economic and social justice. However, in Canada, like in the United States and the United Kingdom, state officials and civil society did not respond to social unrest with state policies aimed at combating racial and gendered inequalities. The conservative push toward "crime prevention" came as a response to civil rights, Black power and other emergent racial and social justice movements as a way to exert control over racialized communities. It was politically useful to mobilize political support by exaggerating the threats posed by "crime" to the safety of the public (Hall et al. 2013; Gilmore 2007; Sudbury 2004a). As such, anti-Blackness — articulated through a focus on Black drug crime — was mobilized as a response to a threat to Canadian society in a time of social unrest, following similar patterns in the United States and the United Kingdom. Following the crises engendered by neoliberalism in the late 1980s, Black people became convenient "folk devils" upon which all of society's fears were scapegoated and projected (Nunn 2002). This was accomplished by means of the War on Drugs.

By the logic of the drug war, drugs were a threat to Canadian society itself. Though drug use had been on the decline since the late 1970s (Khenti 2014), the police, state officials and the media together created a widespread hysteria: drugs, so the newspapers said, were "tear[ing] a gaping hole in the fabric of society" (Kennedy 1989). Yet, instead of massive investment in the needs of society — including social services and addiction support — the communities that were associated with drug crime became the target of widespread hostility and oppression, the enemy of the War on Drugs. The police, supported by the media, associated drugs and violence with the presence of Caribbean communities. One *Toronto Star* article cited former Toronto Police Chief Bill McCormack as saying they specifically targeted drug crimes in Jamaican communities as a grave danger, and decrying "Uzi-toting thugs" who can "use their accents to hide among honest, hard-working people" while "selling the deadly drug that turns children into thieves" (Mascoll 1990). A larger analysis of media responses to the drug war found a repetition of media tropes frantically decrying "murderous posses" of Black Jamaicans selling crack (with the effect of linking Blackness, poverty and cocaine with Jamaicans in the popular imaginary) (Lawrence and Williams 2006). Though drug use remained relatively static across race and class at comparable rates to the years preceding Mulroney's term, the only success of the War on Drugs was to demonize Black life, massively expand Black incarceration and cause irreparable harm to Black communities.

The expanded powers granted to law enforcement officers by the War on Drugs gave police the arsenal necessary to bring into being the contemporary large-scale incarceration of Black communities (Khenti 2014). Perhaps most notably, Canada created a national law enforcement training program called Operation Pipeline, which arguably cemented the practice of racial profiling by law enforcement officers. Derived from a program of the same name run by the Drug Enforcement Agency in the United States and imported by the RCMP in the late 1980s, Operation Pipeline is a training program geared toward the enforcement of drug laws. It has since been used to train Canada Customs officers, provincial police officers and officers in Montréal, Toronto, Calgary, Winnipeg and Vancouver (Tanovich 2006: 89–92). Training methods analyzed by David Tanovich found that literature emphasized highly racialized "profiles" of likely drug traffickers, and included racial and ethnic characteristics, such as dreadlocks, as a means of singling out criminals and criminal organizations, making specific mention of Caribbean men and women (as well as Chinese people and other racial groups) (92). Law enforcement was now granted an expanded scope in the use of racial profiling as a tool to surveil, search and arrest Black persons, those thought (though not demonstrated) to be most involved in the buying or selling of drugs: "[profiling] ultimately became fixated on race, when authorities began to focus on low-income neighbourhoods that were predominately racialized" (87). While both the American and Canadian programs deny that racial profiling is part of their program, Operation Pipeline is nonetheless widely blamed for institutionalizing racist policing practices as part of the War on Drugs in both nations (Alexander 2012; Tanovich 2006: 91–94). The first report of Criminal Intelligence Service Canada (CISC) — used by law enforcement throughout the country — linked Caribbean and other racialized groups to cocaine sales, and CISC has done so repeatedly in subsequent reports (Tanovich 2006: 93–94). In a much less publicized yet highly prevalent form of racial profiling, Black, particularly Caribbean, women are widely represented as drug couriers in airports (a phenomenon which will be more deeply explored in later pages).

The effects of the drug war were disastrous for Black communities. Though not only Black people were arrested for drug infractions, the increased police surveillance and repression of Black communities mandated by drug law enforcement had direct impacts on Black incarceration in the period immediately following Mulroney's War on Drugs. In 1995, a large-scale investigation in Ontario documented a massive influx of Black prisoners during the period spanning 1986–1987 to 1992–1993 (CSR Report 1995). By the end of this period, Blacks were incarcerated at a rate five times higher than their white counterparts. Though the CSR Report found that Black and white communities engaged in crime at comparable rates in that same period, this period saw the rate of incarceration of Blacks increase by over 200 percent, compared to white persons, whose rates rose by just over 20 percent (CSR Report 1995: 69). Black women, though arrested in smaller numbers than Black men, were found to face even more disproportionate rates of incarceration than men. By the end of 1993, Black women were incarcerated at a rate of seven times that of white women (iii). Admissions at Vanier Centre for Women increased the rate of admission of Black women by 630 percent, whereas white women's admissions at the same prison went up by 59 percent (75). Drug laws were the main source of the spike in numbers. The number of prison admissions for Black persons for drug trafficking increased by 1164 percent, compared to an increase of 151 percent for white admissions. The War on Drugs had the effect of caging a previously unimaginable number of Black bodies in Canada, and set the tone for continued public perceptions associating Blackness with criminality.

Drug prohibition today

Although the so-called War on Drugs is often seen as a Conservative policy, the incarceration of Black communities continued to grow, in the background, under Liberal Prime Ministers Jean Chrétien (1993–2003) and Paul Martin (2003–2006) — indeed, the drug war arguably intensified (Gordon 2006). The heavy policing of Black persons, though purportedly practised to combat the leaders of the drug trade, included high rates of arrest and incarceration for petty drug offences. As the focus on drugs increased, so did the levels of Black incarceration. Cannabis-related offences rose 80 percent from 1992 to 2002, mostly for possession, and mostly affecting persons under thirty years old (Gordon 2006: 69). The state investment in the punitive aspect of combating drug crime vastly outweighed the state investment in supporting drug users. In 1992, law enforcement at the federal and provincial levels received $400 million in funding, while treatment services received $88 million (Single, Robson, Xie and Rehm 1996 in Khenti 2014: 192). In 1997, the Liberal government increased the power and authority that had previously been delegated to the police in the *Narcotics Control Act*, and replaced it with the *Controlled Drugs and Substances Act*. This Act allowed police officers a more widespread range of enforcement powers when it came to minor drug cases than those allotted to rape, murder and arson (Gordon 2006: 65). It allowed for "sweeping new police powers of arrest, search and seizure" (Khenti 2014: 191), concretized the maximum penalties for drug related offences and increased the amount of resources for arresting and prosecuting both drug users and drug sellers (Gordon 2006: 65–67). Though the War on Drugs was by this time less publicized, the warfare on those persons profiting the least from the drug trade continued in earnest. Between the early 1990s and 2006, the police-recorded drug crime rate had almost doubled, generally focused on possession and small-time street level dealers (Erickson 1998: 219 in Gordon 2006: 69–70). This continued to correspond to rising Black incarceration rates. By 2003, near the end of two terms of Prime Minister Jean Chretien's leadership, the federal incarceration rate for Blacks was already significantly higher than their proportion of the Canadian population, and had climbed to a rate of 6.3 percent, with Blacks being approximately 3 percent of the population at that time (Sapers 2013, 2014).

The election of Conservative Prime Minister Stephen Harper (2006–2015) brought back visibility to the drug war. Less visible, though, was the Black prison population's increase of almost 70 percent under Prime Minister Harper's reign. Despite relaxing public perceptions on drugs and drug use, the criminalization of drugs was augmented in the framework of a larger "tough on crime" mandate. This era saw a significant investment in building and filling prisons, seemingly at any cost. Prison expansion was given fiscal priority at a time when the government enacted significant austerity measures: social investments were cut across nearly every other sector besides prison and the military, including education, childcare, welfare, pensions, union wages, women's groups, homelessness prevention programs, HIV and Hepatitis C prevention and treatment, and community support organizations for immigrants and Indigenous peoples. Spending on federal corrections grew more than 70 percent between 2003 and 2013, and prison spending exceeded $2.75 billion in the peak-spending year of 2013–2014 (including over $700 million on 2,700 new or retrofitted cells) (Sapers 2015). Most federal funding toward Canada's National Drug Strategy has been channelled to policing efforts; by 2008, more than three-quarters was allotted to law enforcement, rather than treatment or supports (DeBeck, Wood, Montaner and Kerr 2009 in Khenti 2014: 192).

Harper's 2010 National Drug Strategy involved an increasingly punitive drug policy. This carceral investment has been highly effective, not in reducing drug consumption, but in increasing drug-based arrests and creating a massive spike in the arrest and incarceration of Black persons. Between March 2010 and March 2012, the federally incarcerated population grew by nearly 1,000 inmates, which federal corrections investigator Howard Sapers stated is the equivalent of two large, medium-security institutions for males. In this same period, the female prisoner population rose by 20 percent (Sapers 2012). These years saw, too, another spike in the rates of Black women in federal prisons (Sapers 2013). In 2011, more than half of drug arrests (60 percent) involved marijuana, and following that, cocaine. More than three-quarters (76 percent) of those were for possession, but offences for trafficking, production and distribution were also eight times higher than they had been thirty years ago (Statistics Canada 2012 in Mosher and Akins 2015: 338–339). This accelerated with the 2012 passage of legislation requiring mandatory minimum sentences for trafficking marijuana, along with numerous other non-violent crimes. The practice of imposing mandatory minimum sentences has been documented to be ineffective on reducing crime, and very harmful toward incarceration rates of marginalized and racialized communities (Pivot Legal Society 2013).

Disparities are ongoing. In 2016, a judge for the Ontario Superior Court of Justice stated in his ruling on a Black man charged with drug trafficking, "The racial disparities in imprisonment are especially problematic with respect to street level drug dealing" (R v. Reid 2016: para 26). The devaluation of Black life in Canadian society has meant that, despite a massive augmentation of Black communities arrested and incarcerated on drug and other charges in the last two decades, it has not been widely represented as a crisis of racial disparity in Canada (despite Black organizing efforts in several Canadian cities). Black youth, men and women were put behind bars at steadily rising rates amid little outcry and with the silent consent of society at large, including government opposition parties, policy makers and much of the media. The massive spike in Black incarceration is a direct result of successive, ideologically driven and racially enforced drug laws.

Beyond incarceration, the enforcement of drug laws has been fatal at times. Fighting drug crime is not referred to as a "war" by metaphor. The buying and selling of drugs is a consensual transaction. It is a crime that must be proactively sought out by police, not a violent emergency requiring heavy intervention. Still, the policing of even low-level marijuana trafficking is highly militaristic, often taking the form of heavily armed interventions by tactical squads and emergency task forces. For example, Bony Jean-Pierre, a forty-seven-year-old Haitian man, was shot in the head with rubber bullets during a small-scale marijuana bust by the Montréal police tactical squad, and died days later from his injuries (S. Michaud 2016; CBC News April 4, 2016). This form of militarized intervention focused on drug crime has led to several deaths of unarmed Black men (for example, Small 2013).

A misleading profile

Law enforcement of the buying and selling of drugs allow for a significant level of discretion in policing, as both buying and selling drugs are consensual activities for which, by and large, no one calls the police (Alexander 2012: 104). To use the words of an Ontario police performance review, the policing of drugs is "enforcement driven" and a "direct reflection of the priority" of police services (Provincial Benchmarking Committee 2001: 3). This means that the intensified focus on drug policing comes not from any community or socially determined need, but from the police or higher political powers. The decision of whom to search, survey and arrest lies entirely in the hands of law enforcement officials (Alexander 2012: 104).

In a society with a centuries-long history of vilifying Black bodies, it is not surprising that policing efforts focus primarily on Black youth. A 2002 study found that 65 percent of Black drug dealers interviewed reported being arrested at least once, compared to only 35 percent of white drug dealers (Tanner and Wortley 2002 in Gordon 2006: 70). A Black teenager in Montréal is seven times more likely to be seen and arrested by the police for smoking cannabis or selling drugs in public than a young white teen, and this difference in arrest is largely attributable to heightened surveillance of Black youth in public space (Bernard and McAll 2010: 8–9). There is a significant focus on policing Black communities for drug crimes, even though Black persons are by no means more likely to use or profit from drugs than white persons (CSR Report 1995).

In the case of drugs, it is increasingly clear that police do *not*, contrary to their claims, "go where the crime goes." Drug use, as well as the sale of drugs, is in fact more common in white communities (Owusu-Bempah and Wortley 2011). A 2012 survey by the Canadian Alcohol and Drug Use Monitoring Survey (CADMUS), which interviewed 11,090 individuals, found that white youth used more marijuana than Black youth, at a rate of 44.9 percent compared to 38.7 percent, and were nearly three times more likely to use cocaine, at a rate of 5.9 percent versus 2.3 percent of Black youth (CADMUS 2012 in Mosher and Akins 2015: 337). In addition, a study of youth in Toronto found higher rates of marijuana and cocaine use among white students as compared to Black students, and noted that white students were slightly more likely to be selling drugs than their fellow Black students (Toronto Youth Crime Victimization

Survey 2000 in Owusu-Bempah and Wortley 2014). Black youth, then, are far more likely to be arrested and jailed for a crime that is much more prevalent among white youth. Though Black people stand to gain wealth (that is otherwise difficult to access due to their systemic economic marginalization) from participating in illicit economies, the majority of those who make up the profits in the market for illegal drugs are certainly not disenfranchised Black communities (Nunn 2002).

Collateral damage

An enormous amount of human life has been harmed or destroyed by drug prohibition. It could be argued that the loss of life and liberty has been a necessary, if unfortunate, side effect toward the just cause of eliminating the "scourge" of drugs from society. After over one hundred years of vilification, the proposition that drugs are perhaps not a significant source of harm sounds, to some, preposterous and even dangerous. The ideological work of moral reformers and conservative politicians has been well accomplished: drugs are linked not only to race, but to social decline, immorality and degradation as well. Yet, evidence now makes it increasingly obvious that the substantial dangers that have been attributed to illegal drugs are, in fact, the result of drug prohibition (Hart 2013). Indeed, though Black communities have been particularly targeted for incarceration, the harmful effects of the War on Drugs have been felt across society. A high-profile study by the *Lancet* and Johns Hopkins University Commission on Drug Policy and Health examined the scientific evidence on public health issues stemming from drug prohibition in 2016. The study confirmed that it is drug prohibition, not drugs, that has contributed to an enormous loss of life and lack of safety — including lethal violence, criminal networks, the spread of HIV, Hepatitis C and overdose deaths — and has created numerous barriers to health as well as committing human rights violations (Csete et al. 2016). This misattribution of harm extends further: petty theft or violence to pay for drugs is seen as a side effect of a particular substance, rather than an indicator of economic inequality. Middle-class white people, in short, can afford to have drug addictions without needing to resort to theft, as the inflated price of drugs stems from their very illegality. Relatedly, though addiction is commonly associated with the properties of drugs themselves, it has been found to stem not from the properties of "dangerous" substances themselves, but from social isolation, childhood abuse, trauma and/or economic circumstances. People suffering from addiction who have access to financial and familial support, as well as timely treatment, are far less likely to be homeless and destitute (Report of the Global Commission on Drug Policy 2011).

In 2015, the U.N. High Commissioner found that illicit drug use itself was neither a medical condition, nor did it necessarily lead to dependence (in Csete et al. 2016: 1427). Despite widespread and grossly exaggerated messaging by politicians, the church and the media on the horrors resulting from illicit drug use, particularly what are considered "hard" drugs, little pharmacological harm has been documented to accompany the moderate use of illegal drugs. Instead, medical professionals have suggested that treating illicit drugs with the same social policies as tobacco and dangerous foods, in addition to distribution of harm reduction materials, is a far safer, evidence-based approach (Csete et al. 2016: 1427). Out of 246 million persons around the world who used drugs in 2014, only 11 percent experienced problem drug use (U.N. Office on Drugs and Crime 2015 in Csete et al. 2016: 1431). The *Lancet*–Johns Hopkins study found, too, that the application of drug laws in societies with racial bias in policing and arrests leads to social and economic devastation for racialized communities and causes intergenerational effects (Csete et al. 2016).

Just as importantly, the criminalization of drugs is ineffective in reducing drug use or drug availability. Waging a "war" on low-level players, generally focused on poor and vulnerable Black men and women who are almost never the ones making the large-scale profits that come from the drug trade, succeeds in assuring a steady incarceration of Black bodies but accounts for "a negligible impact on the availability of illegal drugs" available on the Canadian market (CSR Report 1995: 156). Over forty years, the American government has spent billions of dollars on anti-drug law enforcement and has seen its incarcerated population grow from 300,000 to over two million people, but the number of drug users has remained relatively stable since 1988 (Alexander 2012; Robinson and Scherlen 2014). Using heavy law enforcement against minor suppliers and couriers to control or stop drug use has consistently been found to be completely ineffective (Csete et al. 2016). Indeed, medical, legal and human rights experts around the world increasingly argue against drug prohibition, instead urging a move toward the gradual decriminalization of non-violent drug crimes and the regulation of illegal drugs, as well as an end to the practice of incarcerating women for drug crimes (Csete et al. 2016). Despite growing global medical consensus on the suffering caused by drug prohibition, those who buy, sell and courier controlled substances continue to be demonized and represented as dangerous to society, regardless of their relative powerlessness in the hierarchy of profits (Lawrence and Williams 2006: 308).

The infectiveness of drug prohibition is now widely documented. Yet, the state has long been aware of this and has consistently ignored scientific evidence. The result of the drug war has not been the protection of society, but the extensive caging of Black communities. Families, communities and lives destroyed or ended is a form of violence that is only beginning to be quantified by international research. Black communities continue to be subjected to the violence of surveillance and arrest, and are still being forced to spend important years of their lives behind bars, separated from family, saddled with criminal records, exposed to trauma and isolation resulting from imprisonment, all for policies that have helped and protected no one inside or outside of the Black community.

Ignorance of this reality on the part of government officials cannot be used as a justification for the continued criminalization of drugs. It is malign negligence, or worse, that enormous amounts of public money continue to be invested in law enforcement, jails and prisons, rather than invested in communities, education, treatment and health services. Decades of state support for drug prohibition in Canada would likely be viewed as "criminal" were it not for an unacknowledged but powerful anti-Blackness, alongside a total disregard that makes the lives of Black, Indigenous, the poor, drug users and/or people with mental health problems expendable. Yet, due to the lack of value for Black lives, restitution for the state violence that is drug prohibition remains unlikely.

THE DESTRUCTION OF BLACK BODIES: POLICE VIOLENCE AND IMPUNITY

The War on Drugs — and the intensified surveillance and profiling that it helped to enable — has wreaked enormous harms on Canada's Black communities. However, Black communities are not only fearful of being stopped or harassed by the police; Black communities live in a state of heightened anxiety surrounding the possibility of bodily harm in the name of law enforcement. A genuine fear of law enforcement officers exists among many in the Black community, a response that is rational given the circumstances. The research of Frances Henry found that young Black men of any class status routinely show their hands as soon as being approached by the police out of fear of being shot (Henry 1994: 214). "Hands up, don't shoot" is not only a chant at rallies, but continues to be a mainstay of Black fear-based responses to police interactions. In a society where many white Canadians think of the police as those who protect their security, Black people, quite legitimately, largely fear for their security in any situation that could involve the police. Parents, in particular, have expressed a genuine concern for the physical safety of their loved ones (Wortley 2006).

These fears, unfortunately, are entirely warranted. Police abuse of Black subjects has been documented by criminologist Scot Wortley's study, which examined 784 incidents of police use of force that were brought to the provincial Special Investigations Unit (SIU) between January 1, 2000, and June 6, 2006. The findings demonstrated that Black populations face a rate of violence by police that is more than five times that of the white population, and were subject to rampant and frequent abuse with little to no access to recourse (Wortley 2006). Though a racial analysis has not been duplicated in the past decade, the number of sexual assault charges reported against police has tripled in the past ten years, the number of investigations of police abuses overall has doubled and, most notably, complaints involving injuries sustained during police interactions have increased fourfold (Gillis 2015a). Yet, despite alarming rates of police abuse and the documented targeting of Black communities, police violence and even killings continue with relatively few consequences for offending officers. The SIU has come under criticism for a lack of independence and for employing ex-police officers to investigate current police officers (Ballingall 2016). Allegations of police impunity are substantiated with hard facts: out of nearly 320 complaints in the year 2013, only four officers were charged (Gillis 2015a). The unit has come under fire for anti-Black and pro-police bias prone to exonerating law enforcement officers. The Toronto City Council, following extensive protests by Black Lives Matter Toronto, voted to review the unit through an anti-racism lens (Gillis 2016a).

The deeply ingrained fear of law enforcement officers is a rational response to the brutal reality that Black lives are taken too often by law enforcement and that these killings go largely unpunished, creating a situation in which Black lives can be taken by police officers with near-total impunity. In Ontario, a shoot-to-kill policy appears to be the driving factor in the policing of the Black community. Black activist Ajamu Nangwaya compiled a list of significant media reports on Black people shot or killed by police in Ontario, some of which are documented below. Lester Donaldson was shot to death in his rooming house in 1988 by a white police officer. The officer was acquitted, though he was later reprimanded for referring to Black persons as "apes" and "niggers" in the context of an internal police investigation (DiManno 2003 in Nangwaya 2011). Michael Wade Lawson, a seventeen-year-old Black man, had his life taken in the same year in Mississauga: he was shot in the back of the head while apparently driving a stolen car. His killers were subsequently acquitted by an all-white jury (Wasun 2008 in Nangwaya 2011). In 1989, Sophia Cook was shot in the back and temporarily paralyzed after missing her bus and riding in the passenger seat of what happened to be a stolen car; though charged, the responsible officer was acquitted in 1994 (Wasum 2008 in Nangwaya 2011). In 1992, Raymond Lawrence was shot twice in the chest and killed by police officers who claimed he had a knife. Although no fingerprints corroborated this, the officers were exonerated (Maloney 1993 in Nangwaya 2011). Tommy Anthony Barnett, twenty-two years old, was shot to death in 1996 with four bullets fired into his chest by officers who claimed he had been unsheathing a sword (Rowley 1996 in Nangwaya 2011). In 1997, Hugh Dawson was shot nine times from three inches away by Officer Rick Shanks while unarmed, sitting in his car with a seatbelt on (Pron 1999 and Pron and Quinn 1999 in Nangwaya 2011). In 2006, an unarmed fifteen-year-old named Duane Christian was shot and killed with five bullets while driving a stolen van (Nangwaya 2011). More recent known cases involve the shooting of Jermaine Carby in 2014, an incident that arose from a "carding" stop. No charges were laid on police despite documented evidence of police tampering with evidence (including the removal for several hours of the weapon allegedly in Carby's possession) (Gillis 2015b, 2015c). And yet another incident is that of Kwasi Skene-Peters in 2015, whose case is still under investigation (Wallace 2015). In each of the above cases, officers either faced no charges, or were exonerated of any wrongdoing.

Police killings of Black persons are not found only in Ontario. Following the death of Anthony Griffin, a Black teenager in Montréal who was shot in the back of the head and killed in 1987, it was revealed publicly that the municipal police had been placing photos of Black people over their shooting practice targets (Henry and Tator 2006: 78). The deaths of young Black men at the hands of the police and the clearing of any wrongdoing for police officers forms a pattern in Montréal. Leslie Presley, a twenty-six-year-old Black Jamaican man was killed in 1990 by the Montréal police at a downtown bar (Collectif Opposé à la Brutalité Policière 2007, henceforth COBP 2007). Fritzgerald Forbes, a Black man of Jamaican descent, died at age twenty-two in 1991 of cardio respiratory failure shortly after being arrested in Park Extension. Marcellus Francois, an unarmed twenty-four-year-old Haitian man, was shot to death with an M16 machine gun despite being unarmed and, indeed, not the man sought by police; the officer responsible was cleared of all charges (COBP 2007). In 1993, a forty-three-year-old Jamaican man named Trevor Kelly lost his life by being shot in the back by the Montréal police (COBP 2007). In 2004, Rohan Wilson, a twenty-eight-year-old Black migrant from Saint Vincent and the Grenadines, died in Montréal's Notre-Dame-de-Grâce borough from what the coroner's report called an "accidental violent death" caused by alcohol intoxication following a police intervention that involved six officers (COBP 2007; Bergeron

2004). Quilem Registre, a Black Montrealer, sped through a stoplight, crashed into a car and was then tasered six times by the police, dying of organ failure four days later in the hospital (CBC News August 29, 2008). In 2014, the police were called on Alain Magloire, a forty-one-year-old Black homeless man in the midst of a mental health crisis, because he was wielding a hammer in distress. He was first hit by a Montréal police squad car, rolled over the hood of the car, and was then shot four times by the Montréal police (Montreal Gazette October 17, 2014; Lalonde 2015). Bony Jean-Pierre, discussed earlier in the text, was shot in the head at close range with rubber bullets in a minor marijuana bust in 2016, and died in the hospital days later (S. Michaud 2016). None of these deaths resulted in convictions for the officers involved. Until 2016, the province of Québec had no oversight body in situations of police force; the Montréal police have been historically investigated by the Sûreté du Québec (SQ), the provincial policing body, and vice versa. This has, for years, been denounced by activists and legal experts as clear conflict of interest. Out of nearly five hundred investigations by outside police forces since 1999, only six charges have been levelled at officers (Wilton 2016). The SQ have themselves been accused of widespread racist and gendered violence: more than forty Indigenous women have so far come forward with allegations of sexual assault, abuse and being driven kilometres outside of inhabited areas to be left in the cold (Leavitt 2016). In 2016, after decades of activism as well as pressure in recent years by Black activists and a coalition of family members of those killed by the police, which was formed in 2010, a new, purportedly neutral investigation body was formed called the Bureau des enquêtes indépendantes (BEI). However, far from being independent, fifteen out of the twenty-two members of the BEI are former police employees and the supervisor of investigations, Patrice Abel, is a former investigator employed by the SQ. The group has come under fire for their lack of impartiality from legal activists, the Black community and family members of persons killed (Riga 2016; Maynard 2017). In Montréal, like elsewhere, the destruction of Black bodies and the ending of Black lives occurs all too frequently without consequences for those who are believed by most to be protecting society.

The use of force against Black persons suffering from mental instability or mental illness is of particular concern.[1] Several Black activist organizations have joined forces to call attention to the issue. In a press conference protesting the numerous recent police killings of Black persons suffering from mental distress and disabilities, the African Canadian Legal Clinic's Anthony Morgan told the press, "Racialized minorities, especially black males, are dramatically overrepresented in incidents of police use of deadly force when confronted with a person in mental distress" (in Gillis 2015d). Research by Canadian sociologists Wendy Chan and Dorothy Chunn confirms that persons with mental health issues are highly vulnerable to violence in the name of law enforcement, particularly if they are racialized (Chan and Chunn 2014). Recent known deaths of Black persons who suffered from mental health issues are recorded, in part, in what follows: Reyal Jardine-Douglas was killed in 2010 and known by police to be suffering from mental distress. O'Brien Christopher-Reid was shot eight times and killed in 2004 amid a mental health crisis, in which witnesses stated that he had a knife but was not moving toward the officers (Grewal 2007). Michael Eligon was shot and killed while leaving a mental health facility in 2012 (Rush 2012). Ian Pryce, a thirty-year-old with schizophrenia, was shot by police in November 2013 while holding a pellet gun (Gillis 2015e). In Montréal in 2014, Alain Magloire, named above, was shot and killed during a mental health crisis. In a highly controversial killing in 2015, Andrew Loku, a Sudanese refugee and father of five living in a building leased by the Canadian Mental Health Association, was killed by the police officers who had been called to assist with his mental health crisis. Loku was holding only a hammer. One of the police officers implicated in the incident attempted to tamper with the videotape of the shooting; it was later found to have gaps in the footage (Nasser 2016). As well, the executive director of the Canadian Mental Health Association, having viewed video footage of the shooting, said the police did not attempt to perform CPR for nearly ten minutes after the shooting (Gillis 2016b). In none of these deaths was the victim armed with a gun, and in each case, the police officers were cleared by SIU investigators (though in the case of Michael Eligon, the Ontario Ombudsman accused the investigators of a pro-police bias) (Nangwaya 2011). Officers were cleared of any wrongdoing in each of the above cases, though relatives and the larger Black community continue to assert the victims would not have been shot to death if they had been white.

It is impossible to know how many more Black people have been killed at the hands of the police across Canada: the information is not released by police, their oversight unions (if they exist) or at the federal level. Ontario's SIU does not keep race-based statistics, nor does Statistics Canada, the Toronto or Montréal police, Correctional Services or the Ministry of Community Safety (Gillis 2015b). But fears felt by persons of African descent are well justified. Black residents of Ontario are ten times more likely to be shot by the police; they are nearly one-third (27 percent) of all the deaths caused by police force and make up over one-third (34.5 percent) of all deaths caused by police shootings, despite being only 3.6 percent of the Ontario population (Wortley 2006: 52).

Though police killings, like other forms of systemic racism, are frequently justified by invoking Black criminality and "dangerousness," this does not stand up to scrutiny. Criminal involvement does not, by any means, provide moral justification for police killings. However, police use of force also does not correlate to rates of Black criminality: while most white persons involved in incidents of police use of force have criminal records, this is not the case for Black Canadians (Wortley 2006: 53). Instead, it is race that impacts police treatment: in one study, it was discovered that when responding to "minor offences," police drew their weapons during arrest four times more often when arresting Blacks than any other group (Stenning 1994 in Henry and Tator 2006: 74). Black people continue to be killed by police in situations that could have been de-escalated by other means and often due to police interventions that would not even have occurred had they been white. Law enforcement officials, however, do not act in isolation from the rest of the criminal justice system, and anti-Black racism does not stop at the level of the streets but extends through to the courthouse, provincial jails and federal prisons.

FROM THE STREET TO THE COURTHOUSE

> Name any essentially similar offence and the case law always seems to find it more serious when a black man commits it. (Toronto-based criminal lawyer Reid Rusonik in Rankin and Winsa 2013)

If systemic racism does not stop at the role of law enforcement officials, neither does the harm inflicted on Black lives. Beyond targeted police profiling and violence, this discrimination continues all the way up the courts. Black-white disparities can be found in pre-trial detention and release conditions, including bail and sentencing. For nearly any crime, not only are people of African descent more likely to be arrested, but they are also much more likely to be detained pre-trial, to have restrictive bail conditions and to receive longer sentencing for the same charge. In the words of Toronto criminal lawyer Reid Rusonik, "Black people go to jail for possessing and selling crack cocaine. White people who sell and use cocaine powder rarely do" (in Rankin and Winsa 2013). Unfortunately, national data is not available, but available studies find the disproportionality in the courts quite dramatic, and not only in terms of disparities surrounding crack and cocaine. In Ontario in 1994, the rate of pre-trial detention for Black people charged with trafficking and importing drugs was twenty-seven times higher than for whites. For drug possession, it was fifteen times higher. Black persons were also found to be three times more likely than whites accused for the same crime to be refused bail and detained pre-trial (CSR Report 1995: iii–iv). This is corroborated by a 2004 a study that found that pre-trial detention was far higher for Black persons, even with all other factors accounted for. The authors noted that this is particularly significant because it is during pre-trial detention that guilty pleas are often coerced, regardless of guilt (Kellough and Wortley 2004). In an analysis of ten thousand arrests for drug possession in Toronto between 1996 and 2001, Black people were almost twice as likely (38 percent) to be taken to the police station for processing than white persons (23 percent) for simple drug possession — and once processed, Black people were two times more likely to be held overnight (Rankin et al. 2002 in Owusu-Bempah and Wortley 2014: 26). In another study in Montréal, it was found that once released pending trials, there were serious disparities in the conditions placed on Black youth versus those of white youth (Bernard and McAll 2008: 12). Black persons released on bail are assigned stricter conditions, such as curfews and mandatory supervision (Kellough and Wortley in Owusu-Bempah and Wortley 2014). At the level of sentencing, white people received far more lenient sentences than Blacks convicted of the same crime, even though whites were far more likely to have a serious criminal record. For drug offences, more than half of Black people found guilty were sentenced to prison, compared to one-third of white people found guilty of a drug offence (CSR Report 1995: vii).

These disparities continue after incarceration. Black prisoners have lower parole grant rates, so are released later in their sentences than other inmates. They also receive fewer temporary absences, and despite being a lower risk of re-offending, are more likely to be held in maximum-security institutions (Sapers 2013 and 2014). Québec's Commission des droits de la personne et droits de la jeunesse report, conducted fifteen years after the Ontario Commission's, corroborated that serious disparities continue. The authors found that independent from the profiling practised by law enforcement officers, which feeds the over-judicialization of racialized persons, there are reasons to question the decisions made during every step of the judicial process because they may have discriminatory impacts (in the laying of charges, criminal convictions, sentencing, conditions for release, etc.) (CDPDJ 2011: 36).

It appears that xenophobia may also be a factor, and that discrimination toward Black persons deemed "foreign" may also exist at the level of the courts as well. In one study, references to country of origin, immigration status, years in Canada and "foreignness," more generally, occurred in a third of non-bail hearings involving Black accused, and in slightly less than one-third of bail hearings (CSR Report 1995: 224–225). The law is neither colourblind nor neutral; instead, it reflects the hierarchies already found in society. Feminist and anti-racist legal scholarship continues to find that the criminal justice system perpetuates, rather than challenges, racial and gendered stratification (Roberts 1993).

THE VIOLENCE OF CAPTIVITY: BLACK LIFE BEHIND BARS

Incarceration is a form of captivity. Besides murder by police — the destruction of the body and the ending of life — it is the ultimate deprivation of liberty that can be inflicted by the state. Prisons are not only places of profound suffering, but they also make any participation in society's social, economic and political life impossible. The populations that make up prisons make clear the fault lines of societal devaluation: there are no federal prisons composed mostly of wealthy, able-bodied, cisgender men. As incarcerated populations grow, jails and prisons are increasingly populated with those who have been deemed disposable: Black and Indigenous communities, people with cognitive disabilities and mental health problems and people with drug addictions. Incarceration does not impact all communities equally. For Black and Indigenous communities, incarceration is merely an extension of practices of captivity that date back centuries. This reality has led Nova Scotian poet, activist and academic El Jones to state that Canadian prisons are both "slavery's afterlife" and "the new residential schools" (Jones 2016).

Today, Canada is in the midst of an explosion of Black incarceration. Between 2005 and 2015, growth in the Black federal prisoner population went up 69 percent — among the highest of any racial group. While Black people make up 3 percent of the population, they are over 9 percent of prisoners in federal corrections facilities (Sapers 2015). Federal prisons are not the only facilities that hold Black communities behind bars at vastly disproportionate rates. Provincial facilities do not publicly publish their race-based statistics (and, indeed, some claim not to collect them), yet from available data the disproportionate jailing of Black populations is equal and often worse at this level. Criminologists Akwasi Owusu-Bempah and Scot Wortley accessed the records of some provincial jails' race-based data by means of numerous Access to Information and Privacy requests for their 2010–2011 populations. Though each province and territory was contacted, only Ontario, Alberta, Nova Scotia and New Brunswick provided data on Black incarceration rates. Black people made up 3.9 percent of Ontario's population, yet they made up 17.7 percent of admissions to Ontario's correctional facilities. In Alberta, they found a ratio of 1.4 percent of the population to 5 percent of admissions, and in New Brunswick a rate of 0.6 to 2.4 (2014: 289). In Nova Scotia in 2014–2015, the Black population was 2 percent of the general population but made up 16 percent of youth jail admissions and 14 percent of adult admissions (Luck 2016). The situation appears to be even more dire in Québec, though no official records have been released. Documentarian Ronald Boisrond stated that, "in the early 80s, there were no Black inmates at the Bordeaux prison. Today, they represent about 40 percent of the population of that prison" (2008 in CDPDJ 2011: 29).

Though nominally intended to be rehabilitative, even a cursory examination of the conditions of Canada's jails and prisons makes clear that the lives of those behind bars are accorded little value and seen, generally, as disposable. Prisons create isolation — parents are separated from their children, and the price of long distance phone calls can be so exorbitant that many prisoners have no contact with the outside world. Further, people who go to jail even for short periods of time often lose their housing and jobs, becoming homeless and destitute once they are released.

Life conditions in provincial jails can only be described as malignly neglectful. Bordeaux jail in Québec, which is noted to have a vastly disproportionate Black population, was found to have horrific and inhumane conditions. It was revealed in 2012 that it was common practice to confine prisoners to their small cells for fourteen hours per day, and that the jail was infested with rats and vermin, among other unhygienic conditions. During summer renovations in one area of the basement, seventy inmates had to share one shower, and others had no shower at all (*Toronto Sun* October 13, 2012). The Ottawa-Carleton Detention Centre has recently been in the media for frequent, unwarranted physical abuse of detainees (*Ottawa Community News* July 25, 2013), and has been accused of housing prisoners in eight-by-ten-foot shower cells on mattresses on the wet floor, and keeping up to one-quarter of its population in solitary confinement (Dimmock 2016).

At the level of federal prisons, conditions continue to decline. The practice of double-bunking, in which two prisoners are placed in a cell made for one, remains endemic in male prisons due to an overcrowding that many critics attribute to Harper's carceral "tough on crime" time in office (Sapers 2012). In Ontario's Grand Valley Institution, where the large majority of federally incarcerated Black women reside (Sapers 2013), prisoners were being held in gymnasiums, with some women being held in an "interview room" that had no running water or toilets (Sapers 2012). As well, Black prisoners face significant racial discrimination once behind bars. Prisons are permeated with the same anti-Black racism that operates in the so-called "free" world outside. Indeed, the exposure of Black prisoners to racist violence at the hands of prison guards has been documented at least since the mid-1990s. In one government-sponsored report, Black male youth reported that prison guards would watch them shower, comment on their genitals and make highly racial and sexualized comments (Commission on Systemic Racism in the Ontario Criminal Justice System 1994). More recently, Black prisoners have reported experiencing racial discrimination in accessing health services and prison employment" (Sapers 2013). Black prisoners also continue to experience high rates of violence at the hands of prison staff. Black prisoners accounted for almost 15 percent of all reviewed use-of-force incidents in 2014, far above their population of 9 percent, which led the federal correctional investigator to conclude that prison staff's use of force is racially discriminatory (Sapers 2012 and 2015). While all prisoners are vulnerable to violence behind bars, the markedly high rates of abuse directed at Black prisoners when compared to the general prison population makes it clear that this violence is rooted in anti-Black racism.

Beyond physical violence, Black prisoners are acutely vulnerable to psychological harm with isolation practices known to inflict unnecessary suffering and cause long-lasting harm. Black (and Indigenous) prisoners face particularly high rates of solitary confinement (Sapers 2013). Canada's use of prolonged solitary confinement, which is regularly imposed on Canadian prisoners for months at a time, has been noted by the World Health Organization to cause or exacerbate health problems and to harm the possibility of rehabilitation (Sapers 2015); it has been compared to torture by the U.N. Human Rights Council and the U.N. Committee Against Torture (Woods 2017). The practice, frequently directed against prisoners with mental health issues, has been called "the most onerous and depriving experience that the state can legally administer in Canada" by Howard Sapers (2015). For people with mental health issues, it has been known to lead to suicide (Woods 2017). Arlene Gallone, a Black woman who was held in solitary confinement in a cell the size of a bathroom stall for a total of nine months in Québec's federal facility, Joliette Institution for Women, has accused the prison of placing her in solitary confinement for such benign instances as banging too loudly on her door or blocking the toilet (Woods 2017). To use her words, "I felt like an animal … You do not lock a dog in cage for three months" (CBC News January 23, 2017). Gallone is currently undertaking a class action lawsuit against Correctional Service Canada on behalf of every prisoner in the province who has been held in solitary confinement for more than seventy-two consecutive hours (Woods 2017).

Though incarceration itself is harmful, subjecting Black and Indigenous people, as well as people with mental health issues to solitary confinement — despite all medical and human rights evidence opposing this practice — makes it clear that prison is a site of violence, not one of healing. In the words of Black feminist and prison scholar Julia Sudbury, who has conducted research with Black incarcerated people in Canadian prisons, the very nature of prison life is immobility and fear. She writes that the experience of being imprisoned is to be exposed to authorities that choose to "administer a judicious degree of pain" on captive subjects whose every movement is subject to strict control (2004c: 154).

AGAINST PRISONS

> Countries do not use prison as a direct, rational measure to reduce crime. Rather, they choose — through a complex process of ideological, moral, political and juridical negotiation — the level of pain that they are willing to inflict on their citizens. (Christie 1982 in Stevens, Stöver and Brentari 2010: 380)

Caging "undesirables" does not actually create a safer or more peaceful society. In fact, in many cases it makes this goal more difficult to attain by exacerbating, rather than directly addressing, the social, economic and racial inequalities at the root of much of what is called "criminal behaviour." Race plays an integral role in deciding who will come to be defined as criminal (Roberts 1993), as does class, mental health and addiction: a significant majority of Canada's incarcerated population is poor and suffering from mental health problems and addiction (Sapers 2015). Still, the underlying principle that prison remains a logical place to house those who defy the Criminal Code remains unquestioned throughout much of society. That some unruly persons must spend significant amounts of their lives behind bars remains common sense, both from those who advocate a "tough on crime" philosophy as well as those pushing for much-needed reforms. The societal investment in incarceration is significant and on the rise. Despite increasingly dire conditions, it costs $108,376 per year to house a man in prison and nearly twice that for a female inmate, while funding for reintegration and release programs continues to be cut (Sapers 2015). Indeed, prison spending has been a priority in an era otherwise characterized largely by spending cuts; a report by the United States

Solicitor General found that money spent by states to keep prisoners behind bars has risen nearly proportionally to the drop in spending on higher education (Dobbin 1999 in Gendreau, Goggin and Cullen 1999). Numerous studies continue to show that, in terms of deterrence, preventing crime and "recidivism," prison sentences do not work, and imprisonment does not significantly affect crime rates (Kovandzic and Vieraitis 2006 and Reiner 2000 in Stevens, Stöver and Brentari 2010; Gendreau et al. 1999). The United States Solicitor General's analysis of fifty studies on 336,052 offenders found that prisons actually slightly increased people's likelihood to commit crimes when compared to community-based rehabilitation, and noted that "prisons should not be used with the expectation of reducing future criminal activity" (Gendreau, Goggin and Cullen 1999). Given the rising rate of people with mental and cognitive disabilities behind bars, prisons are even less equipped to "rehabilitate" mental illnesses, and are frequently causing people further harm and making societal reintegration even more difficult (Sapers 2015).

Prisons allow society to be relieved of "the responsibility of thinking about the real issues afflicting those communities from which prisoners are drawn in such disproportionate numbers" (Davis 2003: 16). As a settler society, the legitimacy of the Canadian state to incarcerate Indigenous peoples at all has been called into question by Indigenous scholars like Patricia Monture-Angus, as, she argues, it is an imposition upon previously existing Indigenous justice systems (in Nichols 2014). Given the increasingly well-documented failures of a carceral approach to crime, a small but growing movement aimed at prison abolition is advocating less punitive ways to address social ills such as violence and addiction. Instead of investing enormous amounts of public resources toward law enforcement and incarceration, prison abolition advocates aim toward societal transformations that would radically address the roots of social ills, including racial, gender and economic inequalities. Due to limitations of scope I will not re-create their arguments here, but the works of critical thinkers such as Ruth Wilson Gilmore (2007), Joy James (2006), Angela Y. Davis (2003) and Julia Sudbury (2004), as well as larger social movements such as Incite! Women of Colour Against Violence (2006) and the Movement for Black Lives (2016) have made innovative and timely interventions about the importance of prison abolition toward attaining racial, gendered and economic justice. Given the harms that incarceration has inflicted on Black communities, it's necessary to reimagine what genuine community safety could mean. In a world defined by rampant, growing economic and racial inequality and increasing incarceration rates, it is only by aiming toward transformative rather than punitive forms of justice that we may begin to imagine a society in which Black communities do not rot away inside juvenile detention centres, jails and prison cells.

CONCLUSION

The agencies that together make up the criminal justice system have been afforded enormous and, in some ways, unparalleled powers to surveil and control Black movement and curtail Black freedom. As fear of Blackness is increasingly articulated as a fear of crime, state powers of criminalization continue to be consolidated and violent technologies of surveillance and punishment continue to have enormous power over the lives of Black folks. The longstanding conflation of Blackness with criminality has not only helped the state devalue Black lives, it has even justified the often-violent deaths of Black community members. Racial profiling and Black incarceration help keep in place a racial hierarchy that has dominated the Canadian landscape for centuries, and Black people with criminal records "are now as systematically excluded from mainstream Canadian life as their early twentieth-century ancestors before them" (Khenti 2014: 194).

This violent imposition upon Black people's lives has always been contested. Since the 1980s and early 1990s, Black communities across Canada have been highly vocal against the failures of the criminal justice system and the racist intimidation and violence that has been inflicted on Black communities by the police. Toronto's Black Action Defence Committee (BADC), formed in the wake of the police killing of Michael Wade Lawson and Lester Donaldson, as well as the shooting of Sophia Cook (Hall and Flavelle 1988; English 1994), have demonstrated an uncompromising stance against racist police violence. In the words of co-founder Dudley Laws (speaking to the *Globe and Mail*), "if police officers in Metro Toronto think that they can come into our community and shoot people in questionable circumstances and kill people unnecessarily, and no action will be taken against them, they are totally wrong" (in Wilson 1989). This organizing, though successful in many ways, was met with popular hostility and organizers were treated as enemies of the state — the mother and aunt of Lawson were even placed on a list of suspected "radicals" and subject to police surveillance, along with other members of the BADC (English 1994). Also Known as X (AKAX), who became an active Black political force in 1990s Montréal after the death of Marcellus Francois and amid anti-Black violent attacks on Black Montrealers by white nationalists, also changed the public landscape and created important discussions within Montréal's Black communities on the role of policing in their cities (Mugabo 2016). More recently, Black Lives Matter Toronto made international headlines by camping out for two weeks outside of police headquarters to address the death of Andrew Loku and to demand an end to the practice of carding and racial profiling (Black Lives Matter "Demands" n.d.). Further, this activism has begun to challenge more broadly the legitimacy of law enforcement and to push the criminal justice system to disinvest in police and prisons (Khan 2017, n.d.). While racialized policing and punishment has, in many ways, been designed toward maintaining the subjection of Black peoples, the Black response continues to be one of subversion, resilience and refusal. However, despite inspirational and important successes, the climate of anti-Blackness across society and state institutions has remained nearly absolute.

CHAPTER FOUR

LAW ENFORCEMENT VIOLENCE AGAINST BLACK WOMEN

Naming their names, telling their stories

There seems to be no sense of urgency when it comes to black women and black trans women, who are also targeted by police. (Pascale Diverlus, co-founder of Black Lives Matter Toronto in Goldsbie 2015)

THE IMAGINED VICTIM OF POLICE SURVEILLANCE, harassment and violence is often presumed to be a young Black male. While Black men have undeniably experienced street checks at enormous rates and make up the large majority of police killings, the law enforcement violence that is experienced by Black women remains largely unseen, a part of a larger, untapped archive of the institutional denigration of Black women's lives. The erasure of the experiences of Black women at the hands of law enforcement is itself a form of violence that "eras[es] the specificity of violence against Black women and Black girls" and places them in a unique danger because it "ultimately supposes that they do not live under a constant threat of harm" from the police (Mugabo 2016: 69).

It is important to place Black women's experiences at the hands of the police as part of a larger Canadian history of state-sanctioned punishment of Black women who fail to be subordinate and docile. This is evidenced most notably in the hanging in the eighteenth century of enslaved woman Marie-Joseph Angélique, who was accused of torching part of the city of Montréal in an attempt to escape bondage (Cooper 2006). While upper-class white women have historically been presented as vulnerable, fragile and requiring patriarchal protection, the construction of Black women has existed beyond and outside the meaning of "woman" itself (Haley 2016). Black "womanhood" has never protected Black women from being forced to perform difficult manual labour, or from the systemic and institutionalized sexual and physical violence structured into the institution of slavery. Although white women in lower classes rarely received the veneration of femininity and motherhood of their upper-class sisters, the very construction of Black femininity itself has always been outside, both rhetorically and practically, of those requiring protection. While some — though not all — white women were believed to be "ladies," the servitude of Black women was elevated to a racial character trait by the trope of Black woman as "Mammy" (Hartman 1997; Austin 1995). The Mammy represented a fictionalized, celibate and idealized — good — Black woman who gratefully raised the white children of her master or employer and performed her servitude willingly. This figure served a dual purpose: it at once justified Black women's economic exploitation and helped remove white culpability from slavery. The Mammy was upheld as "the ultimate … vision of ideal black womanhood — complete submission to the will of whites … who not only acknowledged her inferiority to whites but who loved them" (hooks 1981 in Austin 1995: 432). The Mammy, as an image, had no real relationship to actual Black women, who had always resisted enslavement in large and small ways. Instead, the role that was created for Black women was held in place by the economic, social, political and psychological violence of enslavement, and by the threat (whether implicit or explicit) of punishment in the form of physical or sexual violence for any deviation

An opposing but complementary representation of Black femininity may be seen in the trope of the "Black Jezebel." Characterized by hypersexuality and deviance, this trope historically served the purpose of absolving white, male sexual violence against Black women. As it obscured white men's culpability in the perpetration of acts of violence, it also facilitated hostility toward Black women (Austin 1995). It was Black women, and not the men who harmed them, who were to blame, as their nature made them immoral, wayward and threatening. While these tropes are often identified as emerging from the American South (Hartman 1997), shared views surrounding Black enslaved people crossed borders with white settlers during slavery. For example, antebellum blackface minstrel shows, which featured stereotypical representations of Black womanhood, were common across Canada until the mid-twentieth century (Mathieu 2010).

Today, Black women still face significant danger for being perceived as "uppity." The acceptable social role for Black women established under slavery is still in force by punishment not only in the form of social sanction, but by the violence of law enforcement officers. While strength in women of any race remains subject to criticism within broader society, the perception of arrogance, for Black women, can be harmful or even deadly. "Arrogance" was the reason cited by the transit police who forced a Black twelve-year-old girl off a Montréal city bus when she asked for assistance with directions (CBC News July 29, 2012). In the United States, the highly controversial death of Sandra Bland exemplifies larger patterns of the societal devaluation and punishment of Black women who exhibit strength instead of fear or submission. Bland, who had been publicly vocal of anti-Black police violence, was said to have committed suicide in police custody, a narrative widely contested by her family and the larger Black community. After being arrested for a routine traffic stop that had escalated to abusive treatment by the police, Bland was found hanging from a noose in her cell (Nathan 2016). Her death, an ex-police officer told CNN, occurred because she had been "arrogant" from the very beginning (Edwards 2015). Law enforcement continues to play a significant role in reinforcing the racial and gendered social order. Black women who deviate from their ascribed role as deferent continue to be punished — sometimes by humiliation, physical abuse, sexual assault and neglect — for any deviance from their designated role as subservient, and for failing to perform the submissive, content role of the Mammy.

The violence of settler colonialism, though in many ways distinct, occurred in parallel and in concert with the history of slavery and its afterlives and has resulted in a similar dehumanization of Indigenous girls and women across Canada. Indigenous femininity, too, has received none of the protections granted to white and middle-class Canadian women. High rates of law enforcement violence directed at Indigenous women has made national and international headlines; for example, a Human Rights Watch investigation conducted in British Columbia uncovered systemic neglect and horrific accounts of abuse toward Indigenous women and girls by police, including rape, death threats, violent arrests, the use of tasers on girls as young as twelve years old and other accounts of sexual and physical abuse (Human Rights Watch 2013). A CBC investigation in Val D'Or, Québec, also documented dozens of Indigenous women who described being sexually or physically assaulted by provincial police, as well as being left out in the snow and forced to walk back in dangerous conditions (Dupuis and Panasuk 2016a, 2016b). This violence exists within a larger context of an epidemic state abuse and neglect of Indigenous women and girls, including the internationally criticized neglect in addressing the murder or disappearance of at least 582 Indigenous girls and women across Canada as of 2010 (Native Women's Association of Canada n.d.). It is necessary to frame this violence as a product of ongoing settler colonialism, and as an outgrowth of other state impositions aimed at eradicating Indigenous women that date back centuries (Jacobs 2013). The state violence levelled at Indigenous women is not identical to that experienced by Black women. Yet, Indigenous women, too, have been represented as having deviant sexuality to excuse the harms visited upon them by the state (Razack 2002). This reality is integral in further discussions surrounding the racialized and gendered facets of policing in Canada.

Black Canadian feminist historians Peggy Bristow, Dionne Brand, Linda Carty, Afua Cooper, Sylvia Hamilton and Adrienne Shadd assert strongly that, in the context of the institutional erasure of Black women's lives in Canada, the telling of Black women's individual stories helps us to begin to resuscitate Black women's realities in Canada (1999). The stories of the following women's experiences of abuse at the hands of law enforcement officials in recent years cannot stand in for a concerted, nationwide investigation into the realities of police violence against Black women. Nonetheless, I hope that sharing their experiences can help bring to light the underlying hostility and suspicion to which Black women are subjected by law enforcement officers.

MAJIZA PHILIP

The pending case of Majiza Philip, a Black, Montréal-based woman, helps us see how Black women who do not manifest passivity are subject to arbitrary racist violence at the hands of law enforcement. On November 26, 2014, Philip, a chef and a dance instructor, was out celebrating her twenty-sixth birthday with a white male friend at a downtown club. He was asked to leave the club for excessive drinking, and police arrived to give him a ticket for loitering. Philip stated that she knocked on the window of the police car to let her friend know that she had his jacket when the police began violently assaulting her: "At that moment, this huge tall officer just came and started pushing me, pushing me violently, pushing me back" (CTV News February 19, 2015). She stated she informed him that he was violating her rights, and in response he grabbed her, pushed her face down into the patrol car and hit her. She claims she heard a loud, cracking sound and was subsequently handcuffed and thrown into the cruiser. Philip stated that, despite crying, begging to be un-cuffed and telling them repeatedly that her arm had been broken, they just laughed at her. They then took her to the police station where she was handcuffed to a chair and questioned for hours before finally being released and taken to the hospital. It was at the hospital that she learned that her right humerus bone had been snapped. Philip later discovered that the officers had, without informing her, filed six criminal charges against her, including resisting arrest, assaulting two police officers and obstructing justice, and that a warrant was filed for her arrest (which was later withdrawn). Her white, male friend who had been the subject of the initial incident received two tickets but was not charged or hurt. Philip, however, has refused to accept this dehumanizing treatment and intimidation, and is currently filing a civil suit against the SPVM for racial profiling (CTV News February 19, 2015; CBC News August 5, 2015; Laflamme 2015). The violence and humiliation experienced by Philip, along with the subsequently withdrawn criminal charges, demonstrate that quick escalation, extreme and unnecessary physical force, arrest and criminal charges are not reserved solely for Black men. The description of events also illuminates how Black women's submission is enforced by physical violence, humiliation and legal retribution. In asserting her rights and personhood, she was immediately subject to both psychological and physical sanction by law enforcement officers.

SHARON ABBOTT

Another example of a flagrant police assertion of dominance over a Black woman is the case of Sharon Abbott. In 2007, Abbott, a postal worker in Toronto, was followed by a white police officer, Sergeant Stephen Ruffino, while delivering newspapers at three in the morning. The officer alleged that he was following her because she had been driving without a seatbelt. He stated that he then observed her turning left without signalling and asserted that she was driving erratically, so he pulled her over and asked her for identification. Abbott stated that she was afraid of being assaulted by a man impersonating an officer, and when he asked her several times to come near and identify herself, she instead called her husband, so that there would be a witness to the encounter — an important survival strategy used by many women to counter the threat of sexual assault. At that time, he told her she was under arrest, grabbed her from the car and pushed her roughly against the police car to handcuff her. Abbott asserts that he then threw her onto the ground, used her head as leverage to lift himself up and proceeded to pick her up using her belt, leaving half of her body in the car and half on the ground. Ruffino denied that this occurred. Abbott was then kept handcuffed in the patrol car for approximately an hour and then issued seven tickets for minor traffic violations, six of which were later dismissed. Abbott sustained several injuries, including an abrasion over her left eye, cuts on the inside of her upper lip and bruising from the handcuffs.

Abbott, too, refused to passively accept this violence. She subsequently filed a human rights complaint and won a $5,000 settlement (*Abbott v. Toronto Police Services Board* 2009). The presiding judge found that the officer was guilty of both racial and gendered discriminations toward her, stating that, "I have tried to hypothesize a White woman out delivering papers in the early morning having fairly routine traffic matters escalate into an arrest. I have been unable to do so" (para 44). The judge further found that the sergeant's actions were part of a larger system of violence used to force the subordination of Black persons perceived as "uppity." He found that Sergeant Ruffino's actions were "consistent with a manifestation of racism whereby a white person in a position of authority has an expectation of docility and compliance from a racialized person, and imposes harsh consequences if that docility and compliance is not provided" (para 46, f). Abbott's case, too, is indicative of a more widespread societal attitude that punishes Black women whose confidence threatens the racial and gendered hierarchy that structures Canadian society.

JACQUELINE NASSIAH

The story of Jacqueline Nassiah, too, demonstrates the punishment enacted on Black women who do not or will not embody submission and deference to white law enforcement officers. As well, her story makes visible the xenophobic hostility that Black women receive from the police. In Toronto, in February 2003, Jacqueline Nassiah was shopping when a white security guard accused her of stealing a bra worth less than $10. She denied the charge. When the Peel Regional Police officer arrived on site, she again denied having stolen anything and was then subjected to two body searches and questioned in a verbally abusive manner for over an hour. At one point in the questioning, she later testified, that the officer assumed she did not speak English, threatened to take her to jail and stated, "fucking foreigner ... if you don't tell me where the bra is I'm going to take you [down]" (*Nassiah v. Peel [Regional Municipality] Services Board* 2007). The allegedly stolen bra was never recovered, and a security videotape found no evidence of theft. No charges were laid, and she was subsequently released. Nassiah, in an act of courage, brought the case to the Ontario Human Rights Commission. The Commission ruled in 2007 that the incident was one of racial profiling because it subjected her to a "more intensive, suspicious and prolonged investigation because she is Black" (172), and awarded her $20,000 in damages (Ontario Human Rights Commission 2007). Nassiah's failure to comply — by being unable to produce what she had not stolen — appears to have been seen as a challenge to the authority of the security and police officers, and was punished by psychological and verbal abuse.

AUDREY SMITH

In 1993, Audrey Smith, a thirty-seven-year-old mother of five and Jamaican tourist, was subjected to sexualized humiliation by Toronto police officers. The officers claimed that they had been tipped off that someone fitting her description had crack cocaine in her underwear (Rushowy 1995 in Lawson 2002: 215). Two male officers called a third, female officer to the scene to search her for drugs. According to Audrey Smith, the female officer asked her to unbutton the top of her jumpsuit and subsequently stripped her of her underwear and bent her over, all at a busy corner of an intersection (Abbate 1995 in Lawson 2002: 215). Although no drugs were found, Smith was unable to account for her presence on a park bench at night, so she was then accused of prostitution (Lawson 2002: 217). Her claim stated that the officers left her naked and that, in addition, she had committed no verifiable offence. When the incident was brought to a police tribunal by Smith, the police officer's lawyer attested that she had unclothed herself, and that it was normal that Jamaican women flashed their bottoms to authority figures as a sign of disrespect — an inaccurate and derogatory stereotyping of Jamaicans that was subsequently critiqued by Black community members (McTair 1995 in Lawson 2002: 215). Audrey Smith expressed, "There I was, naked as the day I was born on the street. I have never felt so ashamed and humiliated in my life" (Colbourn 1993 in Mosher 1998: 17). The Black Action Defence Committee called for the dismissal of Police Chief Bill McCormack over what they described as a "dehumanizing, racist, illegal and sexual attack" on Smith (*Sun Sentinel* September 19, 1993). Further outcry came from Jamaican diplomats (*Sun Sentinel* September 23, 1993), but despite all this blowback, the police officers implicated were cleared of any wrongdoing. Smith's presumed hypsersexuality was used both to justify her sexual humiliation and, later, to absolve the police of responsibility for Smith's degrading treatment.

STACY BONDS

In 2008, Stacy Bonds, a twenty-seven-year-old make-up artist based in Ottawa, was subject to a violent sexual assault at the hands of the Ottawa police. While having a conversation with two men in a van on Regent Street in Ottawa, Bonds apparently had a sip from an unknown bottle that she then placed in a garbage can. Law enforcement officers stopped her, apparently thinking she may have been a sex worker soliciting a client, took her name and date of birth, and after running it, told her that she could go. Bonds testified that when she asked the officers why they had stopped her — and insisted on an answer after being ignored — she was arrested for public intoxication (Cobb 2010 in Tanovich 2011). Following this arrest, though she remained non-violent and compliant, she was subjected to hours of violent humiliation and physical and sexual abuse. Bonds' statement details how one of the officers used his knee to deal two violent blows to her kidney area, grabbed her hair and wrenched her head forward (Makin 2010; Tanovich 2011). Next, according to Bonds' account, an officer forced his hand down her pants, her shirt and bra were cut off her body with scissors and she was held down with a plexiglass riot shield. Following these events, she was left half naked in a cell for hours (Makin 2010). She was subsequently charged with public intoxication and assault of an officer, but the charges were thrown out when the judge viewed the video footage capturing the assault (CTV News March 15, 2011).

Bonds, though traumatized after the incident, launched a successful lawsuit against the Ottawa police, in which the judge found that "there is no reasonable explanation ... to have cut Ms. Bonds' shirt and bra off, and there is no reason, apart from vengeance and malice, to have left Ms. Bonds in the cell for a period of three hours and fifteen minutes half naked and having soiled her pants" (Makin 2010). In a rare victory, due largely to the videotaped evidence, the officer implicated was charged with sexual assault (CTV News March 15, 2011). The law enforcement officer's assumption of Bonds' deviant sexuality triggered an enormous level of hostility, manifested in physical violence and her subsequent sexual and psychological humiliation.

CHEVRANNA ABDI

The death of Chevranna Abdi in police custody, along with the coverage surrounding her death, demonstrates the disregard of Black trans women's lives not only by law enforcement but also by the media. In 2003, Chevranna Abdi, a twenty-six-year-old Black transgender woman, died in police custody under highly suspicious circumstances. According to witnesses quoted in the *Hamilton Spectator*, police were called by a neighbour because Abdi was yelling and acting strangely toward others in her building. Abdi was handcuffed and dragged, facedown, down seven flights of stairs by law enforcement officers. The officers claimed that they were "fatigued" from carrying her and forced "to release her legs, letting her lower limbs drag *while they carried her upper body face down*" (Brown 2006, emphasis added). By the time they reached the lobby on the main floor, she was not breathing and subsequently died in police custody (Brown 2006). Her death was ruled accidental by the SIU and blamed on choking due to vomiting "based on cocaine poisoning" (Legal Foundation of the LGBT Law Association of Greater New York 2006: 236). It is difficult to imagine that a death after this seemingly negligent and dehumanizing treatment would not have produced significant outcry from the population if Abdi had been a white middle-class woman in distress. Instead, her HIV status, race and gender identity were used by the media to dehumanize her and sensationalize her death. Throughout the media, she was referred to as an "HIV-positive transsexual" and "either a prostitute or a drug dealer," and her death a "drug-fuelled melee" (Brown 2006). Some coverage went so far as to attribute her death to her being transgender, and unnecessarily reminded readers that "Chevranna Abdi was born a man" (Burman 2003). Abdi's treatment by the police, as well as the media, cannot be seen as separate from her identity as a Black transgender woman — this fact helps to render invisible the responsibility of the police for the violence used against her. Black transgender women often live at the intersection of both the societal demonization of Black women and a societal hostility toward transgender persons. The negation of Abdi's humanity and the sensational treatment of her gender by the media are unfortunately representative of an all-too-common practice of media coverage of transgender persons (Grant et al. 2011). Both Chevranna Abdi's tragic, unnecessary killing and its subsequent coverage clearly illustrate the multiple tropes that uniquely dehumanize Black transgender women. The transmisogyny and anti-Blackness that marks Black transgendered women's lives not only renders them vulnerable to police abuse, but also engenders a disrespect to their person.

LARGER PATTERNS OF PROFILING AND
ABUSE AT THE HANDS OF LAW ENFORCEMENT

Despite its invisibility from the larger public realm, police violence directed at Black women in Canada is not a new phenomenon. In the late 1980s, Black feminist historian Délice Mugabo uncovered an incident in which Mireille Romulus, a Haitian-born mother of two, was handcuffed, beaten and choked on her kitchen floor, called a "nigger" and told to "go back to Africa" in front of her two children by police officers. The officers had claimed to be looking for her sister to settle a debt that she had with a department store. This violence, Mugabo asserts, was relatively commonplace for Black women in Montréal throughout the 1980s and 1990s; it received little attention within broader society (Mugabo 2016: 69–72). Age has not protected Black women any more than it has Black men: in Montréal, two Black women in their seventies identified that they had also been victims of police brutality (Rocha 2005 in Henry and Tator 2006: 78).

Today, there are still significant barriers in trying to highlight Black women's experiences with law enforcement. The Canadian media, in the too-rare moments that it addresses racial profiling at all, focuses largely on police violence against Black men. The default object of racial profiling is often assumed to be male, even when studies do not refer explicitly to gender. The 2012 *Toronto Star* investigation on racial profiling, for example, did not disaggregate data based on gender, and its reports focused largely on the experiences of Black men. Accordingly, reports centred on Black cis or transgender women in Canada are more difficult to find. Beyond the widely documented difficulties in accessing data on racial discrimination in Canada more generally, there exists virtually no systematic data collection on police violence that is based on gender and/or sexuality.

Because of the silence surrounding police profiling of Black women, it is particularly important to highlight the disproportionate and degrading treatment they receive at the hands of the police. Disproportionate stops and use of force, for example, are not only applied to Black men, but women as well. One of the only systematic collections of race-based statistics ever compiled in a Canadian city (conducted over twelve months between 2003 and 2004) was in Kingston. The study revealed that Black women were stopped less often than Black men, but remained slightly more likely to be stopped than white men, and more than *three times* more likely to be stopped than white women (Owusu-Bempah and Wortley 2014: 294, emphasis added). As well, between 2000 and 2006, the rate of cases that Black women brought to Ontario's SIU involving sexual assault and deaths at the hands of police was just over double the rate of cases brought to the SIU by white women (Wortley 2006: 38). One Montréal study on Black youth found that Black girls were three times more likely than white girls to have been arrested two or more times (Bernard and McAll 2008: 18). This limited data suggests that even though it receives far less visibility, state violence toward Black women in the form of racial profiling and police brutality does occur, and it occurs disproportionately (though, of course, "proportionate" police violence is not a viable end goal toward racial and gendered justice).

As Canadian criminologist David Tanovich reminds us, "the issue of gendered violence against racialized women by police and state officials is an under-studied and litigated area in Canada" (2011: 21). The bravery demonstrated by the Black women above — who dared to challenge those with a far more social power than them — cannot be understated. However, for many reasons, including fear of reprisal, expensive legal fees and public scrutiny, many persons who have experienced police abuses chose not to publicize them. Yet, given the high rates of Black women in behind bars and extrapolating from the little data available surrounding law enforcement abuse of Black women, I argue that the cases highlighted above are not likely to be individual aberrations from the norm, but rather are indicative of larger patterns of unexamined police abuse of Black women. This abuse is a continuation of enforcing the gendered and racialized stereotypes about Black womanhood which are now centuries old.

It is important, however, not to mistake Black women's erasure from the cultural landscape for their silence. In addition to the bravery of individual women contesting incidents of police abuse and the largely undocumented everyday resistance of Black women who refuse to be submissive, Black women's activism has also challenged law enforcement violence. In Toronto, Black women have tried to raise the visibility of police violence against Black women as early as the late 1980s and early 1990s. Black women, who were highly active in broader struggles around police violence, publicly decried the impacts of police violence as it impacted Black women. For example, Sherona Hall, co-founder of the Black Action Defence Committee and member of the Women's Coalition Against Racism and Police Violence, spoke frequently to the media regarding the police shooting of Sophia Cook. Hall drew attention to the lack of repercussions for those who harmed Black women, telling a crowd of protesters on International Women's Day in 1990 that, "They are trying to turn back, to take away from us what we have fought for and won" (in Holden

1990). Cook herself, even as she was recovering from her injury, was highly vocal and critical of police violence (*Windsor Star* January 29, 1990; Holden 1990). It is important not to participate in the erasure of Black women's activism that contests the obfuscation of their experiences at the hands of police, despite the lack of attention within mainstream feminism and wider society. There are likely countless more undocumented instances of Black women's vocal resistance that remain untold.

CONCLUSION

The lack of attention paid to Black women's experiences is made possible because of the devaluation of Black women across Canadian society, including within the Black community in many instances. For this reason, Black women's experience of policing abuse must no longer be sidelined or dismissed due to "lack of data." In particular, the realities of trans Black women — and as gender non-binary or non-conforming people — require further attention, both from researchers as well as larger social movements. So that Philip, Abbott, Nassiah, Smith, Bond, and Abdi's experiences are neither forgotten nor repeated, making known the experiences of Black women at the hands of law enforcement must now be taken up as an essential task for researchers, activists and educators.

CHAPTER FIVE

MISOGYNOIR IN CANADA

Punitive state practices and the devaluation of Black women and gender-oppressed people

I invite you to come with me as I aim the spotlight at the obfuscated image of Black women, buried under cobwebs of oblivion, indifference and racism. (Esmerelda Thornhill 1991 in Daenzer 1997: 282)

DESPITE THE ENORMITY OF THE GOVERNING power that anti-Blackness has in Canada and worldwide, the criminalization of Black women cannot be reduced to racial oppression. For cis and transgender women, as well as non-binary and other gender-oppressed individuals, the experience of anti-Black racism is "existentially inseparable" from the lived experiences of gender and class (Brand 1999: 84). As Black feminist scholars Kimberlé Crenshaw and Andrea J. Ritchie astutely point out in their groundbreaking study, *Say Her Name* (2015), by setting the policing of Black men as the standard by which we seek, study and organize against anti-Black violence by law enforcement, we continue to erase Black women's full realities. This erasure, they argue, helps to camouflage and thus protect the status quo while obscuring the persistent, continued state violence experienced by Black women, who are both over-policed and under-protected (Crenshaw and Ritchie 2015). It is urgent to widen our framework by addressing other complex layers of racialized, gendered and xenophobic state violence that are regularly enacted on Black cis and transgender women by the state.

Unique and distinct forms of economic, social and political devaluation — and most notably, acute vulnerability to both intimate and state violence — mean that Black women's lives are defined by intersecting conditions of subjection, invisibility and disposability. For this reason, discussions surrounding the policing of Black women's lives remain frequently absent from discussions about both racial oppression (which often centre Black men) and gender oppression (which centre white women). Black women are still generally not imagined as primary targets of state violence. Yet now, as ever, Black women continue to face state antagonism and repression in their attempts to parent, migrate and make a living, often while surviving or attempting to overcome conditions of acute material deprivation.

Police violence exists as one form of oppression among many, making up only one facet of the larger criminalization of poor Black women's everyday lives. In addition to police harassment and violence, the policing of Black women often takes different forms, and relies on different dehumanizing racial and gendered logics, than those experienced by Black men. Less visible forms of state surveillance and punishment are enacted by police, customs officers and welfare agents, all of whom have enormous power over the day-to-day private and public lives of Black women. Some forms of the policing of the lives of poor Black women — who frequently have their homes searched and neighbours questioned by social service workers seeking evidence of welfare fraud — are often seen as mundane and administrative. Occurring largely in the private rather than the public realm, many forms of state surveillance that target Black women evoke far less public outrage than the police identity checks that plague the lives of young Black men. However, Saidiya Hartman reminds us that violent spectacles are not the only instances that evidence racial and gendered subjection. Rather, violence exists along a spectrum and many of the seemingly benign and mundane "everyday" displays of power in the lives of Black women actually mask a far more violent relationship of domination (1997: 42). The concerted surveillance and punitive targeting of poor Black women — often spanning multiple institutions at once — can be just as violent and harmful as harassment or assault by law enforcement officials.

Earlier pages have already briefly addressed the impacts of the criminal justice system as it impacts Black communities more broadly. It's necessary, though, to address aspects of racialized criminalization that are relatively unique to Black women if we wish to comprehensively understand the policing of Black lives in Canada. Toward addressing the invisibility of Black women's experiences, the term "misogynoir" was coined by queer Black feminist Moya Bailey (2010,

2014) to identify the virulent and often unseen hatred directed at Black women due to the intersection of anti-Blackness, misogyny and racism in society. The term has since been widely adopted by Black feminist scholars and activists to describe the unique forms of systemic discrimination and devaluation that they face. Misogynoir extends across society, including and well beyond the state. This is not intended to erase the fact that state violence against cisgender Black men is also gendered, or to negate the fact that Black men are also highly sexualized due to long-standing, false associations between Black masculinity and rape. Still, highlighting gendered oppression makes visible the multiple and intersecting violences inflicted by patriarchy and white supremacy on those who do not receive any of the benefits from either system.

While all Black women experience misogynoir and are vulnerable to state violence, all Black women do not experience identical forms of oppression. Black women outside of the realm of "respectability" are more vulnerable to victimization by state-sanctioned processes. In particular, Black women who are associated with "deviant" realities such as receiving social assistance, experiencing single motherhood, living with mental illness or being involved with drugs or sex work — realities that are not mutually exclusive — are particularly stigmatized, and therefore their lives are rendered particularly disposable. Negative representations of Black women do not exist in isolation from one another, but are mutually reinforcing. Transgender Black women experience unique marginalization, including massive levels of poverty, housing insecurity, police violence and wider societal hostility, but their lives are too frequently sidelined in discussions of violence against girls and women. In the words of Black, trans activist and feminist Janet Mock, "Trans black women live at the intersection of ... pass her by and pay her no mind" (in Hope 2016). Though little data is available in Canada, more than ten Black trans women had been killed in the first six months of 2016 in the United States, including Skye Mockabee, Deeniquia Dodds and Dee Whigham. Gender oppression extends well beyond the male/female gender binary: intersex, non-binary and gender non-conforming people, while not identifying as women, experience important and under-documented marginalization that often goes unseen by anti-racism efforts that focus solely on the experiences of young Black men.

While negative representations such as that of the Mammy and the Jezebel that were established under slavery have persisted with striking similarity across centuries, important re-articulations of slavery-era misogynoir have continued in more recent times. In *Black Feminist Thought: Knowledge, Consciousness and the Politics of Empowerment*, Black feminist theorist Patricia Hill Collins wrote that contemporary representations or "controlling images" of Black woman-hood, adapted and upgraded somewhat from those created under slavery, continue to allow for the ongoing political, economic and social subjugation of Black women. This includes stereotypical characterizations of Black women as "welfare queens," "hoochies" and negligent mothers, among other tropes of modern Black female deviance. These images serve to shift the blame for Black women's subjugation onto Black women themselves, and make "racism, sex-ism, poverty, and other forms of social injustice appear to be natural, normal, and inevitable parts of everyday life" (1990: 69). While negative associations attached to Black women permeate society at large, they are given legitimacy and reinforced by diverse government agencies. State institutions in Canada have played a key role in perpetuating and reinforcing state violence, systemic exploitation and vulnerability by representing Black women as welfare queens, sex workers and drug mules. These revamped images of Black female deviance and inferiority continue to be used to police Black women's intimate and public lives, as well as to leave Black women who experience sexual or intimate partner violence under-protected.

Under slavery, Black enslaved women working as domestics were subject to nearly constant scrutiny by the white households that held them captive, and both free and enslaved Black women faced intensive surveillance when in public spaces (Nelson 2016c). The ongoing legacy is apparent today in the surveillance and punishment of Black women by social services, law enforce-ment and customs agents, as well as in the skyrocketing rates of Black women's incarceration that collapse any perceived distinction between public and pri-vate realms. Discussions surrounding the criminalization of Blackness must take these articulations of state violence against Black women into account to effectively address and combat the systemic denigration of Black life in Canada.

WELFARE FRAUD, MISOGYNOIR AND THE CRIMINALIZATION OF POVERTY

The devaluation and exploitation of Black women's labour has consistently relegated Black women to the near-bottom of Canada's wage economy. While Black women have historically been represented as contentedly working in service positions for whites, in reality, Black women's lives have been marked by degrading working conditions and extreme poverty, often while being the sole provider for children (Brand 1999). In particular, as addressed earlier, the effects of massive cuts to public spending in recent decades by the federal and provincial governments on welfare and social programs have had significant effects on the economic security of Black women. Though social assistance is characterized as a supportive institution, accessing social assistance has resulted in intensive surveillance by welfare agents, often with highly punitive results. This has been particularly true for racialized women (Boyd 2006: 141). However, the role that anti-Blackness — and misogynoir in particular — has played in the criminalization of poverty in Canada is still widely under-recognized. While Black women have been among Canada's poorest demographics, they have simultaneously been scapegoated not only as the cause of their own marginalization and poverty, but also as a threat to Canadian society as a whole. In particular, amid widespread cuts in social spending in the 1990s, a state-led and media-fuelled frenzy regarding a perceived epidemic of what is referred to as "welfare fraud" cast poor Black women as likely "welfare cheats" and led to a massive increase in state surveillance of poor women's lives, homes and relationships.

In a crisis largely fabricated by government officials and much of the Canadian media, a substantial wave of repression took aim at the perceived attack on social assistance by "fraudsters" and undeserving welfare recipients (Pratt and Valverde 2002). While the resulting highly punitive scrutiny of welfare recipients wreaked enormous harms on the lives of poor women of every background, the public face associated with welfare fraud, and the primary target of the ensuing repression, was the poor Black woman. The widespread societal panic regarding Black women receiving social assistance was not restricted to Canada. In the late 1980s in the United States, negative stereotypes targeted Black women for being "welfare queens." In this stereotype, widely disseminated by Ronald Reagan and other conservative politicians, Black women's poverty was said to exist not as a result of state processes, but because of their inherent criminality, laziness and calculated dependency. Black women were represented as a "moral aberration and an economic drain" in wider society (Collins 1990: 80). Also, Black women were rendered a threat, seen as "deficient ... reproducers of an attendant culture of poverty" (Davis 1998: 70). In Ontario, however, the racist and sexist focus on Black female welfare recipients took a particularly xenophobic turn, and though all Black women were impacted, Somali women bore the brunt of popular hostility and experienced significant state repression.

In the early 1990s, a leaked federal report, later found to be almost entirely baseless, alleged massive Somali involvement in welfare fraud. The report, written by an immigration officer, made unsubstantiated claims that Somali refugees could easily collect up to $100,000 a year from fraudulent claims and stated that it was "extremely generous" to believe even 50 percent "of what a Somali tells you" (in Papp 1993). Despite being disputed widely by the Somali community and found to be both grossly exaggerated and misleading, this state-sponsored report had tangible and long-lasting effects. The ruling Ontario Liberal government, media and politicians frequently repeated the unsubstantiated claims that Somalis were "masters of confusion" engaged in "importing refugees to systematically pillage our vulnerable and exposed social welfare system" (*The Globe and Mail* 1993 in Pratt and Valverde 2002: 152). At that time, the Somali population in Canada was made up largely of single Somali mothers who had fled conflict accompanied by their children; many men had either died in the conflict or were left behind. This demographic was exacerbated by amendments to the *Immigration Act* that made family reunification difficult. As well, Somali women were often expected to send remittances to their family members elsewhere who also had fled conflict (OCASI 2016: 3). Somali refugee women faced widespread suspicion and were accused by media and state officials of sending their welfare money to "tribal warlords." In one case, a large photo of a Somali refugee mother and her children appeared in newspapers with the word "COLLECTOR" written above it (Pratt and Valverde 2002: 153). This form of sensational portrayal is dehumanizing and suggests to the public that Somali female-led households are, in fact, the face of fraud. These representations, while discovered to be largely baseless, nonetheless allowed for racialized profiling and repression that was directed explicitly at Black women.

The widespread social panic directed at Somali refugee women across Ontario was soon bolstered by a significant expansion of state repression. This resulted in enormous harms for poor women of any background, as it provided the backdrop for both massive cuts in social assistance benefits and the criminalization of those receiving welfare. With the aim of breaking a perceived "crisis" in what was termed "economic dependency," Ontario Premier Mike Harris's government (1995–2002) chose not to address the conditions causing widespread racialized and gendered poverty, but instead oversaw massive welfare cuts that reduced benefits by almost one-quarter and disqualified many single women from the program (Pratt and Valverde 2002; Chunn and Gavigan 2006). At the time, a recent government-sponsored study had demonstrated both that welfare fraud was not a significant fiscal issue and that it could be best addressed by making benefits more adequate (Ontario 1988 in Chunn and Gavigan 2006: 222). Rather than following the report's advice, Ontario's provincial government declared a crackdown on welfare fraud. To do so, they substantively expanded Criminal Code prosecutions for actions such as providing false addresses, living common-law without declaring a "spouse," receiving undeclared income and tendering lost/stolen cheques (Mirchandani and Chan 2005).

The criminalization of welfare fraud has been, in effect, the criminalization of poor women's survival strategies. For decades, welfare rates across Canada have been too low to allow women to meet their basic living expenses. It has thus been necessary for many women's very survival to resort to finding additional sources of income (Cox 2001). In 2016, welfare in Ontario was set at a rate of $585 per month — not even enough to cover most one-bedroom apartments (Shields 2016). Given the rising costs of housing and food, it is nearly impossible to survive on the monthly allotment without some form of income supplementation. However, it is this very survival strategy — finding alternative sources of income — that has been criminalized under legislation aimed at ending so-called "welfare fraud."

The reach of the law extends far beyond "fraud," as it in fact criminalizes Black and other racialized and/or poor women for their very conditions of poverty. For example, many people living in poverty and precarious housing are unable to store years of paperwork and identity documents. Yet, many offences under the umbrella of welfare fraud require decades of paperwork to prove innocence, a difficult and sometimes impossible feat while living in poverty (Mirchandani and Chan 2005: 20). Additionally, welfare recipients can be punished for "fraud" even in the case of an administrative error by their welfare agent, which is relatively common (Mosher and Hermer 2005). Despite popular conceptions of widespread fraud, even amid enormous resources allotted to cracking down on welfare fraud, convictions in 2001 to 2002 amounted to 0.1 percent of the combined social assistant caseload, and 1 percent of the total allegations (Mosher and Hermer 2005: 34).

There is no evidence linking Black communities to higher rates of welfare fraud and, indeed, no research indicates that Black women or migrants are more or less likely to use welfare than white Canadians (Shields 2003 in Mirchandani and Chan 2005: 3) Still, the stereotypical face of welfare abuse is often that of the Black single mother, widely denigrated as the cause of her own poverty (Carruthers 1996: 250). Poor women, and in particular racialized poor women, have in recent decades been subject to significant surveillance and enforcement at the level of welfare agents, at rates far higher than men (Mosher and Hermer 2005: 6). In one study, many of the interviewees who had been criminalized by welfare fraud legislation were Black women of African or Caribbean descent (Mirchandani and Chan 2005: 20).

The policing of welfare fraud allows for enormous and far-reaching forms of punishment. Conviction for welfare fraud is not a minor affair. Though actual convictions are rare, punishment, intended to act as a deterrent, is extremely harsh. Even fraud under $5,000 is often punished with incarceration (Mosher and Hermer 2005: 8). As well, one report showed that many accused pleaded guilty merely to avoid prison sentences that would mean leaving their children in the hands of welfare authorities (Martin 1992 in Mirchandani and Chan 2005: 26). The unfettered powers of surveillance granted to welfare agents toward the aim of preventing welfare fraud is itself a form of punishment.

While accorded far less political urgency than other forms of racial profiling, the policing of welfare fraud has allowed for a highly intensive policing of poor racialized women's private lives. Surveillance and intrusion into poor racialized women's residences by welfare agents are part of the mandated "war" on welfare fraud. Following up on tips from anonymous hotlines, dubbed "snitch lines" (Carruthers 1996: 244), eligibility review officers in Ontario possess the ability to enter a woman's house at any time, without a warrant, to "collect evidence." Though the review officers are not, in technical terms, the police, the effect of their investigations are the same, since some charges may lead to prosecutions and incarceration. Welfare fraud investigations allow for a level of state surveillance that surpasses that which is allotted to law enforcement officials for many serious crimes, but they do not require warrants. Investigators are given the arbitrary power to interview children, landlords and neighbours; these broad-reaching surveillance powers breach any imagined right to privacy (Mirchandani and Chan 2005: 28).

As well, investigations into welfare fraud appear to be rife with rights abuses, including "information mishandling, threats and harassments, failure to identify the purposes of the investigation, physical intimidation, and violation of privacy" (Morrison 1995 paraphrased in Carruthers 1996: 244). Welfare recipients are made to be permanently vigilant. Interviews of the neighbours and landlords of welfare recipients may alert a woman's entire social network to her use of social assistance, which may create or exacerbate stigmas (Mirchandani and Chan 2005: 28). Many welfare recipients have reported fearing interactions with neighbours, landlords and teachers, who may retaliate by reporting them for welfare fraud (Mosher and Hermer 2005: 6). Because women can be accused of welfare fraud for not having a reported "spouse in the house," many women fear having a romantic partner stay overnight, and others become trapped in situations of domestic abuse and coercion by partners who threaten to report them and allege fraud (Mosher et al. 2004 and Little 1998 in Chunn and

Gavigan 2006: 227, 231). As well, because welfare agents have a relative degree of discretion in whom to report, poor women receiving welfare are largely at the mercy of the whims of the particular agent, some of whom are highly "punitive and controlling" (Mosher et al. 2004 in Chunn and Gavigan 2006: 230). The presumption of guilt that accompanies social assistance removes any semblance of privacy in poor racialized women's intimate lives. Their lives are "regarded with acute interest, suspicion and often open hostility" and become "everybody's business" (Mirchandani and Chan 2005: 66).

Surprise home visits, invasive questioning of neighbours, call-in reporting hotlines and other forms of hyper-vigilant policing of Black and other marginalized women who are seen to be abusing the welfare system do not apply to those middle-class or wealthy persons who may cheat on their taxes. For similar offences, this demographic is neither widely persecuted, nor publicly demonized (Addario 2002). As well, the focus on racialized and poor women as the face of "system abuse" obscures the actual gravity and pervasiveness of the offence. A report for the Department of Justice found important information:

> More people cheat on their income taxes and lie about their cross-border shopping than defraud the welfare system. Corporate crime, white collar fraud and tax evasion, in Ontario cost the public more every year *than the entire cost of the social assistance system.* (Addario 2002: n.p., emphasis added)

In 2016, the CBC uncovered that Revenue Canada had granted legal amnesty from civilian or criminal prosecution to at least twenty-six millionaires who had stashed over $100 million worth of revenue offshore in an attempt to avoid paying taxes (Cashore et al. 2016). Yet, women living on less than $700 a month are deprived of their fundamental right to privacy as a matter of state practice, can be subject to massive surveillance as the result of an anonymous phone call and are liable to be prosecuted and sentenced merely for not reporting added income that is necessary toward their very survival.

Clear differences of social and political power, based largely on race, class and gender, underwrite this highly differential treatment. If the level of invasive scrutiny faced by Black, Indigenous and other poor racialized women were applied to white, middle-class Canadians, it would be widely decried and seen as a scandalous, Orwellian infringement of the basic rights and freedoms thought to be the right of all Canadians. Indeed, it would be seen as an affront to all Canadians. The state and popular treatment of what is called welfare fraud makes clear that "race becomes part of society's determination of what conduct to define as criminal" (Roberts 1993: 1954). The fact that dark-skinned and poor women thought to be cheating the government are treated by both welfare and the criminal justice system as dangerous criminals exposes the societal fault lines of sexism, racism, classism and xenophobia.

Further, although confronting welfare fraud is represented as saving public money from "abuse," there is a significant financial investment in the intensified surveillance and repression of welfare fraud offences. Welfare cuts and the criminalization of welfare fraud do not demonstrate a commitment to reduce government spending. Instead, they demonstrate how state investment continues to shift away from support and toward the repression and punishment of poor racialized women (Chunn and Gavigan 2006).

Devalued and demonized, Black, Indigenous and other marginalized women receiving social assistance are subject to a persistent and ongoing scrutiny of their day-to-day existence. While Black women on welfare have been represented as threats to Canadian society, significant harms have actually been enacted not by poor racialized women, but by "those who craft, pass, and enforce the laws and policies" (Neve and Pate 2004: 32). Addressing the root causes of poverty — for example, raising welfare rates, guaranteeing minimum incomes, combatting racial inequalities in the economy and raising minimum wage — would undoubtedly be far more effective in ensuring that welfare recipients were not subjected to undue hardships. These are necessary steps toward combatting the criminalization of all poor women who receive social assistance. However, in addition to remedying the economic injustices inherent in the criminalization of poverty, it's necessary to challenge the underlying demonization of Black women as "welfare queens" that has been so successfully employed toward justifying both cuts to social assistance and the criminalization of poverty. Further, ending the extreme levels of scrutiny that Black women face from welfare agents is necessary for any larger push to end racial profiling in Canadian society.

SEXUAL THREATS: THE DEMONIZATION OF BLACK WOMEN IN PUBLIC SPACE

The criminalization of Black women's intimate lives and the policing of their homes and personal relationships by welfare agents extends, too, into the public sphere. Black women have been historically assumed to possess a depraved and animalistic sexuality, seen as "a site of bestiality and illicitness" (James 1996: 143). Under slavery, Black women were frequently described — and bought and sold — using the term "Negro Wench," a term that, in the *Century*

Encyclopedia in 1889 connoted both "a lewd or immodest [European] woman" and "a coloured woman" (in Extian-Babiuk 2006: 32). Indeed, while historically white women could *become* deviant by engaging in particular behaviours, Black women were always and already presumed to be sexually deviant. This served to justify sexual violence toward Black women (Extian-Babiuk 2006: 32; Haley 2016). In addition to justifying sexual violence against Black women, which often occurred in the domestic realm, representations of Black women's sexual deviance have also been used to control Black women's movements in public space. Following the abolition of slavery, prostitution laws became one means of exerting state control over Black women's sexuality and their access to public space, as well as an extension of colonial law over Indigenous women's lives (Sayers 2013).

Today, widespread assumptions that Black women in public are involved in the sex trade reproduce age-old associations between Black women and criminal sexuality. A unifying feature in the aforementioned stories of Stacy Bonds and Audrey Smith, who suffered sexualized abuse at the hands of law enforcement, was the unsubstantiated assumption on the part of the officers that they may have been involved in the sex trade. Though far too little Canadian data addresses this reality, stereotypes linking Black women to prostitution continue to inform law enforcement practices beyond the stories of Audrey Smith and Stacey Bonds. The mere presence of a Black female body in public space is sexualized, and prostitution is frequently assumed. The 2003 Ontario Human Rights Commission report found that Black women reported being profiled as sex workers when in cars with white men (2003: 45). In another study, an African Nova Scotian woman described harassment on the assumption that she was involved in sex work:

> The police were always stopping me for nothing ... If I was on the corner trying to score [get drugs] they assumed I was prostituting ... Nobody gets charged for using drugs, but they were always bugging me ... I just got tired of the cops picking me up. There was no grounds for arrest but they kept picking me up. (Bernard 2001: 15)

In yet another case of assumed prostitution, a Black incarcerated woman named Dominique, who was on vacation when arrested and who was not involved in the sex trade, recounted being falsely accused by the police of stabbing someone due to the presumption that she was a sex worker. She told her interviewer,

> The cops stereotyped me — Black girl from the islands, white boy

— blue collar white boy, so they said "you're a prostitute and we know you trick them and you stab them." They put me in jail and they let the white guy who actually did the stabbing [get] away. (in Reece 2010: 124)

In the United States, both cis and transgender Black women face elevated levels of profiling for possible prostitution offences, which were sometimes justified, after the fact, on the grounds that they had been found to have a condom in their possession (Crenshaw and Ritchie 2015: 22). A report prepared for the United Nations from 2007 found that Black women, particularly Black transgender women, are routinely linked to prostitution and subject to profiling on the streets irrespective of their involvement in sex work. This report showed that they were "subjected to stops, strip searches, and arbitrary arrest and detention on a regular basis" whether they were working or not (Ritchie and Mogul 2007: 21). For trans Black women, the presumption of involvement in sex work is even more pronounced. Trans women face police profiling or arrest under the assumption that they are sex workers so often that it has been given the description "walking while transgender" (Grant et al. 2011). In one American study, the largest-ever survey of transgender and gender non-conforming people, 41 percent of Black trans women reported having been arrested or jailed because of their gender identity, compared to 7 percent of non-racialized trans respondents (Grant et al. 2011: 163). In Canada, no comparable research of this scope exists. However, acclaimed Canadian transgender feminist scholar Viviane Namaste has written that racialized and migrant transgender women are subject to intensive levels of police profiling while walking on the street in Canadian cities (Namaste 2005).

Racial and gendered profiling of possible sex workers can also occur at the hands of border officials. Canadian law allows for the profiling of possible sex workers to stop their migration. For instance, the federal government's 2011 omnibus crime bill, Bill C-10, granted power to immigration officials to profile women possibly involved, or at risk of being involved, in sex work and therefore deny their entry (Citizenship and Immigration Canada 2011). Now empowered with the highly subjective task of determining whether poor, brown or Black women *seem* like possible sex workers, immigration agents may refuse work permits to those deemed vulnerable to exploitation, including exotic dancers, low-skilled workers and "potential victims of human trafficking (Citizenship and Immigration Canada 2011). Given the historical and ongoing stereotyping of Black and other migrant women as involved in prostitution, the movement of poor Black, Asian and other racialized groups of women into Canada, whether or not they plan to work as sex workers, is now more constricted. While it is framed in terms of women's protection, the state-sanctioned profiling accorded to immigration officials with the *Safe Streets and Communities Act* is particularly harmful in a context in which it is already difficult for poor racialized women to migrate legally to Canada.

It is important to historicize and critique the racist and gendered injustice that stereotypes all Black women as likely sex workers. But at the same time, care must be taken to avoid falling into a trap of respectability politics, here defined as the practice of seeking to counter racist stereotypes by upholding Black female "virtue" and sexual morality (Miller-Young 2014: ix). To de-stigmatize Black womanhood by means of distancing good Black women from their "fallen" sisters contributes to yet another form of "sexual policing of black women" (Miller-Young 2014: ix). It places value on the lives and worth only of so-called "upstanding" Black women — that is, Black women who are presumably not involved in the sex trade. This politic promotes a duality between the innocent, respectable Black women who are falsely profiled as prostitutes, in opposition to the bad Black women who do, indeed, exchange sex for money, goods or security. This duality is harmful to all Black women since it makes Black women's humanity contingent on sexual purity. Respectability politics creates only a false sense of security for Black women who happen to fit into the standards of the "virtuous" Black woman. As the stories in the previous chapter demonstrate, law enforcement does not distinguish between "good" and "bad" Black women in public space based on their behaviour. All Black women are suspect.

To stop, then, at countering the stereotypes that link Black women to sex work risks marginalizing those who do earn a living or supplement their income by selling or trading sex. If we accept the framework that Black women do not deserve or police abuse because they are not *actually* involved in the sex trade, then Black women who are involved in prostitution become "deserving" victims of repression, criminalization and violence. This dichotomy places actual Black sex workers outside of the need for security, safety and freedom from policing and arrest. It also helps contribute to the erasure of the still under-documented reality that Black sex workers face significant levels of criminalization and police violence.

There are particular economic and structural conditions that define the lives of Black women in Canada. Largely restricted from high paying positions and positions of power, Black women continue to be relegated to poorly paid service and care work. For this reason, among others, some Black women sell or trade sex as a source of income and/or security. Mireille Miller-Young, author of *A Taste for Brown Sugar*, writes that "marginalized and exploited in the labour market, many young, working-class black women today identify the sex industries as preferred spaces to make a living for themselves and their families" (2014: 12). For a variety of reasons, some Black women chose, instead of welfare or minimum wage labour, the relative autonomy allowed by selling or trading sex. Others do this occasionally or as a means of supplementing their income. The stigmatization of sex work experienced by Black sex workers is accompanied by real material effects, including criminalization and even violence at the hands of law enforcement officials.

Far too little research has been done on the contemporary realities of Black sex workers in Canada. No large Canadian-based studies have yet measured over-policing or police violence toward Black or other racialized sex workers. American data, though, has found that Black sex workers are disproportionately targeted for arrest (Judge and Wood 2014); one study found that 94 percent of those arrested in Brooklyn on grounds of "loitering for the purposes of prostitution" were Black women (Berlatsky 2014). In my own experience as an outreach worker with street-based sex workers in Montréal, I have heard first-hand of at least a dozen examples of profiling, racial slurs, harassment, ticketing and threats levelled at Black cis and trans sex workers by the police. In one case, a Black woman was assaulted by an officer, called a monkey and told she would be shot if she dared to complain.[1] Compelling anecdotal evidence exists that suggests though all sex workers, particularly street-based ones, are vulnerable to police violence, Black and Indigenous sex workers face far higher rates of police harassment and violence than white sex workers do, including racist and sexist language, public strip searches and death threats.[2] To use the words of Monica Forrester, a two-spirit Black and Indigenous sex worker, long-time community activist and outreach worker based in Toronto, "Black sex workers are more harassed by the police, more arrested, and less protected, but nobody's talking about it" (Forrester, personal communication 2017).

The criminalization of Black women involved in sex work, or perceived to be involved in sex work, is particularly acute if they are transgender. Many racialized trans women work in the sex trade due to the results of systemic racism compounded with endemic transphobia, such as structural barriers to education, employment and appropriate, secure healthcare and housing (Namaste 2005). Noting that transsexuality itself was criminalized into the 1960s and 1970s, Viviane Namaste argues that the criminalization of prostitution in Canada continues, albeit more discreetly, to criminalize racialized transgender women in public space. In her words, "Transsexual lives are ordered, governed, and controlled in and through the criminalization of prostitution" (2005: 14). Racialized transgender women in the sex trade routinely face humiliation and abuse by law enforcement officers, both for their gender presentation as well as their actual or perceived involvement in the sex trade (Namaste 2005; Poteat et al. 2015; Grant et al. 2011). As well, research on incarcerated trans people in Ontario found that trans people in the sex trade seem to constitute the majority of those trans people arrested and imprisoned, particularly if they are Black and Indigenous (Scheim et al. 2013). Canadian activist-scholar Nora Butler Burke also observed a pattern of widespread police abuse of trans sex workers in Montréal. She found numerous incidents in which trans, migrant and often racialized sex workers were regularly "verbally berated and threatened, pepper sprayed, beaten and subsequently charged with assaulting an officer" (2016a: 117).

The racialized harms of Canada's prostitution laws have also negatively impacted Indigenous women and Asian migrant sex workers in sometimes distinct and sometimes comparable ways. Indigenous women face particular forms of legal and colonial violence — including, for example, the massive rate of missing and murdered Indigenous women — that cannot be directly paralleled or reduced to the historical or contemporary experiences of Black women. Significant racial and economic discrepancies in the criminalization of prostitution have disproportionately affected Indigenous women, who have been historically targeted for prostitution offences since the creation of the *Indian Act* (Sayers 2013). Anecdotal evidence suggests that Indigenous sex workers are vastly over-represented in street-based sex work (the form of sex work most targeted for arrests by law enforcement officials) (Currie 2000l and Farley and Lynn 2005 in Hunt 2013: 89). Similar to Black women's experiences, negative associations of Indigenous women's sexuality — stemming from their colonial depiction as sexually depraved "squaws" — has been used to justify sexual violence toward Indigenous women and to normalize widespread violence against Indigenous women involved in the sex trade (Hunt 2013). Additionally, migrant sex workers, and in particular Asian sex workers, have been stereotyped as "trafficking victims" while simultaneously being targeted by law enforcement officials for deportation (Maynard 2015; McIntyre 2015).

The stigmatization and erasure of Black women's involvement in the sex trade, both in the media and in advocacy surrounding sex workers' rights, serve to insulate the ongoing marginalization of Black sex workers. Beyond police violence, the criminalization of sex work has meant that sex workers have frequently been targeted for violence by aggressors posing as clients. Research conducted by and for sex worker advocacy groups, numerous government reports, the *British Medical Journal Open*, *The Lancet* and organizations such as the World Health Organization and U.N. AIDS have found an important link between the criminalization of sex work — including the criminalization of clients and third parties like receptionists and security guards — and sex workers' vulnerability to violence (Fraser Committee 1985; Department of Justice of Canada 1989; Rapport de recherche soumis au ministère fédérale de la justice 1994; Krusi et al. 2014; World Health Organization 2005; U.N. AIDS 2009; *The Lancet* 2014). Racialized and Indigenous sex workers remain particularly vulnerable to being targeted for violence, being dehumanized both by the illicit nature of their work and because they are racialized. A racialized Ontario-based trans sex worker described experiencing an acute vulnerability to violence as a criminalized worker, which was further compounded by her race. For her, an inability to challenge violence and aggression by both clients and police existed because "being racialized ... has allowed me to be silent to the physical and sexual abuse I've experienced ... Due to not being believed or [with the belief that] I perpetuated it" (in Fletcher 2013: 69).

While the unique realities of Black sex workers have been largely invisible in Canada, Canada's most infamous sex worker is a Black woman named Terri-Jean Bedford. Bedford, alongside Amy Lebovitch and Valerie Scott, led a 2010 Supreme Court challenge (*Bedford v. Canada* 2010) that aimed to decriminalize sex work as part of a struggle to end violence against sex workers. Bedford exemplifies the opposite of a "respectable" Black woman: she is a retired dominatrix, former drug-user and street-based sex worker, and she commonly appears in public holding a whip (Fine 2013). After she was arrested following a police raid of her "Bondage Bungalow" in Thornhill, Ontario, she spent decades challenging the government until she reached Canada's highest courts and finally overturned the Criminal Code sections that criminalized sex work (Loney 2013).

Despite a victorious Supreme Court decision, sex work remains largely criminalized. After a positive ruling that struck down numerous provisions, the courts granted the government a one-year window to create new laws surrounding the sex trade. The Conservative government ignored national and international evidence that supported decriminalization and instead implemented Bill C-36, the *Protection of Communities and Exploited Persons Act*. Though politicians publicized the bill under the rubric of "decriminalizing women," the legislation actually re-criminalized most aspects of sex work, maintained a loophole which allowed for ongoing arrests of street-based sex workers and increased penalties and surveillance capabilities for law enforcement (Canadian HIV/AIDS Legal Network, Pivot Legal Society and Stella, l'amie de Maimie 2014). The ongoing criminalization of sex work, and particularly some street-based sex work, facilitates the heightened surveillance of Black women — as real or imagined sex workers — and allows for not only ongoing possible criminalization through prostitution laws, but also facilitates other intrusive policing measures like ticketing and arrests for municipal, drug and other minor infractions. As well, ongoing criminalization continues to reinforce vulnerability to violence and exploitation. For this reason, in Canada and worldwide, movements toward the decriminalization of sex work are a necessary step toward racial justice more largely (Davis 2003). The future possibility of decriminalizing sex work offers enormous opportunities to reduce the policing of Black women in public space. Prostitution laws are not the only measures, however, that allow for the heightened policing of Black women by law enforcement agencies. Stigmas making Black women appear "dangerous" are also found in the application of Canadian drug laws.

"THE MULES OF THE WORLD": PROFILING BLACK WOMEN AS DRUG MULES

The plight of Black women is rarely in the first image that comes to people's minds in conversations about the War on Drugs. However, drug law enforcement has played an enormous role in the grossly disproportionate incarceration of Black women. Behind the characterization of Black women as "drug mules," it is possible to see a contemporary form of state-sanctioned violence and misogynoir that has been enabled by the so-called War on Drugs. While the racialized nature of drug law enforcement has already been addressed in earlier pages, the profiling of Black women as "drug mules" reveals gendered aspects of drug law enforcement that render the experiences of Black women unique. The conditions delimiting Black women's involvement in the drug trade, and the state repression of this involvement, are marked by distinct vulnerabilities that expose power differentials at the fault lines of sex, race, class and nationality.

When Prime Minister Brian Mulroney officially declared a War on Drugs in the late 1980s, law enforcement training systematically entrenched the police profiling of young, urban-dwelling Black men as drug dealers (Tanovich 2006). Significantly less discussed is that at the same time, Black Caribbean women were assigned the profile of drug couriers (Tanovich 2006). Available documentation suggests that this profiling is endemic. Though both Canadian and

American law enforcement and border security agencies deny practising racial profiling, a 2000 report by the United States General Accounting Office found that Black women were x-rayed at a rate of nine times that of white women on suspicion of carrying drugs — the highest rate of any other demographic — although they were found to be the least likely to be carrying illegal substances (in Lawrence and Williams 2006: 322). In Canada, one study found that Black travellers in Canada have a search rate of five times higher than white travellers, with seven out of every ten Black travellers detained at the hands of customs officials (Wortley n.d.: 17 in Gordon 2006: 69).

The profiling of Black women as drug mules has an impact both on African-Caribbean women visiting from abroad as well as Canadian or Caribbean-born Black women returning from vacations (Sudbury 2004a). Just as with other crimes, targeted profiling results in disproportionate incarceration: in 1992–1993, only six years after Black women were profiled as drug couriers at the advent of the War on Drugs in 1987, Black women's incarceration in Ontario had already increased sevenfold, a rate significantly higher than the increase of white women in the same time. Additionally, Black-white racial disparities for trafficking and importing had shot up to a rate of twenty-two Black people for every one white person incarcerated, despite no evidence of increased Black involvement in either crime (CSR Report 1995: 89). Complementing this data, in 1993, a study found that 20 percent of women in federal prisons were born elsewhere, that most of them had been charged with the importation of drugs and that they would be subject to deportation upon their release (Kendall 1993 in Boyd and Faith 1999).

Today, while significantly fewer Black women are incarcerated than Black men, over half of Black women incarcerated in federal prisons are serving sentences for nonviolent drug crimes — a rate higher, proportionally, than the rate of Black men incarcerated for drug crimes (Sapers 2013). While there is no evidence that Black women are more likely to import drugs than any other member of society, since the War on Drugs was announced, Black women have borne the brunt of disproportionate surveillance, arrest, incarceration and often, as well, deportation. For this reason, Black women who are actually involved in drug importing are uniquely vulnerable to arrest.

Beyond the aforementioned harms of racial profiling and drug law enforcement, a closer examination of the criminalization of Black women for drug crimes underscores the unique systemic racialized and gendered forms of injustice that they face. The contemporary representation of Black women as "drug mules" makes visible historical tropes denigrating Black femininity. The term mule, widely used in media descriptions of drug couriers, is itself laden with racialized and gendered meaning. Historically, enslaved Black women were seen as more animal than human, with a reduced ability to feel pain and possessing limited intelligence. This was reproduced by the letter of the law (Hartman 1997). Because they were seen as interchangeable commodities rather than full human beings, the labour of Black women has been historically exploited for this perceived lack of humanity. The devaluation of Black women's labour continued long after slavery. In *Their Eyes Were Watching God*, first published in 1937, acclaimed Black anthropologist and writer Zora Neale Hurston famously wrote that — to paraphrase — Black women have been treated as "the mules of the world" (2013: 14). This is perhaps made most visible in the dehumanizing labour conditions, disposability and enormous forms of repression that constrict and threaten the lives of Black women who have imported drugs through customs.

Drug importing — that is, importing small amounts of drugs on one's person — is a relatively unique role in the illicit drug economy. Unlike large-scale and small-scale drug traffickers, drug couriers are generally only paid a small, one-time fee, and are rarely involved in decision-making, or any of the profits resulting from the distribution of drugs (*R. v. Hamilton* 2003; Sudbury 2002). It is a particularly powerless role within drug economies, marked by little financial gain and enormous risk, not only of arrest, but also of fatal overdose in instances where an error occurs with drugs that have been swallowed or otherwise stored inside the body (*R. v. Hamilton* 2003). The power imbalance experienced by drug couriers is highly gendered and accentuated by race.

To understand the racialized and gendered impacts of the intensive and highly punitive targeting of Black women as so-called drug mules, it's necessary to look at the structural impediments that often lead to Black women's involvement in the illicit drug economy. The conditions governing Black women's involvement in importing drugs are generally determined by factors that clearly demonstrate Black women's gendered and racial subordination in society. Julia Sudbury conducted interviews with fifty incarcerated women in the United States, Canada and Britain between 1999 and 2001 and identified that most Black women involved in drug importing identified the main reasons for their involvement as "economic need, threats and coercion, and deception" (Sudbury 2002: 58).

Economic need, Sudbury says, needs to be understood within the larger global context of neoliberal restructuring and the feminization of poverty. As addressed earlier, Jamaica and other countries in the Global South in the 1990s have had most public resources privatized under the watch of the IMF and the World Bank. Global neoliberal reform policies have reduced economic options most substantially for poor women of colour in the Global South, since they generally carry the burden of taking care of children, the elderly and sick relatives (Harrison 1991 in Sudbury 2002: 69). In Canada, as well, Black women remain among the poorest demographics. This economic vulnerability has created "gendered and racialized incentives" — stemming from gendered and racialized vulnerabilities — that severely restrict the economic choices of poor racialized women both in the Global South and the Global North (Sudbury 2004a: 175).

Poor women, of course, are not without agency, but this agency is constricted both by global economic factors as well as by the racial and gender hierarchies within drug economies. In addition to having few legal economic opportunities, those choosing to take the calculated risk of drug importation, particularly racialized women, are highly exploited, poorly paid and treated as disposable within the global drug industry (Sudbury 2004a: 170). The role of couriers in the drug crime hierarchy is one of gender subordination that spans society, and couriers are generally "individuals sufficiently desperate to risk imprisonment for minimal benefit" who are positioned as "throwaways for the upper echelon of illicit drug enterprises" (R. v. Hamilton 2003). Within the drug trade, as in larger society, Black women's labour has little value. Not only are women largely excluded the financial gains found within drug economies, but Black women have also reported being "set up" for arrest as decoys to distract customs agents from the larger, more profitable shipments, serving as "a cheap and replaceable army of labourers" (Sudbury 2002: 69).

In Canada, like in the United States and Britain, Black women's involvement in drug crime generally stems from attempting to overcome situations of extreme poverty, often to support immediate or extended family. Interviews conducted with Black prisoners in 2012–2013 by Correctional Services Canada found that of those who had been interviewed, most Black women incarcerated in the Grand Valley Institution reported being involved in drug crimes to escape poverty (Sapers 2013; see also Pollack 2006). "Puss," a Black incarcerated woman interviewed by Canadian researcher Shoshana Pollack, testified that she got involved in drug crime because she "couldn't give [her] kids a proper meal three nights out of the week" (in Pollack 2006: 77). Further sociological studies confirm that most women who deal drugs do so to economically support themselves and their families (Morgan and Joe 1997; Boyd 1999), and sometimes to subsidize their own drug use (Boyd and Faith 1999).

Sudbury's (2002) research demonstrates that many Black women also become involved in importing and other forms of crime due to abusive relationships. In one example, a Black woman named Diane, who had been incarcerated in an Ontario prison, described not being paid for importing, but instead receiving occasional gifts or jewellery from her deceptive boyfriend, who had not informed her that his previous courier had already been arrested (2002: 68). This pattern is supported by other Canadian findings: some Black women incarcerated in Canada for drug crimes reported being forced to do so by threats to themselves or their families (Sapers 2013).

Black women's disposability is reinforced by the courts. Black travellers are highly scrutinized, and the sentencing of importing — a crime that has been gendered female and raced Black — demonstrates both racialized and gendered disparities when compared to other drug crimes. A study that examined the sentencing of Black female drug importers found that Black women found guilty of importing relatively small amounts of cocaine are treated by the courts as highly dangerous. Despite the fact that importers make exponentially less money than drug traffickers, even first-time offenders charged with importing face far higher sentences than an offender accused of drug trafficking — that is, selling drugs. Those charged with importing were sentenced at an average rate of five years, versus seven months for trafficking (Statistics Canada 2004 in Lawrence and Williams 2006: 309). Within sentencing, couriers, far more so than many other drug offenders, are routinely blamed for the ills ideologically (and erroneously) attributed to drugs. Couriers were said to be "responsible for the gradual but inexorable degeneration of many of their fellow human beings" who were "contribut[ing] to what is nothing short of the destruction of this society" by "placing a 'lethal weapon' in the hands of drug dealers, wreaking havoc on the streets of our cities" and "tear[ing] at the fabric of our society" (Benn supra note 40 at 1, Smith supra note 71 at 1053, R. v. Levy 1997 and R. v. Allen 1997 in Lawrence and Williams 2006: 308). Black women with little social, economic and political power are nonetheless represented as holding enormous amounts of lethal power by the current applications of Canadian drug law. This, of course, is consistent with a larger history of constructing Black women, particularly Black women born elsewhere, as dangerous for Canadian society.

A 2003 Ontario court case attempted to address the racialized and gendered disparities that were seen to lead to so many poor Black women being charged and severely sentenced for drug importing. The plaintiffs, Marsha Hamilton and Donna Rosemarie Mason, both Jamaican women, poor and single mothers without criminal records, were arrested for importing drugs. Both had been offered relatively small lump sums of money to bring cocaine into Canada. Hamilton nearly died because the cocaine she had swallowed in pellets leaked into her bloodstream (*R. v. Hamilton* 2003). The presiding judge, Justice Hill, attempted to instigate change in what he thought to be the overly punitive sentences, given what he identified to be a grossly disproportionate number of poor Black women facing prison sentences for drug couriering in the court over which he presided in Brampton, Ontario. Justice Hill attempted to give them conditional sentences, particularly because Mason was a permanent resident with two Canadian-born children and would have been deported had she received the full conviction (*R. v. Hamilton* 2003). He cited evidence that drug couriers are generally poor and relatively powerless within drug economies and, most notably, he argued that the systemic racial and gendered discrimination experienced by poor Black women was a reason to reduce their sentences. It was a significant legal attempt to redress the effects of systemic racism and gendered discrimination visible in the application of Canadian drug laws. His ruling, however, was overruled by the Court of Appeal, which set the standard for the continued harsh treatment of those found guilty of importation (*R. v. Hamilton* 2004). As a result, the racial profiling of Black women as couriers is likely ongoing, and the discriminatory sentencing enacted on poor Black women remains the status quo.

More recently, in 2011 Jacqueline O'Donahue, a thirty-year-old Jamaican woman recovering from cocaine addiction, was caught importing cocaine from Jamaica to Canada for a drug smuggling ring. O'Donahue stated that she had agreed to bring not drugs, but money into Canada, and that she was told that if she brought $50,000 into Canada, she would receive $2,000 as a one-time fee. However, the agreed-upon terms shifted once the plan was in action. Once she had become stranded in Montego Bay, she claims, the drug smugglers informed her that the plan had changed and she would be importing cocaine, rather than cash. When she resisted, she stated that she was threatened and sexually assaulted multiple times until she acquiesced (*Jamaica Observer* May 20, 2013). She was subsequently caught carrying a large amount of cocaine on her body upon her return. Though she had no criminal record, and despite the extenuating circumstances of coercion and sexual assault, O'Donahue was sentenced to four and a half years in prison due to what the judge reasoned to be the alleged seriousness of her crime. Presiding Judge Chartier's ruling stated that "importation is more serious than trafficking" (Turner 2013), despite the fact that the promised $2,000 flat fee was far lower than the profit that a drug trafficker would have gained from the street value of nearly seven hundred grams of cocaine. Chartier's ruling demonstrates how sexual violence against Black women remains routinely normalized, as well as the way that crimes seen to be associated with Black women are treated as uniquely dangerous within the courts.

Examining the gendered as well as the racial impacts of drug law enforcement makes it clear that drug laws remain less about control over drugs and more about control over certain bodies. The vehement hostility that Canadian courts have levelled at couriers makes clear the lengths to which the exaggerated dangers of prohibited drugs are projected onto poor young Black women. Despite the intense focus of customs agents and other law enforcement officers, the quantity of drugs brought in by drug couriers is negligible when compared to the massive amounts brought in on containers, planes and boats (Lawrence and Williams 2006: 327). While Black women are singled out by customs and law enforcement agents, most of up to twenty-four metric tons of cocaine estimated by the RCMP to enter Canada annually "does not arrive in the bellies of poor black women" (Lawrence and Williams 2006: 327). Though importation rates make up a small percentage (2 percent) of drug related charges, those who are found guilty are likely to be incarcerated and often deported (Boyd and Faith 1999). The harms created by an ideological rather than evidence-based approach to drug use in society continue to legitimate the vilification and dehumanization of Black women.

Black women's subordination is embedded both within the drug trade itself and within the enforcement of drug laws. Canadian prisons are not the only ones that disproportionately cage Black women found guilty of drug importation. In the United Kingdom, in 2001, a massive social panic erupted regarding a perceived influx of "drug mules." Jamaican women became the focal point upon which larger societal issues of crack and gun crimes were blamed. As a result, intensified surveillance focused particularly on Jamaican women resulted in hundreds of targeted arrests of women who had swallowed small drug packages in Kingston (Sudbury 2004a: 170–171). Drug law enforcement has played a significant role in Black women's incarceration in the United Kingdom. While African-Caribbean women make up only 1 percent of the general population, they make up 24 percent of female prisoners; most will be deported to their home countries, where they will be publicly shamed and will face the possibility of enormous reprisals from the drug network (Sudbury 2004a: 169). This demonstrates a larger, more global demonization of Black women, which tropes of "drug mules" have facilitated enormously.

As with much of the War on Drugs, the focus on Black female drug couriers has not achieved many results besides putting more Black women in prison. Drug policy experts have found that law enforcement directed at couriers has no significant impact on drug use or availability (CSR Report 1995: 82; Csete et al. 2016). Many international agencies now recommend reducing and eventually abolishing sentences for importing drugs, as they only perpetuate racialized and gendered inequalities (Csete et al. 2016). In light of available evidence, the focus on arresting and incarcerating Black women for drug crimes is not indicative of a sound policy of public protection, and is instead merely another aspect of the general demonization of Black female life. It is clear, too, that more research and public attention is needed surrounding the application of drug laws as they affect Black women in Canada. Understanding, publicizing and contesting the racial profiling of Black women and their continued discriminatory treatment by the criminal justice system — as well as the racialized and gendered harms of global neoliberal restructuring — all remain crucial elements in addressing the racialized and gendered aspects of drug law enforcement.

SISTERS BEHIND BARS: PRISON AND THE REPRODUCTION OF GENDERED OPPRESSION

Women using social assistance have been widely vilified by the state as being "locked in a lifestyle of dependency" (Government of Ontario 1994: 9 in Pratt and Valverde 2002: 140). But it is a double-bind. Black women are also vilified — and criminalized — when they choose, out of limited options, to labour in informal economies to support themselves and their families. Black women's involvement in informal economies, including the sale of drugs, sexual services and gambling enterprises has largely been motivated by socioeconomic factors, and may be seen as a survival strategy in the face of acute material deprivation (L. Harris 2016). Poor Black women have been incredibly innovative and resourceful, often making difficult decisions under extraordinary circumstances. However, Black women employing economic survival mechanisms are widely demonized and too frequently incarcerated. Black women accused of committing "poverty crimes," such as petty theft, welfare fraud, shoplifting and the sale of sex or drugs, make up a significant percentage of the rapidly rising number of Black women behind bars — at a rate now three times higher than the make-up of Black women in the Canadian population (Sapers 2013; Pollack 2006: 72).

Prison constitutes yet another form of both racialized and gendered violence for Black women. While the systemic lack of protection that stems from racism and gendered oppression is itself a form of harm, the state is often a direct agent of gendered violence. The Commission on Systemic Racism in the Ontario Criminal Justice System found significant racialized disparities between the treatment of Black and white women. Black women reported being exposed to racially imbued sexual harassment and sexual assault by prison staff (1994: 20–21). Black women reported that they were being forced to perform hard physical tasks in the late stages of their pregnancy — forms of labour that white pregnant prisoners at the same stage of pregnancy did not have to do. Black pregnant women were frequently denied the right to take rest and reported that they were being denied access to supplemental vitamins and extra milk that were provided to white pregnant prisoners (80). This demonstrates that norms associated with white femininity and fragility offer protections for white women in ways that continue to be systematically denied to Black women.

Prisons reproduce racial hierarchies at the same time that they reproduce gender norms. This can be seen in the realities faced by Black trans and gender non-conforming prisoners. Trans people in prison have historically been exposed to the state's denial of their gender identity, though recent legislative changes have attempted to rectify some of the worst excesses. Directive 800-5 in the Correctional Service Canada Guidelines designates that "pre-operative" transgender persons must be placed according to their genitals, rather than their actual gender identity (Correctional Service Canada n.d.). This is a form of violence that both polices a strict gender binary and flouts the economic reality facing many trans persons who cannot afford surgery, a normal reality particularly for poor racialized trans women (Namaste 2005). After interviewing gender non-conforming Black prisoners in Canada and the United States, Julia Sudbury found that Black trans prisoners were routinely denied access to hormones and forced to wear incorrectly gendered attire (2009: 16). Trans women in Canada have also complained of horrific conditions and violence, including transphobic slurs and sexual assault (Lupick 2015). Though there are no specific studies on the conditions faced by Black trans women in Canadian prisons, the existence of both racist and transphobic treatment at the hands of Correctional Service Canada makes plain the reality that Black trans women are in a position of heightened marginalization relative to other prisoners. For example, in the United States in 2011, a study found that Black trans women face enormously disproportionate rates of physical and sexual assault in prison compared to white trans women (Grant et al. 2011).

Despite the brilliant activism and research by Black activist scholars and feminists including Rai Reece (2007, 2010), Julia Sudbury (2009) and El Jones, who have begun to draw attention to the impacts of Black women's incarceration, Black women in prison in Canada remain "the silent, forgotten population in our society" (Reece 2007: 279). A deeper understanding of the gendered harms enacted by state incarceration are necessary toward combating racial and gendered injustices in Canadian society more broadly. The profiling and state scrutiny by police and social service agents have had significant impacts on many Black women's dignity and freedom. However, the widespread abuses in addition to the deprivation of liberty in women's prisons reproduce forms of Black women's captivity that are perhaps the most similar to the gendered captivity of enslavement. These forms of violence also impact incarcerated Indigenous women who are behind bars even more disproportionately, particularly in the Prairie Provinces — one of the many legacies of settler colonialism.

Poverty, gendered violence and mental health issues have contributed enormously to the extremely high rates of Black women incarcerated in jails and prison facilities. The criminalization and incarceration of poor Black women has not served toward solving, or even addressing the racialized and gendered forms of injustice that have led to the "evisceration of black women's lives" (Reece 2007: 280). Indeed, targeted state repression has resulted in Black women's increased vulnerability to all forms of violence.

OVER-POLICED, UNDER-PROTECTED: HOW STATE VIOLENCE MAINTAINS BLACK WOMEN'S STRUCTURAL VULNERABILITY TO ABUSE AND EXPLOITATION

An important and too frequently overlooked factor in the criminalization of Black women is how much the enforcement of welfare fraud, prostitution laws and drug laws also reproduce Black women's vulnerability to other forms of violence by aggressors, intimate partners and others. The same representations that have justified state violence against Black women have also been used to deny them access to many forms of state protections. Under slavery and in the years that followed its abolition, the widely held and state-sanctioned representations of Black femininity as inherently degraded were used to deny the fact that violence against Black women was, in fact, violence. This has meant that in addition to being more vulnerable to state violence, Black women are positioned in close proximity to gendered forms of violence. Black women and other gender-oppressed people are not only over-policed, but are also enormously under-protected.

Sexual violence and intimate partner abuse is endemic across race and class in Canada. Every six days, a woman is killed by her intimate partner, and women's anti-violence shelters are often so full that women who are being abused are turned away (Canadian Women's Foundation [CWF] 2014: 1–2). The criminal justice system does little to protect women of any background, and the majority of those experiencing gender oppression do not press charges against their abusers (2). However, Black women experience unique forms of marginalization that render them more vulnerable to domestic violence and sexual assault (James 2007). Black women in Canada "are being subjected to significant levels of sexual violence and sexual coercion with little or no support" (James 2007: 242). While there is still too little data available on the topic, Black girls appear to be subject to higher rates of sexual and physical abuse than white girls (Tanner and Wortley 2002 in Owusu-Bempah and Wortley 2014: 190), and racialized trans women remain highly targeted by hate-motivated violence (Scheim et al. 2013).

While Black women are more vulnerable to experiencing gendered violence, this is compounded by state neglect and by racism and lack of solidarity within the larger (white) feminist and anti-violence against women (VAW) movements (James 2007; Wells 1986). At least as early as the mid-1980s, Black female activists and community workers have been decrying how state-funded VAW organizations have systematically neglected the needs of Black women. Texts written in Canada's first Black women's newspaper, *Our Lives*, identified the relationship between sexism, the unwillingness of white feminists to support Black women's needs and malign neglect on behalf of the state, leading to calls for Black women to organize their own shelters, counselling and anti-sexist struggles (Wells 1986). Thirty years later, Black women continue to report being marginalized within rape crisis and sexual assault centres, being largely denied culturally relevant and appropriate services and being excluded from movements against gendered violence (James 2007). The state has been complicit in de-prioritizing Black women's realities and needs, and anti-violence funding has reproduced the "deep division of access to resources along colour and class lines" apparent within larger Canadian society (James 2007: 242). This replicates long-standing histories of erasing Black women's realities and normalizing violence against them.

Further, many shelters that claim to be geared toward gendered violence continue to hold transphobic policies that do not recognize trans women as women. Black and other racialized trans women face enormous discrimination in accessing housing and experience high rates of homelessness and targeted violence. However, trans women are still frequently denied access to women's shelters because they are not perceived as "real" women, or forced into a secondary violence of being forced to undergo humiliating questions regarding their genitalia to determine their access to safety and protection (ASTT(e)Q: 2011).

State policies further prevent Black gender-oppressed people from accessing protection, both indirectly and directly. Economic cutbacks and disqualification from welfare often force poor Black and other marginalized women to return to violent relationships due to fear of losing housing and/or custody of children (Elizabeth Fry Society n.d.). For this reason, Black women have historically insisted on making economic justice an important part of addressing both racism and gendered violence. A statement written by the Black Women's Collective of Toronto in 1989 insisted, "it is *poverty* which forces women to put up with physical, sexual, psychological and other forms of abuse in the home" (1989: 1, emphasis in original). It is not only the criminalization of welfare fraud, but the criminally low monthly allotment from social assistance services that re-create vulnerability to intimate partner abuse.

Border regulation, a process heavily determined by gender, race and class, has reinforced the vulnerability of Black and other racialized migrant women to gendered violence. Immigration status — and fear of deportation — creates an additional barrier toward seeking help in situations of violence and often stops racialized migrant women from seeking protection (Canadian Panel on Violence 1993 and Musisi and Mukhtar 1992 in Agnew 1998). Asserting labour rights, filing a human rights complaint against exploitative work situations or leaving an abusive private sponsor can often mean a removal order, creating a situation of "relative impunity for gender-based violence" and forming "another systemic, degrading barrier for African Canadian women" (ACLC 2008: 8) Highly visible campaigns led by No One Is Illegal in Toronto and Vancouver and Solidarity Across Borders in Montréal have been pushing their cities to adopt "access without fear" policies (Walia 2013). This would, in effect, give migrants without status the right to access schools, shelters and hospitals without fear of Canada Border Services Agency (CBSA) raids and deportation. Yet, despite (limited) popular support in Toronto and Vancouver, as recently as 2010, a Black Ghanaian woman was deported after CBSA entered a women's shelter in Toronto. CBSA continues to reserve the right to enter women's shelters to detain and deport women (Weese 2011). Extending beyond state practices that sanction migrant women's vulnerability to violence, the ability of the state to arrest and deport women fleeing violence instills fear in migrant women that makes them further isolated from accessing emergency forms of support.

Beyond vulnerabilities caused by immigration policies, Black women's ability to safely access police protection when they are in danger is grossly limited. Because law enforcement is so often a site of harm and trauma within Black communities, Black women and other gender-oppressed people are often unable to access police protection in situations of abuse or exploitation. Black women have been vocally protesting this fact for decades. In the words of Black feminist Josina N. Wells,

> When Black women are battered it is treated lightly by the police and the general community. Racism already dictates the brutalizing of Black people as a whole by police and the government and in the case of Black women, it produces a deadly brand of sexism which sees Black women battered with nothing done about it. There are countless cases of Black women being battered and police treat our complaints with mocking disrespect. (Wells 1986: 7)

Today, racialized women continue to report that they are unlikely to call the police even when experiencing domestic violence, that they feel less protected by the police and that because of their race they will not be taken seriously (Smith 2004 in CDPDJ 2011). Many racialized migrant women feel their experiences of abuse at the level of the criminal justice system serve only to "intensify and compound" the violence they experience from their abusive partners (Erez and Ammar 2003 in Owusu-Bempah and Wortley 2009: 450).

Black women's vulnerability to both state and intimate violence is neither innate, nor is it a "cultural" phenomenon. It has occurred as a result of multiple state-sanctioned processes that have reinforced both racial and gendered hierarchies. The legacy of Black women's resistance to violence against women (and the racist distribution of anti-violence resources) as well as to state violence more largely makes clear that Black women have never accepted the societal position ascribed to them.

CONCLUSION

State violence against Black women exists within a larger continuum of harms resulting from the intersecting oppressions of gender, class, race and, often, nationality. This violence remains shrouded in invisibility, or explained away by widespread beliefs that associate Black women with sexual and criminal deviance. Police violence, while not uncommon, is experienced "as merely one strand in a seamless web of daily gendered/racialized assaults by both state and private actors" and is seen as "unworthy of the focused attention commanded by police brutality against men of color" whose experiences are seen "as a 'direct' form of state violence" (Ritchie 2006: 141). The constant scrutiny, institutional distrust and criminalization of poor Black women that is reinforced by social services, law enforcement, customs agents, the courts and prison staff is still too rarely understood as violence. The societal erasure — and tacit acceptance — of the racialized and gendered surveillance, punishment and abuse levelled at Black women in their everyday lives belies an ongoing and institutionalized disregard for experiences of racism that do not fit within more classical views of racial profiling or gendered violence.

For many Black gender-oppressed people, it's necessary to look to models outside the state for creating real safety and security that do not rely on the police, but instead focus on community-led, transformative forms of justice that are centred on the lives and experiences of Black women and gender non-conforming folks. Being uniquely positioned at the intersections of multiple forms of societal and state violence has allowed Black women to be at the forefront of community-based anti-racist, feminist, queer-friendly and class-conscious responses to gendered and state violence in Canada. This is seen, for example, in the Black Women's Collective in the 1980s, in the words of Black feminist anti-prison activists behind bars (Sudbury 2009) and, today, in the transformative, justice-based Third Eye Collective and the Black queer and trans led activism of Black Lives Matter Toronto. It is only through creating an understanding of racial justice through a lens that acknowledges international and local class and gender disparities that all embodiments of anti-Black racism can be both seen and combated.

CHAPTER SIX

"OF WHOM WE HAVE TOO MANY"

Black life and border regulation

> Immigrant detention and deportation stretch the harmful effects of imprisonment and family separation across national borders. (Loyd, Mitchelson and Burridge 2012: 7)

> Africans were dragged out of their homeland, tied, bound, and brought to the West under torturous duress. Today, coercion has changed in form, content, and direction, thus policing the boundaries and preventing Africans from coming to the West. (Kumsa 2005: 177)

DETENTION AND DEPORTATION ARE A PART of the Black experience in Canada that remains widely under-acknowledged in Canadian society. Black life in Canada is marked by vulnerability to being placed into cages and banished by criminal justice and immigration systems. For Black migrants with precarious citizenship, being in the wrong place at the wrong time can result in not only police harassment or violence, but also indefinite incarceration in immigration detention, and permanent separation from family and community by means of deportation. Indeed, during a moment in which over half of Canada's Black population was born elsewhere, the heightened surveillance, targeted deportations and often-horrific conditions of immigration detention practices that are experienced by Black folks without Canadian citizenship are becoming an increasingly central form of state violence used against Canada's Black communities. For this reason, the role of detention and deportation are central to any analysis of surveillance, confinement and anti-Blackness in Canada.

RACE AND BELONGING

The imposition of different categories of citizenship, in effect, delineate who "belongs" to the realm of humane treatment and state protections, and who is excluded — deemed "temporary," "illegal" and disposable. (Dis)ability, sexuality, race and class have historically played an integral role in determining which migrants were desirable and which should be excluded. These exclusions were enforced and sustained by punitive practices such as detention and deportation (Walia 2013). As much as immigration penality is presented as a race-neutral practice, in reality, poor and racialized migrants are the ones who experience the harms of indefinite incarceration and removal to countries that they barely know or where their lives are endangered. That this is seen as just and reasonable only demonstrates the effective power of the dehumanization of those whose race, class and place of birth have made their lives expendable to the general public. While all Black people in Canada have been dehumanized, regardless of place of birth, Black people who are non-citizens have been cast even further outside of any sense of national belonging.

Since the abolition of slavery, Black people have largely been represented as an unwanted population in Canada. Of course, when enslaved Black people entered Canada with the legal status of chattel, there was little populist or state hostility toward them. However, the arrival of free Blacks has always been contentious and, indeed, often represented as possibly dangerous. Only a few decades after Black peoples' bodies and lives ceased to be reduced to property, Canada's first prime minister, Sir John A. Macdonald, decried in 1868 the "frequency of rape committed by Negroes, *of whom we have too many in Upper Canada*" (in Backhouse 2005: 115, emphasis added). Throughout much of Canadian history, immigration control in Canada has been structured by an underlying, sometimes unspoken assumption that there are simply *too many* Black people in this country. While I will not revisit here the great lengths that state officials took in the first half of the twentieth century to prevent Black migration, racially motivated detention and deportation practices have a long history. In one instance, in 1925, a Jamaican teenage girl was detained upon her arrival in Canada and treated as a prisoner, subsequently suffering a nervous breakdown (Calliste 1993: 138–139). Representation of Black people as sexually deviant and dangerous underwrote numerous targeted deportations in this era.

While anti-migrant, xenophobic sentiment impacts all racialized migrants and refugees, anti-Blackness continues to play a substantive role in both public sympathies and state support for asylum seekers. In the 1970s, almost fifteen hundred Haitians were targeted for removal by the Canadian government. Most had fled repression, possible imprisonment and death at the hands of Canadian-supported dictator Francois "Papa Doc" Duvallier (1957–1971), or his son Jean-Claude "Baby Doc" Duvallier (1971–1986) (Mills 2013: 413). A widespread challenge by the Haitian left in Québec succeeded, after significant public efforts, in staying just over half of the deportation orders. Many others, however, were deported, fled the country or became undocumented and went underground (some who had publicly criticized the Canadian government were subjected to raids by the local police and subsequently deported) (Mills 2013: 434). In the ensuing years, targeted expulsions of Black migrants have continued *en masse*. Since the 1990s, Jamaicans have been among the most deported groups of migrants from Canada (Burt et al. 2016: 3).

Similarly, despite Canada's reputation as a safe haven for refugees, following a massive influx of Somali asylum seekers fleeing the civil war in the early 1990s, Somali refugees received far less institutional and community support than previous large influxes of refugees (OCASI 2016). Somalis were falsely represented by state officials in Canada as fraudulent and dangerous and were consequently targeted by Citizenship and Immigration Canada (CIC), which added unique additional barriers to their migration that were not applied to most other asylum seekers (except Afghan refugees, who were treated similarly). The CIC imposed a five-year waiting period before these migrants would be eligible to apply for permanent residency (Pegg 2004). As a result, by the late 1990s more than ten thousand Somali asylum seekers were restricted from receiving the protections of full Canadian citizenship, held for years in a legal limbo and unable to get permanent resident status or sponsor family members. This endured until a successful *Charter* challenge was mounted by Somali refugees in 2000 (OCASI 2016: 2–3). As post-9/11 Islamophobia intensified the scrutiny of Arab and Muslim migrants, Somalis, who are at the intersection of anti-Blackness and Islamophobia, have faced significant challenges toward asylum and citizenship. Today Somalis face particular difficulties in family reunification. Frequently, documents that establish family relationships are not accepted, and there are delays and increased costs because Somalis are frequently forced to undergo extensive DNA tests to bring their families to Canada (OCASI 2016: 2).

In the present, Black migration remains subject to unique barriers. Displaced continental Africans continue to face particular difficulties accessing asylum in

Canada. Despite the widespread celebration of the acceptance of 25,000 Syrian refugees by Canada in 2016–2017, migration advocates and African refugees have argued that the same welcome has not been accorded to African asylum seekers, who make up half of the world's refugee population needing resettlement. The government has been accused of discriminatory and restrictive measures that restrict the ability of asylum seekers from sub-Saharan African nations to be sponsored into Canada, even as Syrian refugees are (rightly) processed and relocated with relative speed (Black 2016). Wait times for private sponsorships originating in Africa (and many countries in the Middle East) span up to six years, creating what the Canadian Council for Refugees (CCR) has called "a two-tier system" (in *Canadian Press* February 14, 2016). Canada's processing of refugees is the slowest in Africa, particularly in the East and Central African nations — including Somalia, Eritrea, Sudan, Rwanda and Burundi — which are covered by Canada's visa office in Nairobi (CCR 2011).

These racially configured processing times have real effects. While many would-be African asylum seekers have lived for years in camps under brutal conditions, slow processing times have led many sub-Saharan African asylum seekers to try to enter Canada, the United States and Europe through irregular and dangerous means, often with fatal consequences. In the words of Zerit Teclehaimanot, an Eritrean refugee attempting to sponsor family members, "our people are crossing the Sahara and the Mediterranean Sea in large numbers. Many of them passed away in the sea. Why are they taking a lot of risk? Because the international community is not taking initiative to help them" (in Black 2016).

In examining contemporary practices of detention and deportation, we can see that tropes of anti-Blackness that were created centuries ago are reproduced within the racialized surveillance and punishment of Black migrant and refugee communities. Today, popular and state-sanctioned fears of "too many" Black people residing in Canada continue to govern the targeted prevention of Black migration and the detention and removal of Black migrants. Continually reproduced tropes of Black peril not only maintain the disposability of Black labourers but also justify highly punitive border control measures against people of African descent. The meanings attached to Blackness continue to have a particular power to categorize some human beings as dangerous, "deportable" and disposable.

THE CRIMINALIZATION OF MIGRATION

Most Canadians would likely denounce, at least publicly, the notion that certain people should be indefinitely placed behind bars or removed from the country solely because of their race. Yet, far fewer are willing to contest the practices of incarceration via immigration detention, or the deportation of those living in Canada without full Canadian citizenship. It is often accepted as common sense that states have the moral authority to determine who may or may not be a citizen and to enforce that authority by means of immigration control measures, such as detention and deportation. Within popular discourse it is seen as fair, if unfortunate, that the extension of humane treatment has a limit, and that non-citizens fall outside of any legal or moral claims to basic human dignities, like protection from exploitation or freedom from violence (Balibar 2015). This is not to overstate the protections of citizenship — Black citizens, we have seen, have *de facto* remained outside many of the protections of formal equality. But immigration status provides yet another means to construct and entrench society's hierarchies, and to deny poor and racialized people the rights that are at least formally accorded to Canadian citizens. Indeed, immigration status remains a *de jure* and state-sanctioned way to take certain people's rights away and subject them to labour exploitation as well as the violence of indefinite captivity and expulsion (Sharma 2006; Walia and Tagore 2012).

Many Canadians pride themselves on Canada's apparently benevolent acceptance of refugees. However, refugee status is increasingly difficult to attain. The number of accepted refugees dropped by 30 percent between 2006 and 2012 (Citizenship and Immigration Canada 2014). The rejection of asylum is increasingly the norm even for highly persecuted individuals fleeing warfare or environmental disaster. Changes to the *Immigration and Refugee Protection Act* (IRPA) under Bill C-31, passed in 2012, include restriction of appeals and have led critics to allege that even more asylum seekers will be removed from Canada into dangerous situations (Justice for Refugees and Immigrants Coalition 2012).

The restriction of refugee status is paralleled by other restrictions imposed by Canadian immigration policy. A series of immigration reforms under the Conservative government's reign (2008–2015) has led to a significant drop in the number of permanent residents accepted into Canada. In 2000, 79 percent of immigrants became citizens, while only 26 percent become citizens in 2008 (Walia and Chu 2015: 2). Reflected in these figures are imposed reductions in the forms of migration most obtainable by poor people from the Global South. The number of family-class migrants dropped by 20 percent or fourteen thousand between 2006 and 2011. This drop was followed by a three-year moratorium until 2014, and is now capped at five thousand applications per year. These changes, negatively affecting poor would-be migrants, occurred alongside legislative changes that favour wealthy families from the United States and Europe (Walia and Chu 2015: 15). These changes have made it more difficult for poor racialized persons to legally attain citizenship. Gender, race, class and ability continue to play a significant role in the determination of who will gain access to the legal protections of citizenship and who will be excluded — and thus exposed to a high risk of indefinite jailing or expulsion from one's country, family and community.

The percentage of Black migrants relative to the broader undocumented and precarious population is unknown. However, unique barriers to legal Black migration suggest that it is not an insignificant number. Adding to this, Black migrants and refugees from Africa and the Caribbean face particularly acute forms of displacement due to the legacies of the transatlantic slave trade, colonization and, in more recent decades, neoliberal globalization (which has impacted sub-Saharan Africa most acutely). There are, as well, other factors creating undocumented and precarious Black populations in Canada. Refugee acceptance rates for Somalis have dropped from around 90 percent in the early 1990s to 57 percent in 2015, despite widely documented conditions of ongoing and widespread famine (OCASI 2016: 1). Further, the *Toronto Star* reported that recent fee increases and immigration testing have led to a significant drop in Caribbean and East African people's ability to attain citizenship (Keung 2015). As well, LGBTQI* African refugees seeking asylum from persecution based on sexual identity have been noted to face still quite significant barriers toward attaining refugee status. This is because of Eurocentric determinations that are used to gauge genuine "queerness" and border officials who often do not recognize regionally distinct and unique forms of African non-heterosexual identity that differ widely across the continent and are often not recognized by Western standards (Massaquoi 2013: 47). It is still all too common for LGBTQI* Africans to have their refugee claims denied even while fleeing homophobic violence, persecution and death threats (for example, see Goldie 2017; Keung 2016a). Together, these factors put displaced people of African descent into highly precarious positions. While the root causes of displacement are ongoing, many displaced people of African descent who make it to Canada will not be accepted as refugees or permanent residents and will, therefore, be highly vulnerable both to indefinite detention and deportation.

The demonization of Black and other migrants of colour hides from view the realities that lead some people to become undocumented or to be issued a deportation order. While people deemed "illegal" are often highly stigmatized as dangerous in some way, the large majority of people who are placed in immigration detention or deported from Canada are failed refugee claimants. A 2014 investigation by the *Toronto Star* found that Canada deports, on average, over ten thousand persons per year, and that between 2004 and 2013, a large majority (70 percent) of those deported were failed refugee claimants (Oved 2014). The fact that thousands of people per year are incarcerated or removed from the country because their refugee claims were rejected does not indicate widespread deception on the part of asylum seekers, but that increasingly restrictive immigration and refugee policies have made it more difficult for displaced people to be granted asylum (Walia and Tagore 2012). In addition, despite enormous barriers toward the official means of applying for refugee status, those forced to leave their country of origin by paying human smugglers are subject to automatic detention because this is considered a form of "irregular arrival" in Canada (Walia and Tagore 2012). In effect, this criminalizes people fleeing situations under extreme duress.

Criminalizing immigration does not prevent people from migrating. It simply renders this migration more dangerous and makes their lives, once they get to Canada, more precarious. The aforementioned anti-migrant reforms in recent years have not stopped migration to Canada, but instead have resulted in a rise of undocumented or otherwise precarious persons living and working in Canada (Hussan 2014: 2). Despite the challenges they face, people who have been forced to cross borders into countries like Canada are rarely lauded for their bravery or courage. Instead, they are widely represented — and treated by the state — as criminals. Criminalization, which is defined as "the attachment of the criminal label to the activities of groups which the authorities deem it necessary to control" (Hall et al. 2013: 187), has allowed for poor and racialized migrants to be largely excluded from the realm of public sympathies. Non-citizens seeking sanctuary, whose refugee claims have failed or who have overstayed their visas, or even those who are merely missing particular paperwork, are branded as "illegal" and considered to be risks to the nation-state requiring surveillance and punishment (Pratt 2005).

The use of the term "illegal" is itself highly racialized; it is rarely used to characterize, for example, Australian students working in Canada without permits (Walia and Tagore 2012). Further, though a human being may be deemed "illegal," the alleged crime has no victim: "within common discourses, the victim of this criminal act is the state, and the alleged assault is on its borders" (Walia 2013: 5). The criminalization of Black and brown migration has allowed for the policing, incarceration and removal of massive numbers of people living in Canada.

While all poor racialized migrants are vulnerable to highly punitive border regulation and enforcement, long-standing historical associations between Blackness, danger and crime places Black migrants in a situation of particularly acute vulnerability in being discovered, and as a result, detained and expelled from the country. Visibility is vulnerability for people with precarious citizenship status, and the presence of Black persons in public space is heavily scrutinized by law enforcement. However, because the police have a collaborative relationship with immigration enforcement, the extremely high rate of "random" identity checks of Black people explored in earlier pages places undocumented Black persons at an increased risk of discovery, apprehension, detention and deportation. This risk is significant: an Access to Information and Privacy request conducted by No One Is Illegal Toronto found that the Toronto police reported approximately one hundred persons per week to CBSA during a six-month period in 2014–2015. Over 80 percent of those calls were, in fact, status checks, based on nothing but suspicion based on visible assessments, which points clearly to racial profiling (Hussan 2015). In one such incident, "random" traffic spot checks in Toronto's poor, Black neighbourhood at Jane and Finch resulted in the detention and deportation of twenty-one undocumented persons (CBC News August 16, 2014). Black migrants are dehumanized and rendered criminal by the societal meanings attributed to both race and place.

IMMIGRATION DETENTION: INDEFINITE AND ARBITRARY CAPTIVITY

It is not a theoretical argument to say that migrants of colour are criminalized. Indeed, common features of life in immigration detention include solitary confinement, orange prison jumpsuits and strip searches (Kennedy 2017). The state repression experienced by poor, racialized migrants in immigration detention is, in many ways, virtually identical to imprisonment, only less regulated and more arbitrary. Detention — the incarceration of non-citizens — is a form of confinement that is similar to the massive incarceration of Indigenous and Black populations in provincial and federal penal institutions. But unlike prison, immigration detention is technically not considered to be punitive, but administrative. Incarcerated migrants are not serving sentences or accused of any crime, but are incarcerated because they lack adequate identity documents or are deemed to be a security risk or a flight risk. Anyone who is undocumented — that is, anyone who has overstayed a tourist or work visa, is a failed refugee claimant or has been forced to arrive by "irregular" means (for example, on a boat or by paying a smuggler) — may be subject to immigration detention (Walia and Tagore 2012). Immigration detention in Canada has a significant scope and scale: nearly ninety thousand migrants were detained without charge between 2006 and 2014 (Walia and Chu 2015: 20). Each year, an average of eleven thousand migrants, a large number of whom are racialized, are held in immigration detention in Canada, including over eight hundred children (Walia and Chu 2015: 20).

Though immigration detention is often imagined as a place for dangerous migrants, less than 5 percent of migrants in detention have been deemed possible "security threats" (End Immigration Detention Network 2016a). Instead, a significant majority of those held in detention are failed refugee claimants who are deemed a "flight risk." Yet, the designation of "flight risk," which allows for the detention of migrants presumed unlikely to appear for their deportation date, places those claiming refugee status in an impossible position. To attempt to become a refugee, it is necessary to exhibit a genuine fear of being forced to return to one's country of origin. However, if a failed refugee claimant exhibits a very legitimate fear of forced return, they are likely to be subject to "preventative" detention — even if their deportation is not imminent (Walia and Tagore 2012). In effect, they are punished with incarceration for the "crime" of manifesting trauma.

Another reason for detention results from changes to the *Immigration and Refugee Protection Act* (IRPA) that have granted immigration officers an increased ability to detain any non-citizen if they are "unsatisfied" with a person's identity at any point during the refugee claim process. This is the case even though it is widely known that many asylum seekers have been forced to flee their country of origin without their proper identity documents. Those who have often spent months or years fleeing persecution, then, are placed behind bars for periods lasting from several hours to several years. This is not because of any demonstrable threat that they pose, but for administrative purposes that serve to punish migrants for conditions resulting from their displacement (Walia and Tagore 2012).

Detention is experienced as a form of harm and violence. Most detainees who are failed refugee claimants have escaped from horrific and violent situations abroad only to be placed behind bars in their place of attempted refuge. Healthcare practitioners have criticized the detention of migrants, stating that it could exacerbate mental and physical health issues of those who have experienced warfare and persecution in their home countries. Dr. Rachel Kronick, an Ontario psychiatrist who frequently treats migrants, told the *Toronto Star*, "detention harms people" (in Keung 2016b). Detention exacerbates post-traumatic stress disorders and depression, conditions that are vastly more common in detained asylum seekers compared to those who are not in immigration detention (Cleveland et al. 2012 in Global Detention Project 2012).

Immigration detention is supposed to be non-punitive — it is governed by the IRPA and not the Criminal Code. But in reality, immigration detention is largely indistinguishable from the incarceration of prisoners convicted of crimes, and those held captive have fewer legal protections than prisoners (Hussan 2014). Because migrants are not serving sentences, they are not able to challenge any charges against them (because there are none). They do not have the right to legal representation and will not have a trial — only a detention review every thirty days. Further, the conditions of immigration detention are highly punitive. There are three designated immigration detention centres in Canada, yet migrants are held in hundreds of locations across Canada. Up to one-third of detainees are held in provincial prisons, mostly in maximum-security institutions (Silverman n.d. in Hussan: 2014). Just like prisoners in Canadian jails and prisons, mandatory isolation and segregation are common features of the incarceration of non-citizens, who are sometimes locked in one cell for twenty hours a day (Hussan 2014: 4). Migrants with physical or mental health problems are, as a matter of practice, frequently housed in provincial jails (Draaisma 2016).

Life in immigration detention is dehumanizing, and every aspect of day-to-day living is subject to total state control. In 2008, the Toronto Immigration Holding Centre was found to have dealt with overcrowding issues by using blankets and sleeping bags on the floor (AGC Report to Parliament 2008 in Hussan 2014). In the Centre de prévention de l'immigration de Laval (which, in English, means "immigration prevention centre") outside of Montréal, detainees have limited circulation and no activities beyond television, with rigid rules governing all their behaviour (Cleveland et al. 2012 in Global Detention Project 2012). In Central East, a jail in Lindsay, Ontario, that detains the largest number of non-citizens in Canada, between 2015 and 2016, the jail was in full or partial lockdown as a result of staff shortages on over 260 occasions, during which all inmates and detainees were confined to their cells, often for days at a time (Kennedy 2017). When detained migrants are transported, they are shackled, placed in leg irons and handcuffed, which serves to "subjugate and humiliate migrants" as well as to "cast them as deviant" and reinforce their "illegality" (Walia and Tagore 2012: 76).

It is unknown how many children are in detention in Canada at any given time. The hundreds *documented* to be held in detention each year may only be a smaller amount of a larger, uncounted group of minors considered to be "accompanying their parents" as guests — thus not, technically, in detention and therefore not accounted for under CBSA statistics (CBSA 2011 and Nakache 2011 in Global Detention Project 2012). However, since the other option is often for migrants to give up custody of their children and have them placed in state care, the children's designation as "guests" does not change the brutal fact of the incarceration of children. Under section 60 of the IRPA, the detention of minors is supposed to be a last resort. But it is not uncommon for mothers and their children to be held without charge for indefinite periods of time for reasons such as having unconfirmed identities. One such example is Glory Anawa (also known as Glory Ochigbo), a Black woman who had fled Cameroon and subsequently resided in Toronto's Immigration Holding Centre from 2013 until 2015, most of it while caring for an infant. At the time of her incarceration, she was three months pregnant. Once she had given birth, her son Alpha spent the first several years of his life in a detention centre surrounded by barbed wire. Because Anawa did not have adequate documentation issued by the Cameroonian government, the CBSA refused to release her, fearing she would disappear and remain in the country undocumented. Her son was born in Canada and was therefore officially a Canadian citizen and not, by technical determinations, in detention. However, his release would have resulted in possibly permanent separation from his mother (Cain 2016). Instead, he spent his infancy incarcerated: Alpha's first words were "radio check," the words that were spoken by immigration guards at shift change (R. Browne 2015). After being detained for nearly three years, Anawa was finally deported to Cameroon, accompanied by her son. Anawa's case is illustrative of the extremely punitive and exacting nature of immigration detention, which allows for a mother and baby to spend nearly three years incarcerated merely because of missing paperwork.

Anawa's case is also indicative of one of the most appalling features of detention in Canada: Canada has no maximum length of immigration detention. The average length of immigration detention averages approximately twenty-five days for men and fifteen days for women (Hussan 2014). Unlike a prison sentence, which has an end date, loopholes in Canada's immigration legislation allow detention to continue indefinitely. This is a situation unique to Canada among most Western nations (Hussan 2014). According to a recent *Toronto Star* report, while the average stay in immigration detention is approximately twenty days, over a hundred detainees currently in immigration detention have spent at least three months behind bars. Further, one-third of those in immigration detention have been detained for more than a year (Kennedy 2017). Numerous Black migrants have been held, without charge, for years at a time, and their stories make clear the inhumanity of immigration detention practices in Canada.

One case exemplifying the brutality of indefinite detention is that of Michael Mvogo, a Black man from Cameroon, who spent almost a decade in an immigration detention centre after being picked up at a Toronto homeless shelter (Black 2015). After being charged with possessing $10 worth of crack cocaine in 2006 and serving a jail sentence, he was not released but was kept in immigration detention for almost ten more years. For a significant percentage of that time, he was kept isolated in solitary confinement (Logan 2015). While technically he was no longer being punished for any crime, he continued to be held because the CBSA could not confirm his identity. Because they could not confirm his identity, they could not deport him, despite failed attempts to send him to the U.S., Haiti and Guinea (Logan 2015). His identity was finally verified and he was subsequently deported in 2015 (Black 2015). Like so many others facing indefinite detention, Mvogo's decade-long incarceration was officially justified as an issue of paperwork, not of any danger posed to individuals or society more broadly. Mvogo not only experienced jail for a crime that would have been far less likely to be punished had he been white, but he was then also subject to nearly a decade of so-called non-punitive incarceration.

In a similar case of grossly extended immigration detention, a Black migrant widely believed to be Mbuyisa Makhubu — a South-African anti-apartheid icon — was held without charge in an immigration jail from 2004 to 2016. Makhubu is widely believed to be the now-infamous teenager who was photographed during the 1976 Soweto uprisings while carrying the body of a dead child killed by the South African police. His refugee claim was rejected in the 1990s and he was subsequently picked up by an immigration officer in 2004. After refusing to provide his name, the man believed to be Makhubu remained in detention, as his identity had not been entirely confirmed by CBSA (Keung 2014). His cousin, who lived in South Africa, told CBC News that she believes he would not confirm his identity because of the trauma he experienced in South Africa years ago: "He is still afraid that maybe when he comes to the country, they are going to kill him because the time he was here the police were killing people" (Arsenault 2015). Despite significant international press and criticism by human rights experts, including the United Nations, his detention continued until he was finally deported in 2016 (Arsenault 2015).

Risk and danger have been so effectively attributed to "foreigners" that even in the absence of law breaking, they may legally be subjected to unspecified lengths of incarceration in often-nightmarish conditions. This injustice has been frequently contested by detained migrants. In the summer of 2016, in Lindsay and the Toronto East Detention Centre in Scarborough, approximately sixty largely Black and brown migrants held a hunger strike that lasted, for some, nearly two months, to protest their indefinite detention (Keung 2016c). Among them was Alvin Brown, a Jamaican man who had lived in Canada since early childhood but had been in detention since 2011 after serving a jail sentence for robbery. His incarceration in immigration jail was administrative; at the time of the hunger strike he had already spent five years in detention because Jamaica would not issue his travel documents. He told the *Toronto Star* that his reasoning for participating in the strike was that, "It is cruel for them to punish us, torture us and lock us away indefinitely. It must end now" (Keung 2016c).

Detention, while violent in and of itself, can often have fatal consequences. The death of Abdurahman Ibrahim Hassan, a Somali refugee with mental health issues who arrived in Canada in 1993, illustrates the tragic circumstances that can result from Canadian detention practices. Hussan had been granted asylum, but because of some mental health issues, he had never finished attaining his permanent resident status. Because he was Somali — and Canadian legislation renders it difficult to deport Somali peoples — Hassan spent over three years in immigration detention (Keung 2016c). Following a mental health crisis at the Peterborough Regional Health Centre, where he was being detained, Hassan was restrained by police officers and died as they held a rolled towel over his face on June 11, 2015. The officers were cleared of any wrongdoing (Special Investigations Unit 2016). Intersecting devaluations occurred that resulted in Hassan's life being taken, including indefinite detention, the ongoing practice of detaining migrants with mental health problems and, more broadly, the societal disregard for the treatment of racialized migrants behind bars.

Deaths of Black and brown migrants behind the bars of immigration jails are not uncommon; at least fourteen have died while behind bars since 2000. This number includes a sixty-four-year-old Burundian asylum-seeker named Melkioro, a Black man who committed suicide after being held in immigration jail. He had been held for over a year, facing no charges and with no access to trial (End Immigration Detention Network 2016b). His suicide demonstrates the inhumane conditions and malign neglect imposed upon those who are criminalized merely for being present in Canada without proper documentation.

Though all incarceration is harmful, it is particularly jarring that this level of deprivation may be inflicted on human beings for "administrative" purposes alone. Even beyond the social costs accrued by perpetuating such injustice, the financial cost of maintaining a migrant in immigration jail is $239 per day (Keung 2016b). This represents a significant financial investment in jailing migrants at a time of cuts to refugee health benefits, and demonstrates the financial as well as political commitment to this form of state violence as opposed to a commitment to the well-being and safety of migrants in Canada. The proportion of Black migrants held in detention is unknown, as the CBSA rarely reveals details publicly about migrants in detention, aside from numbers alone (Oved 2014). Syed Hussan of the End Immigration Detention Network confirmed that though they do not keep official demographic statistics, the majority of calls to their detainee hotline were from Caribbean and West African men (Hussan July 14, 2016). Regardless, the massive scale and scope, as well as the conditions of racialized and Black migrants in detention, make clear that immigration detention is a form of racialized state violence. For this reason, detention of non-citizens is a central facet of Black incarceration in Canada.

DOUBLE PUNISHMENT: RACE, CRIME AND DEPORTATION

> So long as negroes are in this country ... crime will continue and increase, in proportion as the negro population increases. (*Edmonton Evening Journal* 1911 in Mathieu 2010: 24)

The criminalization of racialized and Black peoples' movement across borders is deeply harmful. It's difficult not to see the moral abhorrence of the widespread practice of incarcerating undocumented, largely racialized migrants and jailing asylum seekers for solely administrative purposes, as is their deportation to highly dangerous circumstances. Yet, it is equally important not to neglect the injustices wreaked on those migrants who *have* been found guilty of a crime. Indeed, many migrant justice movements have based their public appeals on the notion that though they are called illegal, migrants are not criminals. Many American regularization campaigns, for example, have often focused on regularization for migrants *without* criminal records (Escobar 2008). While this may be an effective way to rouse public sympathies, this strategy also abandons the widespread injustices levelled at those migrants that the state deems to be criminals.

A critical race analysis of criminalization reminds us not to abandon those seen as deviant or criminal to disproportionate punishment for their apparent transgressions. Race, after all, and Blackness in particular, largely determines who is seen, caught, arrested, charged, found guilty and sentenced for breaking the law (Alexander 2012). Race also influences which crimes are most heavily targeted and punished (Roberts 1993).

The banner of "crime" has been directed at many individuals and activities and used to exclude or deport those seen as dangerous for "various combinations of moral, racial and ideological reasons" throughout Canada's immigration history (Pratt and Valverde 2002: 137). However, just as ideas surrounding Black subservience played an integral role in the creation of Canada's temporary work programs, widely held beliefs linking Blackness to criminality have been central toward the creation of Canada's contemporary deportation policies directed at so-called criminal foreigners.

In 1994, two highly mediatized incidents of interracial violence took place in Ontario. In one, two Black men attempted a robbery at the Just Desserts restaurant, and a white woman named Georgina Leimonis was killed. The second incident involved the fatal shooting of white police officer Constable Todd Baylis (Burt et al. 2016: 6). Following these incidents, an anti-Black and particularly anti-Jamaican backlash took place. A widespread and highly mediatized panic took hold regarding fears of violent crimes committed by Black people born outside of Canada. This panic was unsubstantiated; legal historian Clayton Mosher notes that there is "objective proof that Jamaican crime was not a serious problem in Canada" (1998: 11). Still, the media-fuelled hysteria focused on an unsubstantiated perception of a spike in Black, foreign-born criminals, which resuscitated numerous tropes regarding Black criminality, Black danger and Black outsiders invading Canada (Barnes 2002). The two incidents were believed to stand in for a larger crisis regarding Black communities and Canada's immigration system. The words of *Toronto Sun* writer Christie Blatchford exemplified the climate well; she stated that the incident "provided Canadians with a window into the shambles that is their federal immigration department, it is also a sure thing that this is just the tip of the proverbial iceberg" (Blatchford 1994 in Foster 1996: 209). The ensuing outcry focused specifically on Jamaican men, while largely ignoring the fact that the men had come to Canada as children, some as infants, and that one of them was actually from Trinidad (Pratt 2005: 140; Mosher 1998: 11).

Jamaicans were not only targeted by the media, but also by law enforcement and border control. In July 1994, in response to the perceived crisis, Minister of Citizenship and Immigration Sergio Marchi put forward a so-called "Criminals First" legislation and created an RCMP–Immigration Canada taskforce to track down and remove those perceived to be dangerous (Barnes 2002; Pratt 2005).

Drafted as a part of the "Criminals First" legislation, the passage of Bill C-44, subsection 70 (5), in 1995 amended the IRPA so that permanent residents who had been found guilty of committing what was designated a "serious" offence could be deemed a danger to the public, stripped of their permanent residency and issued a removal order (in addition to serving a prison sentence) (Barnes 2002: 193). The practice is referred to as "double punishment" by migrant justice advocates (Boctor 2013; Maynard 2010) because migrants must first serve time behind bars for the offence, then additionally face a second punishment of detention and deportation, unlike their Canadian counterparts who would be nominally considered "rehabilitated" after serving jail time and released back to their communities.

Directly following the passage of this legislation, Black migrants were targeted with large-scale deportations. By September 1995, almost five hundred migrants convicted of crimes had been declared a danger to the public and deported, and a significant majority of those were Jamaican nationals (Jakubowski 1997 in Barnes 2002: 194). In the initial two years after the amendment, the rate of deportations to Jamaica was five times higher than to the next recipient country, which was Trinidad (Barnes 2002: 194). These statistics illuminate a racially motivated witch-hunt that targeted "a specific racial group with the specific aim of cleansing the community of those perceived as a 'danger to the public'" (Falconer and Ellis 1998: 24 in Barnes 2002: 194). Indeed, by 2001, Black persons made up made up 60 percent of the persons deported from Ontario since 1995, becoming the population expelled most frequently for criminality (ACLC 2001). Large numbers of those deported had spent much of their lives in Canada (ACLC 2001). In 2001, following another public backlash based on fears of Black "foreign" crime, the IRPA removed the right to appeal from permanent residents sentenced to imprisonment for two years and over. This amendment occurred despite the fact that the legislation had already been flagged by the U.N. Committee on the Elimination of Racial Discrimination for enacting disproportionate deportations of migrants of African descent (Concluding Observations of the Committee on the Elimination of Racial Discrimination 2002 in ACLC n.d.).

The trend of deporting Black (and brown) migrants for criminal offences has only continued. Bill C-43, titled the *Faster Removal of Foreign Criminals Act*, was passed in 2013 and focused on speeding up the deportation of migrants convicted of crimes, making increasingly small-scale offences "deportable." Following this amendment, the charge of "serious criminality" has become increasingly flexible. Offences with a six-month sentence, as minor as shoplifting, dangerous driving, causing a public disturbance, threatening to damage property or mischief, now all constitute "serious criminality." The Canadian Bar Association has deemed many of these added offences to be problematic since their applications by the criminal justice system are highly discretionary. This bill also removed any possibility for a humanitarian and compassionate consideration, which means deportations under this Act cannot be stayed regardless of the circumstances of the crime committed or the life conditions, family ties and community associations of the individual (Canadian Bar Association 2012; *Faster Removal of Foreign Criminals Act* 2013).

The ideological power of invoking (Black) criminality is effective, and legislative changes facilitating the deportation of foreign-born persons continue to be justified by invoking the protection of Canadian citizens from threats to their safety. Former Immigration Minister Jason Kenney justified the most recent amendments to the IRPA by claiming they would "protect Canadians from criminal and security threats" (2012). Though Kenney's words were technically racially neutral, the unspoken association between Blackness and criminality is never far from the surface. More than two decades after the Toronto shootings, Jamaicans continue to constitute the most deported group from Canada for criminal offences (Burt et al. 2016: 3). Between 2000 and 2013, Canada deported almost 2,800 people to Jamaica for criminality (Bronskill 2016), at a rate averaging two hundred Jamaicans per year (Burt et al. 2016: 3). Double punishment may apply to any migrant without full citizenship in Canada, yet it renders Black communities particularly vulnerable due to the aforementioned widespread practices of anti-Black racial profiling and the ongoing collaboration between police services and CBSA.

Despite the fact that these deportations were justified on the grounds of "serious criminality," the constitution of "serious criminality" is not an objective category and its application is highly discretionary (Pratt 2005: 141). A large majority of deportations of "serious criminals" have not been related to violence or organized crime, but to drugs. Indeed, despite popular associations between Jamaicans and gangs, in the nearly twenty-year period from 1997 to 2015, only eleven Jamaican nationals have been removed for involvement in organized crime (Burt et al. 2016: 6).

While official discourse has rationalized these deportations as the removal of security threats, the deportations so disproportionately levelled at Black communities have, in large part, been for relatively minor crimes. A significant portion of those expelled to the Caribbean have been found to constitute a danger for minor trafficking convictions, in the absence of either violence or weapons (Pratt and Valverde 2002: 145). As covered earlier, while white communities appear to have equal or higher rates of both drug sales and drug use, drug charges are disproportionately levelled at Black persons due to heightened surveillance and arrest patterns by police. Yet, Black migrants in particular face consequences unheard of by white Canadians. The Toronto Deportation Pilot Project found that between 2003 and 2006, two-thirds of Jamaican deportees involved in the research project had been removed for drug violations (in Burt et al. 2016: 8). Between 2012 and 2013, more than eighty persons were deported to Jamaica for drug offences, including eleven for marijuana (Burt et al. 2016: 15), a substance on the brink of legalization and noted to be less dangerous than alcohol.

In the case of any involvement with law enforcement officials (a frequent occurrence for those with African features), the bureaucratic difference between holding permanent resident status and full citizenship creates a staggering divergence in one's life trajectory. While the practice of double punishment is framed around danger and risk, the deportation of those found guilty of crimes is more about exerting control over Black communities. Rather than protecting society from "dangerous criminals," double punishment has instead been a highly effective means of addressing public and state concerns that there are simply *too many* Black people.

Though the initial public justification of double punishment focused largely on the dangerousness of Black *men* — and Jamaican men have been "the faces" and the primary targets of deportations for criminality — Black women are not, by any means, excluded from Canadian double punishment practices. The racist and sexist stereotyping of Black women that was detailed earlier, in which the state has profiled single Black mothers as "welfare queens" or as "drug mules," has not only resulted in criminalization, but also in double punishment (Barnes 2002: 198; Sapers 2013).

The story of Debra Spencer makes clear that double punishment often has little to do with "dangerous" individuals and is instead used to remove people whose lives have been deemed disposable. Born in St. Vincent, Spencer suffered sexual abuse and neglect as a child until she was adopted by a Canadian family when she was eight years old. A permanent resident and mother of two Canadian children, she suffered from addiction and mental health issues as well as developmental challenges. As a result, she was not able to complete an application for Canadian citizenship. After witnessing her boyfriend commit a murder, she was charged as an accessory and convicted in 2014. She served two-thirds of her sentence, then was released and served a deportation order.

When she received notice of her pending deportation, she became so upset that her parole officer put her back in prison because of a perceived elevated risk of self-harm (despite the fact that incarceration has been found to exacerbate mental illness). Her family, along with the Elizabeth Fry Society (who had been advocating on her behalf), said to the press that this deportation placed her at enormous risk, since she had no knowledge of the country, no family, no resources and lived with severe trauma and mental health challenges (CBC *News* November 20, 2015; Moore 2015). Her family told the press that Spencer was not fully aware of what was happening to her, and her sister told freelance journalist Erin Moore (CBC *News* November 20, 2015), "She spent almost her whole life here. She has family here. Her children are here" and further asked "What is it that makes her less valuable and disposable like that?" Regardless, Spencer was deported in 2015.

In addition to the fact that "serious criminality" is rarely associated with dangerous activities, the notion that permanent residents are "foreign criminals" erases the reality that Black permanent residents have quite often spent a significant portion of their lives in Canada. Indeed, the concept of "foreignness" — particularly when linked with Blackness — is infused with such power that it obscures the fact that permanent residents are quite often the products of Canadian society. A considerable number of permanent residents have grown up, gone to school, worked and raised families in Canada for most, if not all, their lives. Even those permanent residents who *could* legitimately be called dangerous were often brought up here. It is not abnormal for Black persons who have resided most of their lives in Canada to be permanent residents and not full Canadian citizens (Burt et al. 2016; ACLC 2008). There are many reasons for this. The process undertaken to achieve full Canadian citizenship is a slow process for many families and individuals, filled with burdensome legal costs and bureaucratic details. It is not abnormal for extended families to live and raise children here as permanent residents, while applying for citizenship status a few at a time. It is common to see families made up of differing levels of citizenship for often fairly long periods of time while working, living, going to school and building relationships. This appears to be particularly true for Black women (ACLC 2008).

New barriers to achieving citizenship, such as new language tests, have reduced the ability of Black migrants to receive their full citizenship from permanent residency. A fivefold increase in the fee to obtain citizenship has also lessened the ability of poorer permanent residents to obtain their citizenship; it has jumped from $100 to $630 total per person, a substantial sum for a low-income family (Keung 2015). This means that, as a group, Black migrants are becoming ever more vulnerable to extremely punitive consequences for actions committed with some regularity across society. Actions which would have few, if any, consequences for a white citizen continue to be used to deem Black migrants without full citizenship too dangerous to reside in Canada, and to forcibly remove them from family and community to a largely unknown, sometimes highly dangerous land.

While Black permanent residents experience punishment on an entirely different scale than white citizens, for refugee claimants, being found guilty of a criminal offence can have particularly perilous outcomes. This can result, in some instances, in extremely long and indefinite stays in immigration detention centres or deportation to extremely dangerous and life-threatening situations. Immigration legislation surrounding refugee claimants deigns to protect refugees from deportation if they have fled countries with deportation moratoriums or temporary bans due to their grave human rights situations. Yet, refugees found guilty of committing crimes are, in some cases, being deported regardless of moratoriums. Though refugee claimants are not supposed to be removed to countries with deportation bans except in the case of crimes against humanity, a *Toronto Star* report found that deportation bans have been nullified even in cases in which a claimant is found guilty of a low-level crime, such as shoplifting (Oved 2014). Situations that would, for a white citizen, likely end with a fine or a warning can mean expulsion to the world's most dangerous countries for refugee claimants, placing their lives in grave danger. This includes a significant number of predominantly Black countries, including Haiti, the Democratic Republic of Congo, Zimbabwe, Somalia and the Central African Republic (as well as Palestinian Territories, Iraq and Afghanistan) (Oved 2014).

Between 2004 and June 2014, failed refugee applicants convicted of criminal offences have been deported to several highly dangerous countries during deportation moratoriums or temporary deportation bans: fifty-five were deported to the Democratic Republic of the Congo, two hundred sixty-two to Haiti, sixty-nine to Zimbabwe, four to the Central African Republic, thirty-seven to Somalia, sixty-three to Mali and significant numbers to majority Black countries with atrocious human rights records and significant state repression, such as Eritrea, South Sudan and Sudan (Oved 2014). Though Canada no longer has the death penalty, the state continues to remove refugee claimants to countries where the possibility of death is high.

Because of the ongoing conditions in Somalia, the deportation of Somali refugee claimants is rare. Instead, Somali claimants found guilty of a criminal offence frequently face indefinite detention in Canadian immigration jails, standing in for deportation as a second punishment with no set end date (Hussan 2015). However, deportation to Somalia does occur, while rare, under conditions that are alarming. Somalia is considered so dangerous due to the lack of infrastructure and security that Canadian officials are banned from travelling there when accompanying deportees. However, instead of granting unconditional amnesty for Somali asylum seekers, state officials instead place Somali deportees in highly vulnerable conditions to secure their removal from the country. According to a 2014 CBC News report, since CBSA agents were not themselves allowed to enter Somalia, the agents would drop deportees off in Kenya. From there, the CBSA hired third parties — in effect, human traffickers — and paid them tens of thousands of dollars in cash to smuggle deported Somalis into the country of Somalia. This effectively absolved the Canadian immigration agents of any responsibility for monitoring or ensuring the safety of the deportees (CBC News November 4, 2014).

In one example, Saeed Ibrahim Jama, a permanent resident in Canada who had never lived in Somalia, was issued a deportation order in 2012 after serving a prison sentence of just over two years for drug trafficking and resisting arrest. He was brought into the city of Mogadishu, a city ravaged by civil war, where he was subsequently kidnapped and held at gunpoint by a gang until his parents paid a ransom to secure his release (CBC News November 4, 2014). Another case demonstrating the practice of abandoning Somali deportees to situations of extreme violence is that of Mohamed Barre Bulle. Bulle, convicted of assault with a weapon and drug possession, was left in 1998 by his CBSA-hired third-party on a deserted airstrip in a desert in Northern Kenya with very little food or water. He was subsequently attacked by a hyena and nearly died. He was then forced to make his way to Somalia, where he was held for months as a suspected spy until he was finally released (CBC News November 4, 2014). These cases, though rare, are nonetheless the direct result of state policies.

That Black and racialized migrants can be punished by such extreme measures due to minor criminal offences demonstrates the violent effects of Canadian policies that allot differentiated rights and protections to subjects based on hierarchical levels of citizenship. Many Canadian citizens are incarcerated for serious and even quite violent offences and subsequently return to their families and communities after time served. To deport and even smuggle refugees deemed "criminal" — who have often already served jail or prison sentences — back into civil wars as a (second) punishment for a criminal offence is to inflict suffering on a scale utterly incomparable to that of a prison sentence. The brutal disregard for human life found in this deportation practice demonstrates how little import the preservation of Black life has in Canadian state policies.

The publicly supported state practice of double punishment makes visible the public consensus that Black and other racialized migrants deserve more extreme and retributive forms of punishment than other members of society do. Though most Canadians have at some point broken a law, the power of racism and xenophobia continue to reduce human beings to "foreign," Black and "criminal" threats to be expelled no matter their time spent living in Canada. Indeed, Black persons born abroad are ultra-vulnerable to arrest and often excluded from legal rights and protections that many Canadians consider inalienable. The power of the demonization of Blackness disguises the structural racism at work and, as such, the suffering enacted onto Black communities by their disproportionate confinement and banishment from society is widely regarded as "just." Former Immigration and Citizenship Minister Jason Kenney embodied this sentiment well when he told the House of Commons, "Should that permanent resident being removed following deportation have family members in Canada, they are not required to stay here. *They are welcome to go back to their country*" (House of Commons 2013, emphasis added). Canada's role in supporting neoliberal interventions that have forced people to flee their homes, of course, remains always invisible. Kenney's words clearly demonstrate how little import is accorded to Black suffering by the Canadian state. As border control and the criminal justice system operate in tandem to dole out banishment as a tool to "solve" crime, the expenses of detention and removal continue to be preferred over investment in secure housing, employment and community reintegration.

"PASSPORT BABIES": BLACK MOTHERHOOD AS A DRAIN ON THE NATION

Race does not operate in isolation to determine who, in the eyes of Canadian border regulation, is seen as deportable. Age-old ideas surrounding Black women's reproductivity have continually cast Black motherhood as a threat and as a possible contaminant to Canadian society. Canada's immigration system continues to focus on stereotypes of Black women's sexual immorality, looseness and proclivity to have children. This has created a particular hostility toward Black, female-headed families within Canadian immigration policy that dates back to the early twentieth century (Browne 2002; Lawrence and Williams 2006). This hostility to Black motherhood, of course, exists across institutions;

in the 1960s, Black women in Nova Scotia were labelled as "prolific child bear-
ers" by the RCMP (*Canadian Press* July 20, 1994). Today, Black reproduction
continues to be seen as a threat and a contaminant, and this can be seen in the
state's representation of Black migrant mothers as both calculating and parasitic,
the mothers of "passport babies."

The case that most exemplifies how Black motherhood has been denigrated
by the immigration system is that of Mavis Baker. Though dating back to 1999,
the case remains highly relevant to discussions surrounding the relationship
between deportations and popular representation of Black migrant women,
Black single mothers and persons living with mental illness. Baker arrived in
Canada at twenty-six years old in 1981, without citizenship, and worked as a
live-in domestic for eleven years. At this point, she became ill with postpartum
depression and was unable to work, so she applied for social assistance. This
application alerted immigration authorities to Baker's "illegal" presence and she
was issued a deportation order in 1992. She applied for a humanitarian consideration to a permanent residence claim on the grounds that she had sole custody
of two Canadian-born children (her two others lived with their Canadian father)
and to avoid putting strain on her continuing mental illness (*Baker v. Canada
[Minister of Citizenship and Immigration]* 1999). The application for a humanitarian claim was denied, and again at the Federal Court and the Federal Court of
Appeal, until she finally won the right to have her humanitarian claim heard at
the Supreme Court of Canada. It was a highly publicized and controversial case,
in large part because it allowed a look into the highly discriminatory assessment
by her immigration officer, G. Lorenz, whose notes were used by the officer that
oversaw her hearing and rejected her claim. Lorenz's notes included a strong
focus on what he appears to find her sexual immorality:

> PC is unemployed — on Welfare. No income shown — no assets.
> Has four Cdn.-born children — four other children in Jamaica —
> HAS A TOTAL OF EIGHT CHILDREN … The PC is a paranoid
> schizophrenic and on welfare. She has no qualifications other than
> as a domestic. She has FOUR CHILDREN IN JAMAICA AND
> ANOTHER FOUR BORN HERE. She will, of course, be a tremen-
> dous strain on our social welfare systems for (probably) the rest of her
> life. There are no H&C factors other than her FOUR CANADIAN-
> BORN CHILDREN. Do we let her stay because of that? I am of the
> opinion that Canada can no longer afford this type of generosity.
> (*Baker v. Canada [Minister of Citizenship and Immigration]* 1999: para
> 4, emphasis in original)

Though the judgement was eventually overruled and found to be prejudicial by the Supreme Court, it is important to note that it was widely supported by public opinion. Surveillance scholar Simone Browne's analysis of the press surrounding the issue found widespread support for Baker's removal. Baker had become a national figure of undesirability and her case lent public support to a tightening of immigration restrictions for racialized migrant women who gave birth to children, derogatorily and widely referred to as "passport babies" (Browne 2002: 104–105). The *Baker v. Canada* case helped reveal a Canadian trope that treats the procreation of Black women as criminal and as a security threat — the very association between Black women and "passport babies" characterizes Black migrant women's sexuality as "corrupting, maddening and imbued with excessive fertility" (Browne 2002: 98). That Baker became a folk devil in the courts and the public just over fifteen years ago demonstrates the power of sexism, ableism, anti-Black racism and xenophobia in determining who is deserving and undeserving of rights such as state protection and family unity. It is difficult to imagine that a white middle-class woman with many children could be seen as a threat to society or the nation.

Despite the negative press and initial court judgements, Mavis Baker defeated her removal order at the level of the Supreme Court on the basis of Canada's international obligations to protect the best interests of children (*Baker v. Canada* 1999). This victory should have, in theory, protected future migrant women in similar situations from such deportations. However, a 2008 legal analysis of the post-*Baker* treatment of Black women by Canada's immigration system found that immigration officers have continued to resist applying the *Baker* ruling in determining an applicant's eligibility (Rowe 2008: 344). Indeed, the legacy of separating Black mothers from their children and representing Black women as mothers of "passport babies" lives on well into the present.

The Canadian immigration system is still marked by an ongoing systemic lack of regard for keeping Black mothers with their children. One present-day example is Herlet Gokhul, a forty-year-old single mother from Jamaica. In 1990, Gokhul, then a teenager, had fled a sexually abusive relative in Jamaica and spent the next twenty years working and living in Canada, trying to attain citizenship. She worked as a live-in nanny for free for four years, then worked sixteen-hour days seven days a week at a donut store, while also being the sole parent of her son. CBSA ordered her deportation in 2011 after Immigration and Citizenship Canada denied the application she made on humanitarian and compassionate grounds. She was deported back to Jamaica, where she had no job and no family support, without her son (Jeffords 2013; Yuen 2013). Gokhul's case makes clear the links between the disposability of poor Black women, the labour exploitation of Black migrant women in Canada and the lack of support or protection allotted to Black mothers by Canada's immigration system.

It is difficult to know how many more unnamed Black women live, work and create community in Canada only to be subject to deportation and forced to leave their children behind. The African Canadian Legal Clinic has written that while the deportation of mothers forced to leave behind their children is an issue that could affect any migrant, Black mothers are disproportionately affected by this due to the combined factors of systemic racial and gendered discrimination (ACLC 2008: 9).

Further, moves toward stricter border regulations continue to be justified by evoking the image of Black women as possible threats who would harm Canada by giving birth to "passport babies." In 2012, when Immigration Minister Jason Kenney pushed for a crackdown on what he referred to as "birth tourism," he named women from "French-speaking African nations" as well as Chinese women as the most likely culprits (Brean 2012). He stated, despite having no statistical evidence demonstrating the frequency of the practice, that a crackdown was necessary, insisting that "regardless of how often it happens, it undermines the value of Canadian citizenship" and that it was a "pretty blatant violation of Canada's generosity" (Brean 2012). It is clear that the systemic disregard for Black motherhood — originating under slavery — has remained relatively intact in Canada's immigration system.

AGAINST BORDER REGULATION

Citizenship, as it exists today, remains a legitimate, widely and formally accepted form of exclusion, allotting rights and protections to some and withholding it from others who then fall victim to state violence by virtue of their designation as "outsiders." The immigration system has become part of the "tough on crime" mandate that continues to focus on surveillance and punishment of racialized migrant communities, African and Caribbean communities in particular. Detention and deportation are indeed acts of state violence against vulnerable, unwanted and unprotected state subjects, and the devaluation of Black life is nearly total in the absence (and even in the presence) of full citizenship. Canadian research on the family members of deported persons has found that the deportation of a family member is experienced similarly to a death in the family. The families left behind report financial stress, depression, fear and anxiety (Toronto Deportation Pilot Project in Burt et al. 2016: 8). Deportees, who frequently have no knowledge of their "home" country, are frequently unable to secure housing, education, healthcare or employment (Burt et al. 2016: 23). The forced separation of Black families from their loved ones — often justified by the invocation of Black crime — is merely another articulation of the familial separation that has its origins in slavery.

There is a deep hypocrisy in the punitive treatment of Black migration in a society that formerly sanctioned the forced traffic of Black bodies who entered Canada's borders as property to be bought and sold. Indeed, just as Black enslaved people who ran away from captivity were punished with incarceration and other state-sanctioned violence, African-descended migrants the world over continue to be placed in captivity in immigration detention as punishment for fleeing the impoverishment, persecution, starvation and warfare that has resulted from slavery, colonialism and neocolonialism. The Canadian state continues to neglect its responsibility for the enormity of human suffering caused by centuries of violent dispossession of labour, culture and resources across Africa, the Caribbean and the larger Global South. Rather than atonement through reparations and regularization — and a divestment from involvement in exploitative extraction of African and Caribbean commodities — Canada's neocolonial debt is disavowed by the state. Instead, innumerable Black and brown people are placed in cages, expelled from the country or granted the ability to stay only contingent on conditions of extreme duress. Further, the borders that separate Canada, Mexico and the United States are colonial impositions that separate families and communities from one another, and border regulation itself negates Indigenous sovereignty over the historical lands of Inuit, Metis and First Nations peoples (Walia 2013: 7).

As much as prisons do not stop crimes, immigration controls do not work to keep people out of Canada or other countries of the Global North. Strict border controls do not address "push factors" that drive people from their homes and families; they only result in more danger for those forced to migrate, who "resort to staggering feats of ingenuity, courage and endurance to assert their right to move and to flee" (Hayter 2004: 152). Yet, enormous suffering is continually inflicted on racialized migrant communities by Canadian detention and deportation practices. After decades of concerted activism, many large Canadian cities including Vancouver, Toronto and Montréal, begin to push toward adopting the framework of becoming "sanctuary cities" — that is, cities in which immigration status does not bar access to health, social and education services. It is clear that the cruelty of border regulation — and the differential rights that accompany it — need not be viewed as an immutable and permanent facet of Canadian a global society. However, despite the symbolic importance of these statements, the practice of the exclusion of migrants from social, political and economic life and their vulnerability to detention and deportation has still remained largely unchanged, for the present. Understanding and combatting anti-Black racism and other prominent forms of racism institutionalized within Canadian society involves not only destabilizing dominant assumptions surrounding race, crime, policing and prisons in society, but also questioning the legitimacy of citizenship to govern human worth.

This is a moment of a particular and global urgency that requires us to address anti-Blackness through a framework critical of border regulation. Border controls have been continually fortified across Western states, particularly since the 1990s; this has resulted in the tragic and unnecessary deaths of displaced migrants trying to cross borders (Loyd, Mitchelson and Burridge 2012: 7). In particular, the Mediterranean Sea, which divides Europe and Africa, continues to absorb the bodies of African migrants paralleling the deaths of captured Africans who jumped or were thrown overboard during the Middle Passage.

Given the widespread growth of anti-migrant sentiment, racism and Islamophobia worldwide — including "Brexit" and the rise of Donald Trump — it is urgent to counter the scapegoating of racialized and Black migrants worldwide and move toward open borders. Yet, in Canada this cannot be accomplished without acknowledging the important and persistent legacy of anti-Blackness in immigration control, detention and deportation policies.

CONCLUSION

In the present moment, as Blackness is, as ever, rendered alien and other, immigration controls continue to delineate the limits of Black freedom and Black mobility. Despite a history in Canada dating back four centuries, Black communities are always seen as "non-Canadian, always other, always elsewhere, recent, unfamiliar, and impossible" (McKittrick 2006: 99). The state has played an important role in maintaining this otherness by entrenching it in law through the means of border regulations that have kept Black migrants precarious, exploitable, jailable and removable. Particularly for Black communities, there are many overlaps between crime and migration policies that blur the lines between the two as distinct methods of punishment for those who are abandoned by state protections (Loyd Mitchelson and Burridge 2012: 8). As much as prisons serve as one of the most extreme ways to banish citizens, immigration penalty allows for an even more severe form of banishment of those deemed "unwanted." As a result, Black life, for non-citizens is marked by a constant vulnerability to arbitrary punishment, indefinite, brutal detention with no fixed end date, and permanent exile, as well as violence and death.

CHAPTER SEVEN

DESTROYING
BLACK FAMILIES
Slavery's afterlife in
the child welfare system

WHILE MOST TRADITIONAL ACCOUNTS OF PROFILING, policing and punishment address the criminal justice system and, more rarely, immigration penalty, child welfare agencies have played a significant role in the policing of Black life. Under the banner of protection, in many Canadian cities Black children and youth are removed at appalling rates from their families and placed in state care or foster homes, where they experience trauma, isolation and a wide array of other harms. Further, family and community ties are shattered and sometimes demolished by the loss of so many Black children and youth who are apprehended by the state. Given the grossly disproportionate removal of Black children from their families when compared to the general population, it's necessary to understand the child welfare system as a site of racist state violence against Black families and against Black communities more largely (Roberts 2002).

The surveillance and punishment of Blackness — slavery's afterlife — is readily apparent in the realities of child welfare in Canada. Indeed, though officially tasked with ensuring the safety and well-being of marginalized children in the event that their families are unable to do so, since its inception the child welfare system has re-created forms of racialized surveillance, captivity and familial dislocation that originated under slavery. Child welfare agencies are granted enormous powers to monitor, control and divide Black families, and confine Black youth into state institutions or foster care. Further, the current crisis of Black child apprehension and placement makes up part of a long history of the destruction of Black family bonds. The separation of Black parents and children — what Saidiya Hartman calls "the enforced 'kinlessness' of the enslaved" (1997: 67) — that was a defining feature of slavery lives on, in modified forms, in the present-day functioning of the child welfare system.

A HISTORY OF BLACK CHILD WELFARE

Widely held beliefs that today cast Black families as unfit and requiring white supervision date back centuries, not decades. The separation of Black mothers from their babies and the subsequent denial of familial relationships to many enslaved Black people played an important role in the maintenance of white supremacy that is reproduced today in the child welfare system. Children's aid societies were established in the late nineteenth century and were a part of the first explicit child welfare legislation. The provinces granted these new institutions the legislative authority to remove neglected children from their homes (Schumaker 2012: 32). Yet, the interventions, based on "friendly visits" from white middle-class women, were tied to the notion of protecting upper classes and were tasked with the mission to impose (British) European morality on marginalized women and families who were seen as immoral (Swift 1995). The monitoring of lower-class and marginalized families was deeply tied into the goal of continued dominance for the ruling classes. Indeed, "the concern of the child savers was not only for the difficult conditions endured by the street urchins and children of the poor, but also for the safety of their own children, accumulating property, and preservation of social stability" (Schumaker 2012: 32). The sanctification of white children, in contrast to the denigration of Black children, underwrote the structuring of many provincial child welfare programs in the early twentieth century. This frequently resulted in the segregation of Black children from white children (Lafferty 2013: 72).

The federal child welfare branch was also implicated in policing race and class. Created in 1920, it was originally a division of the Department of Health, headed by Helen MacMurchy (Mancuso 1999: 93). MacMurchy held some of the more extreme dehumanizing racist beliefs. She was a vocal and active eugenicist who advocated for the institutionalization and sterilization of the "feeble-minded," a pseudo-scientific category that stood in for the racialized, poor, immoral, mentally ill and otherwise undesirable persons (McLaren 1990). MacMurchy worked closely with the Women's Branch of the aptly named Immigration and Colonization Department to ensure the careful monitoring of the population (Mancuso 1999: 93). White female social workers were trained in the surveillance of the population with a particular focus on immigrant communities. Their occupation was professionalized partly because of "the need to have trained experts police new arrivals" (A. McLaren 2008: 198).

There is too little available research on the treatment of Black youth and families by child welfare agencies in the early to mid-twentieth century. Still, a discernible legacy of pathologizing Black families and removing their children can be gleaned. Black families often faced extreme levels of poverty as a result of segregation, but had always resisted in large and small ways the removal of Black youth and children from their communities. However, as a result of racism, would-be Black foster families desiring to take in Black children have historically been discriminated against and unduly overlooked by child welfare agencies (Bernard and Bernard 2002; Dubinsky 2008). At the same time, Black children in care were largely unwanted in white society.

Nova Scotia could be said to be have the most visible and concerted history of anti-Blackness within the child welfare system. In the late nineteenth and early twentieth centuries, orphanages were reluctant to accept Black children. Though a few accepted children of all races, others refused "coloured" children outright. It was not uncommon for Black infants to be denied entry and even be left to die (Taylor 2015: 29–30). Mobilization on the part of the Black community led to proposals to create a special home to protect Black children (Taylor 2015: 30). State officials were eager to segregate Black children entirely and place them into the newly created Nova Scotia Home for Colored Children, which was founded to ensure the protection of the province's "neglected and destitute coloured children" (Lafferty 2013: 65–66, 80). Though the Black community was proud of the existence of this home, as it served as a testament to Black survival (Lafferty 2013), it is undeniable that the circumstance that required its creation was the acute systemic racism that kept Black children and their families outside of the protection of society at large. Black children were seen as less evolved and thus a danger to white children. Their integration with other children was undesirable to child welfare workers (Lafferty 2013: 72, 82).

Segregation did not protect Black children from abuse. Indeed, significant and long-standing state neglect played an important role in the often-horrific conditions faced by the children who lived in this home. In 1947, a staff report to the province demonstrated that there were only three staff and two bathrooms for sixty children, as well as inadequate food and sleeping space — yet, the province responded with inaction (Taylor 2015: 40). Silence on the part of the province continued despite numerous allegations of serious child abuse and beatings of young girls in the 1950s (Taylor 2015: 44). The Home, in some moments, received almost three times less funding per child than other similar childcare homes in the province, despite repeated requests to the province for equal funding from the 1940s through to the end of the 1970s (Taylor 2015: 37–39). Girls who attended the Home in the 1970s reported sexual violence as commonplace, and that many young women had been impregnated by staff. Researcher Wanda Taylor also wrote that "countless" former residents, many of whom had never spoken to each other, recounted that when babies died, they were buried in the woods behind the Home (Taylor 2015: 45–46).

In 1980, the per diems allotted to the Home were finally raised to $27.88, but by this time children in other wards received $55 (Taylor 2015: 39). Continued neglect on the part of the province and the staff meant that Black children were subjected to overcrowding and denied basic education, hygiene and care (Taylor 2015). Hundreds of residents of the orphanage suffered physical, psychological and sexual abuse by its staff from the 1920s until it closed in the 1980s. Black children endured lasting trauma from being separated from their siblings, being forced to work without pay, enduring sexual and psychological violence and neglect (Taylor 2015). This state-sanctioned and institutionalized violence extended the horrors of slavery long past abolition for many African Nova Scotians. This horrific history has only started to be revealed to the wider public more recently, following a fifteen-year legal battle won by former residents. The province of Nova Scotia agreed to a settlement and issued a public apology. A public inquiry will be launched in the future to continue to uncover what transpired in the Home (*Canadian Press* July 7, 2014).

In the 1960s and early 1970s, Black children in Nova Scotia also began to be placed *en masse* into white homes (Bernard and Bernard 2002). Because of this, while some were spared the horrific abuse endemic at the Home for Colored Children, generations of African Nova Scotian youth in care were denied access to their culture and heritage and subjected to racism, and experienced isolation within white families who had no cultural sensitivity training or ties with their community and culture (Bernard and Bernard 2002).

While the atrocities of the Nova Scotia Home for Colored Children were not replicated elsewhere, anti-Black racism nonetheless functioned within child welfare policies in other Canadian cities as well. In the 1940s, children with "Negroid blood" were deemed non-adoptable in Canada (Landsdowne 1949 in Dubinsky 2008: 270). In the 1950s, the Toronto Children's Aid Society placed children of "Negroid appearance" in institutions rather than in foster homes for the same reason (Schwalbe 1958 in Dubinsky 2008: 278). In the 1960s and 1970s, many Black mothers working as domestics in Toronto and interviewed for a study on the topic reported having conflictual relationships with child welfare agencies that continued to have "a strong presence" in their lives (Daenzer 1997: 278).

The city of Montréal had a unique approach for dealing with Black children placed in state care, which stems from a different articulation of anti-Black racism than the one found in other Canadian cities. The adoption of Black children into white families was widely promoted in the 1950s and 1960s, but these adoptions were facilitated by the Open Door Society, an organization created by self-proclaimed white liberals who believed that cross-racial adoption was key to a post-racial future through "integration" (Dubinsky 2008). Over three hundred children, most of them Black, were adopted by white families between 1955 and 1969. While this organization claimed that the practice helped combat racism, the underlying assumption was that Black children, like Indigenous and Asian children, would be better off in white families, clearly showing the founders' racial biases. The so-called integration that they promoted was indeed unidirectional. In 1961, a Toronto-based periodical called the *Star Weekly* mused, "The white Anglo-Saxon has lost supremacy. Couldn't our future citizens of mixed race brought up in white homes, *knowing the best of both backgrounds instead of the worst*, be Canada's ambassadors for peace? (in Dubinsky 2008: 269, emphasis added). Their casting of white families as the foundation for the "best of both backgrounds" and as a way to "salvage" children from the comparatively worse fate of being brought up in Black homes was a belief shared by organizations promoting such adoptions. Notes taken by social workers at the time indicated that many adoptive parents saw their child's Blackness as an unfortunate blight to be transcended or overcome. "Full Negro" children remained the least popular children to adopt (Dubinsky 2008: 275).

Despite the work of the Open Door Society, Black mothers in mid-twentieth-century Montréal were discouraged by child welfare workers from giving up their children, because their Blackness made them undesirable and therefore unlikely to be adopted (Dubinsky 2008: 280). Not only were Black youth treated as pathological, but long-standing historical tropes surrounding Black femininity were also re-created in the representation of Black mothers. An examination of social workers' notes on their Black female clients reveals that Black mothers in the 1970s were labelled as "stubborn," "aggressive" and "challenging." The caseworkers also derided Black women for their perceived audacity in complaining about racial discrimination (Dubinsky 2008: 281). This racial experiment, while seen as progressive by white adopters who self-identified as "liberal," was met with ambivalent responses and some resistance from the Black community. In one instance, during a meeting between Black students of Sir George Williams University and Open Door Society, one Black student demanded that the white parents "give us back our children" (anonymous interview in Dubinsky 2008: 283). Interracial adoption, of course, has a larger history within the child welfare system's treatment of Indigenous families.

While Black and Indigenous communities each have a distinct historical and contemporary relationship with the state, both communities face high rates of child apprehension from state-funded child welfare agents, and both communities' children suffer the consequences of the systemic racism that tears them away from their families "for their own good" (Pon, Gosine and Phillips 2011). Indeed, child welfare in Canada developed as a tool to further settler colonialism. In the 1960s, interracial adoption of Indigenous children occurred on a much larger scale across Canada. Child protection agencies began an *en masse*, largely non-consensual apprehension of Indigenous children from their families, sending them to be adopted (most often by white families) and causing enormous, physical, emotional and spiritual harm to both individual children and their communities (Truth and Reconciliation Commission 2015, henceforth TRC 2015; Blackstock 2007). This practice, aimed at "assimilating" Indigenous children, is often referred to as the "60s Scoop" and is now seen as a form of cultural genocide. However, similar dynamics persist into the present: Indigenous children and youth, representing 5 percent of the population, make up 30 to 40 percent of all children in state care in Canada and up to 80 percent of youth in the system in Manitoba (Blackstock 2011). There are more Indigenous youth in care today than at any time in recorded history (Blackstock 2011). Today, the legacies of both of Indigenous genocide and slavery are still firmly entrenched within child welfare systems.

The legacy of racism in child welfare has not gone unseen by Black communities. In 1970, the radical Uhuru Movement called for a separate Black child welfare system and denounced the racism that entrenched policies preventing Black families from adopting Black children (Dubinsky 2008: 283). Similarly, the Nova Scotia Association of Black Social Workers fought to have Black children placed with Black families (Bernard and Bernard 2002). However, by the 1980s, the sheer number of Black children in state care was already at a crisis point in many Canadian cities. For example, in the mid-1980s in Montréal, 50.9 percent of all child placements from the "ethnic" population were children of Caribbean descent (Review of the Main Issues in the Delivery of Service to Ethnic and Visible Minorities in a Social Service Centre 1986 in Rambally 1995: 85) and in the early 1990s, Black anglophones were over-represented in youth care at a rate of nearly 400 percent (Hutchinson et al. 1992: 7 in Clarke 2010).

Today, national figures on Black youth in care are not collected. Yet, in areas with significant Black populations, the number of Black youth held in care is jarring. In Ontario, Black Canadians are in care at five times the rate of their percentage of the population in the province (Ontario Association of Children's Aid Societies [OACAS] 2015). In Toronto, Black youth make up 8 percent of the youth population but represent more than 40 percent of the population of youth in care (Contenta, Monsebraaten and Rankin 2014). In contrast, the white youth who make up more than half of the youth population represent only 37 percent of the in-care population (Contenta, Monsebraaten and Rankin 2014). In an unnamed urban centre in Ontario with a Black population of 8 percent, 65 percent of the youth in care are Black (Child Welfare Anti-Oppression Roundtable 2009: 1).

Though racial data is not systematically publicized in Québec, both anglophone and francophone Black youth are significantly overrepresented in care in Montréal (CDPDJ 2011: 84; Rambally 1995; Bernard and McAll 2009). One study conducted in Montréal found that one-third of English-speaking youth in care were Black (Rambally 1995: 87) and another found that Haitian children are three times more likely to be placed in care than other French-speaking children (Belony 2007). More recently, in 2008, Black English-speaking youth made up almost one-third of youth in placement within the main anglophone youth protection service agencies (Côte-des-Neiges Black Community Association 2016). While these numbers are jarring, statistics alone can do little to represent the harms enacted on Black children, Black families and the Black community as a whole.

BLACKNESS AS RISK: POLICING BLACK FAMILIES

To be Black is to be perceived as a risk. Negative associations with Blackness — that Black people are aggressive, prone to violence, dishonest and lacking intelligence — are compounded in the child welfare system by an important lack of empathy toward Black youth or their parents. This pathologization, which dates back centuries, permeates decision-making across the entirety of the child welfare system (OACAS 2016). Contrary to negative stereotypes and tropes about Black families commonly propagated via the media and popular culture, the massive overrepresentation of Black youth in state care is not a product of dysfunctional Black culture. Black families are not comparatively more abusive. Numerous studies have confirmed that the over-representation of Black youth in care is largely a product of both racial profiling in reporting to child welfare agencies and systemic discrimination (CDPDJ 2011; OACAS 2016). Black families are closely scrutinized, and widely held, often-unconscious beliefs that Black families are unfit and pathological play an important role in the apprehension of Black children from their parents (Roberts 2002). The profiling of Blackness that spans across schools, law enforcement and social services — which can rightly be described as a large-scale and widely diffused mass surveillance across state institutions — is readily apparent in the over-reporting of Black families to child welfare agencies. Over-reporting fuels the over-representation of Black youth in the child welfare system.

While the overall rates of child abuse by white and Black families are relatively similar, Black families are reported to youth protection agencies at a significantly higher rate than white families (OACAS 2015). According to one Montréal study, they are flagged to child welfare at a rate that is double that of other children (Dufour and Lavergne 2009 in CDPDJ 2011: 83). This profiling extends across institutions; schools and law enforcement agencies account for a significant percent of the (over-)reporting of Black families to child welfare agencies (Bernard and McAll 2007 in CDPDJ 2011; Child Welfare Anti-Oppression Roundtable 2009). According to one source cited by the *Toronto Star*, calls from schools and the police account for approximately 40 percent of reporting (Contenta, Monsebraaten and Rankin 2014). Racist beliefs and policies institutionalizing these views are the only way to explain such rates. A 2009 Ontario report with data from nearly half of Ontario's welfare agencies found that, "in both [the school and child welfare] systems, racialized children *are negatively perceived and thus negatively impacted*" (Child Welfare Anti-Oppression Roundtable 2009: 3, emphasis added).

Cases abound of racial bias in the assessment of whether or not Black youth are "at risk" of abuse or neglect. In one case, a child welfare worker recounted how one Black youth was reported to child welfare by his school for having a roti packed as a lunch because it was perceived as "not healthy or sustainable for this child" (in Contenta, Monsebraaten and Rankin 2014). In an interview with the *Toronto Star*, Everton Gordon, the executive director of the Jamaican-Canadian Association confirms having witnessed racial profiling when it comes to the reporting of Black families by law enforcement officers. He identifies the practice as one part of a larger pattern of the police vilifying Black communities (Contenta, Monsebraaten and Rankin 2014). Racism also informs reporting that occurs from medical institutions. One Ontario-based study reported that Black mothers who are HIV-positive would routinely be reported to child and family services by hospital staff, regardless of demonstrable parental abilities and involvement and management of their illness (in OACAS 2016: 62).

Every time a Black family is reported, it is placed on the case file and increases the risk that they will be investigated or end up in court. For this reason, there are enormous risks to Black children and their families that result from conscious or unconscious racial bias in reporting. Racial profiling in the over-reporting of Black families to child welfare services across state institutions has been compared by Black community members as having a similar effect as does the widespread practice of police street checks and documentation experienced by a significant proportion of Black people in Canadian cities (OACAS 2016: 60).

Class also affects reporting rates; medical professionals are more likely to report a child with bruises for possible abuse when their family is poor than when the child is from a wealthier family (Clarke 2010). Since Black families face disproportionate levels of poverty, poor Black families are therefore at higher risk of coming into contact with child welfare agencies and, subsequently, of being found unfit to parent. This is not to explain away racial disparities by pointing toward economic factors; rather, intersecting realities of class- and race-based discrimination impact Black families together. Race and poverty are so closely interrelated that they are analytically inseparable in addressing systemic racial injustice within child welfare apprehension (Roberts 2002: 97).

The Commission des droits de la personne et des droits de la jeunesse identified over-reporting of Black families as one of the most important factors leading to the over-representation of Black youth in care (CDPDJ 2011). However, being reported is only the beginning of what becomes a pattern of increased involvement with child welfare agencies, within which mistreatment of Black youth and their families is common. The power granted by the state to social workers — 94 percent of whom are white women of European backgrounds — allows them an enormous influence over the lives and futures of the families that fall under their dominion as "caseloads" (Fallon, MacLaurin, Trocmé and Felstiner 2003 in Pon, Gosine and Phillips 2011: 395). Following any complaint, child welfare workers can enter and search people's homes, interview doctors, teachers and family friends and are granted the authority to make life-altering decisions around the fitness of families (Public Legal Education and Information Service of New Brunswick 2007). Indeed, considering that many child removals take place without any laws having been broken, the policing and surveillance powers — up to and including child removal — granted to child welfare workers over poor Black families are significant. In many ways, the welfare system has been deputized with powers more commonly associated with law enforcement agencies, and has similar or even more substantive ability to surveil, curtail and control Black people's lives, livelihoods and families. In fact, for Black families, there is no clear separation between child welfare and law enforcement agencies: child welfare workers often visit the homes of Black families with the presence of police officers due to the fact that Black families are imagined to be "criminals and dangerous" (Pon, Phillips, Clarke and Abdillah in OACAS 2016). Many child welfare workers appear to be influenced (whether consciously or unconsciously) by a tendency to pathologize Black parents.

Beyond profiling and invasive surveillance, the experiences of Black families with child welfare agents have often been degrading and racist encounters. For decades, Black families have raised concerns about their treatment by the child welfare system and its staff (OACAS 2015 and 2016). Trinidadian-Canadian social worker Rae Tucker Rambally, who wrote extensively on the Canadian social services system, criticized the racism and cultural ignorance that often underwrites the assessment and treatment of Black families by child welfare agents (Rambally 1995: 88). Social workers investigating claims have labelled families as negligent for having pantries filled with foods of a Caribbean diet such as rice, corn and beans (La Presse 2008 in CDPDJ 2011). An Ontario study found that service users who do not share the same set of cultural values, or have different backgrounds (race, class, sexuality) than case investigators are defined as "different." Those differences are perceived as being both inferior and "risky" within the child welfare system (Child Welfare Anti-Oppression Roundtable 2009: 3). Being perceived as a risk has enormous consequences. Black women in Toronto reported having contacted Children's Aid Societies (CAS) for support only to have their children removed from their custody, and many reported being closely monitored, assumed to be "guilty" and judged harshly due to their race (Clarke 2010).

Decisions made by child welfare agents that were influenced by the race of the person or family involved appear to continue up the chain; the decisions made about which cases are selected for investigation and which ones are sub-stantiated have also been shown to be influenced by anti-Blackness and other forms of racism (Lavergne et al. 2009: 71, 74). In Ontario, people with African features are twice as likely to be investigated after being reported (Yuan et al. 2003 in OACAS 2015). In Québec, one study found that Haitian youth were more likely to be coded as "urgent" in their file processing, more likely to be removed on an "emergency" basis, twice more likely not to be returned home, more likely to have their file referred to court and more often placed in care (Bernard and McAll 2009 in CDPDJ 2011: 82). Black children also tend to stay involved in state care for far longer than white children. In 2008, 45 percent of Black children involved with the Toronto CAS spent more than twelve months in care, twice as long as white or Asian youth (Contenta, Monsebraaten and Rankin 2014). Black youth are more likely to be placed out-of-home and are less likely to be reunited with their families. They are also more likely to spend their childhood growing up in foster care without finding another home or being adopted (OACAS 2016; Clarke 2010).

Further, the punishment levelled by law enforcement at Black people who do not manifest docility to whites is reproduced, too, within child welfare. Black parents who question the involvement of child welfare agencies — that is, who do not willingly accept a role subservient to child welfare — are far more likely to be labelled non-compliant, be subjected to judicial action, be criminalized and lose their children (Rambally 1995: 91; Contenta, Monsebraaten and Rankin 2014). A recent study published by OACAS found that many Black women and caseworkers recounted that child welfare workers simply would not allow Black mothers to advocate on behalf of themselves, stating, "often the system refuses to engage with the [Black] woman" (OACAS 2016: 74). Some Black women are even criminalized as a result of trying to advocate on their family's behalf, due to stereotypes regarding the so-called "angry Black woman" (OACAS 2016: 74). While all social workers may not harbour ill will or bad intentions toward racialized communities (though some undoubtedly do), racism nonetheless continues to inform decision-making, which, for Black families, means the potential temporary or permanent loss of their loved ones (OACAS 2016). This is compounded by further systemic injustices that contribute to the massive apprehension of Black youth from their families.

(RE)PRODUCING "NEGLECT": NEGLECTFUL BLACK FAMILIES OR NEGLECTFUL STATE POLICIES?

An important fact remains: vulnerable children, of course, need to be protected from neglect and abuse. However, neglect and abuse differ markedly from one another. The large majority of child removals in Black families occur under the umbrella of "neglect," not as a result of any form of abuse. While less than a quarter of Black youth in care are there due to physical or sexual abuse, 70 percent are apprehended due to what social workers deem to be neglect (or for violence between parents) (Contenta, Monsebraaten and Rankin 2014). In her book *Manufacturing "Bad Mothers,"* author Karen Swift points out that though "neglect" appears to be a racially neutral category, it is actually used to create and maintain racial divisions "without an appearance that is explicitly racial" (Swift 1995: 127). For this reason, it's important to examine the systemic racism that is obscured behind what is called "child neglect."

Black poverty is directly related to the rates of child apprehension. Black families are too often assigned the designation of "neglectful" and have their children apprehended simply due to conditions resulting from poverty (CDPDJ 2011: 81). Child neglect, unlike physical, sexual or emotional abuse, is not a harmful or malicious action. Neglect resulting from a lack of food, space or parental presence is generally a consequence of poverty and/or unemployment (Schumaker 2012: 7; Swift 1995). In addition, poverty not only determines *if* a child will be removed, but also for how long (Lindsey 1992 in OACAS 2015). To understand the interplay between these removals and the wider context in which they take place, one can look at the major cuts to family supports and social welfare during Ontario Premier Mike Harris's tenure and the concurrent lowering of the threshold for child neglect under the law. These events corresponded with a massive increase in child removals in Ontario (Contenta, Monsebraaten and Rankin 2014). Such cuts and policies cement the racialization of poverty; however, we still see the moral responsibility for the often-destitute conditions faced by Black and Indigenous families shifted from the state to the family. Still, "neglect" is individualized and treated as a family problem, rather than a direct result of systemic discrimination.

The high rate of poverty in Black communities stems largely from structural racism, and a full two-thirds of Black children in Canada live in poverty (Galabuzi 2007 in ACLC 2012). Discriminatory treatment within child welfare agencies is compounded and exacerbated by inequitable access to safe housing, employment, nutrition and childcare, all of which affect the ability to provide a nurturing home environment. Black immigrant families, for example, are often concentrated in areas with high rates of substandard and dilapidated housing (Curling and McMurtry 2008). In 2000, unsuitable housing was the cause of nearly 20 percent of child apprehensions by the Ontario CAS and the reason that 10 percent of the children were not returned to their families (Easton 2001 in Clarke 2010). Children may also be removed due to neglect because of factors like little food in the home, inadequate seasonal clothing or the presence of peeling or lead-based paint (Contenta, Monsebraaten and Rankin 2014). While these are all concerning issues, they are also poverty-based issues. In a recent analysis of the involvement of Haitian children in state care in Montréal, it was found that, while these children were largely removed because their families were determined to be neglectful, this determination stems largely from the precarious socioeconomic factors of Haitian families (Belony 2007). It is clear that, while the Black family is often the object of negative stereotyping and therefore stigmatized and viewed with suspicion, it is not cultural or innate inferiority that has caused the massive apprehension of Black children. Material conditions, compounded with racial discrimination within child welfare, are what actually lead to the removal of so many Black children.

Alongside Black families, Indigenous families are also deemed unfit at massive rates due to being assessed as neglectful (Lavergne et al. 2009: 72). A significant body of Canadian research has critically assessed the removal of Indigenous children under the guise of neglect (Trocmé et al. 2006 in Blackstock 2011; Schumaker 2012). Rates of child abuse are not significantly higher than they are in white families, but still, neglect is used as the justification for the majority of Indigenous youth currently in care (Trocmé et al. 2006 in Blackstock 2011). Cindy Blackstock, a prominent Indigenous child welfare activist, has documented that the conditions of deprivation and extreme poverty that lead Indigenous homes and families to be deemed neglectful directly result from deliberate government policies (2010). The Canadian government has deliberately, massively underfunded on-reserve schools, housing and child welfare initiatives and agencies, allotting them significantly fewer resources than those dedicated to white Canadians. The government has also neglected issues such as the lack of sanitation and clean drinking water or the lack of available and affordable healthy food in many communities. It has dedicated a scant amount to culturally appropriate programming addressing issues of substance use, despite this being rooted in the intergenerational trauma stemming from centuries of violent state actions (Blackstock 2011). Removing tens of thousands of Indigenous children from their homes under the guise of neglect is therefore profoundly cynical, as it punishes Indigenous communities for a poverty that is continually imposed upon them by the Canadian government.

Similarly, to label poor Black families as neglectful obscures the failure of the child welfare system and other key government agencies to implement an *effective* social intervention that would, at its core, systemically address the racial inequality keeping so many Black families in poverty. The racialization of poverty is not a random occurrence, but the result of state policies. It is deeply harmful that Black children lack adequate nutrition, safe housing and the basic materials required to survive and thrive. Poverty harms people both physically and psychologically. To "intervene" is indeed necessary to avoid undue harm to young persons of any race. However, the chosen form of intervention speaks to how little import is placed on keeping poor Black families together. Currently, the state favours children being apprehended from their families over address-ing economic and racial inequality.

The investment in removing children from their families instead of providing economic support and maintaining family integrity demonstrates the ongoing disposability of Black, Indigenous and other racialized and poor people's lives. The failure to address poverty head on by the child welfare system and other government agencies is both harmful and ineffective (Lindsey and Shlonsky 2008 in Schumaker 2012: 7; Blackstock 2011). Child welfare agencies, though granted the power to remove children, do not address the systemic factors that lead to child removal. This results from funding priorities and the lack of coordination or concerted efforts with other relevant agencies (ACLC 2012). Indeed, until 2013, Ontario's CAS funding was directly tied to the number of children removed and placed rather than to the prevention of family separa-tion. This has been widely criticized by both Black and Indigenous community members (ACLC 2012; Blackstock 2007; OACAS 2016).

The state-mandated remedies for neglect make clear the lack of a coher-ent and systemic response toward alleviating the conditions of child poverty. When a family's poverty is labelled as neglect, the children and their parents are made to undergo counselling. Parents are often given strict conditions to meet to have their children returned, often without the necessary support to access affordable and acceptable housing and better paid employment. While necessary measures toward addressing "neglect," these are seen as falling out-side of these agencies' mandates (Rambally 1995: 91). Black parents who are unable to move into more "appropriate" housing may, therefore, end up losing custody of their children for an extended period of time (Clarke 2010). Poor households, particularly those led by single parents, find themselves unable to reconcile meeting the requirements of child welfare agents, such as ensuring more supervision of their children, with maintaining employment to cover basic needs like shelter and food (Rambally 1995). The so-called protection offered by child welfare agencies does not adequately focus on prevention and support, or on the structural factors that entrench Black communities in poverty and/ or marginalize them. Therefore, "protection" often has the opposite effect of exposing Black children to further harm. Black families, whose poverty largely results from gendered and racialized state practices, do not receive support in improving their economic conditions and maintaining the integrity of their family. Instead, they are punished by the dismantling of their family structure. To paraphrase Dorothy Roberts, author of *Shattered Bonds: The Color of Child Welfare,* child welfare policy today reflects the political choice to address dire child poverty in Black (and Indigenous) communities by punishing parents and their children instead of directly confronting the structural causes of racial and economic inequality. For this reason, despite the good intentions of some of those within the system, the child welfare system remains "a racist institution" (Roberts 2002: 99). Though it is important that young persons are not in immediate danger in their family homes, the racial discrimination underwriting the entire child welfare system means that many Black youth are placed in care in situations where support and prevention could have kept their families intact.

CASE STUDY: DRUG USE AND
THE PUNISHMENT OF BLACK MOTHERS

Although long-standing beliefs regarding the unfitness of Black families are visible within the institution of child welfare, racist and sexist stereotypes regarding Black women as "bad mothers" have played an important role in the removal of Black children. Both Indigenous and Black women, particularly those who are single mothers, continue to be targeted by "mother blame" — a phenomenon through which child welfare authorities place the blame on women for the structural factors that inhibit their lives, such as poor housing, poverty and male violence against women (Pon, Gosine and Phillips 2011; Swift 1995). Women, Canadian criminologist Susan C. Boyd notes, are "held personally responsible for the outcomes of their pregnancies and mothering, regardless of negative social and environmental factors" (Boyd 1999: 16). Not only are poor Black women blamed for their marginalization, but they are also punished for it accordingly.

Black women have historically been tasked with the role of taking care of white children at the expense of their own families, yet Black motherhood has been historically widely denigrated (Roberts 1995). Since the 1980s, the demonization of Black motherhood has been accomplished, in part, by the association of Black mothers with illicit drugs. Stereotypes of Black women as welfare queens who produce "crack babies" extend throughout popular culture and the welfare and criminal justice systems (Roberts 1995: 384). Joy James observes that Black mothers have long been widely treated as a source of social decay as mothers and parents, "alleged to reproduce or breed criminals and deviants" (1996: 144). This is enormously visible in the hostility and neglect that Black mothers face within the child welfare system, particularly in the situations faced by Black mothers who use drugs.

Black women and Black mothers are not more likely to use drugs than other members of society; maternal drug use is relatively even across race and class

(Boyd 1999). However, race and class have significant impacts on who is most likely to be flagged by social services or doctors for drug use. The first ever in-depth Canadian study on mothers and illicit drug use, conducted by Boyd in 1993–1994, found that women who use illicit drugs vary in age, race and class. It found, equally, that women disadvantaged by race and poverty experienced the large majority of the punitive consequences of this, such medical intervention, arrest and child apprehension (Boyd 1999: 212).

While drug use can have an impact on the health outcome of pregnancies, as well as on the ability to parent, the surveillance of Black mothers suspected of drug use does not demonstrate concern for pregnant Black mothers or their children; rather, it is a racialized and gendered surveillance practice that devalues Black motherhood. Unlike in the United States, women cannot be prosecuted in Canada for using drugs while pregnant (though, in a few cases, women have been forced to attend drug treatment facilities against their will — see Nelson 2013: 195–196). African-American mothers are far more likely to be subjected to "random" drug testing than white mothers, in some cases without their knowledge or consent (Martin 2015 in OACAS 2016; Roberts 1993). For this reason, a poor and racialized woman who has used drugs is significantly more likely to be made to undergo drug testing — and subsequently lose her parental rights — than a middle-class white woman who has used drugs.

Poor women, particularly those who are Black, Indigenous or racialized, may be subject to punitive child removal by child welfare for drug use regardless of whether or not it had any impact on their parenting. In one estimate, 70 percent of child protection cases involve parental alcohol or drug use (Bramham 2016). Most child protection agencies report that they do not rely solely on drug tests to determine whether or not children should be removed, but would need further evidence that parenting had been compromised. However, individual lawyers who take child welfare cases and organizations such as the Family Lawyers Association told an Attorney General investigator that drug tests using hair samples were "highly relied on," a "material factor in the outcome" of cases and were "a significant factor in deciding whether children were returned to their parents, both at case conferences and at trial" (Ontario Ministry of the Attorney General 2015: para 26 and 27, henceforth Ontario Ministry 2015). This suggests race, more than any actual demonstrable risk opposed to a child, determines not only whether or not Black women will be forced to undergo drug testing, but additionally that a positive drug test could result in the temporary or permanent loss of children.

This injustice is compounded by the fact that Motherisk — the private company responsible for the drug tests on mothers and young children that were used by child welfare agencies in child removal cases across the country until 2015 — was exposed for relying on faulty technology and a lack of oversight that led to a significant rate of false positives (Mendleson 2015). This meant that evidence of drugs or alcohol was found in hair samples where none may have been consumed and that, in other cases, the amount of substances used may have been grossly overestimated. While tens of thousands of samples were taken and tested between 2005 and 2015, the results were found by the Ontario Attorney General to be "neither accurate nor reliable" (Ontario Ministry 2015: para 45). The drug tests were found to have had a "black hair bias," which meant that persons with black hair may demonstrate concentrations of drugs up to ten times higher than those found in other hair colours (Bramham 2016).

The fact that Black women are more likely to have black hair than white women, compounded with the stigmatization and surveillance of Black women by social services, suggests that Black (and Indigenous) women are likely to have made up a significant over-representation of those who lost their young babies or children due to faulty drug testing. Whether or not this will be addressed or remedied is an ongoing question; possible re-openings of many apprehension cases that involved Motherisk are currently being considered by some provinces and rejected by others (Donkin 2016). The moral implications of this widely under-reported, under-challenged injustice are far-reaching and illustrative of an overall climate of state negligence toward poor Indigenous and Black women in Canada.

While there is a clear and enormous injustice faced by Black women falsely accused of using drugs during pregnancy or while parenting, the lack of support and castigatory treatment of women who use drugs during pregnancy or while parenting also demonstrate how child welfare agencies are far more punitive than supportive in their functioning. Surveillance and child apprehension continue to be the main solution for mothers and children deemed "at risk." African Nova Scotian researcher Wanda Bernard interviewed numerous poor drug-using Black women who had had their children apprehended by child welfare. Many respondents reported that there were inadequate, nearly nonexistent culturally appropriate services aimed at helping them get their children back (Bernard 2001). As well, many reported a climate of constant threats from child welfare agents. Women had also lost their children for breaking highly stringent conditions, such as having trace amounts of marijuana in their bodies. One woman told Bernard,

I knew that Children's Aid was going to take my daughter, because I saw them take my friend's kids. They made me go for drug testing, and to go for the 28-day program. I did all that … so I could keep my kids. I gave up crack and alcohol, but I didn't think marijuana would hurt me. I used it to take the edge off. But the minute they found traces of it [marijuana] in my urine, they came and took her … They said they had no choice because I was warned and had signed an agreement. (13)

Many drug-using Black mothers in Nova Scotia reported having more support in prison than from their social workers (Bernard 2001). Drug-using Black mothers, as social pariahs, have been both punitively targeted and widely neglected by a system that is nominally committed to supporting their well-being.

This is not to downplay the fact that parental addiction can be harmful to the well-being of children. Instead, it is to demonstrate that a punitive approach is significantly more harmful to family well-being than one of support. An examination of the science of maternal illicit drug use demonstrates that a non-punitive approach, with adequate support including non-judgmental prenatal care and concerted social and economic support, is more effective in minimizing risk than punitive measures (Colten 1980 and Murphy and Rosenbaum 1999 in Boyd 2006: 142; Boyd 1999). Through extensive medical and sociological research, Boyd found that the focus solely on punishing mothers for maternal drug use often creates further family instability. She contrasts this to what is called the "social model of care": non-judgemental social and economic support, which has far more effective health outcomes than surveillance and punishment (Boyd 1999: 133). In extreme situations in which women and their extended families are unable to care for their children, it is clear that some form of intervention is necessary. Yet, the form of intervention is important, as many social factors, particularly poverty, influence health outcomes far more significantly than illicit maternal drug use (Boyd 1999). Too often, child welfare agencies fail women and their children by failing to address the conditions that do not change in their lives, such as extreme poverty or lack of child-rearing support, which are ongoing even when they are "clean." Indeed, poverty is a far more influential factor of harm during pregnancy than is drug use, and the moral panic surrounding drugs serves as a distraction from the systemic inequities of race, class and gender in society that act as the main barriers to the preservation of healthy families (Boyd 2006: 142). Boyd and others continue to advocate for changes in state responses surrounding maternal drug use, and for supportive rather than punitive means of maintaining the health of both marginalized, drug-using women and their children. Though too little data exists to make definitive claims on the realities or the enforcement of maternal drug use specific to Black populations in Canada, it is nonetheless clear that improvements to the support provided to mothers who use or have used drugs, as well as attempts to eradicate maternal poverty, would be enormously helpful to Black women who use drugs, since they make up one of the most highly stigmatized demographics in Canada.

THE VIOLENCE OF LIFE "IN CARE"

While the removal of children is officially labelled as part of child protection, child welfare apprehensions rarely benefit Black youth or Black families. Indeed, the conditions of life "in care" are appalling and frequently have a negative impact on children and youth of any ethnic and racial background. In the province of Ontario, a commission that examined two groups of children who had spent three years in care found that one in five had changed homes more than three times (Contenta, Monsebraaten and Rankin 2014). Almost 70 percent of homeless youth come from state care, either foster homes or group homes (Monsebraaten 2012). A provincial survey conducted in 2014 found that more than half of youth in state care for more than two years had moved between three or more schools since birth, with a significant number of them having changed schools between five and seven times. This explains, in part, why only 44 percent of children in foster care graduate from high school, compared to 81 percent of their peers (Public Safety Canada 2012: 4). Alarmingly, upward of 50 percent of youth in care who are five and older are prescribed behaviour-altering medications (Contenta, Monsebraaten and Rankin 2014). However, while child apprehension is deeply life altering and damaging for a significant number of families of all backgrounds, the structural features of child welfare "result in racially disparate harms to families" (Roberts 2002: 97). Though all poor families are at risk of harm from overzealous child removal, Black (and Indigenous) families are being "systematically demolished" (Roberts 2002: viii).

Beyond the general harms enacted on all poor families by overly punitive and unsupportive child removal, there are distinct racial injustices that are felt by Black youth and children removed from their families — and the Black community as a whole — as a result of the separation of so many families (Roberts 2002). Transracial adoptions that remove Black youth from Black environments and bring them into white homes and communities can be highly damaging. Black youth are separated from their blood families and are not often placed in Black homes. In Toronto, fewer than one in ten Caribbean youth and less than 4 percent of African youth are placed in homes with Black foster parents

(Statistics Canada 2014 in Contenta, Monsebraaten and Rankin 2014). In the 1960s, the National Association of Black Social Workers condemned the transracial adoption of African-American children and youth, calling it a form of cultural genocide (OACAS 2016: 38). Some studies have found that transracial adoptions can be detrimental to Black children and youth. White caregivers, even those who mean well, may reinforce racial stereotypes and are often unequipped to support Black youth with the realities of racialized hostility, isolating them from community-based protection and survival skills. This often results in feelings of anxiety, self-hate and despair for the adopted children (Chipungu and Bent-Goodley 2004 in OACAS 2016: 39).

Separation from their culture affects Black youth's sense of belonging and fosters feelings of isolation and alienation, particularly in the current educational and cultural context that erases or leaves out Black culture and history. As stressed by the African Canadian Legal Clinic,

> Children of African descent learn about their identity from within the home and community. African Canadian children that are removed from their homes, schools, religious institutions, friends, and families are thus disengaged from their cultural background and denied the opportunity for optimal development and functioning. (ACLC 2012: 12)

In a racially hostile society, cultural knowledge is crucial for the development of self worth and community. Black children in care often do not receive the relevant cultural education at home. This constitutes a violent form of cultural destruction that puts itself squarely in the lineage of the violent history of linguistic and cultural destruction experienced by those Black communities who were subjected to centuries of slavery. Removing Black children from Black communities is a form of racial violence that can cause psychological and emotional harm. In the words of one Black youth in the care system, "I've lost my culture. I don't know anything about my Black culture because I've only been in White homes" (OACAS 2016: 68).

Beyond isolation and cultural alienation, Black youth who are apprehended and placed in state care are subjected to racially discriminatory treatment. Many have reported differential treatment in foster homes, as well as being surveilled and viewed with suspicion at group homes (Clarke 2010). Black youth have reported that they experience significantly more disciplining than white youth for comparable actions, and are far more likely to be criminalized as a result (OACAS 2016: 76).

All youth in care are far more likely to be involved in the criminal justice system. In a study conducted by the Office of Child and Family Service Advocacy, it was found that almost half of youth in detention reported a history of involvement with child welfare (2007 in Public Safety Canada 2012). Another study focused particularly on Black male youth found that child welfare involvement was associated with "high-rate, chronic offending" (Directors of Child Welfare Committee 2004 in Public Safety Canada 2012: 3). In the context of the high rate of profiling of Black youth in public space, the likelihood of Black youth being criminalized once they are removed from their families is heightened. For LGBTQI* Black youth, this is further accentuated. For those experiencing hostility at home, CAS can be yet another place that they experience gendered, racial and homophobic discrimination (OACAS 2016: 83). American data suggests that youth in care and shelters experience "harassment, discomfort, insensitivity, rejection, and feelings of isolation," while also being far more likely than heterosexual and cisgender youth to have lived in care. Further, they experience higher rates of contact with the criminal justice system (Dank et al. 2015).

The cost of keeping one child in state care for a year comes up to approximately $60,000 — more than double the average annual income of most Black families, and likely far more than the price of investing in culturally appropriate parenting classes and housing support, for example (OACAS 2016: 83). While poor Black families are often held to impossible standards if they wish to keep their families intact, Black children who are taken into state "care" are only exposed to a heightened vulnerability to psychological and emotional harms, and are funnelled toward future criminalization.

CONCLUSION

Though child apprehension is not officially intended to be punitive, the placement of a Black child or adolescent in state care is often disastrous for the youth, their family and Black communities as a whole. The child welfare system remains "a state-run program that disrupts, restructures, and polices Black families" (Roberts 2002: viii). Whether as "wards of the state," in foster care or in adoptive homes, Black youth are made to suffer enormously by a society mired in prejudice and structural racism that holds little regard for their lives and safety.

Despite enormous institutional barriers toward addressing the injustices of the Canadian child welfare system, Black communities across the country have invested enormous amounts of energy toward changing the conditions faced by Black families and fighting for safety and dignity in the treatment of Black children and youth. The Nova Scotia Association of Black Social Workers has created programs to help Black foster children in white homes learn about their culture and background (Bernard and Bernard 2002). Black social workers in Montréal, as well, have mobilized both to document and address anti-Black racism in the welfare system (Rambally 1995), and long-standing Black community centres like Montréal's Côte-des-Neiges Black Community Association run support programs to provide community-based support for Black families. Today, many within the Black community continue to advocate for Black-run child welfare offices. Others contend that Black communities would be better served by an agency that focuses on reducing involvement with the child welfare system and supporting the well-being of Black children, youth and families more broadly instead (OACAS 2016: 84).

Trauma, poor education outcomes and poor life outcomes are experienced by youth of all backgrounds in state care (OACAS 2016: 83), and it is clear that child welfare requires significant institutional changes toward the actual protection of all poor families and children needing support. However, child welfare agencies have, since their inception, further entrenched white supremacy by destroying, on a large scale, the familial and communal networks of Black and Indigenous people. They have helped to establish a system of widespread surveillance, punishment and criminalization of Black families more broadly. Because of this, nothing short of a radical transformation of the institution — grounded in principles of economic and racial justice — is likely to reverse the trend of family dislocation and provide redress for the countless Black youth whose futures have been constricted, or even destroyed, by the child welfare system.

CHAPTER EIGHT

THE (MIS)EDUCATION OF BLACK YOUTH

Anti-Blackness in the school system

Schools act as carceral spaces that familiarize Black children with the processes of pathologization and criminalization. (Black's Lives Matter Toronto "Freedom School" n.d.)

A large number of African Canadian students are receiving an education that is separate and unequal. (African Canadian Legal Clinic 2012: 21)

ON SEPTEMBER 30, 2016, THE MOTHER of a Black first grade student missed several calls from her daughter's school in Mississauga, a suburb of Toronto. When she called back, a school official passed the phone to a police officer, who informed her that her six-year-old daughter had been placed in handcuffs. Upon arriving at the school, the mother learned that the police had been called in by school staff because her daughter had been reportedly acting in a violent manner. The two police officers had handcuffed the girl — who weighed a total of forty-eight pounds and was unarmed — by attaching her hands and her feet together at the wrists and ankles. While the girl's mother said that her daughter had been treated like a "dog" or a "monster" and not a human child (*Toronto Star* February 6, 2017), Peel Regional Police spokesperson Sergeant Josh Colley defended the fact that a young Black child had been handcuffed by stating that it had been done for "the safety of other students and ultimately the child" (Cheung and Sienkiewicz 2017). School officials issued no immediate apology, and Sgt. Colley told the media that it was "disgusting" that this behaviour could be construed as racist. The family's lawyer, however, alongside the African Canadian Legal Clinic, went on to file complaints against both the school and the police for anti-Black racism (Westoll 2017).

It is difficult to imagine how any child weighing forty-eight pounds could be thought to pose such a danger to anyone, let alone in the presence of school officials and two police officers. Only by attending to the ongoing governing power of anti-Blackness can we make sense of how two armed men could decide to handcuff an unarmed child, likely one-quarter of their size, in the name of "safety." What this incident illustrates is that, in the eyes of white society and state institutions, Black children are not conceived of as children at all, and are attributed with supernatural, dangerous abilities far beyond their age, size and physical capabilities. The way that Black children and youth are treated — and the way that their suffering is largely ignored or unseen — makes clear that anti-Blackness over-determines their experiences within the education system and beyond.

Education is one of the bedrocks of Canadian society. Legislated as "a fundamental social good," it is intended to provide both socialization and opportunities to develop youth's minds and relationships, and to help them build their futures (OHRC 2003: 18). This is largely rhetorical; schools continue to be underfunded and under-resourced, and teachers are widely devalued and poorly compensated. Nonetheless, publicly funded education is generally understood as creating options and facilitating advancement in society. For many Black students, though, schools are places where they experience degradation, harm and psychological violence (Codjoe 2001). Even as education environments continue to under-serve many communities from different backgrounds, there are unique dimensions to the experiences of Black youth, who experience schools as carceral places characterized by neglect, heightened surveillance and arbitrary and often extreme punishment for any perceived disobedience (Wun 2015; Salole and Abdulle 2015). Schools in Canada remain permeated with anti-Blackness. Because Black youth are so often not seen or treated *as children*, schools too often become their first encounter with the organized and systemic devaluation of Blackness present in society at large.

THE EVACUATION OF BLACK CHILDREN
FROM THE CONSTRUCTION OF "INNOCENCE"

In order to fully grasp the current treatment of Black youth and children across Canadian institutions, it's necessary to look at how Black childhood has been historically represented (and denied), both by the state and more broadly. The state's negation of Black childhood innocence has been an important part of the maintenance of white supremacy. In Canadian society, and Western society more broadly, since the end of the nineteenth century, children have been construed as innocent, vulnerable and in need of the state's protection. The concern for children's welfare was correlated to the state's focus on build- ing the nation, accompanied by "an emerging belief that children represented the future of the young dominion, and their healthy growth and development became inextricably linked to the welfare of Canadian society" (Schumaker 2012: 26). As the symbol of society's future, young persons were seen as requir- ing and deserving protection, guidance and societal investment. However, the purported innocence of children, and thus the worthiness of ensuring their secu- rity and protection, was largely determined by their race. Youthful innocence, according to historian Robin Bernstein, was raced white (Bernstein 2011: 5).

Many children have always been formally or informally excluded from this and have fallen outside of those seen as vulnerable and deserving of safety. While the protection of (white) children was, in many ways, more ideological than actual — many poor white children remained vulnerable to a multiplicity of harms — Black children have, *as a group*, been excluded from even the very conception of childhood purity or vulnerability. That Black and Indigenous children were considered property in earlier Canadian history testifies to the delineations of sanctified childhood. At the turn of the twentieth century, white toddlers were associated with attributes such as purity, innocence and fragility, qualities denied to Black and Indigenous children (Lafferty 2013: 72). The preservation of white childhood innocence has often taken place at the expense of the safety and security of Black children. In Nova Scotia, the vulnerability of white children was invoked to push forward the exclusion of Black children from many public and church-based institutions: "For members of the white community, segregation of the black child was thus a natural and logical part of child saving, just as was maintaining religious separation" (Lafferty 2013: 72). Innocent (white) childhood could be protected, in part, by maintaining distance from the corrupting force of "uncivilized" and immoral Black children.

Their innocence negated, Black children were therefore denied the pro- tections that would safeguard it. The new articulation of (white) childhood innocence meant that while white children were construed as requiring nurturing and protection, Black children were thought to be impervious to suffering; this thinking was a relic of an era in which enslaved children were not, as a whole, considered "children." Bernstein states, "pain, and the alleged ability or inability to feel it, functioned in the mid-nineteenth century as a wedge that split white and black childhood into distinct trajectories" (Bernstein 2011: 20). This belief has ramifications to this day; though segregation is formally over, the de-sanctification of Black childhood is ongoing.

Today, Black children and youth remain outside the construction of innocence, as well as that of childhood itself, and the suffering that they are exposed to is frequently erased or negated. In a large-scale study of American police officers' perceptions of Black children, psychologists found that racially motivated dehumanization plays a significant role in the designation of innocence. To use their words,

> As the perception of innocence is a central protection afforded to children … it follows that this social consideration may not be given to the children of dehumanized groups … in equal measure as they are given to their peers … In this context, dehumanization serves to change the meaning of the category "children." (Goff et al. 2014: 527)

In other words, Black children are still not considered to really be children. The authors found that once Black children reached the age of ten, they were perceived as "significantly older and less innocent than other children of any age group" (527). Childhood itself takes on a different meaning depending on race, and the category of "innocent youth" continues to be raced white. This has substantial and harmful effects: "The evidence shows that perceptions of the essential nature of children can be affected by race, and for Black children, this can mean they lose the protection afforded by assumed childhood innocence well before they become adults" (American Psychological Association 2014). Not only are Black children and youth denied the protections that accompany presumptions of innocence and vulnerability, but in the present, they are also still imbued with the quality of danger. Black youth, like Black adults, are frequently attributed with "superhuman" capabilities, believed (by whites) to possess supernatural qualities that transcend the laws of nature and to have a decreased ability to experience pain (Hoffman, Trawalter and Waytz 2015).

There are numerous publicized cases that illustrate the impact that dominant conceptions of Black (non-) children can have. One must only look at the killings of Tamir Rice or Aiyana Jones, Black children killed by police in the United

States. In Canada, a similar picture emerges. The above-cited handcuffing of the six-year-old Black girl in her school is only one example of how Black youth are widely treated as if they are threatening and possibly dangerous even to adults. A staff official working in an Ontario youth penal institution reported that staff members became so concerned when Black youths would socialize together that multiple staff meetings had to be called to address widespread fears that the Black youth were organizing a riot (Commission on Systemic Racism in the Ontario Criminal Justice System 1994: 22). Neither did their youth protect two Black children from having the car they were inside of pepper-sprayed in 2015. In this incident, two girls aged seven and ten were treated in the hospital after their father was pepper-sprayed by the police while seated in front of them in a car. He and his wife had described the incident to the press as a traffic stop that was random, non-violent, non-criminal and unwarranted (CTV News December 22, 2015). Black children and youth are frequently exposed to traumatic and violent state actions, with little regard to their vulnerability, because their suffering is not conceived of as suffering. Today, it remains the case that Black youth of all genders, sexual identities and abilities are forced to suffer a severe punishment for merely existing in an anti-Black society.

Though these examples make visible how police and corrections staff consciously or unconsciously dehumanize Black youth, this fundamental disregard for young Black lives is endemic across state institutions. Black children are often the receptacles of the negative projections of a society mired in the fear of Black bodies. Societal hostility is often woven into everyday life for young Black persons; everywhere they go, they encounter psychological violence in terms of systemic disregard, surveillance, suspicion and the presumption of guilt. The demonization of Black youth and children is visible in the hostility, surveillance, punishment and neglect in the fabric of the education system.

ABANDONMENT AND CAPTIVITY: EDUCATION POLICY AS A TOOL TOWARD WHITE SUPREMACY

Historically, Canada's public education system has been an explicit tool toward the advancement of white supremacy, and public schools have been a site of both abandonment and captivity for Black youth. The segregated schooling of Black children and the explicit disinvestment in the education of Black youth in most parts of Canada (excluding Québec) was "a direct by-product of the system of chattel slavery" and was used to strip African people of their humanity and turn them into vehicles of cheap labour (Hamilton 2011: 98). In the nineteenth century, Black children, it was believed, would have a morally corrupting influence on white children (K. McLaren 2008: 7). In the words of an Ontario school trustee, it was better to "cut their children's heads off and throw them into the ditch" than "have them go to school with niggers" (in Walker 2010: 36). The practice of segregated and unequal schooling, while not practised in all provinces, lasted well into the late twentieth century. Although the Supreme Court in the United States outlawed segregation in schools in 1954, the practice continued in Nova Scotia and Ontario until much later, and the last segregated school in Canada did not close until 1983 (Hamilton 2011: 101). Even in Nova Scotia's "integrated schools," Black students had to use separate entrances, exits and washrooms throughout the 1950s and 1960s (BLAC 1994: 26).

Slavery, followed by centuries of segregation in the school system in many provinces, left an indelible legacy of racism in publicly funded Canadian education institutions, visible in a lasting inequity between Black and white educations in Canada. In Nova Scotia, upon integration, many Black schools were defunded and closed. Black students had to be bussed long distances to attend white schools, thus bearing the entire burden of integration (BLAC 1994: 51). In Nova Scotia in 1969, only 3 percent of Black students graduated from high school and only 1 percent of the graduates attended university (Pratt 1972 in Bombay and Hewitt 2015: 31). A survey conducted in 1962 by the Institute of Public Affairs in Nova Scotia found that most Black adults had education levels between grades four and nine (in BLAC 1994). The researchers identified several contributing factors to these lower levels of schooling, such as the harassment of Black students, poverty, derogatory comments by teachers affirming that Black students stayed in lower grades and were likely to fail, the low number of Black teachers and the absence of Black history in the curriculum (BLAC 1994: 27).

That education was a tool of white supremacy is visible, as well, in the legacy of settler colonialism. The violent dehumanization, forced assimilation and genocide enacted en masse on Indigenous children by means of residential schools from 1883 until the late 1990s cannot be seen as separate from the development of publicly funded education, and must be understood as foundational toward the development of white supremacy. Between 1867 and 1912, half of the children in residential schools died, with an average of 42 percent of the pupils dying per year (Churchill 2004 in Thobani 2007: 120). Though officially called "schools," the Truth and Reconciliation Commission has noted that residential schools were educational in name only and, in truth, functioned as part of a violent, "coherent policy to eliminate Aboriginal people as distinct peoples and to assimilate them into the Canadian mainstream against their will" (TRC 2015: 3). At least 150,000 Indigenous children were forced into these schools, which were rife with state-sanctioned acts of monstrous violence including continuous sexual, physical and emotional abuse; this abuse was enacted by state agents as cogs in a larger genocidal attempt to eradicate Indigenous culture and, indeed, the very survival of Indigenous persons (TRC 2015: 105). Generations of stolen children experienced trauma so severe that it endangered the physical and mental health of not only those who attended residential schools, but also their children and grandchildren as well (TRC 2015). Indigenous children continue to face significant dehumanization, measurable by the particularly acute disinvestment in their success and well-being compared to other children: only one in four graduate high school, and federal funding for on-reserve schools is 40 percent less than for other children, and 70 percent less for on-reserve high schools (Matthew 2000 in Blackstock 2011). The living legacies of slavery and colonization persist today in the (mis)education of Black and Indigenous children and youth that continues to expose education institutions as fundamentally white supremacist institutions.

"SECOND GENERATION SEGREGATION": STREAMING BLACK STUDENTS

Though education is seen as a "public good" and is allegedly race-neutral, informal practices throughout the school systems in Canada continue to stream students based on race. Of course, class has also played a significant role in education inequalities for youth of all backgrounds, and wealth disparities reproduce unequal outcomes between children of wealthy and poor families as well (Canadian Council on Learning 2006). However, while race and class are inextricably linked — Black families being among the poorest in Canada — it would be a mistake to reduce the streaming of Black youth and children to an issue of class. While systemic barriers resulting from poverty impact youth of all racial backgrounds, Black youth face unique and acute disadvantages because of long-standing associations linking Blackness to a lack of intelligence, and inferiority more generally.

Black youth continue to be disproportionately streamed into lower education tracks as a result of both individual prejudice and systemic factors. Racial stereotypes held by teachers play a significant role in the streaming of Black students (Codjoe 2001; Dei et al. 1997). Instructors continue to hold racial stereotypes, or "assumptions of separate racialised groups possessing distinct mental and physical abilities," that affect their interactions with Black youth (Small 1994: 105 in Codjoe 2001: 354). For example, Black students in

Alberta have expressed that instructors give African-descended students the "silent treatment" or try to dissuade them from higher education by expressing their uncertainty, for example, that "a Black could study to become a doctor" (Codjoe 2001: 350, 354). This treatment, widespread in many Canadian cities, has an important role in the experiences and development of Black students and their education.

According to a survey of Black students' needs, teacher expectations play a significant role in the academic engagement of Black students (Livingstone 2010: 12). Black youth in major cities across the country have consistently named their teachers' low expectations as a major factor when it comes to their overall engagement. They report that they are pressured into vocational training or into adult education, that they are not encouraged to finish on the regular academic track and that they are steered away from challenging courses (Livingstone 2010: 2; BLAC 1994: 42; Dei et al. 1997). To use the words of a Black student, Black youth often feel their presence is unwanted: "they don't care about Black students. They don't care if you are there or not" (BLAC 1994: 63). In a 2006 census survey, only 54 percent of Black youth reported that they felt supported by teachers (Rankin, Rushowy and Brown 2013). This lack of support affects more than academic achievement; the Ontario Human Rights Commission states that it is often "in relation to their teachers that children begin to develop a perception of themselves and of the world around them" (OHRC 2003: 18). Discriminatory treatment at this young age, then, can enact lasting damage on development.

When they are being streamed into lower track education programs, Black students are disproportionately assigned to learning platforms that have inadequate resources. In Québec, students with Caribbean backgrounds are three times more likely to be identified as SHSMLD (students with handicaps, social maladjustments or learning difficulties) and subsequently placed in separate classes for "at risk" students. This designation is decided by school officials, a practice that has been associated with racial profiling as it gives "substantial discretionary power to school personnel in terms of deciding which students it should be applied to" (CDPDJ 2011: 67). Similarly, Caribbean and other racialized students are frequently placed in closed "welcoming classes" for new immigrants, a practice that the CDPDJ found to be ill-suited and deficient to meeting their students' needs, causing delays in transitioning students into regular classes. In one instance, a Haitian student in elementary school was placed in a welcoming class solely because he was Haitian, without any other evaluation. A judge found him to have been a victim of racial profiling (*Mondestin v.*

Commission scolaire de la Pointe-de-l'Île 2010 in CDPDJ 2011: 68–72). Following streaming in high school, Black students are then frequently directed, or pushed, into the adult sector to receive their high school diplomas (CDPDJ 2011: 74).

Streaming has been documented in several other Canadian cities. In Halifax, Black students are massively over-represented in what are called "individual program plans" (IPPS). In 2015, the results of a random sample taken of students placed in IPPs in the Halifax Regional School Board exposed that almost half of the IPP students were Black (Ryan 2016). The phenomenon has also been documented in Toronto (Rushowy 2015), where Black students make up 13 percent of the student body but only 3 percent of those labelled "gifted," compared to white students, who are one-third of the student population but more than half of those labelled "gifted" (Maharaj 2014).

The informal yet demonstrable practice of streaming students according to race has been aptly coined "second generation segregation" because of the ongoing inequities that it perpetuates (Mickelson 2007). Streaming students into different tracks is demonstrably inequitable, as students in higher tracks are generally afforded more resources as well as a wider variety of teaching methods (BLAC 1994: 42). The practice cements inequalities rather than challenging them (Cameron and Hamlin 2015; Maharaj 2014). This disinvestment in Black youth has definite effects on their future opportunities as well as on their own sense of self-worth. The privileging of the lives and worthiness of white students demonstrates the ongoing societal devaluation of Black childhood. The racially differential treatment experienced by Black youth also demonstrates a concerted lack of empathy for the feelings and dignity of Black students on the part of instructors.

In addition to experiencing a lack of support and active streaming into lower tracks of education opportunities, Black students contend with erasure, which is itself arguably a form of violence. Both invisibility within curriculums and the predominantly white demographic make-up of educators continue to negatively affect Black students. Besides one Africentric school established in Toronto after much community agitating (Brown 2014) and the newly available African-Canadian studies material in Nova Scotian high schools (Hamilton 2011: 107), most education institutions lack content highlighting Canada's history of slavery and segregation, and overlook the history of Black institutions and Black resilience more largely (BLAC 1994; CDPDJ 2011; Livingstone 2010; Henry 1993). Not only are Black students not seeing themselves reflected and celebrated in the curriculums, but the lack of racial representation in school staff is also significant. Québec, for example, continuously misses the mark of its already too-low targets for racial diversity in the makeup of educators (CDPDJ 2011). Being taught by largely white instructors and, therefore, being denied positive Black role models within institutions of learning only further cements the lower status of Black students.

SCHOOL DISCIPLINE POLICIES, RACIALIZED SURVEILLANCE AND PUNISHMENT

Black students are not only treated as if they are inferior, but they are also frequently treated as if they are a threat inside of education settings. The presence of Black children and youth remains unwelcome and undesirable in many public schools, and their movements are closely monitored and subject to correction. While racism and harassment from other students has long played a vital role in making Black youth and children feel unwanted in many Canadian public schools (Codjoe 2001), school disciplinary policies have helped to cement the undesirability of Black students that is apparent within the education system. Black youth face heightened surveillance and disciplinary measures at massively disproportionate rates compared to their white peers.

Over the years, schools have become an increasingly carceral experience for Black, Indigenous and other racialized students, in terms of both the general environment and disciplinary practice. In addition to experiencing overtly racist treatment from teachers (Livingstone 2010: 18), Black students have likened their treatment by school officials to their experiences with the police (CDPDJ 2011). Montréal-based Black youth frequently report being treated by teachers as if they are in a gang solely because of their skin colour. School and security staff often dissuade them from gathering in groups and subject them to heightened surveillance and frequent identity checks (Livingstone 2010; CDPDJ 2011). In sum, Black youth are often treated as suspects instead of as the children they are, in the very place where children get socialized and educated. Experiencing this typecasting and demonization is deeply harmful to Black youth who are still in their formative years. The feelings of exclusion and pain cause emotional harm and limit Black students' ability to thrive in the public education setting (Wong, Eccles and Sameroff 2003 in Livingstone 2010: 21). Formal and informal school discipline policies are forms of policing and criminalizing of Black children and youth that position them as "captive objects" within schools (Wun 2015).

The assumption that Black youth are less innocent than white youth, and that their mere presence harbours danger, colours disciplinary practices in public schools across the country. While repressive school practices affect all youth, racialized youth are most heavily targeted. Handled by school officials as if they are "threatening" (CDPDJ 2011: 59), Black students are subjected to much more extreme disciplinary measures than white students. In a school in Durham, Ontario, an investigation by the provincial Human Rights Commission found that Black students in the Ontario school system were nearly eight times more likely to face discipline than white students (Szekely and Pessian 2015b).

Suspension and expulsion play an important role in banishing Black youth from schools, particularly for young Black males. Across many Canadian cities, youth of African descent are suspended or expelled at disproportionately high rates. In schools, as elsewhere in society, race plays an important role in the administration of punishment, even in the case of similar offences (Ferguson 2000, Morris 2005 and Skiba et al. 2002 in Morris and Perry 2016). Systemic racism and discrimination, as opposed to a propensity for "bad behaviour," explain the significant differences in the ways that Black and white students are disciplined.

In Toronto, between 2011–2012 and 2015–2016, almost half of the students expelled from the Toronto District School Board were Black, and only 10 percent of those expelled were white students (Naccarato 2017). Similarly, during the 2006–2007 school year, Black students in Toronto were three times more likely to be suspended than white students (Rankin, Rushowy and Brown 2013). Age doesn't seem to be a protective factor when it comes to this trend. Younger Black students have not been exempt from punitive treatment either, quite the opposite. In the same year, nearly half of all suspensions and 14 percent of expulsions in Toronto were doled out to elementary school students (Rankin and Contenta 2009c). The rates remain particularly high for younger Black students in Toronto. They represented 15 percent of the seventh- and eighth-grade student body, but nearly 40 percent of suspensions. Among this population, one in seven Black students had been suspended at least once, compared to one in twenty white students (Rankin, Rushowy and Brown 2013).

In Halifax, during the 2015–2016 school year, Black students made up 8 percent of the student body but 22.5 percent of total suspensions (Ryan 2016). The rate of suspensions has changed a little since the 1980s, and has been protested as an injustice by the Black community dating back at least decades (BLAC 1994). A similar picture emerges in the province of Québec, where Black and other racialized students also face disproportionate rates of suspension and expulsion. The CDPDJ found that Black students, particularly Haitians, were frequently suspended and expelled in a discriminatory fashion for minor infractions, such as being late. The commission stated that they were subjected to a "zero tolerance" framework that other students did not face (2011). This exemplifies perfectly the functioning of racialized punishment: actions that result in a minor sanction when committed by a white youth are punished by disproportionately extreme measures when committed by a Black child or youth. Indeed, despite favourable comparisons to the United States that are frequently drawn throughout popular culture, the suspension rates of Black youth in many Canadian schools are comparable to those found in the United States; according to the United States Department of Education, Black students are suspended at a rate three times higher than white students (in Wong 2016).

These expulsions fuel a cycle of miseducation and abandonment. Special schools for expelled students are disproportionately attended by Black students (ACLC 2012; Rankin and Contenta 2009a and 2009b; CDPDJ 2011). These schools have been criticized for offering too few hours and classes for students to be able to fulfill the requirements for passing all of their courses (ACLC 2012; Rankin and Contenta 2009b), effectively stunting their ability to further their studies or even stay engaged in the education system.

The heightened discipline directed at Black youth that creates a hostile learning environment extends beyond the treatment of Black students into the entire Black family. Black parents, as well, frequently suffer from discriminatory treatment and from the encroachment of policing in education institutions. This was seen most recently when Nancy Elgie, an eighty-two-year-old white school board trustee, was forced to resign after calling a Black mother named Charline Grant a "nigger" at the close of a York school board meeting in November 2016 (Price 2017). A lawyer serving the Black community in Toronto reported that parents, particularly Black women, are often met with hostility and aggression:

> The parents are absolutely targeted. The kids will get slapped with a suspension, but the parents will get do-not-trespass notices and be themselves subject to fairly aggressive measures ... [The] underlying racist stereotyping by principals and teachers ... crystallizes with the Black mother. All we have is someone trying to talk about what is happening. But it is immediately interpreted as violent, hysterical and threatening. (in Bhattacharjee 2003: 41)

Black parents end up on the receiving end of trespassing orders and have been reported to the Children's Aid Society for "offences" that have included, for example, challenging school officials on whether a child needs medication for attention deficit disorder (Bhattacharjee 2003: 41).

Even as Black students are targeted with disproportionate disciplinary measures, the same concerted attention is not necessarily granted toward protecting them from the often extreme and daily racism that many Black youth have reported experiencing from their peers (Codjoe 2001). A nine-year-old Nova Scotian Black girl told acclaimed researcher Dr. Wanda Bernard that she often skipped school because of unchecked racism from her peers: "They make me hate myself" (Bernard in Noble-Hearle 2014). In one case in 2017, Adrienne Charles, the mother of two elementary-school-aged Black children in Montréal, was forced to go to the media in addition to filing complaints against the school because school officials refused to take concerted action to address the virulent racism from white students that her sons experienced (Perron 2017). While Black youth and children face heightened surveillance and extremely limited tolerance for even minor disobedience, the racist hostility of white students appears to be granted far more leniency. School discipline policies both place Black youth under constant surveillance and render "the complexities of their lives, pain, and suffering" — the result of structural, institutional and interpersonal racism — invisible (Wun 2015: 174).

THE SCHOOL-TO-PRISON PIPELINE

While the informal school environment is itself highly carceral for Black youth, formal surveillance and criminalization also occur within public schooling. School disciplinary policies work in conjunction with the racialized surveillance of Black youth across multiple institutions that "begins in school and is directly connected to practices that continue outside of schools" (Meiners 2009 in Salole and Abdulle 2015: 129). Not only do disciplinary policies mimic youth's treatment by law enforcement officers, but schools also expose youth to further encounters with police or security guards. In Québec, the task of the surveillance and discipline of (disproportionately Black) students is increasingly contracted out to private security firms (CDPDJ 2011). In Toronto, mandated police presence in schools has made Black and other racialized youth increasingly vulnerable to criminalization. Further, even in the absence of mandated police presence, police are frequently called into Toronto schools, and will often handcuff Black youth for relatively minor infractions (Bhattacharjee 2003: 58). The punitive and carceral atmosphere of schools was cemented in 2008 when, in addition to heightening surveillance policies, including cameras at school, lockdown policies and hall monitors, the School Resource Officer (SRO) program was launched within the Toronto District School Board and twenty-nine uniformed police officers were placed inside of Toronto schools

(Salole and Abdulle 2015: 131). This was contested by many parents, teachers and community members as contributing to a hostile environment for marginalized students. Following years of these policies, a survey of largely Black, school-aged youth in Toronto found that youth reported feeling that they were constantly under surveillance while at school (Salole and Abdulle 2015: 143).

Beyond the increasingly prison-like atmosphere of many public schools, disciplinary policies in schools, particularly suspensions and expulsions, contribute directly to the grossly disproportionate encounters between Black youth and the criminal justice system. Suspensions and expulsions have extremely damaging effects on all youth and can be life changing. A recent American study found that school discipline, particularly suspension, leads to poorer academic achievement in Black youth and "is a major source of the racial achievement gap and educational reproduction of inequality" (Morris and Perry 2016; CDPDJ 2011). Yet, beyond inequality, expulsion and suspension correlates quite directly with their likelihood to end up behind bars. This dynamic has been coined the "school to prison pipeline." Black legal scholar Kimberlé Crenshaw explains, "It is well-established in the research literature and by educational advocates that there is a link between the use of punitive disciplinary measures and subsequent patterns of criminal supervision and incarceration" (Crenshaw 2015: 5). Though it takes place only in schools, the concept of the school-to-prison pipeline encapsulates the multiple state agencies that lead to students being pushed out of school and to their incarceration. This is why Michelle Alexander defines the school-to-prison pipeline as the numerous institutional forces that "collectively under-educate and over-incarcerate students of colour at disparate rates" (2012: 104).

This is not only an American phenomenon. The link between school discipline, system involvement and incarceration is a Canadian reality as well (Salole and Abdulle 2015). The African Canadian Legal Clinic has found that school officials often contact the police to instigate criminal charges against Black youth for minor infractions and they are then given court conditions that prevent them from coming near their school (ACLC 2012). Students who are suspended and expelled are also more frequently found in public spaces. Black students in public spaces face extremely high rates of police surveillance and harassment, which often lead to arrest. Black students have substantially higher rates of arrests than their white peers (Charest 2009; Bernard and McAll 2010; CDPDJ 2011). In 2009, a *Toronto Star* analysis found that the Toronto schools that had the highest suspension rates tended to be in parts of the city that also had the highest rates of provincial incarceration (*Toronto Star* 2009 in

ACLC: 2012). It is essential to locate some of the responsibility for the massive incarceration of Black youth within the school system.

PUSHED OUT OF SCHOOL: FUGITIVITY AND RESISTANCE

White-run public schools largely remain a site of racialized violence for many marginalized students. Black youth are exposed to a "hostile environment" in which they undergo "psychological damage, emotional pain, and ... personal humiliation" due to racially discriminatory treatment (Codjoe 2001: 349, 351) by those tasked with their education. For this reason, many youth disengage from school entirely. While it is frequently referred to as "dropping out," this language disguises the structural racism both inside and outside of the education system that impacts Black children's ability to remain in school. It presumes an individual problem found in these Black boys and girls, while erasing the contextual factors within school and society that contribute to this phenomenon (Dei et al. 1997). For this reason, "dropping out" or "low academic achievement" can more accurately be described as the result of a concerted "push-out." The concept of the "push-out" has become an important reframing of the crisis by Black activists and researchers alike: Black youth are pushed out by various school structures and policies that neglect their needs, single them out and cause them to disengage (Dei et al. 1997; Crenshaw 2015).

Indeed, Black students continue to be pushed out of school at significant rates. While the rate of high school completion rose in the past decade and the racial gap narrowed, Black students continue to have a higher drop-out rate than the rest of the population (McAndrew, Ledent and Ait-Said 2005 and Torczyner 2010 in Livingstone 2010; Dei et al. 1997). Data from the Toronto school board found that, overall, Black students had the lowest graduation rate of any group — 65 percent for the 2006 to 2011 cohort (Szekely and Pessian 2015b). A similar picture emerges in Québec, where nearly half of the province's Black students continue to drop out of high school. In 2004, a study demonstrated that a group of Black students in Québec who started high school between 1994 and 1996 had a 51.8 percent graduation rate, compared to 69 percent for the population as a whole (McAndrew and Ledent 2004 in Hampton 2010: 106). The push-out of Black youth, while impacting all youth of African descent in important ways, is nonetheless not experienced identically by all Black students.

Public discussions about racial inequality in schools tend to focus more on the experience of Black boys. Even when gender is not specified, it is the young, Black, cisgender boy who is often pictured when the topic of systemic racism in the education system is raised. This attention is warranted because it is true that, empirically, both in the United States and in Canada, Black boys represent the highest percentages of drop-outs, suspensions and expulsions (Crenshaw 2015; Ryan 2016). Yet, a more complex story emerges when looking at these trends from an intersectional perspective. The experience of school "push-out" takes different forms for those Black youths who are also marginalized by their gender, sexual minority status, (dis)ability and immigration status. Racist violence directed at Black girls may be less visible, but it is not less harmful. Existing research and data "often fail to address the degree to which girls face risks that are both similar to and different from those faced by boys" (Crenshaw 2015: 8). To leave these experiences out risks insulating or invisibilizing the discrimination experienced by Black girls.

Gender remains "a crucial variable in the construction of inequality for Black youth" in Canadian schools (Dei et al. 1997: 102). Like boys, Black girls in Canada have also expressed experiencing school "as a system of domination" (Dei and James 1998:102). Though it appears to be at a lesser rate than Black boys, Black girls are impacted by discriminatory disciplinary practices as well. For example, in 2008, a Black girl attending a Durham area school was arrested in her school by the police and criminally charged for allegedly slapping another student. She denied the allegations and her family subsequently complained to the Ontario Human Rights Tribunal, which found there was indeed a racial disparity in her treatment by the school officials (Szekely and Pessian 2015a and 2015b). In Ontario, two Black female students were suspended from school for "weapon possession" because they had brought nail files to school (Bhattacharjee 2003: 3). A questionnaire given to Black youth of all genders in Calgary, Halifax and Toronto found no difference between them in terms of racialized devaluation experienced by boys and girls. Both reported being treated as if they were "stupid" and identified this as one of their most stressful experiences in the context of their education (James et al. 2010: 94). For Black girls, streaming occurs along the lines of both race and gender: Black girls reported being channelled into both racialized and gendered segments of the labour market and discouraged from taking math and sciences (Dei et al. 1997: 102). While Black culture and contributions are largely absent from the curriculum, what does exist focuses only on the contributions of Black men (Dei et al. 1997). Less visible forms of violence experienced by Black girls at school often go unaddressed and unseen by traditional measures. One American study by critical race scholar Connie Wun found that, while Black girls are subject to comparatively fewer suspensions and expulsions than Black boys, they reported experiencing heightened surveillance and discipline that are more difficult to measure with statistics. They reported that even for the smallest of movements in class, their movements and behaviours were constrained and punished (2015: 183).

Black girls, like Black women, are impacted not only by racialized and gendered criminalization, but also by neglect across state institutions (Ritchie 2012; Wun 2015). Inaction in the case of conflicts between students at school can also be a form of racialized and gendered violence toward Black girls. Though more research is necessary, Black girls report experiencing high levels of sexual harassment at school (Dei et al. 1997: 100) and, in general, face higher rates of sexual assault than white girls (Tanner and Wortley 2002 in Owusu-Bempah and Wortley 2014). These racialized and gendered experiences create unique barriers for Black girls in completing their education (Crenshaw 2015: 27). Indeed, while Black girls remain vulnerable to both heightened surveillance and punishment as well as sexual harassment and violence, their unique needs within the Canadian education system still go too often unaddressed.

Black and other racialized youth who are gender or sexual minorities experience school as a particularly hostile environment. The combination of the school system's policies and inaction or silence surrounding racism, transphobia and homophobia exacerbates the risks of discrimination, violence and abuse for LGBTQI* youth. The school system's status quo indeed creates and upholds the conditions that end up fuelling perhaps the most extreme conditions of a structural "push-out." Gender and sexual minority youth of all racial backgrounds are already pushed out of schools at an enormous rate. A large-scale Canadian study found that up to half of students who were sexual minorities reported having experienced sexual harassment at school. Trans students face appallingly high levels of harassment, including bullying, sexual harassment and violence. Over one-quarter of transgender students reported hearing teachers make transphobic comments on a daily or weekly basis. Almost half of transgender students have skipped school due to feeling unsafe (Taylor and Peter 2011).

Youth of colour who are gender and sexual minorities face particularly high rates of physical harassment and assault at school because of the multiple layers of stigmatization they face (Taylor and Peter 2011). This push-out is particularly violent and dangerous since youth who are gender and sexual minorities, especially those who are racialized or Indigenous, also face the highest rate of homelessness in Canada (Abramovich 2015). For racialized gender and sexual minorities, homelessness vastly increases their chances of being criminalized and incarcerated. This amounts to an even more direct demonstration of the dynamics of the school-to-prison pipeline. The way the Canadian education system functions is far from the sole factor in the extreme hardship, violence and neglect faced by Black youth who are sexual minorities. Yet, exclusion from secure housing and employment, combined with rejection and violence in the education system, puts Black, Indigenous and other racialized sexual minority youth in situations of extreme precarity.

Beyond gender- and sexuality-based oppression, youth with disabilities face enormous challenges in the school system. Youth who are navigating marginalization because of their race while also living with one or many physical or mental disabilities are very vulnerable to multiple forms of systemic discrimination. For one, navigating race and mental health are related in many ways. One reason for this is that racism contributes to mental health issues in racialized communities, particularly the kind of racial discrimination faced by racialized immigrants (Rollock and Gordon 2000 and Ontario Human Rights Commission 2012 in Chan and Chunn 2014: 41). That said, without recognizing this vulnerability, Black youth are disproportionately labelled as "special needs," a term that encompasses students with mental health issues as well as those with linguistic or behavioural challenges (Ryan 2016; CDPDJ 2011).

The intersection of race and disability places Black students labelled as disabled at a heightened risk of being pushed out of school. The Ontario *Safe Schools Act* (2001–2008), which created harsher and more punitive suspension and expulsion policies until it was repealed, resulted in a massive spike of expulsions that impacted Black students and students with disabilities most severely (Bhattacharjee 2003). Though information specifically addressing race, disability and expulsions is not tallied, observers called it "a logical inference" that suspensions and expulsions would "impact even more heavily on Black students in special needs classes" and noted that, "moreover, other factors such as poverty and immigrant/refugee status may further compound the impact" (Bhattacharjee 2003: 50). In one case, it was reported that a fourteen-year-old Black student with an intellectual disability was suspended because his teacher was struck by an object in a classroom that was darkened because of a film screening. The vice principal questioned the student for over an hour before the police were called. Although all charges were dropped, this student's suspension lasted three months (Bhattacharjee 2003: 3) Once out of school and spending more time in public spaces, both Black persons and persons with mental health issues are more likely to be treated with excessive force by police officers as well as being more likely to be arrested and put behind bars (Chan and Chunn 2014: 50). Despite the recent abolition of the *Safe Schools*

Act and "zero tolerance" policies in Ontario, students with disabilities are still vulnerable to being punished for their disability. New "exclusions" permitted by Ontario's *Education Act* allow Ontario principals to remove special needs children from school indefinitely if they do not have the resources to support them. The government has neither set limits nor imposed any tracking of this practice (Robinson 2016).

Black migrant youth who are undocumented continue to be excluded from schools in several Canadian cities. Because of the clandestine nature of living in Canada without papers, it is difficult to examine the experiences of Black and other racialized students who live without legal immigration status and who seek to access the education system. Following years of organizing by migrant justice activists, Vancouver and Toronto have adopted "Don't ask, don't tell" policies as part of efforts aimed at ensuring that all city residents, including people without full immigration status, can access essential services (housing, healthcare, education, social services, emergency services) without fear of being detained or deported. In principle, adopting these policies should mean that non-status students are able to go to school. That said, significant barriers remain. Toronto has since seen incidents in which students without papers were apprehended at school and deported, alongside their families (Community Social Planning Council of Toronto 2008). In the province of Québec, the Ministry of Education has recently granted some leeway toward allowing non-status students to attend school by adopting non-binding guidelines in the spirit of "Don't ask, don't tell." However, since they are non-binding, the ongoing fear of apprehension and deportation means that many non-status children, most of whom are Black and brown, are still unlikely to attend school at all as they continue to be at risk of discovery and removal (Collectif éducation sans frontières 2013).

Despite being exposed to both systemic and individual hostility within the education system, as well as violence from their peers, school officials and teachers beginning at a young age, Black youth continue to apply survival strategies and find ways to navigate exceedingly complex situations. Resistance tactics employed by Black students take many forms, both large and small. Widely acclaimed ethnographer George J. Sefa Dei, who, with his assistants, has conducted ethnographic research on Black students in Ontario, has argued that in the face of acute racial domination, "oppositional behaviours," including adopting unique dress and language styles that conflict with dominant society, are ways in which Black youth subvert the hegemonic norms being imposed upon them in schools (Dei et al. 1997: 25). Further, he has argued that given the experiences of Black youth in public schools, "dropping out and the behaviours associated with 'fading out' of school (e.g., 'truancy,' lack of interest and participation in school, etc.) can be seen as forms of resistance" (1997: 25). This sentiment is echoed in the work of critical education scholar Damien M. Sojoyner, who has argued against pathologizing Black youth who choose to leave hostile and violent school environments, recasting this as akin to "fugitivity" since, in effect, Black youth are fleeing sites of racial violence (in Allen 2016).

While disengagement can be a form of resistance amid limited options, engaging within education institutions can also be a form of resisting the racial violence that often predominates the school environment. Black youth also engage in school clubs and activities to try to create social change within school institutions (Dei et al. 1997: 25). For example, for decades, Black youth across the province of Nova Scotia have participated in celebrating Black history and African contributions, countering the too-frequent absence of Black realities found in schools (Oostveen n.d.). In addition, many Black youth who have been pushed out of high school go on to achieve high rates of graduation in adult education settings, GED and trade schools (BLAC 1994; CDPDJ 2011). Despite the conditions of imposed upon them, Black youth continue to resist their denigration in a multitude of ways.

CONCLUSION

Historically, Black communities did not passively accept segregation in schools, but actively contested it until it ended. At the same time, Black families have always, despite enormous obstacles, worked toward finding ways to educate their children formally or informally, regardless of the abandonment of Black youth by wider society (Hamilton 2011; Cooper 1999). Indeed, Black families and Black educators have played an important role toward redressing the systemic injustices experienced by Black youth and children. Schools founded specifically to address and remedy anti-Blackness, which can be found in Toronto and Halifax, only exist because of decades of concerted organizing (Hampton 2010).

Toronto's Africentric Alternative School, founded in 2009 as a product of Black community mobilizing and developed to counter the erasure of Black realities found in the mainstream school system, has been remarkably successful. Performance in standardized tests is well above average, with students testing above the provincial average in reading, writing and math (James 2011). The "Freedom School" organized by Black Lives Matter Toronto in the summer of

2016, though not a year-round institution, was created to counter the violence enacted by the education system and to teach Black youth about their own histories. The initiative pays great mind to Black folks marginalized by gender, sexuality and ability as well, unlike other educational settings Black youth find themselves in (Black Lives Matter "Freedom School" n.d.).

Yet, histories of resilience and overcoming obstacles are not nearly enough, and cannot stand in for institutional change. "Positive racial identity" and the knowledge of Black history and present-day realities remain important in coping with daily racial hostility and humiliation in schools (Codjoe 2001: 370). But deeper institutional transformations that tackle systemic racism from an intersectional framework are required, both to address the general societal disinvestment in education that affects students of all backgrounds as well as to redress the racism structured into the education system.

Decades after the integration of Canada's last segregated school, Black students continue to be pushed out of schools and streamed into poverty, low-waged work and youth correctional facilities. Not only are schools underserving young Black minds, but they are also functioning as one arm of the carceral system that grips entire segments of the Black community. The systemic abandonment felt by so many Black youth is psychologically harmful — a student's school experience can have "a major effect on his or her self-image and self esteem and on his or her development in later life" (OHRC 2003: 18). The realities facing Black youth in the school system are neither well known outside of the Black community, nor widely seen as a crisis, yet they are, to use the words of Afua Cooper, a "national disgrace" (in *Radio Canada International* 2016).

It is urgent to counter the devaluation and vilification of Black youth in the school system with a focus away from carceral trends in the education system and toward a system that invests in nurturing, rather than punishing, Black youth.

FROM "WOKE" TO FREE

Imagining
Black futures

> In the poetics of struggle and lived experience, in the utterances of
> ordinary folk, in the cultural products of social movements, in the
> reflections of activists, we discover the many different cognitive maps
> of the future, of the world not yet born. (Kelley 2002: 9–10)

THE CONDITIONS OF BLACK LIFE TODAY are products of technologies and
structures of violence, surveillance and abuse geared toward Black subjection
that have their roots in the transatlantic slave trade and have been embedded
in state practices and institutions for centuries. If dominant representations
of Blackness have remained markedly similar since the era of the transatlantic
slave trade, similar conditions of racial domination, as well, persist into the
present. This includes, but goes well beyond, economic exploitation. Indeed,
while Black people's labour has been exploited from slavery through to the
present — an uncontentious and devastating reality — the exploitation of Black
labour "is just one kind of use within an open, violent and infinite repertoire
of practices" that are used against Black populations (King 2014: n.p.). Many
of the conditions that characterized slavery — racialized surveillance in the
public and private realms, arbitrary separation from familial and kin relationships, forced displacement, vulnerability to arbitrary physical punishment and
violence, captivity and premature death — can today be found across diffuse
state institutions. There is a particular kind of pathologization that has served
to justify often-vicious acts of psychological and physical violence against Black

229

people of all ages. Today, as the policing of Blackness is ubiquitous across the criminal justice system, the immigration system, social services, child welfare and schools, even young Black children are protected from neither the excesses of arbitrary and violent repression, nor from the "banal and everyday" rituals of racial domination in most aspects of their day-to-day lives.

Still, if powerful technologies of anti-Black oppression date back centuries, so too, does the Black radical tradition (Robinson 1983). If an anti-Black social order has attempted to impose a deviant uniformity and interchangeability onto people of African descent in Canada — to collapse Black existence into a living, breathing embodiment of pathology and crime — actual Black communities have been multiple, plural and resistant. For this reason, resistant cultural practices have been enormously vast and diverse. Within Canada's African diaspora, one can find innumerable legacies of Black resistance, large and small, far beyond those touched upon in this book.

Policing Black Lives has detailed many different aspects of how the state directly and indirectly inflicts spiritual, economic, psychological and physical harm onto Black communities: the able-bodied, the migrant, the young, the disabled, the mentally ill, the cis and transgender, the law-abiding and the law-breaking. In the face of such injustice, it is particularly necessary to imagine a different society than the one in which we find ourselves. As Black historian Robin D.G. Kelley reminds us, effective knowledge production around race and racial justice has always been intertwined with political struggle (2002: 9). So, to conclude, I turn to the harnessing of the Black radical imagination that can be found in the present moment.

As this book goes to print, activists and Black community members are formulating important visions for Black futures across the country and, indeed, around the world. What would it look like to imagine a future of Black freedom, of lives unencumbered by the everyday and spectacular moments of suffering caused by the racially structured institutions that govern society? What would it mean to chip away at — or abolish entirely — the systemic forms of violence that are enacted regularly onto Black people's lives? Many responses to state violence against Black lives are being created, as they always have been, in hushed conversations while babies nap, in meetings, on the streets, in conference calls, at dinner tables and in classrooms.

Countless escaped enslaved people — and in particular, Marie-Joseph Angélique — set the terms of Black resistance and refusal. Later, individuals like Halifax's Rocky Jones and Toronto's Sherona Hall, and groups like Montréal's AKAX and Toronto's Black Action Defence Committee, have in many ways been the forerunners of contemporary Black activism. Today, with heightened visibility for queer and trans Black folks, Black people of all genders continue to fight immigration detention and deportations, police street checks, incarceration, child removal, the push-out of Black children and youth from schools and the subordination of Black women's experiences to those of Black men.

Further, the necessity of institutions often taken for granted, such as the police, is being questioned from a renewed radical framework for racial and economic justice. What would it look like to disinvest the incredible amount of public funds that are currently diverted toward police and prisons and invest, instead, in community-run, community-based institutions that serve people's very real need for security, education and dignity? These questions are being asked by a new generation of Black activists — for example, Black Lives Matter Toronto co-founder Janaya Khan (2017) and Halifax-based activist, scholar, poet and prison abolitionist El Jones.

In *Are Prisons Obsolete?* (2003), Angela Y. Davis suggests that the decriminalization of sex work and drugs are necessary steps toward the eventual abolition of prisons and other repressive state institutions that target racialized, poor and otherwise dispossessed people. Moving toward these goals, both of which are supported by growing bodies of evidence internationally, could have far-reaching implications for Black communities in Canada by removing some of the major justifications for widespread surveillance, incarceration and deportation. For example, even a reduction in the powers granted to law enforcement in the *Controlled Drugs and Substances Act* would likely significantly reduce present processes of Black criminalization.

However, reforms that do not also challenge the underlying systemic racism that creates disparities in the distribution of wealth and power in the first place are unlikely to effect meaningful change. Without a transformation of the existing political conditions that render so many lives expendable, meaningful justice is unlikely to manifest itself. Significant celebrated and hard-fought reforms in the late 1980s and early 1990s were brought to women's federal prisons following the *Creating Choices* report, which exposed the horrific violence that incarcerated women had been exposed to behind bars. Yet, because the dehumanization of Canada's Indigenous and Black populations was left intact, the rates of incarceration of women from both groups have only risen.

Similarly, tireless efforts on the part of migrant justice organizers, researchers and legal advocates against Canadian detention practices have led the federal government to commit to an ambiguous set of reforms. These reforms, though important and likely life saving, also resulted in a commitment of $138 million to build more detention centres, and left broader injustices found within Canada's border practices unquestioned and intact, including the practice of indefinite detention. In another ambiguous reform, the federal government's plan to decriminalize some parts of the sale and possession of cannabis leaves much of the architecture of racialized surveillance and punishment intact, and actually increases the potential sentences for driving under the influence of marijuana and selling cannabis to teenagers. Further, the practice of police "street checks" — and the massive intrusion into Black people's lives that they allow for — also remain firmly in place.

Michelle Alexander, author of The New Jim Crow (2012), urges us to tie activism about legal reforms to efforts that combat the deeper, racialized nature of "justice" and "crime" in our societies. She argues that, though important, legal reforms that take place without addressing the demonization of Black communities are unlikely to result in major gains against institutionalized racism or even racist policing and incarceration. Without addressing the racist root, she argues, new justifications and systems for racial control will likely take the place of the old (2012: 239–240). It is important to remain vigilant of the evolving nature of racism in any society characterized by racial hierarchies. Without a change of what Alexander calls the "public consensus" on how Black persons are perceived and treated, short-term reforms are unlikely to end the devaluation of Black lives that is embedded within state practices. This continued devaluation, instead, will breed new forms of subjugation as some older ones are eliminated through reforms.

Any legal reform, then, must be tied into concerted efforts toward seeing, naming and concertedly countering the demonization of Black life that permeates both state institutions and wider society. If not, we are unlikely to stop the seemingly limitless forms of harm enacted by state institutions that cause so many lives to be stifled, shortened, endangered and lost needlessly. This deeper, more fundamental struggle needs to centre Black leadership and Black realities, even as it links with non-Black communities and addresses many forms of oppression. However, neither reform nor Black leadership are immune to being co-opted by the status quo of the intersecting logics of white supremacy, patriarchy, heterosexism and capitalism that are found within society and within (some) transformative movements themselves. Seeking a transformation of this kind, Davis pushes for a conception of racial justice that moves beyond the traps of reform and incorporation and toward a radical transformation of the very fabric of today's societies. While acknowledging the importance of reform as a short-term strategy, she argues that the challenge that faces us in the twenty-first century "is not to demand equal opportunity to participate in the machinery of oppression," but to "identify and dismantle those structures in which racism continues to be embedded" (2005: 26). Additionally, drawing from W.E.B. Du Bois's concept of abolition democracy, Davis argues that it is necessary to envision more than the abolition of racist *institutions*. The governing power of racism, she argues, is unlikely to be transformed in the absence of creation — that is, the simultaneous building of new and more just institutions (2005: 68–70). Davis urges us, in short, to struggle not only for the abolition of slavery's afterlives, but for also for genuine emancipation from all forms of oppression.

Much of Black activism today is focused on winning reforms with tangible benefits, such as an overhaul of the bodies that investigate police violence. Yet, many young Black activists, too, are moving simultaneously beyond reform and imagining futures that dually reimagine and restructure institutions outside of the bounds and limitations of white supremacy and anti-Blackness.

Black Lives Matter, the Critical Resistance network and INCITE! Women of Color Against Violence are only a few of many contemporary abolition movements in the Americas that identify the multiple and diverse locations of state-sanctioned harm — in prisons, but also extending across the criminal justice, immigration, child welfare, social services and education systems (see also CR10 Collective 2010; INCITE! 2006). These efforts, geared toward radically transforming these diverse institutions, stand to benefit Black populations as well as all other marginalized folks, including Latinx people, Arab and Muslim peoples, sexual minorities, poor people of any background and people living with disabilities.

In Canada, any struggle for economic, racial and social justice must necessarily address ongoing settler colonialism. In a white settler colony like Canada, it's not possible to talk about abolition — not only of prisons but also of the enduring legacy of slavery in all state institutions — without simultaneously supporting Indigenous decolonization movements. Given the historical relationship between slavery (and its afterlives) and settler colonialism, it should come as no surprise that recent racial justice organizing has seen a renewed effort in creating Black-Indigenous solidarity. Examples of recent Black organizing efforts in Canada that have focused on supporting anti-colonial Indigenous movements include the occupation of the offices of Indigenous and Northern Affairs Canada by Black Lives Matter and Idle No More in Toronto in April 2016. This action was aimed at pressuring the government to address the suicide crisis in Attawapiskat that resulted from acute state neglect (*Democracy Now!*

May 20, 2016; Khan n.d.). A future in which Black liberation movements are tangibly connected to Indigenous struggles for land and bodily sovereignty holds enormous potential to enrich and expand how racial justice is practised in Canada.

Though this book deals primarily with the topics of oppression, violence, pain and death, I leave us here with an affirmation of life. While recognizing the structures that oppress us, I also urge us to look beyond the current structure of society and the suffering therein. Black, Indigenous and racialized feminists have, for years, insisted that it is necessary to maintain the ability to look toward transformative racial and economic justice beyond the necessary, if inadequate, reforms of particularly harmful state policies. Many liberatory possibilities articulated in the present moment appear, perhaps, utopic; many of us continue to take for granted modern, state-sanctioned sources of human suffering, such as borders, prisons, policing and state surveillance, as if they were ahistorical institutions and practices and not man-made ones. It may be hard to imagine a world in which institutions like prisons and borders do not figure prominently — or at all — in our landscapes, and in which Black lives across the age, gender and ability spectrums are not systematically devalued. Yet, the visionary platform recently created by the Movement for Black Lives (2016) — an organization made up of over fifty Black organizations in the United States and supported by Black Lives Matter Toronto — reminds us that the attainment of investing in economic, racial and gender justice is a matter of priority. It is a matter, that is, of prioritizing life over death, of investing in education, health and safety over criminalization and cages. This is not an expression of naïve hope, only an insistence that we must refuse to surrender our imaginations, even amid the backdrop of Black suffering and death that seems unstoppable. The fact that radical changes may be necessary to achieve racial and economic justice should not deter us from believing that we can, and should, work toward a society that deprioritizes, disinvests and dismantles institutions that mandate the violent subordination of our most vulnerable.

NOTES

Introduction — On state violence and Black lives

1. See Nasser (2016) for Andrew Loku, Gillis (2015c) for Jermaine Carby and CBC *News* (August 29, 2008) for Quilem Registre.
2. Throughout *Policing Black Lives*, I use the terms sexual minority or LGBTQI* interchangeably toward inclusively encompassing a diverse array of sexual and gender identities including those who are lesbian, gay, bi-sexual, two-spirit, trans, intersex and gender non-conforming. At times, I more specifically address transgender or trans women toward the aim of addressing the unique forms of oppression that trans women experience in society. Otherwise, the word "women" should be considered inclusive of both cis and transgender women. On some occasions, I use the term "gender-oppressed," following Julia Sudbury's usage (2009), in an attempt to encompass the ways that patriarchy impacts women as well as those outside of traditional gender binaries — meaning, in effect, all of those who are not cisgender men.
3. After being largely erased from the national imaginary, due to the diligent activism of her surviving family members, Viola Desmond has been featured on Canadian stamps and most recently has been slated to appear on paper currency in 2018 (K. Harris 2016).
4. See Chapter Six for more information.
5. Notably, following the death of Abdirahman Abdi, there was a coast-to-coast national day of action organized by Black activists in six cities across Canada, including Toronto, Winnipeg, Vancouver, Hamilton, Kitchener-Waterloo, Edmonton and Ottawa (Migdal 2016).
6. See, for example, Isaacs (2016) on Black/Palestinian solidarity after Mike Brown's death in Ferguson, Missouri, and Carless (2015) on Black Lives Matter activism in Brazil.

Chapter One — Devaluing Black life, demonizing Black bodies: Anti-Blackness from slavery to segregation

1. Archives of Ontario, Ministry of Government and Consumer Services, "Peggy: Difficult Property," retrieved at <archives.gov.on.ca/en/explore/online/slavery/peggy.aspx>.

Chapter Three — Arrested (in)justice: From the streets to the prison

1. Parts of this section were published in a different form in an op-ed in the *Toronto Star* on July 31, 2016, entitled "Let death of Abdirahman Abdi be last of its kind."

Chapter Five — Misogynoir in Canada: Punitive state practices and the devaluation of Black women and gender-oppressed people

1. Details from an in-person conversation.
2. Telephone correspondences with Nora Butler Burke (2015), former coordinator of ASTT(e)Q (Montréal); Liam Michaud (2016), former street outreach worker at CACTUS Montréal (a harm reduction organization by and for sex workers); Monica Forrester

(2017), coordinator of Maggie's (Toronto) drop-in and outreach services; and Stephanie Lareau (2016), coordinator of Stella (Montréal), confirm that each has witnessed and heard of more extreme levels of surveillance, harassment and police abuse, including racist and sexist language, public strip-searches and death threats, levelled at both Black and Indigenous sex workers.

REFERENCES

Abdi, Ali A. 2005. "Reflections on the Long Struggle for Inclusion: The Experiences of People of African Origin." In Tettey, Wisdom J., and Korbla P. Puplampu (eds.), *The African Diaspora in Canada: Negotiating Identity & Belonging*. Calgary: University of Calgary Press. 49–60.

Abeni, Cleis, Aashna Malpani, Mari Brighe, Trudy Ring and Dawn Ennis. 2016. "These Are the Trans People Killed in 2016." *Advocate*. <advocate.com/transgender/2016/7/19/these-are-trans-people-killed-2016#slide-2>.

Abramovich, Alex. May 25, 2015. "It's About Time Canada Stood up for Homeless LGBT Youth." *Huffington Post*. <huffingtonpost.ca/alex-ilona-abramovich/lbgt-homeless-shelter-toronto_b_6933278.html>.

Abramovich, Ilona Alex. 2012. "No Safe Place to Go—GBTQ Youth Homelessness in Canada: Reviewing the Literature." *Canadian Journal of Family and Youth/Le Journal Canadien de Famille et de la Jeunesse* 4.1: 29–61.

ACLC (African Canadian Legal Clinic). 2001. *Eliminating racism: Linking local and global strategies for Change, immigration and refugee issues: Promoting full participation and reversing the tide of Criminalization and Expulsion*. Brief to U.N. World Conference Against Racism. Toronto: African Canadian Legal Clinic.

———. 2008. *Report to CEDAW Committee in Consideration of Canada's 7th Periodic Report under the Convention on the Elimination of All Forms of Discrimination against Women*. Toronto: African Canadian Legal Clinic.

———. 2012. *Canada's Forgotten Children: Written Submissions to the Committee on the Rights of the Child on the Third and Fourth Reports of Canada*. Toronto: African Canadian Legal Clinic.

———. n.d. *Disaggregated Data Collection (Race-Based Statistics)*. Toronto: African Canadian Legal Clinic.

Addario, Lise. September 21, 2002. *Six Degrees from Liberation: Legal Needs of Women in Criminal and Other Matters, Chapter 1: Legal Aid and Other Legal Needs of Women Accused (Cont'd)*. National Council of Welfare, Justice and the Poor: Department of Justice, Government of Canada.

African Nova Scotian Affairs. 2014. *African Nova Scotians Today*. Province of Nova Scotia.

Agnew, Vijay. 1998. *In Search of a Safe Place Abused Women and Culturally Sensitive Services*. Toronto: University of Toronto Press.

Akuffo, Edward Ansah. 2012. *Canadian Foreign Policy in Africa: Regional Approaches to Peace, Security, and Development*. Farnham, Surrey: Ashgate Publishing.

Alexander, Michelle. 2012. *The New Jim Crow: Mass Incarceration in the Age of Colorblindness*. New York: The New Press.

Allen, Ryan M. (producer). 2016. "Damien M. Sojoyner, First Strike: Educational Enclosures in Black Los Angeles." *New Books Network*. <newbooksnetwork.com/damien-m-sojoyner-first-strike-educational-enclosures-in-black-los-angeles-u-of-minnesota-press-2016/>.

Alves, Jaime Amparo, and João Costa Vargas. 2017. "On deaf ears: anti-black police terror, multiracial protest and white loyalty to the state." *Identities* 24.3: 254–274.

American Psychological Association. March 6, 2014. "Black Boys Viewed as Older, Less Innocent Than Whites, Research Finds." Press release. Washington: American Psychological Association.

Amnesty International. December 6, 2012. "Canada: Surveillance of Indigenous Protests and Rule of Law." *Amnesty Canada Blog.* <amnesty.ca/blog/canada-surveillance-of-indigenous-protests-and-rule-of-law>.

———. August 11, 2015. "Global Movement Votes to Adopt Policy to Protect Human Rights of Sex Workers." *Amnesty.org.* <amnesty.org/en/latest/news/2015/08/global-movement-votes-to-adopt-policy-to-protect-human-rights-of-sex-workers/>.

Arsenault, Adrienne. June 5, 2015. "Mystery Man's Identity Still Murky after Decade in Canadian Detention." CBC *News.* <cbc.ca/news/world/mystery-man-s-identity-still-murky-after-decade-in-canadian-detention-1.3100781>.

ASTT(e)Q (Action Santé Travesti(e)s et Transsexuel(le)s du Québec). 2011. *Taking Charge: A Handbook for Health Care and Social Service Providers Working with Trans People.*

Austin, David. 2013. *Fear of a Black Nation: Race, Sex and Security in Sixties Montreal.* Toronto: Between the Lines.

Austin, Regina. 1995. "Sapphire Bound!" In Kimberlé Williams Crenshaw, et al. (eds.), *Critical Race Theory: The Key Writings That Formed the Movement.* New York: The New Press. 426–40.

Backhouse, Constance. 1985. "Nineteenth-Century Canadian Prostitution Law: Reflection of a Discriminatory Society." *Histoire sociale/ Social History* 18.36: 387–423.

———. 1999. *Colour-Coded: A Legal History of Racism in Canada, 1900–1950.* Toronto: Osgoode Society for Canadian Legal History by University of Toronto Press.

———. 2005. "What Is Access to Justice?" In Julia Bass, W.A. Bogart and Frederick H. Zemans (eds.), *Access to Justice for a New Century: The Way Forward.* Toronto: Law Society of Upper Canada. 113–46.

Bailey, Moya (moyazb). March 14, 2010. "They Aren't Talking About Me …" *Crunk Feminist Collective.* <crunkfeministcollective.com/2010/03/14/they-arent-talking-about-me/>.

———. 2014. "More on the Origin of Misogynoir." *Moyazb.* <moyazb.tumblr.com/post/84048113369/more-on-the-origin-of-misogynoir>.

Bakan, Abigail, and Daiva Stasiulis. 1997. *Not One of the Family: Foreign Domestic Workers in Canada.* Toronto: University of Toronto Press.

———. 2008. "Marginalized and Dissident Non-Citizens: Foreign Domestic Workers." In Barrington Walker (ed.), *The History of Immigration and Racism in Canada: Essential Readings.* 264–78.

Balfour, Gillian. 2006. "Introduction." In Elizabeth Comack and Gillian Balfour (eds.), *Criminalizing Women: Gender and (in)Justice in Neo-Liberal Times* Eds. Black Point, Winnipeg: Fernwood Publishing. 154–70.

Balibar, Étienne. 2015. *Citizenship.* Malden: MA Polity Press.

Ballingall, Alex. April 17 2016. "The SIU Police the Police — but a Problem Exists in Who They Staff." *Toronto Star.* <thestar.com/news/gta/2016/04/17/the-siu-police-the-police-but-a-problem-exists-in-who-they-staff.html>.

Bannerji, Himani. 2000. *The Dark Side of the Nation: Essays on Multiculturalism, Nationalism and Gender.* Toronto: Canadian Scholars' Press.

Barnes, Anne-Marie. 2002. "Dangerous Duality the 'Net Effect': of Immigration and Deportation on Jamaicans in Canada." In Wendy Chan and Kiran Mirchandani (eds.), *Crimes of Colour: Racialization and the Criminal Justice System in Canada.* Toronto: University of Toronto Press. 191–204.

Bauer, G., N. Nussbaum, R. Travers, L. Munro, J. Pyne and N. Redman. May 30 2011. "We've Got Work to Do: Workplace Discrimination and Employment Challenges for Trans People in Ontario." *Trans PULSE E-Bulletin* 2.1. <transpulseproject.ca/wp-content/uploads/2011/05/E3English.pdf>.

Beckles, Hilary McD. 2013. *Britain's Black Debt: Reparations for Caribbean Slavery and Native Genocide.* Kingston: University of West Indies Press.

Belony, Esther. 2007. "La Prise En Charge Des Enfants De L'immigration Haïtienne Par La Direction de la Protection de la Jeunesse: Une Analyse Comparative." Québec: Université du Québec: Institut national de la recherche scientifique, Maîtrise en démographie.

Ben-Moshe, Liat, Allison C. Carey and Chris Chapman, eds. 2014. *Disability Incarcerated: Imprisonment and Disability in the United States and Canada.* New York: Palgrave Macmillan.

Bergeron, Maxime. March 3, 2004. "La Mort De Rohan Wilson Soulève Beaucoup De Questions." *La Presse.* <collections.banq.qc.ca:81/lapresse/src/pages/2004/03/03/A/82812_20040303LPA10.pdf>.

Berlatsky, Noah. October 1, 2014. "Black Women Profiled as Prostitutes in NYC." *Reason. com.* <http://reason.com/archives/2014/10/01/nypd-profiles-sex-workers-too>.

Bernard, Candace, and Wanda Thomas Bernard. 2002. "Learning from the Past/ Visions for the Future: The Black Community and Child Welfare in Nova Scotia." In Brian Wharf (ed.), *Community Work Approaches to Child Welfare.* Toronto: University of Toronto Press, Higher Education Division. 116–28.

Bernard, Wanda Thomas. May 2001. *Including Black Women in Health and Social Policy Development: Winning Over Addictions — Empowering Black Mothers with Addictions to Overcome Triple Jeopardy.* Halifax: Maritime Centre of Excellence for Women's Health.

Bernard, Léonel, and Christopher McAll. 2008. "La Surreprésentation Des Jeunes Noirs Montréalais." *Revue du Cremis* 1.3: 15–21.

_____. 2009. "Pauvreté et 'Protection.'" *Revue du CREMIS* 2.4 (Automne): 26–30.

_____. 2010. "Jeunes Noirs et Systeme de Justice." *Revue du CREMIS* 3.1 (Hiver): 7–14.

Bernstein, Robin. 2011. *Racial Innocence: Performing Childhood and Race from Slavery to Civil Rights.* E-book, Project MUSE Web ed. New York: New York University Press.

Berthomet, Stéphane. April 4, 2014. "Profilage Racial En Techniques Policières?" *Collectif Opposé à la Brutalité Policière.* <https://cobp.resist.ca/documentation/profilage-racial-en-techniques-polici-res>.

Bhattacharjee, Ken. 2003. "The Ontario Safe Schools Act: School Discipline and Discrimination." *Ontario Human Rights Commission.* <ohrc.on.ca/sites/default/files/attachments/The_Ontario_Safe_Schools_Act%3A_School_discipline_and_discrimination.pdf>.

Birmingham, David. 2008. *The Decolonization of Africa.* London: Routledge.

BLAC (Black Learners Advisory Committee). 1994. BLAC *Report on Education: Redressing*

Inequity-Empowering Black Learners. Halifax: Black Learners Advisory Committee.

Black, Debra. August 22, 2015. "Canada Border Services Agency Confirms Identity for 'Man with No Name.'" *Toronto Star.* <thestar.com/news/immigration/2015/08/22/canada-border-services-agency-confirms-identity-for-man-with-no-name.html>.

———. February 28, 2016. "Is Ottawa Treating All Refugees Fairly?" *Toronto Star.* <thestar.com/news/immigration/2016/02/28/is-ottawa-treating-all-refugees fairly.html>.

Black Lives Matter Toronto. n.d. "Demands." n.d. <blacklivesmatter.ca/demands/>

———. n.d. "Freedom School." <freedomschool.ca/impact/>

Black Women's Collective of Toronto. 1989. "Proposal to March 8th Coalition for IWD 1989" *Rise Up! A Digital Archive of Feminist Activism.* <riseupfeministarchive.ca/wp-content/uploads/2016/08/blackwomenscollective-1989-proposaltoMarch8coalitionToronto.pdf>.

Blackstock, Cindy. 2007. "Residential Schools: Did They Really Close or Just Morph into Child Welfare?" *Indigenous Law Journal* 6.1: 71–78.

———. 2011. "The Canadian Human Rights Tribunal on First Nations Child Welfare: Why If Canada Wins, Equality and Justice Lose." *Children and Youth Services Review* 33.1: 187–19.

Blatchford, Christie. June 15, 2015. "Controversial 'Carding' Practice Is an Invaluable Source of Intelligence for Police, If Done Right." *National Post.* <news.nationalpost.com/full-comment/christie-blatchford-controversial-carding- practice-is-an-invaluable-source-of-intelligence-for-police-if-done-right>.

Block, Sheila, and Grace-Edward Galabuzi. 2011. *Canada's Colour Coded Labour Market: The Gap for Racialized Workers.* Ottawa: The Wellesley Institute, Canadian Centre for Policy Alternatives.

Boctor, Lillian. 2013. *Twice Removed: Double Punishment and Racial Profiling in Canada.* Documentary. <youtube.com/watch?v=XyJGfnmkzcU>.

Bolaria, B. Singh, and Peter S. Li. 1988. *Racial Oppression in Canada.* Toronto: Garamond Press.

Bombay, Amy, and Kevin Hewitt. 2015. *A Report from the Committee on Aboriginal and Black/African Canadian Student Access and Retention: A Focus on Financial Support.* Halifax: Committee on Aboriginal and Black/African Canadian Student Access and Retention.

Boyd, Susan, and Karlene Faith. 1999. "Women, Illegal Drugs and Prison: Views from Canada." *International Journal of Drug Policy* 10: 195–207.

Boyd, Susan C. 1999. *Mothers and Illicit Drugs: Transcending the Myths.* Toronto: University of Toronto Press, 1999.

———. 2006. "Representation of Women in the Drug Trade." In Gillian Balfour and Elizabeth Comack *Criminalizing Women: Gender and (in)Justice in Neo-Liberal Times.* Black Point, Winnipeg: Fernwood Publishing.

Bramham, Daphne. March 9 2016. "'Unreliable' Tests May Have Led to Apprehension of B.C. Children." *Vancouver Sun.* <vancouversun.com/Daphne+Bramham+Unreliable+tests+have+apprehension+children/11777160/story.html>.

Brand, Dionne. 1991. *No Burden to Carry: Narratives of Black Working Women in Ontario, 1920s–1950s.* Toronto: Women's Press.

———. 1999. "Black Women and Work: The Impact of Racially Constructed Gender Roles on the Sexual Division of Labour." In Enakshi Dua and Angela Robertson (eds.),

Scratching the Surface: Canadian Anti-Racist Feminist Thought. Toronto: Canadian Scholars' Press and Women's Press. 83–96.

———. 2008. "'We Weren't Allowed to Go into Factory Work until Hitler Started the War': The 1920s to the 1940s." In Barrington Walker (ed.), *The History of Immigration and Racism in Canada: Essential Readings.* Toronto: Canadian Scholars' Press. 239–249.

Brean, Joseph. March 5, 2012. "Tory Crackdown on 'Birth Tourists' Will Eliminate Canadian Passport Babies." *National Post.* <news.nationalpost.com/news/canada/passport-babies-canada>.

Brem, Maxwell. 2006. "Migrant Workers in Canada: A Review of the Canadian Seasonal Agricultural Workers Program." *The North-South Institute.* Policy brief.

Bristow, Peggy. 1999. "'Whatever You Raise in the Ground You Can Sell It in Chatham': Black Women in Buxton and Chatham, 1850–65." In Peggy Bristow, Dionne Brand, Linda Carty, Afua P. Cooper, Sylvia Hamilton, Adrienne Shadd (eds.), *"We're Rooted Here and They Can't Pull Us Up": Essays in African Canadian Women's History.* Toronto: University of Toronto Press.

Bristow, Peggy, Dionne Brand, Linda Carty, Afua P. Cooper, Sylvia Hamilton and Adrienne Shadd (eds.) 1999. *"We're Rooted Here and They Can't Pull Us Up": Essays in African Canadian Women's History.* Toronto: University of Toronto Press.

Bronskill, Jim. March 14, 2016. "Deportations to Jamaica, Honduras Could End up Hurting Canada: Federal Studies." *CBC News.* <cbc.ca/news/politics/deportations-jamaica-honduros-1.3490185>.

Brown, Barbara. February 25, 2006. "Drug-Fueled Melee Subject of Inquest." *Hamilton Spectator.*

Brown, Louise. February 26, 2014. "Africentric High School Students Thrive in Pioneering Program." *Toronto Star.* <thestar.com/yourtoronto/education/2014/02/26/africentric_high_school_students_thrive_in_pioneering_program.html>.

Brown, Maureen J. 2004. "In Their Own Voices African Canadians in the Greater Toronto Area Share Experiences of Police Profiling." African Canadian Community Coalition on Racial Profiling.

Browne, Rachel. June 18, 2015. "What Are Babies Doing Behind Bars in Canada?" *Macleans.* <macleans.ca/news/canada/what-are-babies-doing-behind-bars-in-canada/>.

Browne, Simone. 2002. "Of 'Passport Babies' and 'Border Control': The Case of Mavis Baker v. Minister of Citizenship and Immigration." *Atlantis: Critical Studies in Gender, Culture & Social Justice* 26.2: 97–108.

———. 2015. *Dark Matters: On the Surveillance of Blackness.* Durham and London: Duke University Press.

Bryan, Patrick E. 1984. *The Haitian Revolution and Its Effects.* Oxford: Heinemann.

Burman, John. February 25, 2003. "Woman's Death No Surprise to Friends; Victim Had Tough Life with Gender Identity." *The Hamilton Spectator.*

Burman, Jenny. 2007. "Deportable or Invisible? Black Women in the Space of 'Removal'" In Katherine McKittrick (ed.), *Black Geographies and the Politics of Place.* Toronto: Between the Lines. 177–92.

Burt, Geoff, Mark Sedra, Bernard Headley, Camille Hernandez-Ramdwar, Randy Seepersad and Scot Wortley. 2016. *Deportation, Circular Migration and Organized Crime: Jamaica Case Study.* Research Report 2016–R007. Ottawa: Government of Canada, Public

Safety Canada.

Butler Burke, Nora. 2015. Former coordinator of ASST(e)Q. Personal correspondence.

———. 2016a. "Connecting the Dots: National Security, the Crime-Migration Nexus and Trans Women's Survival." In Yolanda Martínez-San Miguel and Sarah Tobias (eds.), *Trans Studies: The Challenge to Hetero/Homo Normativities*. New Brunswick: Rutgers University Press.

———. 2016b. "Double Punishment: Immigration Penality and the Daily Lives of Migrant Trans Women." Dissertation. Concordia University.

Cahill, Barry. 1994. "Slavery and the Judges of Loyalist Nova Scotia." *University of New Brunswick Law Journal* 43: 73–135.

———. 1999. "The Black Loyalist Myth in Atlantic Canada." *Acadiensis* 29.1 (Autumn): 76–87.

Cain, Patrick. September 22, 2016. "Immigration Detention 'Woefully Unsuited for Children,' Report Charges." *Global News* <globalnews.ca/news/2953723/immigration-detention-woefully-unsuited-for-children-report-charges/>.

Calliste, Agnes. 1993. "Race, Gender and Canadian Immigration Policy: Blacks from the Caribbean, 1900–1932. *Journal of Canadian Studies* (Winter) 28.4. 131–48.

———. 1995. "The Struggle for Employment Equity by Blacks on American and Canadian Railroads." *Journal of Black Studies* 25.3: 297–317.

———. 1996. "Antiracism Organizing and Resistance in Nursing: African Canadian Women." *CARS Canadian Review of Sociology/Revue canadienne de sociologie* 33.3: 361–90.

Cameron, David and Daniel Hamlin. 2015. "Applied or Academic: High Impact Decisions for Ontario Students." *People for Education*. Toronto: People for Education.

Canadian Press. July 20, 1994. "RCMP issues apology for spy reports on NS Blacks." *Canadian Press NewsWire*. Toronto.

———. July 7, 2014. "Survivors of Alleged Abuse at Orphanage Win Settlement." *Macleans.* <macleans.ca/news/need-to-know/survivors-of-alleged-abuse-at-halifax-orphanage-win-major-settlement/>.

———. February 14, 2016. "Canada's two-tier system: Syrians not the only ones fleeing adversity at home, experts and refugees say." <nationalpost.com/news/canada/canadas-two-tier-refugee-system-syrians-not-the-only-ones-fleeing-adversity-at-home-experts-and-migrants-say/wcm/f83c337f-2ee9-4905-b186-0f6caa99b1c9>.

Canada Human Rights Reporter. 2003. *Driving While Black*. Nova Scotia: *Halifax Regional Police Service v. Johnson*, C.H.R.R. D/307.

Canadian Association of Social Workers. 2005. *Income of Black Women in Canada*. Ottawa.

Canadian Bar Association. 2012. *Bill C-43, Faster Removal of Foreign Criminals Act*. Ottawa. <cba.org/CMSPages/GetFile.aspx?guid=a12bce4d-aaf4-4bfa-b6ac-5b2514ac973f>.

Canadian Council on Learning. 2006. *The Social Consequences of Economic Inequality for Canadian Children: A Review of the Canadian Literature*.

Canadian HIV/AIDS Legal Network, Pivot Legal Society and Stella l'amie de Maimie. 2014. *Reckless Endangerment: Q & A on Bill C-36: Protection of Communities and Exploited Persons Act*. <chezstella.org/docs/en/billc36_info.pdf>.

Carless, Will. November 3, 2015. "Brazil's 'Black Lives Matter' Struggle — Even Deadlier." *Global Post*. <pri.org/stories/2015-11-03/brazils-black-lives-matter-struggle-even-more-dire>.

Carmichael, Stokely, and Charles V. Hamilton. 1967. *Black Power: The Politics of Liberation in America*. New York: Vintage Books.

Carruthers, Errlee. 1996. "Prosecuting Women for Welfare Fraud in Ontario: Implications for Equality." *Journal of Law and Social Policy* 11, Article 10: 241–62.

Carty, Linda. 1999. "African Canadian Women and the State: Labour Only Please!" In Peggy Bristow, Dionne Brand, Linda Carty, Afua P. Cooper, Sylvia Hamilton and Adrienne Shadd (eds.), *"We're Rooted Here and They Can't Pull Us Up": Essays in African Canadian Women's History*. Toronto: University of Toronto Press. 193–229.

Cashore, Harvey, Dave Seglins, Frederic Zalac, and Kimberly Ivany. March 8, 2016. "Canada Revenue Offered Amnesty to Wealthy KPMG Clients in Offshore Tax 'Sham.'" CBC *News*. <cbc.ca/news/business/canada-revenue-kpmg-secret-amnesty-1.3479594>.

CBC News. August 29, 2008. "Montreal Family Wants Public Inquiry after Coroner Says Taser Use Avoidable." CBC *News*. <cbc.ca/news/canada/montreal/montreal- family-wants-public-inquiry-after-coroner-says-taser-use-avoidable-1.734475>.

———. July 29, 2012. "Human Rights Complaint over Montreal Girl Forced Off Bus." CBC *News*. <cbc.ca/news/canada/montreal/human-rights-complaint-over-montreal-girl-forced-off-bus-1.1281664>.

———. August 16, 2014. "CBSA Immigration Arrests During Spot Checks Stir Controversy." CBC *News*. <cbc.ca/news/canada/toronto/cbsa-immigration-arrests-during-spot-checks-stir-controversy-1.2738337>.

———. November 4, 2014. "To No Man's Land: The Story of Saeed Jama's Deportation to Somalia." CBC *News*. <cbc.ca/radio/thecurrent/a-story-of-deportation-to-somalia-and-canada-s-voice-at-war-1.2907289/to-no-man-s-land-the-story-of-saeed-jama-s-deportation-to-somalia-1.2907291>.

———. August 5, 2015. "Montreal Woman, Allegedly Roughed up by Police, Discovers She Faces Criminal Charges." CBC *News*. <cbc.ca/news/canada/montreal/montreal-woman-allegedly-roughed-up-by-police-discovers-she-faces-criminal-charges-1.3180894>.

———. November 20, 2015. "Nova Scotia Woman Ordered Deported to Country She Hasn't Seen since Childhood." CBC *News*. <cbc.ca/news/canada/nova-scotia/deportation-debra-spencer-not-justice-advocates-say-1.3326741>.

———. April 4, 2016 "Jean-Pierre Bony, Man Shot During Montreal North Drug Bust, Has Died." CBC *News*. <cbc.ca/news/canada/montreal/montreal-north-drug-raid-1.3520308>

———. January 23, 2017. "Quebec Woman Suing over Solitary Confinement 'Hell'" CBC *News*. <cbc.ca/news/canada/montreal/quebec-solitary-confinement-class-action-1.3947921>.

CCR (Canadian Council for Refugees). 2011. "Nairobi: Long Delays — Statement on Responding to African Refugees." <ccrweb.ca/files/nairobistatement.pdf>.

———. 2016. "Refugees Welcome Here: Three Key Issues." <ccrweb.ca/sites/ccrweb.ca/files/rrd-3-issues-march-2016.pdf>.

CDPDJ (Commission des droits de la personne et des droits de la jeunesse Québec). 1984. *Enquête sur les Allégations de Discriminations Raciale dans l'industrie Du Taxi À Montréal: Rapport Final*. Montréal.

———. 2011. Profilage racial et discrimination systémique des jeunes racisés: Rapport de la consultation sur le profilage racial et ses consequences. Bibliothèque et Archives nationales du Québec.

Césaire, Aimé. 2000. *Discourse on Colonialism*. New York: Monthly Review Press.

Chan, Wendy. August 1, 2011. "Canada: Punishing the Undeserving Poor." *Open Democracy*. <opendemocracy.net/5050/wendy-chan/canada-punishing-undeserving-poor>.

Chan, Wendy, and Dorothy Chunn. 2014. *Racialization, Crime, and Criminal Justice in Canada*. Toronto: University of Toronto Press.

Charbonneau, Louis, and Cynthia Osterman. January 23, 2012. "U.N. Probes New Charges of Peacekeeper Sex Abuse in Haiti." *Reuters*. <reuters.com/article/us-haiti-un-i dUSTRE80M26920120123>.

Charest, Mathieu. 2009. *Mécontentement Populaire Et Pratiques D'interpellations Du* SPVM *Depuis 2005: Doit-on Garder Le Cap Après La Tempête?* Montréal: SPVM.

Cheung, Adrian, and Alexandra Sienkiewicz. February 3, 2017. "Mississauga Mom Launches Complaint after Police Handcuff Her 6-Year-Old Daughter." CBC *News*. <cbc.ca/news/canada/toronto/mississauga-mom-launches-complaint-after-police-handcuff-her-6-year-old-daughter-1.3964827>.

Child Welfare Anti-Oppression Roundtable. 2009. *Anti-Oppression in Child Welfare: Laying the Foundation for Change* Toronto.

Choudry, A., Jill Hanley, Steve Jordan, Eric Shragge and Martha Stiegman. 2009. *Fight Back: Workplace Justice for Immigrants*. Black Point, Winnipeg: Fernwood Publishing.

Choudry, Aziz, and Adrian A. Smith. 2016. *Unfree Labour? Struggles of Migrant and Immigrant Workers in Canada*. Oakland: PM Press.

Chunn, Dorothy E., and Shelley A.M Gavigan. 2006. "Welfare Fraud to Welfare as Fraud: The Criminalization of Poverty." In Gillian Balfour and Elizabeth Comack (eds.), *Criminalizing Women: Gender and (in)Justice in Neo-Liberal Times*. Black Point, Winnipeg: Fernwood Publishing. 217–35.

Citizenship and Immigration Canada. 2011. *Backgrounder — Safe Streets and Communities Act: Protecting Vulnerable Foreign Nationals against Trafficking, Abuse and Exploitation*. Ottawa. <cic.gc.ca/english/department/media/backgrounders/2011/2011-09-20.asp>.

———. 2013. *Backgrounder — 2014 Immigration Levels Planning: Public and Stakeholder Consultation*. Ottawa. <cic.gc.ca/english/department/media/backgrounders/2013/2013-06-21.asp#annexD>.

———. 2013. *Faster Removal of Foreign Criminals Act, Backgrounder*. Ottawa.

———. 2014. *Temporary Foreign Worker Program Work Permit Holders by Program, 2004 to 2013*. Ottawa.

Clairmont, Donald H. J, and Dennis W. Magill. 1999. *Africville: The Life and Death of a Canadian Black Community*. Toronto: Canadian Scholars' Press.

Clarke, Jennifer. 2010. "The Challenges of Child Welfare Involvement for Afro-Caribbean Canadian Families in Toronto." *Children and Youth Services Review* 33.2: 274–83.

COBP (Collectif Opposé à la Brutalité Policière). 2007. "D'anthony Griffin À Mohamed Anas Bennis: Enquête Sur 40 Personnes Tuées Par La Police De Montréal En 20 Ans (1987–2006)." *Collectif Opposé à la Brutalité Policière*. <cobp.resist.ca/node/15>.

Codjoe, Henry M. 2001. "Fighting a 'Public Enemy' of Black Academic Achievement: the persistence of racism and the schooling experiences of Black students in Canada." *Race Ethnicity and Education* 4.4: 343–375.

Cole, Desmond. May 19 2016a. "The Shame of Our Disposable Workers." *Toronto Star*.

<thestar.com/opinion/commentary/2016/05/19/the-shame-of-our-disposable-workers.html>.

———. July 29, 2016b. "We Need Not Wait to Judge Police Behaviour in Abdi's Death. *Ottawa Citizen*. <ottawacitizen.com/opinion/columnists/cole-we-need-not-wait-to-judge-police-behaviour-in-abdis-death>.

Collectif éducation sans frontières. 2013. "Statement on Quebec Ministry of Education Guidelines." *Solidarity Across Borders*. <solidarityacrossborders.org/en/enfants-sans-papiers-declaration-du-collectif-education-sans-frontieres-au-sujet-des-directives-du-ministere-de-leducation>.

Collins, Patricia Hill. 1990. *Black Feminist Thought: Knowledge, Consciousness, and The Politics of Empowerment*. New York: Routledge.

Comack, Elizabeth, and Gillian Balfour, eds. 2006. *Criminalizing Women: Gender and (in) Justice in Neo-Liberal Times*. Black Point, Winnipeg: Fernwood Publishing.

Comack, Elizabeth. 2012. *Racialized Policing: Aboriginal People's Encounters with the Police*. Black Point, Winnipeg: Fernwood Publishing.

Commission on Systemic Racism in the Ontario Criminal Justice System. 1994. *Racism Behind Bars: The Treatment of Black and Other Racial Minority Prisoners in Ontario Prisons*. Toronto.

———. 1995. *Report of the Commission on Systemic Racism in the Ontario Criminal Justice System*. Toronto.

Commission to Promote Sustainable Child Welfare. 2011. *A New Approach to Funding Child Welfare in Ontario: Final Report*. Toronto.

Community Social Planning Council of Toronto. June 2008. *The Right to Learn: Access to Public Education for Non-Status Immigrants*. <socialplanningtoronto.org/wp-content/uploads/2009/02/right_to_learn.pdf>.

Contenta, Sandro, Laurie Monsebraaten and Jim Rankin. December 12, 2014. "Ontario's Most Vulnerable Children Kept in the Shadows." *Toronto Star*. <thestar.com/news/canada/2014/12/12/ontarios_most_vulnerable_children_ kept_in_the_shadows.html>.

Cooper, Afua. 1999. "Black Women and Work in Nineteenth-Century Canada West: Black Woman Teacher Mary Bibb" In Peggy Bristow, Dionne Brand, Linda Carty, Afua P. Cooper, Sylvia Hamilton, Adrienne Shadd (eds.),*"We're Rooted Here and They Can't Pull Us Up": Essays in African Canadian Women's History*. Toronto: University of Toronto Press. 143–70.

———. 2006. *The Hanging of Angélique: The Untold Story of Canadian Slavery and the Burning of Old Montréal*. Toronto: HarperCollins.

Correctional Services Canada. n.d. "Guidelines: Gender Dysphoria" Guideline 800-5, Corrections and Conditional Release Act, Sections 3, 3.1, 4, 69, 70 and 85–89. Correctional Services Canada. <csc-scc.gc.ca/politiques-et-lois/800-5-gl-eng.shtml >

Côte-des-Neiges Black Community Association. October 8, 2016. "Presentation at United Nations Working Group on People of African Descent." Montréal.

Coulthard, Glen S. 2014. *Red Skin, White Masks: Rejecting the Colonial Politics of Recognition*. Minneapolis Minnesota: University of Minnesota Press.

Cox, Rachel. 2001. *Welfare Rights Are Women's Rights: Report on the Consultation Held by the National Association of Women and the Law on the Gosselin Case*. Halifax/Montréal/

Ottawa/Vancouver: National Association of Women and the Law.

Crawford, Charmaine. 2003. "Sending Love in a Barrel: The Making of Transnational Caribbean Families in Canada." *Canadian Woman Studies* 22.3: 104–09.

Creese, Gillian, and Brandy Wiebe. 2009. "Survival Employment: Gender and Deskilling among African Immigrants in Canada." *IMIG International Migration* 50.5: 56-76.

Crenshaw, Kimberlé Williams. 1995. "Mapping the Margins: Intersectionality, Identity Politics, and Violence against Women of Color." In Kimberlé Williams Crenshaw, et al. (eds.), *Critical Race Theory: The Key Writings That Formed the Movement*. New York: The New Press. 357–83.

CR10 Publications Collective. 2008. *Abolition Now! Ten Years of Strategy and Struggle against the Prison Industrial Complex*. Oakland, Edinburgh: AK Press.

Crenshaw, Kimberlé Williams. 2015. *Black Lives Matter: The Schott 50 State Report on Public Education and Black Males*. Cambridge: Schott Foundation for Public Education.

Crenshaw, Kimberlé Williams, and Andrea J. Ritchie. 2015. *Say Her Name: Resisting Police Brutality Against Black Women*. New York: African American Policy Forum.

Csete, Joanne and Adeeba Kamarulzaman, Michel Kazatchkine, Frederick Altice, Marek Balicki, Julia Buxton, Javier Cepeda, Megan Comfort, Eric Goosby, João Goulão, Carl Hart, Thomas Kerr, Alejandro Madrazo Lajous, Stephen Lewis, Natasha Martin, Daniel Mejía, Adriana Camacho, David Mathieson, Isidore Obot, Adeolu Ogunrombi, Susan Sherman, Jack Stone, Nandini Vallath, Peter Vickerman, Tomáš Zábranský and Chris Beyrer. 2016. "Public Health and International Drug Policy." *Lancet* 387.10026.

CSR Report (Report of the Commission on Systemic Racism in the Ontario Criminal Justice System). 1995. Toronto.

CTV News. March 15, 2011. "Ottawa Cop Charged with Sex Assault in Stacy Bonds Case." *CTV News*. <ottawa.ctvnews.ca/ottawa-cop-charged-with-sex-assault-in-stacy-bonds-case-1.618831>.

———. February 19, 2015. "Woman Claims Police Officer Broke Her Arm." *CTV News*. <montreal.ctvnews.ca/woman-claims-police-officer-broke-her-arm-1.2243954 >.

———. December 22, 2015. "Quebec Police Pepper Spray Man in Front of His Children." *CTV News*. <ctvnews.ca/canada/quebec-police-pepper-spray-man-in-front-of-his-children-1.2711256>.

CUPE (Canadian Union of Public Employees). January 8, 2015. "Fact Sheet: Temporary Foreign Workers Program and the Live-in Caregiver Program." <cupe.ca/fact-sheet-temporary-foreign-workers-program-and-live-caregiver-program>.

Curling, Alvin, and Roy McMurtry. 2008. *Community Perspectives Report: Review of the Roots of Youth Violence Report*. Toronto: Ministry of Children and Youth Services.

CWF (Canadian Women's Foundation). 2014. "Fact Sheet: Moving Women out of Violence." <canadianwomen.org/sites/canadianwomen.org/files//FactSheet-VAWandDV_19_08_2016_formatted_0.pdf>

Daenzer, Patricia M. 1997. "Challenging Diversity, Black Women and Social Welfare." In Patricia Marie Evans and Gerda R. Wekerle (eds.), *Women and the Canadian Welfare State: Challenges and Change*. Toronto: University of Toronto Press. 269–90.

Dank, Meredith, Lilly Yu, Jennifer Yahner, Elizabeth Pelletier, Mitchyll Mora and Brendan Conner. 2015. *Locked In: Interactions with the Criminal Justice and Child Welfare Systems for LGBTQ Youth, YMSM, and YWSW Who Engage in Survival Sex*. Urban Institute.

Daschuk, James. 2013. *Clearing the Plains: Disease, Politics of Starvation, and the Loss of Aboriginal Life*. Regina: University of Regina Press.

Davis, Angela Y. 1998. "Race and Criminalization: Black Americans and Punishment Industry." In Joy James (ed.), *The Angela Y. Davis Reader*. Malden: Blackwell Publishers. 61–73.

———. 2003. *Are Prisons Obsolete?* New York: Seven Stories Press.

———. 2005. *Abolition Democracy*. New York: Seven Stories Press.

———. 2015. "Slavery and the Prison Industrial Complex." *American Program Bureau*. <youtube.com/watch?v=BasNj57GvTA>.

Dei, George J., Josephine Mazzuca, Elizabeth McIsaac and Jasmin Zine. 1997. *Reconstructing 'Dropout': A Critical Ethnography of the Dynamics of Black Students' Disengagement from School*. Toronto: University of Toronto Press.

Dei, George J. Sefa and Irma Marcia James. 1998. "'Becoming Black': African-Canadian Youth and the Politics of Negotiating Racial and Racialised Identities." *Race Ethnicity and Education* 1.1: 91–108.

Department of Justice of Canada. 1989. *Street Prostitution: Assessing the Impact of the Law*. Ottawa.

Democracy Now! May 20 2016. "Part 1: Canada's Indigenous and Black Lives Matter Activists Unite to Protest Violence and Neglect." <youtube.com/watch?v=71OUZp0kHOY>.

Dimmock, Gary. October 3, 2016. "Inside the Ottawa Jail's Shower Cells: 'Nothing Short of Disgusting.'" *Ottawa Citizen*. <ottawacitizen.com/news/local-news/0325-jail>.

Donkin, Karissa. March 10, 2016. "New Brunswick Will Review Cases Involving Motherisk Testing." *CBC News*. <cbc.ca/news/canada/new-brunswick/new-brunswick-motherisk-testing-1.3484697>.

Donovan, Ken. 2014. "Female Slaves as Sexual Victims in Île Royale." *Acadiensis* 43.1: 147–156.

Draaisma, Muriel. May 26, 2016. "Stop Transfer of Immigration Detainees to Provincial Jails, Lawyers Tell Minister." *CBC News*. <cbc.ca/news/canada/toronto/lawyers-legal-specialists-immigration-detainees-ontario-jails-1.3601390>.

Dubinsky, Karen. 2008. "'We Adopted a Negro': Interracial Adoption and the Hybrid Baby in 1960s Canada." In Robert Rutherdale and Magda Fahrni (eds.), *Creating Postwar Canada: Community, Diversity, and Dissent, 1945–1975*. Vancouver: University of British Columbia Press. 268–288.

Dupuis, Josée, and Anne Panasuk. March 31 2016a. "Après Val-D'or, D'autres Femmes Autochtones Brisent Le Silence." *Radio-Canada*. <ici.radio-canada.ca/nouvelles/societe/2016/03/31/001-femmes-autochones-abus-policiers.shtml>.

———. May 13, 2016b. "More Quebec Indigenous Women Break Their Silence About Police Abuse." *CBC News*. <cbc.ca/news/indigenous/quebec-investigation-alleged-abuse-aboriginal-women-1.3577527>.

Edwards, David. July 22, 2015. "CNN Panel Explodes after Ex-Cop Says Sandra Bland Died Because She Was 'Arrogant from the Beginning.'" *Raw Story*. <alternet.org/media/cnn-panel-explodes-after-ex-cop-says-sandra-bland-died-because-she-was-arrogant-beginning>.

Egan, Kelly. April 19, 2015. "Profs, Moms, Lawyers Alarmed at Jail Conditions at Innes Road." *Ottawa Citizen*. <ottawacitizen.com/opinion/columnists/

egan-profs-moms-lawyers-alarmed-at-jail-conditions-at-innes-road>.

End Immigration Detention Network. March 22, 2016a. "Family of Man Who Died in Immigration Detention Seeking Answers." Media advisory. <endimmigrationdetention.com/2016/03/22/family-of-man-who-died-in-immigration-detention-seeking-answers/>.

―――. April 22, 2016b. We Remember, We Resist ― No More Deaths! No More Detentions! No One Is Illegal Toronto. Press release. <toronto.nooneisillegal.org/node/996>.

Elizabeth Fry Society. n.d. "Facts Sheet Human and Fiscal Costs of Prison." <efsmanitoba.org/Facts-Sheet.page>.

Engler, Yves, and Anthony Fenton. 2005. *Canada in Haiti: Waging War on the Poor Majority.* Vancouver: Red Publishing.

Engler, Yves. 2015. *Canada in Africa: 300 Years of Aid and Exploitation.* Black Point, Winnipeg: Fernwood Publishing.

English, Kathy. February 11, 1994. "Metro police Probed Black 'Activists' Mississauga Teen's Slaying Prompted Confidential Study Laws Hearing Told." *Toronto Star.*

Escobar, Martha. 2008. "No One Is Illegal." In Critical Resistance (ed.), *Abolition Now! Ten Years of Strategy and Struggle against the Prison Industrial Complex.* Oakland: AK Press. 57–69.

Extian-Babiuk, Tamara. 2006. "'To Be Sold, a Negro Wench': Slave Ads of the Montreal Gazette, 1785–1805." Dissertation. McGill University.

Fanon, Frantz. 2008. *Black Skin, White Masks.* E-book, EBSCOhost. London: Pluto Press.

Federici, Silvia. 2012. *Revolution at Point Zero Housework, Reproduction, and Feminist Struggle.* Oakland, Brooklyn: PM Press; Common Notions: Autonomedia.

Fine, Sean. December 20, 2013. "The Victor: Terri-Jean Bedford Spent 20 Years Fighting Prostitution Laws." *Globe and Mail.* <theglobeandmail.com/news/national/the-victor-terri-jean-bedford-spent-20-years-fighting-prostitution-laws/article16081828/>.

Fitzpatrick, Meagan. May 9, 2012. "Inmates in Canada Will Pay More Money for Their Room and Board." *CBC News.* <cbc.ca/news/politics/inmates-to-pay-more-for-room-and-board-1.1156979>.

Fleras, Augie. 2014. *Racisms in a Multicultural Canada: Paradoxes, Politics, and Resistance.* Waterloo: Wilfrid Laurier University Press.

Fletcher, Tor. 2013. "Trans Sex Workers: Negotiating Sex, Gender and Non-Normative Desire." In Emily van der Meulen and Elya M. Durisin (eds.), *Selling Sex: Experience, Advocacy, and Research on Sex Work in Canada.* Vancouver: University of British Columbia Press. 65–73.

Forrester, Monica. 2017. Co-ordinator at Maggie's drop-in centre (Toronto). Personal communication.

Foster, Cecil. 1996. *A Place Called Heaven: The Meaning of Being Black in Canada.* Toronto: HarperCollins.

Foster, Thomas A. 2011. "The Sexual Abuse of Black Men under American Slavery." *Journal of the History of Sexuality* 20.3: 445–64.

Fraser Committee. 1985. *Fraser Committee Report.* Ottawa: Ministry of Justice of Canada.

Galabuzi, Grace-Edward. 2006. *Canada's Economic Apartheid: The Social Exclusion of*

Racialized Groups in the New Century. Toronto: Canadian Scholars' Press.

Galtung, Johan. 1969. "Violence, Peace, and Peace Research." *Journal of Peace Research* 6.3: 167–91.

Gendreau et al. 1999. *The Effect of Prison on Criminal Behaviour: Research Summary.* Ottawa: Solicitor General.

Gendreau, Paul, Claire Goggin and Francis T. Cullen. 1999. "The Effects of Prison Sentences on Recidivism, 1999-3." Ottawa: Solicitor General.

Gillis, Wendy. May 10, 2015a. "Investigations against Police Double in Past Decade." *Toronto Star.* <thestar.com/news/crime/2015/05/10/siu-investigations-against-police-double-in-past-decade.html>.

———. August 16, 2015b. "How Many Black Men Have Been Killed by Toronto Police? We Can't Know." *Toronto Star.* <thestar.com/news/crime/2015/08/16/how-many-black-men-have-been-killed-by-toronto-police-we-cant-know.html >.

———. July 21, 2015c. "No Charges against Police in Death of Jermaine Carby." *Toronto Star.* <thestar.com/news/crime/2015/07/21/no-charges-against-peel-police-in-death-of-jermaine-carby.html>.

———. July 9, 2015d. "Police Must Address Race Factor in Fatal Shootings, Say Community Groups." *Toronto Star.* <thestar.com/news/crime/2015/07/09/police-must-address-race-factor-in-fatal-shootings-say-community-groups.html>.

———. January 3, 2015e. "Mother Remembers Ian Pryce, Shot by Police in 2013 with a Pellet Gun in His Hand." *Toronto Star.* <thestar.com/news/crime/2015/01/03/mother_remembers_ian_pryce_shot_by_police_in_2013_with_a_pellet_gun_in_his_hand.html>.

———. April 1, 2016b. "Councillors Want Review of SIU through 'Anti-Black Racism' Lens." *Toronto Star.* <thestar.com/news/crime/2016/04/01/councillors-want-review-of-siu-through-anti-black-racism-lens.html>.

———. May 5, 2016b. "Mental Health Group Raises Questions About Police Response to Loku Shooting." *Toronto Star.* <thestar.com/news/crime/2016/05/05/mental-health-group-raises-questions-about-police-response-to-loku-shooting.html>.

Gilmore, Ruth Wilson. 2007. *Golden Gulag: Prisons, Surplus, Crisis, and Opposition in Globalizing California.* Berkeley: University of California Press.

———. November 9, 2015. "Organized Abandonment and Organized Violence: Devolution and the Police." <vimeo.com/1464506862015>.

Gira Grant, Melissa. May 26, 2016. "Amnesty International Calls for an End to the Nordic Model of Criminalizing Sex Workers." *Nation.* <thenation.com/article/amnesty-international-calls-for-an-end-to-the-nordic-model-of-criminalizing-sex-workers/>.

Global Commission on Drug Policy. June 2011. *War on Drugs: Report of the Global Commission on Drug Policy.* Geneva.

Global Detention Project. 2012. "Canada Immigration Detention Profile." <globaldetentionproject.org/countries/americas/canada>

Goff, Phillip Antiba, Matthew Christian Jackson, Brooke Allison Lewis Di Leone, Carmen Marie Culotta and Natalie Ann DiTomasso. 2014. "The Essence of Innocence: Consequences of Dehumanizing Black Children." *Journal of Personality and Social Psychology* 106.4: 526–45.

Goldie, James. January 17, 2017. "Canada to deport lesbian refugee to country where being gay is a crime." *Xtra.* <dailyxtra.com/canada-to-deport-lesbian-refugee-to-country-where-being-gay-is-a-crime-72855>.

Goldsbie, Jonathan. May 13, 2015. "Police Carding: Racist, Anti-Black, and Useless." *Now Toronto.* <nowtoronto.com/news/police-carding-racist-anti-black-and-useless/>.

Gordon, Lewis R. 1995. *Bad Faith and Antiblack Racism.* Atlantic Highlands New Jersey: Humanities Press International.

———. 1997. *Her Majesty's Other Children: Sketches of Racism from a Neocolonial Age.* Lanham, MD: Rowman & Littlefield.

Gordon, Todd. 2006. "Neoliberalism, Racism, and the War on Drugs in Canada." *Social Justice* 33.1 (103): 59–78.

Gordon, Todd, and Jeffery R. Webber. 2008. "Imperialism and Resistance: Canadian Mining Companies in Latin America." *Third World Quarterly* 29.1: 63–87.

Government of Canada. n.d. "Key Events in Black Canadian History." <canada.ca/en/canadian-heritage/campaigns/black-history-month/key-events.html>.

———. n.d. "Permanent Mission of Canada to the United Nations: Haiti." *Global Affairs Canada.* <canadainternational.gc.ca/prmny-mponu/canada_un-canada_onu/positions-orientations/regions/haiti.aspx?lang=eng>.

Grant, Jaime, Lisa A. Mottet, Justin Tanis, Jack Harrison, Jody L. Herman and Mara Keisling. 2011. *Injustice at Every Turn: A Report of the National Transgender Discrimination Survey.* Washington: National Center for Transgender Equality and National Gay and Lesbian Task Force.

Grewal, Sam. November 7, 2007. "Hospital Couldn't Hold Shooting Victim." *Toronto Star.* <thestar.com/news/gta/2007/11/07/hospital_couldnt_hold_shooting_victim.html>.

Grizzle, Stanley G. 1998. *My Name's Not George: The Story of the Brotherhood of Sleeping Car Porters: Personal Reminiscences.* Toronto: Umbrella Press.

Haley, Sarah. 2016. *No Mercy Here: Gender, Punishment, and the Making of Jim Crow Modernity.* Chapel Hill: University of North Carolina Press.

Hall, Joseph, and Dana Flavelle. December 11, 1988. "'Disgusted' Blacks Want Provincial Probe." *Toronto Star.* <search.proquest.com.proxy3.library.mcgill.ca/docview/435838225?accountid=12339>.

Hall, Stuart, Chas Critcher, Tony Jefferson, John Clarke and Brian Roberts. 2013. *Policing the Crisis: Mugging, the State, and Law and Order.* Second Edition. New York: Palgrave Macmillan.

Hamilton, Sylvia. 1999. "Naming Names, Naming Ourselves: A Survey of Early Black Women in Nova Scotia." In Peggy Bristow, Dionne Brand, Linda Carty, Afua P. Cooper, Sylvia Hamilton, Adrienne Shadd (eds.). *"We're Rooted Here and They Can't Pull Us Up: Essays in African Canadian Women's History.* Toronto: University of Toronto Press.

———. 2011. *"Stories from the Little Black School House."* In Ashok Mathur, Jonathan Dewar, Mike DeGagné (eds.), *Cultivating Canada: A Reconciliation through the Lens of Cultural Diversity.* Ottawa: Aboriginal Healing Foundation. 91–112.

———. 2014. *And I Alone Escaped to Tell You.* Kentville: Gaspereau Press.

Hampton, Rosalind. 2010. "Black Learners in Canada." *Race & Class* 52.1: 103–10.

Haney-López, Ian F. 1994. "Social Construction of Race: Some Observations on Illusion, Fabrication, and Choice." *29 Harv C.R.-C.L. L. Rev 1.*

Hannah-Moffat, Kelly, and Margaret Shaw, eds. 2006. *An Ideal Prison? Critical Essays on Women's Imprisonment in Canada*. Black Point, Winnipeg: Fernwood Publishing.

Harris, Kathleen. December 8 2016. "Black Rights Activist Viola Desmond to Be 1st Canadian Woman on $10 Bill." *CBC News*. <cbc.ca/news/politics/canadian-banknote-woman-1.3885844>.

Harris, LaShawn. 2016. *Sex Workers, Psychics, and Numbers Runners*. The New Black Studies Series. Chicago: Univeristy of Illinois Press.

Hart, Carl. 2013. *High Price: A Neuroscientist's Journey of Self-Discovery That Challenges Everything You Know About Drugs and Society*. New York: HarperCollins.

Hartman, Saidiya. 2007. *Lose Your Mother: A Journey Along the Atlantic Slave Route*. New York: Farrar, Straus and Giroux.

Hartman, Saidiya V. 1997. *Scenes of Subjection: Terror, Slavery, and Self-Making in Nineteenth-Century America*. New York: Oxford University Press.

Hayter, Teresa. 2004. *Open Borders: The Case against Immigration Controls*. London, Ann Arbor: Pluto Press.

Henry, Annette. 1993. "Missing: Black Self-Representations in Canadian Educational Research. *Canadian Journal of Education/Revue canadienne de l'education* 18.3: 206–22.

Henry, Frances. 1994. *The Caribbean Diaspora in Toronto: Learning to Live with Racism*. Toronto: University of Toronto Press.

Henry, Frances, and Carol Tator. 2006. *Racial Profiling in Canada: Challenging the Myth of 'a Few Bad Apples.'* Toronto: University of Toronto Press.

Hill, Daniel Grafton. 1981. *The Freedom-Seekers: Blacks in Early Canada*. Agincourt: Book Society of Canada.

"HIV and Sex Workers." 2014. *Lancet*. Series. <thelancet.com/series/HIV-and-sex-workers>

Hodge, Jarrah. 2006. "'Unskilled Labour': Canada's Live-in Caregiver Program." *Undercurrent* 3.2: 60–66.

Hoffman, Kelly M., Sophie Trawalter and Adam Waytz. 2015. "A Superhumanization Bias in Whites' Perceptions of Blacks." *Social Psychological and Personality Science* 6.3: 352–59.

Holden, Alfred. March 4, 1990. "Sophia Cook Was Given a Standing Ovation." *Toronto Star*. <search.proquest.com.proxy3.library.mcgill.ca/docview/436160574?accoun tid=12339>.

hooks, bell. 1992. *Black Looks: Race and Representation*. Boston: South End Press.

Hope, Clover. May 29, 2016. "Janet Mock: 'Trans Black Women Live at the Intersection of Pass Her by and Pay Her No Mind.'" *Jezebel.com*. <jezebel.com/janet-mock-trans-black-women-live-at-the-intersection-1773879179>.

House of Commons. 2009. *Part II: Non-Status Workers*. Ottawa: Parliament of Canada. <parl.gc.ca/HousePublications/Publication.aspx?DocId=3866154&Language=E& Mode=1&Parl=40&Ses=2&File=141#_ftn4)>.

———. February 6, 2013. "Jason Kenney on Faster Removal of Foreign Criminals Act." *Government Orders, House of Commons*. Ottawa: Parliament of Canada. <openparliament. ca/debates/2013/2/6/jason-kenney-2/only/>.

Hsiung, Ping-Chu,n and Katherine Nichol. 2010. "Policies on and Experiences of Foreign Domestic Workers in Canada." *Sociology Compass* 4/9: 766–78.

Hudson, Peter. 2010. "Imperial Designs: The Royal Bank of Canada in the Caribbean." *Race and Class* 52.1: 33–48.

Human Rights Watch. 2013. *Those Who Take Us Away: Abusive Policing and Failures in Protection of Indigenous Women and Girls in Northern British Columbia, Canada.*

Hunt, Sarah. 2013. "Decolonizing Sex Work: Developing an Intersectional Indigenous Approach." In Emily van der Meulen and Elya M. Durisin (eds.), *Selling Sex: Experience, Advocacy, and Research on Sex Work in Canada.* Vancouver: University of British Columbia Press. 82–100.

Hunt, Sarah, and Naomi Sayers. March 25, 2015. "Cindy Gladue Case Sends a Chilling Message to Indigenous Women." *Globe and Mail.* <theglobeandmail.com/opinion/cindy-gladue-case-sends-a-chilling-message-to-indigenous-women/article23609986/>.

Hurston, Zora Neale. 2013. *Their Eyes Were Watching God.* Harper Perennial Modern Classics.

Hussan, Syed. 2014. "Indefinite, Arbitrary and Unfair: The Truth About Immigration Detention in Canada." End Immigration Detention Network.

———. June 20, 2015. "Who Killed Abdurahman Ibrahim Hassan? Black Lives, Racisms, Police & Immigration." Toronto Media Co-op. <toronto.mediacoop.ca/blog/hussansk/33683>.

———. February 23, 2016. "4 Racial Profiling Incidents in Canada That Will Shock You." *Medium.* <medium.com/@hussansk/4-racial-profiling-incidents-in-canada-that-will-shock-you-8f309c93f646>.

———. July 14, 2016. Personal communication.

Iadicola, Peter, and Anson D. Shupe. 2003. *Violence, Inequality, and Human Freedom.* Lanham: Rowman & Littlefield Publishers.

INCITE! Women of Color Against Violence, ed. 2006. *Color of Violence: The Incite! Anthology.* Cambridge: South End Press.

———. n.d. "Law Enforcement Violence against Women of Color & Trans People of Color: A Critical Intersection of Gender Violence and State Violence." *INCITE! Women of Color Against Violence.* <incite-national.org/sites/default/files/incite_files/resource_docs/3696_toolkit-final.pdf)>.

Isaacs, Anna. 2016. "How the Black Lives Matter and Palestinian Movements Converged." *Moment.* March-April. <momentmag.com/22800-2/>.

Jacobs, Beverley. February 13, 2013. "Decolonizing the Violence Against Indigenous Women." *Decolonization: Indigeneity, Education & Society.* <decolonization.wordpress.com/2013/02/13/decolonizing-the-violence-against-indigenous-women/>.

Jamaica Observer. May 20, 2013. "Jamaican Woman Sentenced for Cocaine in Canada." <jamaicaobserver.com/news/Jamaican-woman-sentenced-for-cocaine-in-Canada>.

James, Carl, David Este, Wanda Thomas Bernard, Akua Benjamin, Bethan Lloyd and Tana Turner. 2010. *Race & Well-Being: The Lives, Hopes, and Activism of African Canadians.* Black Point, Winnipeg: Fernwood Publishing.

James, C.L.R. 1989. *The Black Jacobins: Toussaint L'ouverture and the San Domingo Revolution.* Second Edition Revised. New York, Toronto: Vintage Books.

James, Joy. 1996. *Resisting State Violence: Radicalism, Gender, and Race in U.S. Culture.* Minneapolis, London: University of Minnesota Press.

James, Llana. 2007. "Censure and Silence: Sexual Violence and Women of the African Diaspora." In Notisha Massaquoi and Njoki Nathani Wane (eds.), *Theorizing Empowerment: Canadian Perspectives on Black Feminist Thought.* Toronto: Inanna

Publications and Education. 228–44.

James, Royson. November 4, 2011. "James: Africentric School's Legacy of Success Must Graduate to High School." *Toronto Star*. <thestar.com/news/gta/2011/11/14/james_africentric_schools_legacy_of_success_must_graduate_to_high_school.html>.

Jeffords, Shawn. July 27, 2013. "Woman Deported to Jamaica, Leaves Son Behind." *Toronto Sun*. <torontosun.com/2013/07/27/woman-deported-to-jamaica-leaves-son-behind>.

Jones, Burnely "Rocky," and James St. G Walker. 2016. *Burnely "Rocky" Jones Revolutionary: An Autobiography*. Halifax: Roseway.

Jones, El. May 21, 2016. "New Residential Schools and Slavery's Afterlife." *Halifax Examiner*. <halifaxexaminer.ca/featured/new-residential-schools-and-slaverys-afterlife/#—>.

Judge, Shana M., and Mariah Wood. November 6, 2014. "Panel Paper: Racial Disparities in the Enforcement of Prostitution Laws." *Association for Public Policy Analysis and Management: Global Challenges, New Perspectives*.

Justice for Refugees and Immigrants Coalition (Amnesty International, Canadian Association of Refugee Lawyers, Canadian Civil Liberties Association, Canadian Council for Refugees). 2012. "Protect Refugees from Bill C-3: Joint Statement." <http://ccrweb.ca/en/protect-refugees-c31-statement>.

Justicia for Migrant Workers. n.d. "The Seasonal Agricultural Workers Program." <justicia4migrantworkers.org/bc/pdf/sawp.pdf>

Katz, Jonathan. August 17, 2016. "U.N. Admits Role in Cholera Epidemic in Haiti." *New York Times*. <nytimes.com/2016/08/18/world/americas/united-nations-haiti-cholera.html?_r=2>.

Kazemipur, Abdul Mohammed, and Shiva S Halli. 2001. "Immigrants and 'New Poverty': The Case of Canada." *International Migration Review* 35.4: 1129–56.

Kelley, Robin D.G. 2000. "Introduction: A Poetics of Anticolonialism." *Discourse on Colonialism*. New York: New York University Press. 7–28.

———. 2002. *Freedom Dreams: The Black Radical Imagination*. Boston: Beacon Press.

Kellough, Gailwort, and Scot Wortley. 2004. "Racializing Risk: Police and Crown Discretion and the Overrepresentation of Black People in the Ontario Criminal Justice System." In Anthony Harriott, Farley Brathwaite and Scot Wortley (eds.), *Crime and Criminal Justice in the Caribbean and among Caribbean Peoples*. Kingston: Arawak Publications. 173–205.

Kennedy, Brendan. March 17, 2017. "Caged by Canada: Part 1." *Toronto Star*. <http://projects.thestar.com/caged-by-canada-immigration-detention/part-1/>.

Kennedy, Kaley. February 27, 2012. "More Prisons, Higher Profits." *Dominion*. <dominionpaper.ca/articles/4333>.

Kennedy, Mark. December 30, 1989. "Drugs: Cocaine, Crack Tear a Gaping Hole in the Fabric of Society." *Ottawa Citizen*: TC34. *Canadian Newsstream*.

Kenney, Jason. June 20, 2012. "Speaking Notes for the Honourable Jason Kenney, P.C., M.P. Minister of Citizenship, Immigration and Multiculturalism." Government of Canada.

Keung, Nicholas. July 11, 2014. "Mysterious Man in Canadian Jail Is Mbuyisa Makhubu, Says Brother of Anti-Apartheid Icon." *Toronto Star*. <thestar.com/news/immigration/2014/07/11/mysterious_man_in_canadian_jail_is_mbuyisa_makhubu_says_brother_of_antiapartheid_icon.html>.

———. March 24, 2015. "Canada Faces Dramatic Drop in Citizenship, Prompting Concerns About Disengaged Immigrants." *Toronto Star*. <thestar.com/news/

immigration/2015/03/24/canada-faces-dramatic-drop-in-citizenship-prompting-concerns-about-disengaged-immigrants.html>.

———. September 20, 2016a. "Gay Asylum Seeker Fears for Her Life If Deported to Uganda." *Toronto Star*. <thestar.com/news/immigration/2016/09/29/gay-asylum-seeker-fears-for-her-life-if-deported-to-uganda.html>.

———. May 17, 2016b. "Healthcare Providers Urge Ontario to End Immigration Detention." *Toronto Star*. <thestar.com/news/immigration/2016/05/17/healthcare-providers-urge-ontario-to-end-immigration-detention.html>.

———. July 15, 2016c. "Police Cleared in Immigration Detainee's Death." *Toronto Star*. <thestar.com/news/immigration/2016/07/15/police-cleared-in-immigration-detainees-death.html>.

Khan, Janaya. n.d. "We Need to Come Together, but Not with the State." *Janaya Khan*. <http://janayakhan.com/2016/07/12/need-come-together-not-state/>

———. March 31, 2017. "Janaya Khan: The Criminal Justice System Is Broken: Should the Police Be Abolished?" *Fusion*. <fusion.net/the-criminal-justice-system-is-broken-should-the-polic-1793898217>

Khenti, A. 2014. "The Canadian War on Drugs: Structural Violence and Unequal Treatment of Black Canadians." *International Journal on Drug Policy* 25.2: 190–95.

Kidd, Sean A. 2003. "Street Youth: Coping and Interventions." *Child and Adolescent Social Work Journal* 20.4: 235–61.

King, Tiffany Lethobo. 2013. "In the Clearing: Black Female Bodies, Space and Settler Colonial Landscapes." Dissertation. University of Maryland.

———. June 10, 2014. "Labor's Aphasia: Toward Antiblackness as Constitutive to Settler Colonialism." *Decolonization: Indigeneity, Education & Society*. <decolonization.wordpress.com/2014/06/10/labors-aphasia-toward-antiblackness-as-constitutive-to-settler-colonialism/>.

Kitossa, Tamari. 2005. "*Malleus Maleficarum Africanus:* The Criminalization of African Canadians and 'Due Process' as a Property of Whiteness." In L.A Visano (ed.), *Law and Criminal Justice: A Critical Inquiry*. Toronto: APF Press. 153–72.

———. 2016. "Making Sense of Repression in Police Studies: Whither theorizing in the descent toward fascism." *Radical Criminology: An Insurgent Journal* 6.

Krusi, Andrea, Katrina Pacey, L. Bird, Chrissy Taylor, Jill Chettiar, Darcie Bennett, J.S. Montaner, Thomas Kerr and Kate Shannon. 2014. "Criminalisation of Clients: Reproducing Vulnerabilities for Violence and Poor Health among Street-Based Sex Workers in Canada — a Qualitative Study." *BMJ Open* 4.6.

Kumsa, Martha K. 2005. "Between Home & Exile: Dynamics of Negotiating Be-Longing among Young Oromos Living in Toronto." In Wisdom J. Tettey and Korbla P. Puplampu (eds.), *The African Diaspora in Canada: Negotiating Identity & Belonging*. Calgary: University of Calgary Press. 175–203.

Lafferty, Renee, N. 2013. "Race Uplift, Racism, and the Childhood Ideal: Founding and Funding the Nova Scotia Home for Colored Children, 1850–1960." In Renée Lafferty (ed.), *The Guardianship of Best Interests: Institutional Care for the Children of the Poor in Halifax*. Montreal & Kingston, London, Chicago: McGill-Queen's University Press. 63–87.

Laflamme, Nathalie. August 5, 2015. "Woman Says Arrest and Charges Were Racial

Discrimination." *Montreal Gazette.* <montrealgazette.com/news/local-news/woman-says-arrest-and-charges-were-racial-discrimination,>.

Lalonde, Michelle. January 12, 2015. "Police Shooting of Alain Magloire: What You Need to Know." *Montreal Gazette.* <montrealgazette.com/news/local-news/timeline-on-police-shooting-of-alain-magloire>.

Lareau, Stephanie. December 9, 2016. Outreach co-ordinator at Stella, l'amie de Maimie. Personal correspondence.

Lavergne, Chantal, Sarah Dufour, Janet Sarniento, Marie-Ève Descôteaux. 2009. "La Réponse Du Système De Protection De La Jeunesse Montréalais Aux Enfants Issus Des Minorités Visibles." *Intervention* 131 (Hiver): 233–41.

Lawrence, Bonita. 2005. "Rewriting Histories of the Land: Colonization and Indigenous Resistance in Eastern Canada." In Serene Razack (ed.), *Race, Space, and the Law: Unmapping a White Settler Society.* Toronto: Between the Lines. 21–46.

Lawrence, Sonia N., and Toni Williams. 2006. "Swallowed Up: Drug Couriers at the Borders of Canadian Sentencing." *University of Toronto Law Journal* 56.4: 285–332.

Lawson, Erica. 2002. "Images in Black: Black Women, Media and the Mythology of an Orderly Society." In Wane Njoki N., Katerina Deliovsky and Erica Lawson (eds.), *Back to the Drawing Board: African-Canadian Feminisms.* Toronto: Sumach Press. 199–223.

Leavitt, Sarah. March 31, 2016. "More Aboriginal Women Allege Abuse at Hands of Quebec Provincial Police." CBC *News.* <cbc.ca/news/canada/montreal/quebec-police-aboriginal-indigenous-sex-abuse-allegations-1.3512459>.

Leech, Garry M. 2012. *Capitalism: A Structural Genocide.* London: Zed Books.

Legal Foundation of the LGBT Law Association of Greater New York. December, 2006. "South Africa Embraces Freedom to Marry." In *Lesbian/Gay Law Notes.* 226–240. <nyls.edu/documents/justice-action center/lesbiangay_law_notes/ln0612.pdf>.

Lewis, Stephen. 1992. *Stephen Lewis Report on Race Relations in Ontario.* Toronto: Ontario Advisor on Race Relations.

Liberal Party of Canada. 2015. "Statement by Liberal Party of Canada Leader Justin Trudeau on the Anniversary of Multiculturalism." <liberal.ca/statement-by-liberal-party-of-canada-leader-justin-trudeau-on-the-anniversary-of-multiculturalism/>.

Livingstone, Anne-Marie. 2010. *Black Youth's Perspectives on Educational Challenges and Policy.* School of Social Work, McGill University.

Logan, Nick. August 26, 2015. "'Man with No Name' Detainee Deported from Canada: Source." *Global News.* <http://globalnews.ca/news/2185233/man-with-no-name-detainee-deported-from-canada-source/>.

Loney, Heather. December 20, 2013. "Who Is Terri-Jean Bedford, the Dominatrix Fighting Canada's Prostitution Laws." *Global News.* <globalnews.ca/news/1043102/who-is-terri-jean-bedford-the-dominatrix-fighting-canadas-prostitution-laws/>.

Loyd, Jenna M., Matt Mitchelson and Andrew Burridge. 2012. "Introduction Borders, Prisons, and Abolitionist Visions." In Jenna M. Loyd, Matt Mitchelson and Andrew Burridge (eds.), *Beyond Walls and Cages: Prisons, Borders, and Global Crisis.* Athens: University of Georgia Press. 1–18.

Luck, Shaina. May 20, 2016. "Black, Indigenous Prisoners over-Represented in Nova Scotia Jails." CBC *News.* <cbc.ca/news/canada/nova-scotia/black-indigenous-prisoners-nova-scotia-jails-1.3591535>.

Lupick, Travis. December 13, 2015. "Living Nightmare for Transgender Inmate at All-Male Prison." *Toronto Star.* <thestar.com/news/canada/2015/12/13/living-nightmare-for-transgender-inmate-at-all-male-prison.html>.

MacEwen, Angella, and Christine Saulnier. 2010. *The Cost of Poverty in Nova Scotia.* Halifax: Canadian Centre for Policy Alternatives, Nova Scotia Office.

Mackey, Frank. 2010. *Done with Slavery: Rhe Black Fact in Montreal, 1760–1840.* Montreal & Kingston, London, Chicago: McGill-Queen's University Press.

Macklin, Audrey. 1992. "Foreign Domestic Worker: Surrogate Housewife or Mail Order Servant?" *McGill Law Journal* 37.3: 6781–60.

Maharaj, Sachin. March 4, 2014). "Streaming in Schools Cements Inequality." *Toronto Star.* <thestar.com/opinion/commentary/2014/03/04/streaming_in_schools_cements_inequality.html>.

Makin, Kirk. December 17, 2010. "Strip-Searched Ottawa Woman Sues Police." *Globe and Mail.* <theglobeandmail.com/news/national/strip-searched-ottawa-woman-sues-police/article1320301/>.

Michaud, Liam. 2016. (Former) street-worker at Cactus-Montreal. Personal communication.

Mancuso, Rebecca. August 31, 1999. "'This is our work': The Women's Division of the Canadian Department of Immigration and Colonization, 1919–1938." Dissertation. McGill University. <nlc-bnc.ca/obj/s4/f2/dsk2/ftp03/NQ64614.pdf.>

Manuel, Arthur, and Grand Chief Ron Derrickson. 2015. *Unsettling Canada.* Toronto: Between the Lines.

Movement Advancement Project (MAP) and Center for American Progress. 2015. "Paying an Unfair Price the Financial Penalty for Lgbt People of Color." <lgbtmap.org/unfair-price-lgbt-people-of-color>.

Marquis, Greg. 1995. "Vancouver Vice: The Police and the Negotiation of Morality, 1904–1935." In Hamar Foster and John McLaren (eds.), *Essays in the History of Canadian Law Volume VI: The Legal History of British Columbia and the Yukon.* Vol. 6. Toronto: The Osgoode Society and University of Toronto Press. 242–74.

Martinot, Steve, and Jared Sexton. 2003. "The Avant-Garde of White Supremacy." *Social Identities* 9.2: 169–81.

Mascarenhas, Roland. June 29, 2015. "In Defence of Carding, and the Police." *National Post.* <http://news.nationalpost.com/full-comment/roland-mascarenhas-in-defence-of-carding-and-the-police>.

Mascoll, Philip. February 25, 1990. "Murderous Posses Gain Metro Foothold." *Toronto Star*: A1. *Proquest Canadian Newsstream.*

Mascoll, Phillip. January 9, 2007. "A fighter for Justice Wherever She Went." *Toronto Star.* <http://search.proquest.com.proxy3.library.mcgill.ca/docview/439132330?accountid=12339>.

Massaquoi, Notisha. 2013. "No Place Like Home: African Refugees and the Emergence of a New Clear Frame of Reference." In S.N. Nyeck and Marc Epprecht (eds.), *Sexual Diversity in Africa: Politics, Theory, and Citizenship.* Montreal & Kingston, London, Chicago: McGill-Queen's University Press. 37–53.

Mathieu, Sarah-Jane. 2010. *North of the Color Line Migration and Black Resistance in Canada, 1870–1955.* Chapel Hill: University of North Carolina Press.

Maynard, Robyn. June 8, 2010. "Double Punishment for Villanueva." *The Dominion.*

<dominionpaper.ca/articles/3475>

———. 2015. "Fighting Wrongs with Wrongs? How Canadian Anti-Trafficking Crusades Have Failed Sex Workers, Migrants, and Indigenous Communities." *Atlantis: Critical Studies in Gender, Culture & Social Justice* 37.2: 40–56.

———. July 31, 2016. "Let death of Abdirahman Abdi be last of its kind." *Toronto Star.* thestar.com/opinion/commentary/2016/07/31/let-death-of-abdirahman-abdi-be-last-of-its-kind.html

——— 2017. "Initiatives face au profilage racial" *Revues droits et libertés, Ligue des droits et libertés,* 35: 2. < http://liguedesdroits.ca/?p=4088>

McCalla, Andrea, and Vic Satzewich. 2002. "Settler Capitalism and the Construction of Immigrants and 'Indians' as Racialized Others." In Wendy Chan and Kiran Mirchandani (eds.), *Crimes of Colour: Racialization and the Criminal Justice System in Canada.* Toronto: University of Toronto Press. 25–44.

McCormack, Mike. July 20, 2015. "Baseless Accusations of Police Racism Harm Toronto." Editorial. *Toronto Star.* <thestar.com/opinion/commentary/2015/07/20/baseless-accusations-of-police-racism-harm-toronto.html>.

McIntyre, Catherine. May 13, 2015. "Migrant Sex Workers Caught up in Ottawa Sting Facing Deportation, Further Exploitation: Activists." *National Post.* <http://news.nationalpost.com/news/canada/migrant-sex-workers-caught-up-in-ottawa-sting-facing-deportation-further-exploitation-activists>.

McKittrick, Katherine. 2006. *Demonic Grounds: Black Women and the Cartographies of Struggle.* Minneapolis: University of Minnesota Press.

McLaren, A. 1990. *Our Own Master Race: Eugenics in Canada, 1885–1945.* Oxford: Oxford University Press.

McLaren, Angus. 2008 "Stemming the Flood of Defective Aliens." In Barrington Walker (ed.), *The History of Immigration and Racism in Canada: Essential Readings.* Toronto: Canadian Scholars' Press. 189–204.

McLaren, Kristin. 2003. "British-Canadian Myths of Purity and Segregated Schools in Mid-Nineteenth Century Canada West." *Historical Papers: Canadian Society of Church History.* 73–85.

———. 2004. "'We Had No Desire to Be Set Apart': Forced Segregation of Black Students in Canada West Public Schools and Myths of British Egalitarianism." *Histoire sociale/ Social History* 37.73: 27–50.

———. 2008. "'We Had No Desire to Be Set Apart': Forced Segregation of Black Students in Canada West Public Schools and Myths of British Egalitarianism." In Barrington Walker (ed.), *The History of Immigration and Racism in Canada: Essential Readings.* Toronto: Canadian Scholars' Press. 2008. 69–81.

McQuigge, Michelle. February 14, 2016. "Canada Is a Two-Tier System: Syrians Not the Only Ones Fleeing Adversity at Home, Experts and Refugees Say." *National Post.* <nationalpost.com/news/canada/canadas-two-tier-refugee-system-syrians-not-the-only-ones-fleeing-adversity-at-home-experts-and-migrants-say/wcm/ f83c337f-2ee9-4905-b186-0f6caa99b1c9>.

———. January 8, 2017. "Pride Toronto Votes to Adopt Demands from Black Lives Matter and Ban Police Floats from Parades." *National Post.* <news.nationalpost.com/toronto/ pride-toronto-votes-to-adopt-demands-from-black-lives-matter-and-ban-police-floats-

from-parades>.

Mendleson, Rachel. March 12, 2015. "Motherisk Review Could Have Canada-Wide Implications." *Toronto Star.* <thestar.com/news/crime/2015/03/12/motherisk-review-could-have-canada-wide-implications.html>.

Michaud, Shaun. April 21, 2016. "Two Police Shootings, Eight Years Apart, One Fed Up Montreal Borough" *Vice News.* <news.vice.com/article/eight-years-after-fredy-villanueva-was-shot-and-killed-by-police-in-montreal-north-a-memorial-for-jean-pierre-bony>.

Mickelson, Roslin Arlin. 2007. "First and Second Generation School Segregation and Maintenance of Educational Inequality." In Richard Teese, Stephen Lamb and Marie Duru-Bellat (eds.), *International Studies in Educational Inequality, Theory and Policy.* E-book ed.: Springer. 357–73.

Migdal, Alex. August 24, 2016. "Black Lives Matter Protests Death of Abdirahman Abdi across Canada." *Globe and Mail.* <theglobeandmail.com/news/national/black-lives-matter-protests-death-of-abdirahman-abdi-in-cities-across-canada/article31531189/>.

Migrant Sex Workers Project. *Report on Migrant Sex Workers Justice and the Trouble with "Anti-Trafficking": Research, Activism, Art.* <migrantsexworkers.com/report.html>.

Miller-Young, Mireille. 2014. *A Taste for Brown Sugar: Black Women in Pornography.* Durham: Duke University Press.

Millet, Kris. 2015. "Project Traveller and the Criminalization of Somali Canadian Youth." M.A. research paper. Trent University.

Mills, Sean. 2013. "Quebec, Haiti, and the Deportation Crisis of 1974." *Canadian Historical Review.* 94.3: 405–35.

———. 2016. *A Place in the Sun: Haiti, Haitians, and the Remaking of Quebec.* Montreal & Kingston, London, Chicago: McGill-Queen's University Press.

Mirchandani, Kiran and Wendy Chan. 2005. *The Racialized Impact of Welfare Fraud Control in British Columbia and Ontario.* Ontario: ProQuest ebrary.

Monsebraaten, Laurie. May 14, 2012. "Ontario's Youth Leaving Care Hearings Call for Fundamental Change to Child Welfare System." *Toronto Star.* <thestar.com/news/article/1177881--ontario-s-youth-leaving-careh>.

Montreal Gazette. October 17, 2014. "Montreal Officers Won't Face Charges in Shooting of Homeless Man." <montrealgazette.com/health/Montreal+officers+face+charges+shooting+homeless/10168315/story.html>.

Moore, Erin. November 20, 2015. "Family Fears for Woman Deported to St. Vincent." CBC *News.*

Morgan, Patricia, and Karen Ann Joe. 1997. "Uncharted Terrain." *Women & Criminal Justice* 8.3.

Morris, Edward W., and Brea L Perry. 2016. "The Punishment Gap: School Suspension and Racial Disparities in Achievement." *Social Problems:* 68–86.

Mosher, Clayton James. 1998. *Discrimination and Denial: Systemic Racism in Ontario's Legal and Criminal Justice Systems, 1892–1961.* Toronto: University of Toronto Press.

Mosher, Clayton James and Scott Akins. 2015. "Drugs and Drug Control in Canada." In Anita Kalunta-Crumpton (ed.), *Pan-African Issues in Drugs and Drug Control: An International Perspective.* Farnham, Surrey: Ashgate Publishing.

Mosher, Janet and Joe Hermer. 2005. *Welfare Fraud: The Constitution of Social Assistance as*

Crime. Ontario: Report Prepared for the Law Commission of Canada.

Movement for Black Lives. 2016. "Platform." <https://policy.m4bl.org/platform>.

Mugabo, Délice Igicari. 2015. "Rebirth of the Slick: Transformative Justice and New Black Feminist Possibilities in Montreal." Paper presented at the American Studies Association Conference.

———. 2016. "Geographies and Futurities of Being: Radical Black Activism in a Context of Anti-Black Islamophobia in 1990s Montreal." Masters thesis. Concordia University.

Murphy, Emily F. 1973. *The Black Candle*. Toronto: T. Allen.

Naccarato, Lisa. April 11, 2017. "Almost Half of TDSB Students Expelled over Last 5 Years Are Black, Report Says." *CBC News*. <cbc.ca/news/canada/toronto/almost-half-of-tdsb-students-expelled-over-last-5-years-are-black-report-says-1.4065088>.

Namaste, Viviane K. 2005. *Sex Change, Social Change: Reflections on Identity, Institutions, and Imperialism*. Toronto: Women's Press.

Nangwaya, Ajamu. February 7, 2011. "Factsheet on Police Containment of and Violence in the African Community." *Toronto Media Co-op*. <toronto.mediacoop.ca/blog/ajamu-nangwaya/6183>.

Nasser, Shanifa. April 30, 2016. "Police Officers' Conduct Threatened Credibility of SIU Probe into Andrew Loku Death: Report." *CBC News*. <cbc.ca/news/canada/toronto/police-officers-conduct-threatened-credibility-of-siu-probe-into-andrew-loku-death-report-1.3559597>.

Nathan, Debbie. April 21, 2016. "What happened to Sandra Bland?" *The Nation*. <thenation.com/article/what-happened-to-sandra-bland/>.

Native Women's Association of Canada. n.d. *Fact Sheet: Missing and Murdered Aboriginal Women and Girls*. <https://nwac.ca/wpcontent/uploads/2015/05/Fact_Sheet_Missing_and_Murdered_Aboriginal_Women_and_Girls>.

Nelson, Charmaine A. 2016a. "From African to Creole: Examining Creolization through the Art and Fugitive Slave Advertisements of Eighteenth- and Nineteenth-Century Canada and Jamaica." Art Gallery of Ontario, McCready Lecture on Canadian Art. <youtube.com/watch?v=Gq1-5ERv0oI>.

———. 2016b. "Canadian Fugitive Slave Advertisements: An Untapped Archive of Resistance." *Early Canadian History*. <https://earlycanadianhistory.ca/2016/02/29/canadian-fugitive-slave-advertisements-an-untapped-archive-of-resistance/>.

———. 2016c. *Slavery, Geography and Empire in Nineteenth-Century Marine Landscapes of Montreal and Jamaica*. London, New York: Routledge, Taylor & Francis Group.

Nelson, Erin. 2013. *Law, Policy and Reproductive Autonomy*. Oxford: Hart Publishing.

Nease, Kristy. July 26, 2016. "Ottawa Police Union President Calls Racism Speculation in Fatal Arrest 'Inappropriate.'" *CBC News*. <cbc.ca/news/canada/ottawa/matt-skof-abdirahman-abdi-amran-ali-1.3695349>.

Neve, Lisa, and Kim Pate. 2004. "Challenging the Criminalization of Women Who Resist." In Julia Sudbury (ed.), *Global Lockdown: Race, Gender, and the Prison-Industrial Complex*. New York: Routledge.

Nichols, Robert. 2014. "The Colonialism of Incarceration." *Radical Philosophy Review* 17.2: 435–55.

Noble-Hearle, Misha. November 21, 2014. "'Killing Us Softly': Wanda Thomas Bernard on Racism in Nova Scotia." *Dalhousie University News*. <dal.ca/

news/2014/11/21/-killing-us-softly---wanda-thomas-bernard-on-racism-in-nova-scot.html>.

Non-Status Women's Collective of Montreal. November 27, 2015. "Open Letter from the Non-Status Women's Collective of Montreal." *Solidarity Across Borders.* <solidarityacrossborders.org/en/open-letter-from-the-non-status-womens-collective-of-montreal>.

Nunn, Kenneth B. 2002. "Race, Crime and the Pool of Surplus Criminality: Or Why the 'War on Drugs' Was a 'War on Blacks'" 6 J. *Gender, Race & Justice* 381–445.

OACAS (Ontario Association of Children's Aid Societies). 2016. *One Vision One Voice: Changing the Ontario Child Welfare System to Better Serve African Canadians.* <oacas.org/wp-content/uploads/2016/09/One-Vision-One-Voice-Part-1_digital_english.pdf>.

———. 2015. *One Vision One Voice: Changing the Child Welfare System for African Canadians* <oacas.org/what-we-do/government-and-stakeholder-relations/one-vision-one-voice/#tab-2)>.

OCASI (Ontario Council of Agencies Serving Immigrants). March 2016. *Somali Refugee Resettlement in Canada.*

OHRC (Ontario Human Rights Commission). 2003. Paying the Price: *The Human Cost of Racial Profiling.* Toronto.

———. May 17, 2007. "Tribunal Rules Racial Profiling in Case against Peel Police."

———. 2013. *Policy on Removing the "Canadian Experience" Barrier: Introduction.* <ohrc.on.ca/en/policy-removing-%E2%80%9Ccanadian-experience%E2%80%9D-barrier>.

———. 2016. *Speaking out on Racial Discrimination.* Ontario Human Rights Commission. <ohrc.on.ca/tl/node/17971>.

Okeke-Iherjirika, Philomina, and Denise L. Spitzer. 2005. "In Search of Identity: Intergenerational Experiences of African Youth in a Canadian Context." In Wisdom J. Tettey and Korbla P. Puplampu (eds.), *The African Diaspora in Canada: Negotiating Identity & Belonging.* Calgary: University of Calgary Press. 205–24.

Ontario College of Family Physicians. 2013. *Poverty: A Clinical Tool 2013.* Toronto.

Ontario Ministry of the Attorney General. 2015. *Report of the Motherisk Hair Analysis, Independent Review.* The Honourable Susan E. Lang (Independent Reviewer). <attorneygeneral.jus.gov.on.ca/english/about/pubs/lang/>.

Oostveen, Joanne. n.d. "Began with a Group of Youth." *Chronicle Herald.* <http://thechronicleherald.ca/community/bedford-sackville/1186550-began-with-a-group-of-youth>.

Orkin, Aaron M., Morgan Lay, Janet McLaughlin, Michael Schwandt and Donald Cole. September 17, 2014. "Medical Repatriation of Migrant Farm Workers in Ontario: A Descriptive Analysis." *Canadian Medical Association Journal.* <cmajopen.ca/content/2/3/E192.full>.

Orleans News. July 25, 2013. "Inmates Abused at Ottawa Innes Jail: Report." *Ottawa Community News.* <ottawacommunitynews.com/news-story/3909012-inmates-abused-at-ottawa-innes-jail-report/>.

Otero, Gerardo, and Kerry Preibisch. 2015. *Citizenship and Precarious Labour in Canadian Agriculture.* Canadian Centre for Policy Alternatives.

Our Lives: Canadas First Black Women's Newspaper 1.4. 1986.

Oved, Marco Chown. August 20, 2014. "Canada Deports People to Wars, Repressive

Regimes." *Toronto Star*. <thestar.com/news/gta/2014/08/20/canada_deports_people_to_wars_repressive_regimes.html>.

Owusu-Bempah, Akwasi, and Scot Wortley. 2009. "Unequal before the Law: Immigrant and Racial Minority Perceptions of the Canadian Criminal Justice System." *Journal of International Migration and Integration* 10.4: 447–73.

———. 2011. "Crime and Justice: The Experiences of Black Canadians." In Barbara Perry (ed.), *Diversity, Crime, and Justice in Canada*. Oxford: Oxford University Press. 127–150.

———. 2014. "Race, Crime, and Criminal Justice in Canada." *Oxford Handbook of Ethnicity, Crime and Immigration*: 281–320.

Oxman-Martinez, Jacqueline, Jill Hanley et al. 2004. *Another Look at the Live-in-Caregivers Program: An Analysis of an Action Research Survey Conducted by PINAY, the Quebec Filipino Women's Association with the Centre for Applied Family Studies*. Montréal: Metropolis.

Palmater, Pamela. November 6, 2011. "Unbelievable, but Undeniable: Genocide in Canada." *Rabble.ca*. <rabble.ca/blogs/bloggers/pamela-palmater/2011/11/unbelievable-undeniable-genocide-canada>.

Palmer, Howard. 1982. *Patterns of Prejudice: A History of Nativism in Alberta*. Toronto: McClelland and Stewart.

Papp, Leslie. October 29, 1993. "Report's Tone Called Racist Mcleod Defends Welfare Document Accusing Somalis of 'Pillaging.'" *Toronto Star*: A13. *Canadian Newsstream*.

Pedwell, Terry. October 17, 2012. "Pregnant Woman's Treatment in Ottawa Jail Has Mothers Calling for Inquiry." *Globe and Mail*. <theglobeandmail.com/news/national/pregnant-womans-treatment-in-ottawa-jail has-mothers-calling-for-inquiry/article4619179/>.

Pegg, Shawn. 2004. *Disability, Culture and Service Engagement among Chinese, Somali and Tamil Communities in Toronto*. Toronto: Roeher Institute.

Perron, Louis-Samuel. March 3, 2017. "Cri Du Cœur D'une Mère À Bout De Ressources." *La Presse*. <http://plus.lapresse.ca/screens/cb9f1a97-5b50-4152-82b7-7439c81b0768%7C_0.html>.

Pivot Legal Society. 2013. "Throwing Away the Keys: The Human and Social Cost of Mandatory Minimum Sentences." Vancouver. <pivotlegal.org/throwing_away_the_keys_the_human_and>.

Pollack, Shoshana. 2006. "Therapeutic Programming as a Regulatory Practice in Women's Prisons." In Gillian Balfour and Elizabeth Comack (eds.), *Criminalizing Women: Gender and (in)Justice in Neo-Liberal Times*. Black Point, Winnipeg: Fernwood Publishing.

Polyani, Michael, Lesley Johnston, Anita Khanna, Said Dirie and michael kerr. 2014. "The Hidden Epidemic: A Report on Child and Family Poverty in Toronto." *Social Planning Toronto*. <socialplanningtoronto.org/the_hidden_epidemic_a_report_on_child_and_family_poverty_in_toronto>.

Pon, Gordon, Kevin Gosine and Doret Phillips. 2011. "Immediate Response: Addressing Anti-Native and Anti-Black Racism in Child Welfare." *International Journal of Child, Youth & Family Studies* 2.3/4.

Poteat, Tonia, Andrea L. Wirtz, Anita Radix, Annick Borquez, Alfonso Silva-Santisteban, Madeline B. Deutsch, Sharful Islan Khan, Sam Winter and Don Operario. 2015. "HIV Risk and Preventive Interventions in Transgender Women Sex Workers." *Lancet* 385.9964: 274–86.

Pratt, Anna. 2005. *Securing Borders: Detention and Deportation in Canada*. Vancouver:

University of British Columbia Press.

Pratt, Anna, and Mariana Valverde. 2002. "From Deserving Victims to 'Masters of Confusion': Redefining Refugees in the 1990s." *Canadian Journal of Sociology* 27.2 (Spring): 135–61.

Previl, Sean. January 9, 2017a. "Black in Halifax? You're Three Times More Likely to Undergo Police Check." *Global News*. <globalnews.ca/news/3169332/black-in-halifax-youre-three-times-more-likely-to-undergo-police-check/>.

———. January 11, 2017b. "Halifax RCMP Conduct Street Checks on Black People More Than Halifax Police." *Global News*. <globalnews.ca/news/3174730/halifax-rcmp-conduct-street-checks-on-black-people-more-than-halifax-police/>.

Price, Neil. February 22, 2017. "Why Nancy Elgie's Resignation Is No Victory for the Black Community." *Now Toronto*. <nowtoronto.com/news/nancy-elgie-resignation-no-victory-for-toronto-black-community/>.

Provincial Benchmarking Committee. 2001. *Review of Proposed Police Performance Measurements*. Toronto.

Public Health Agency of Canada. 2008. "Breaking the Links between Poverty and Violence against Women: A Resource Guide." *Public Health Agency of Canada*. <phac-aspc.gc.ca/sfv-avf/sources/fem/fem-breakinglinks-defaireliens/index-eng.php>.

———. 2008. National Clearinghouse on Family Violence.

Public Legal Education and Information Service of New Brunswick. 2007. *What Parents Should Know About Child Protection*. Fredricton.

Public Safety Canada: National Crime Prevention Centre. 2012. *A Statistical Snapshot of Youth at Risk and Youth Offending in Canada*. Ottawa.

Radio Canada International. July 12, 2016. "Black Drop-out Rate in Canada 'a National Disgrace': Professor Afua Cooper." <rcinet.ca/bhm-en/2015/01/30/english-black-drop-out-rate-in-canada-a-national-disgrace-professor-afua-cooper/>.

Rambally, Rae Tucker. 1995. "The Overrepresentation of Black Youth in the Quebec Social Service System: Issues and Perspectives" *Canadian Social Work Review* 12.1 (Winter): 85–97.

Rankin, Jim. August 7, 2012. "Toronto Police Tavis Stop of Four Teens Ends in Arrests, Captured on Video." *Toronto Star*. <thestar.com/news/gta/2012/08/07/toronto_police_tavis_stop_of_four_teens_ends_in_arrests_captured_on_video.html >.

Rankin, Jim, Kristin Rushowy and Louise Brown. March 22, 2013. "Toronto School Suspension Rates Highest for Black and Aboriginal Students." *Toronto Star*. <thestar.com/news/gta/2013/03/22/toronto_school_suspension_rates_highest_for_black_and_aboriginal_students.html>.

Rankin, Jim, and Sandro Contenta. June 6, 2009a. "Suspended Sentences: Forging a School-to-Prison Pipeline" *Toronto Star*. <thestar.com/news/gta/article/646629>.

———. June 7, 2009b. "Expulsion Class Gives Students Another Chance." *Toronto Star*. <thestar.com/news/gta/2009/06/07/expulsion_class_gives_students_another_chance.html>.

———. June 8, 2009c. "Are Schools Too Quick to Suspend?" *Toronto Star*. <thestar.com/news/gta/2009/06/08/are_schools_too_quick_to_suspend.html >.

Rankin, Jim and Patti Winsa. March 9, 2012. "Known to Police: Toronto Police Stop and Document Black and Brown People Far More Than Whites." *Toronto Star*. <thestar.

com/news/insight/2012/03/09/known_to_police_toronto_police_stop_and_
document_black_and_brown_people_far_more_than_whites.html>.

———. March 1, 2013. "Unequal Justice: Aboriginal and Black Inmates Disproportionately
Fill Ontario Jails." *Toronto Star*. <thestar.com/news/insight/2013/03/01/unequal_
justice_aboriginal_and_black_inmates_disproportionately_fill_ontario_jails.html>.

———. July 26, 2014. "Carding Drops but Proportion of Blacks Stopped by Toronto Police
Rises." *Toronto Star*. <thestar.com/news/insight/2014/07/26/carding_drops_but_
proportion_of_blacks_stopped_by_toronto_police_rises.html>.

Rapport de recherche soumis au ministère fédérale de la justice. 1994. *Étude Sur Les Violences
Envers Les Prostituées a Montréal*. Montréal.

Razack, Sherene. 2004. *Dark Threats and White Knights: The Somalia Affair, Peacekeeping,
and the New Imperialism*. Toronto: University of Toronto Press.

Razak, Sherene H. 2002. "Gendered and Racial Violence and Spatialized Justice: The Murder
of Pamela George." In Sherene H. Razak (ed.), *Race, Space and the Law: Unwrapping a
White Settler Society*. Toronto: Between the Lines: 121–56.

Reece, Rai. 2007. "Canadian Black Feminist Thought and Scholar-Activist Praxis." In
Notisha Massaquoi and Njoki Nathani Wane (eds.), *Theorizing Empowerment: Canadian
Perspectives on Black Feminist Thought*. Toronto: Inanna Publications and Education.
266–84.

Reece, Raimunda D. 2010. "Caged (No)Bodies: Exploring the Racialized and Gendered
Politics of Incarceration of Black Women in the Canadian Prison System." Dissertation,
York University.

Riddell, William Renwick. 1920. "Slavery in Canada." *Journal of Negro History* 5.3.

Riga, Andy. June 27, 2016. "Ex-Cops Dominate New Agency That Investigates
Police Shootings." *Montreal Gazette*. <montrealgazette.com/news/local-news/
ex-cops-dominate-new-body-that-investigates-police-shootings>.

Ritchie, Andrea J. 2006. "Law Enforcement Violence Against Women of Color." In Incite!
Women of Color Against Violence (ed.), *Color of Violence: The Incite! Anthology*. Boston:
South End Press. 138–56.

Ritchie, Andrea J. and Joey L. Mogul. December 2007. *In the Shadows of the War on Terror:
Persistent Police Brutality and Abuse of People of Color in the United States: A Report
Prepared for the United Nations Committee on the Elimination of Racial Discrimination
on the Occasion of its Review of the United States of America's Second and Third Periodic
Report to the Committee on the Elimination of Racial Discrimination*. United Nations
Human Rights Office of the High Commissioner. <http://www2.ohchr.org/english/
bodies/cerd/docs/ngos/usa/USHRN15.pdf>.

Ritchie, Andrea J., Joey L. Mogul and Kay Whitlock. 2011. *Queer (in)Justice: The
Criminalization of LGBT People in the United States*. Boston: Beacon Press.

Richie, Beth. 2012. *Arrested (in)Justice: Black Women, Violence, and America's Prison Nation*.
New York: New York University Press.

Roberts, Dorothy E. 1993. "Crime, Race and Reproduction." *Faculty Scholarship* 1383.

———. 1994. "Deviance, Resistance, and Love." *Faculty Scholarship* 1386.

———. 1995. "Punishing Drug Addicts Who Have Babies: Women of Color, Equality,
and the Right of Privacy" In Kimberlé Williams Crenshaw, et al. (eds.), *Critical Race
Theory: The Key Writings That Formed the Movement*. New York: The New Press. 384–426.

————. 2002. *Shattered Bonds: The Color of Child Welfare*. New York: Basic Civitas Books.

Robinson, Cedric J. 1983. *Black Marxism: The Making of the Black Radical Tradition*. London: Zed Press.

Robinson, Matthew B., and Renee G. Scherlen. 2014. *Lies, Damned Lies, and Drug War Statistics: A Critical Analysis of Claims Made by the Office of National Drug Control Policy*. Albany: State University of New York Press.

Robinson, Michael. February 15, 2016. "School Exclusions Can Give Special-Needs Students the Boot — Indefinitely." *Toronto Star*. <thestar.com/yourtoronto/education/2016/02/15/school-exclusions-can-give-special-needs-students-the-boot-indefinitely.html>.

Rodney, Walter. 1982. *How Europe Underdeveloped Africa*. Washington: Howard University Press.

Rodriguez, Dylan. 2007. "Forced Passages." In Joy James (ed.), *Warfare in the American Homeland: Policing and Prison in a Penal Democracy*. Durham: Duke University Press. 35–57.

Rowe, Roger. 2008. "Baker Revisited 2007." *Journal of Black Studies* 38.3: 338–45.

Rush, Curtis. March 2, 2012. "Toronto Police Shooting of Michael Eligon: A Timeline." *Toronto Star*. <thestar.com/news/crime/2012/03/02/toronto_police_shooting_of_michael_eligon_a_timeline.html>.

Rushforth, Brett. 2014. *Bonds of Alliance: Indigenous and Atlantic Slaveries in New France*. Project MUSE, Web ed. Chapel Hill: University of North Carolina Press.

Rushowy, Kristin. October 7, 2015. "End Streaming in Schools, Report to Toronto Trustees Recommends." *Toronto Star*. <thestar.com/yourtoronto/education/2015/10/07/end-streaming-in-schools-report-to-toronto-trustees-recommends.html>.

Rutland, Ted. Forthcoming. *Displacing Blackness: Planning, Power, and Race in Twentieth-Century Halifax*. Toronto: University of Toronto Press.

Ryan, Haley. May 26, 2016. "'It's Sad:' Data Shows Halifax's Black Students Suspended at Higher Rate." *Ottawa Metro*. <metronews.ca/news/halifax/2016/05/26/data-shows-halifax-black-students-suspended-at-higher-rate.html>.

Salole, Abigail T., and Zakaria Abdulle. 2015. "Quick to Punish: An Examination of the School to Prison Pipeline for Marginalized Youth." *Canadian Review of Social Policy* 72: 124–68.

Sangster, Joan. 2002. "Defining Sexual Promiscuity: 'Race,' Gender, and Class in the Operation of Ontario's Female Refuges Act, 1930–1960." In Wendy Chan and Kiran Mirchandani (eds.), *Crimes of Colour: Racialization and the Criminal Justice System in Canada*. Toronto: University of Toronto Press. 45–64.

Sapers, Howard. 2012. *Annual Report of the Office of the Correctional Investigator 2011–2012*. Ottawa.

————. 2013. *Annual Report of the Office of the Correctional Investigator 2012–2013*. Ottawa.

————. 2014. *A Case Study of Diversity in Corrections: The Black Inmate Experience in Federal Penitentiaries Final Report by the Office of the Correctional Investigator*. Ottawa.

————. 2015. *Annual Report of the Office of the Correctional Investigator, 2014–2015*. Ottawa.

Sayers, Naomi. December 28, 2013. "Canada's Anti-Prostitution Laws: A Method for Social Control." *Kwe Today*. <https://kwetoday.com/2013/12/28/canadas-anti-prostitution-laws-a-method-for-social-control/>.

Scheim A., M. Cherian, G. Bauer and X. Zong. April 22, 2013. "Joint Effort: Prison Experiences of Trans Pulse Participants and Recommendations for Change." *Trans Pulse e-Bulletin* 3.3.

Schumaker, Katherine. 2012. "An Exploration of the Relationship between Poverty and Child Neglect in Canadian Child Welfare." Dissertation. University of Toronto.

Sharma, Nandita. 2001. "On Being Not Canadian: The Social Organization of 'Migrant Workers' in Canada." *The Canadian Review of Sociology and Anthropology* 38.4: 415–39.

———. 2006. *Home Economics: Nationalism and the Making of 'Migrant Workers' in Canada.* Toronto: University of Toronto Press.

Sharpe, Christina. 2016. *In the Wake: On Blackness and Being.* Durham, London: Duke University Press.

Shepard, R. Bruce. 1997. *Deemed Unsuitable: Blacks from Oklahoma Move to the Canadian Prairies in Search of Equality in the Early 20th Century, Only to Find Racism in Their New Home.* Toronto: Umbrella Press.

Shields, Simon. 2016. "Welfare (Ontario Works) Law: Chapter 12 — Fraud and Prosecutions." <isthatlegal.ca/index.php?name=fraud.welfare_law_ontario>.

Shiva, Vandana. 1997. *Biopiracy: The Plunder of Nature and Knowledge.* E-resource ed. Toronto: Between the Lines.

Silvera, Makeda. 1989. *Silenced: Makeda Silvera Talks with Working Class West Indian Women About Their Lives and Struggles as Domestic Workers in Canada.* Toronto: Sister Vision Press.

Silverman, Jason H. 1985. *Unwelcome Guests: Canada West's Response to American Fugitive Slaves, 1800–1865.* Millwood: Associated Faculty Press.

Simpson, Audra. 2016a. "Whither Settler Colonialism?" *Settler Colonial Studies* 6.4: 438–445.

———. 2016b. "The State Is a Man: Theresa Spence, Loretta Saunders and the Gender of Settler Sovereignty." *Theory & Event* 19.4.

Sium, Aman. November 22, 2013. "'New World' Settler Colonialism: 'Killing Indians, Making Niggers.'" *Decolonization: Indigeneity, Education & Society.*

Small, Peter. March 1, 2013. "Murder Charge Thrown out against Toronto Police Officer." *Toronto Star.* <thestar.com/news/crime/2013/03/01/murder_charge_thrown_out_against_toronto_police_officer.html>

Smith, Andrea. 2005. *Conquest: Sexual Violence and American Indian Genocide.* Brooklyn: South End Press.

Smith, Malinda. 2006. *Beyond the 'African Tragedy': Discourses on Development and the Global Economy.* Aldershot: Ashgate Publisher.

Spade, Dean. 2011. *Normal Life: Administrative Violence, Critical Trans Politics, and the Limits of Law.* Brooklyn: South End Press.

Special Investigations Unit. July 15, 2016. "Siu Director Concludes Charges Unwarranted in Death of Immigration Detainee Case Number: 15-Ocd-118." Mississauga: Special Investigations Unit. <siu.on.ca/en/news_template.php?print=y&nrid=2697>.

Statistics Canada. 2007a. *The Haitian Community in Canada.*

———. 2007b. *The African Community in Canada.*

———. 2011. *Immigration and Ethnocultural Diversity in Canada.*

———. 2012. *Canada at a Glance: Population.*

————. 2013. *Immigration and Ethnocultural Diversity in Canada.*

Stevens, Alex, Heino Stöver and Cinzia Brentari. 2010. *Harm Reduction: Evidence, Impacts and Challenges.* Lisbon: European Monitoring Centre for Drugs and Drug Addiction.

Stiell, Bernatte and Kim England. 1997. "Domestic Distinctions: Constructing Difference among Paid Domestic Workers in Toronto." *Gender, Place & Culture: A Journal of Feminist Geography* 4.3339–60.

Sudbury, Julia. 2002. "Celling Black Bodies: Black Women in the Global Prison Industrial Complex." *Feminist Review* 70.1 (April): 57–74.

————. 2004a. "'Mules,' 'Yardies,' and Other Folk Devils: Mapping Cross-Border Imprisonment in Britain." In Julia Sudbury (ed.), *Global Lockdown: Race, Gender, and the Prison-Industrial Complex.* New York: Routledge. 167–184

————. 2004b. "From the Point of No Return to the Women's Prison: Writing Contemporary Spaces of Confinement into Diaspora Studies." *Canadian Woman Studies* 23.2: 154–63.

————. 2009. "Maroon Abolitionists: Black Gender-Oppressed Activists in the Anti-Prison Movement in the U.S. And Canada." *Meridians* 9.1: 1–29.

Sun Sentinel. September 19, 1993. "Police Leave Woman Naked." <articles.sun-sentinel.com/1993-09-19/news/9309190054_1_sexual-attack-jamaican-mccormack>.

————. September 23, 1993. "Jamaica Blasts Strip-Search." <articles.sun-sentinel.com/1993-09-23/news/9309220744_1_strip-searched-jamaican-busy-intersection>.

Swift, Karen. 1995. *Manufacturing 'Bad Mothers': A Critical Perspective on Child Neglect.* Toronto: University of Toronto Press.

Symons, Gladys L. 2002. "Police Constructions of Race and Gender in Street Gangs." In Wendy Chan and Kiran Mirchandani (eds.), *Crimes of Colour: Racialization and the Criminal Justice System in Canada.* Toronto: University of Toronto Press. 115–26.

Szekely, Reka, and Parvaneh Pessian. August 6, 2015a. "Parents Warn Black Youth Are Being Racially Profiled in Durham Schools." *Durham Region News.* <durhamregion.com/news-story/5787027-parents-warn-black-youth-are-being-racially-profiled-in-durham-schools/>.

————. August 6, 2015b. "Ontario Human Rights Tribunal Finds There Is a 'Racial Disparity' in Durham." *Durham Region News.* <durhamregion.com/community-story/5787114-ontario-human-rights-tribunal-finds-there-is-a-racial-disparity-in-durham/>.

Tanovich, David M. 2004. "E-Racing Racial Profiling." *Alberta Law Review* 41.4: 905–33.

————. 2006. *The Colour of Justice: Policing Race in Canada.* Toronto: Irwin Law.

————. 2011. "Gendered and Racialized Violence, Strip Searches, Sexual Assault and Abuse of Prosecutorial Power." *Criminal Reports* 79: 132–50.

Taylor, C., and T. Peter. 2011. *Every Class in Every School: The First National Climate Survey on Homophobia, Biphobia, and Transphobia in Canadian Schools. Executive Summary.* Toronto: Egale Canada Human Rights Trust.

Taylor, Wanda. 2015. *Nova Scotia Home for Colored Children: The Hurt, the Hope and the Healing.* Halifax: Nimbus Publishing.

Tettey, Wisdom J., and Korbla P. Puplampu. 2005. "Ethnicity and the Identity of African-Canadians: A Theoretical and Political Analysis. In Wisdom J. Tettey and Korbla P. Puplampu (eds.), *The African Diaspora in Canada: Negotiating Identity & Belonging.* Calgary: University of Calgary Press. 25–48.

Thobani, Sunera. 2007. *Exalted Subjects: Studies in the Making of Race and Nation in Canada.* Toronto: University of Toronto Press.

Thompson, Vincent Bakpetu. 1987. *The Making of the African Diaspora in the Americas, 1441–1900.* White Plains, New York: Longman.

Thomson, Aly. February 6, 2017. "Halifax Police Bow out of Pride Parade Amid 'National Debate.'" *Toronto Star.* <thestar.com/news/canada/2017/02/06/halifax-police-bow-out-of-pride-parade-amid-national-debate.html>.

Thomson, Colin A. 1979. *Blacks in Deep Snow: Black Pioneers in Canada.* Don Mills: J.M. Dent.

Thornhill, Esmeralda M. A. 2008. "So Seldom for Us, So Often against Us: Blacks and Law in Canada." *Journal of Black Studies* 38.3: 321–37.

Tony Wong, T. S. November 11, 1989. "Mothers Demand Answers." *Toronto Star.* <http://search.proquest.com.proxy3.library.mcgill.ca/docview/436066768?accountid=12339>.

Toronto Public Health. October 2013. *Racialization and Health Inequities in Toronto.* <toronto.ca/legdocs/mmis/2013/hl/bgrd/backgroundfile-62904.pdf>.

Toronto Star Editorial Board. February 6, 2017. "A 6-Year-Old Should Never Be Placed in Handcuffs." *Toronto Star.* <thestar.com/opinion/editorials/2017/02/06/a-6-year-old-should-never-be-placed-in-handcuffs-editorial.html>.

Toronto Sun. October 13, 2012. "'Unhygienic' prison conditions leads to less time for prisoner." <torontosun.com/2012/10/13/unhygienic-prison-conditions-leads-to-less-time-for-prisoner>.

TRC (Truth and Reconciliation Commission of Canada). 2015. "Honouring the Truth, Reconciling for the Future Summary of the Final Report of the Truth and Reconciliation Commission of Canada." Ottawa. <trc.ca/websites/trcinstitution/File/2015/Honouring_the_Truth_Reconciling_for_the_Future_July_23_2015.pdf>.

Trocmé, N. Della Knoke, and Cindy Blackstock. 2004. "Pathways to the Overrepresentation of Aboriginal Children in Canada's Child Welfare System." *Social Service Review* 78.4: 577–601.

Trocmé, Nico, Bruce MacLaurin, Barbara Fallon and Della Knoke. 2006. *Mesnmimk Wasatek: Catching a Drop of Light. Understanding the Overrepresentation of First Nations Children in Canada's Child Welfare System: An Analysis of the Canadian Incidence Study of Reported Child Abuse and Neglect (FNCIS-2003).* Ottawa: First Nations Child and Family Caring Society of Canada.

Trudeau, Justin. March 9, 2015. "Canadian Liberty and the Politics of Fear." *Liberal Party of Canada.* <liberal.ca/canadian-liberty-and-the-politics-of-fear/>.

Trudel, Marcel. 1960. *L'esclavage Au Canada Francais.* Quebec: Les presses de l'universite de Laval.

Tuck, Eve, and K. Wayne Yang. 2012. "Decolonization Is Not a Metaphor." *Decolonization: Indigeneity, Education & Society* 1.1 (2012): 1–40.

Tulloch, Headley. 1975. *Black Canadians: A Long Line of Fighters.* Toronto: NC Press.

Turner, James. May 17, 2013. "Drug Mule Cries as Judge Rejects Sob Story." *Winnipeg Sun.* <winnipegsun.com/2013/05/17/drug-mule-cries-as-judge-rejects-sob-story>.

"U.N. AIDS Guidance Note on HIV and Sex Work." 2009. Joint United Nations Programme on HIV/AIDS. <unaids.org/sites/default/files/sub_landing/

JC2306_UNAIDS-guidance-note-HIV-sex-work_en.pdf>

U.N. CESCR (United Nations Committee on Economic, Social and Cultural Rights). 2016. "Concluding Observations on the Sixth Periodic Report of Canada (Advance Unedited Version)." 2016. United Nations Human Rights Office of the High Commissioner. <http://tbinternet.ohchr.org/Treaties/CESCR/Shared%20Documents/CAN/E_C-12_CAN_CO_6_23228_E.pdf>

United Nations Committee on the Elimination of Racial Discrimination (CERD). 2012. *Consideration of Reports Submitted by States Parties under Article 9 of the Convention: Concluding Observations of the Committee on the Elimination of Racial Discrimination.* New York, Geneva.

Valverde, Mariana. 2008. "Racial Purity, Sexual Purity, and Immigration Policy." In Barrington Walker (ed.), *The History of Immigration and Racism in Canada: Essential Readings.* Toronto: Canada Scholars' Press. 175–88.

Vowel, Chelsea. 2016. *Indigenous Writes: A Guide to First Nations, Métis and Inuit Issues in Canada.* Winnipeg, Manitoba: High Water Press.

Walcott, Rinaldo. 2003. *Black Like Who? Writing Black Canada.* Toronto: Insomniac Press.

———. 2014. "The Problem of the Human: Black Ontologies and 'the Coloniality of Our Being.'" In Sabine Broeck and Carsten Junker (eds.), *Postcoloniality–Decoloniality–Black Critique: Joints and Fissures.* Frankfurt, New York: Campus Verlag.

Walia, Harsha. 2013. *Undoing Border Imperialism.* Oakland: AK Press/Institute for Anarchist Studies.

Walia, Harsha, and Omar Chu. 2015. *Never Home: Legislating Discrimination in Canadian Immigration.* Vancouver: No One Is Illegal.

Walia, Harsha, and Proma Tagore. 2012. "Prisoners of Passage: Immigrant Detention in Canada." In Jenna Loyd, Matt Mitchelson and Andrew Burridge (eds.), *Beyond Walls and Cages: Prisons, Borders, and Global Crisis.* Athens: University of Georgia Press. 74–90.

Walker, Barrington, ed. 2008. *The History of Immigration and Racism in Canada: Essential Readings.* Toronto: Canada Scholars' Press.

———. 2010. *Race on Trial: Black Defendants in Ontario's Criminal Courts, 1858–1958.* Toronto: Published for the Osgoode Society for Canadian Legal History by University of Toronto Press.

Walker, James St. G. 2008. "Land and Settlement in Nova Scotia." In Barrington Walker (ed.), *The History of Immigration and Racism in Canada: Essential Readings.* Toronto: Canadian Scholars' Press. 49–65.

Wallace, Kenyon. July 25, 2015. "Man Shot Dead in Entertainment District Wanted for First-Degree Murder." *Toronto Star.* <thestar.com/news/crime/2015/07/25/siu-investigating-shooting-in-entertainment-district.html>.

Ware, Syrus, Joan Rusza and Giselle Dias. 2012. "It Can't Be Fixed Because It's Not Broken: Racism and Disability in the Prison Industrial Complex." In Liat Ben-Moshe, Chris Chapman and Allison C. Carey (eds.), *Disability Incarcerated.* New York: Palgrave Macmillan. 163–84.

Wayne, Michael. 1995. "The Black Population of Canada West on the Eve of the American Civil War: A Reassessment Based on the Manuscript Census of 1861." *Histoire sociale/Social History* 28.56: 465–86.

Weese, Bryn. February 11, 2011. "Women's Shelters No Longer Off-Limits to Immigration

Officers." *Toronto Sun.* <torontosun.com/news/canada/2011/02/11/17234471.html>.

Wells, Josina N. 1986. "Shelter Whitewash." *Our Lives: Canada's First Black Women's Newspaper* 1.4.

Wente, Margaret. October 29, 2002. "Death, Guns and the Last Taboo." *Globe and Mail.* <theglobeandmail.com/news/national/death-guns-and-the-last-taboo/article757409/>.

Westoll, Nick. February 3, 2017. "Mother Upset after 6-Year-Old Daughter Handcuffed by Police at Mississauga School." *Global News.* <globalnews.ca/news/3224634/mother-upset-after-6-year-old-daughter-handcuffed-by-police-at-mississauga-school/>.

Whitfield, Harvey Amani. 2004. "African and New World African Immigration to Mainland Nova Scotia." *Journal of the Royal Nova Scotia Historical Society* 7 102.IX: 102–11.

———. 2006. *Blacks on the Border: The Black Refugees in British North America, 1815–1860.* Lebanon: University Press of New England.

———. 2010. "Slavery in English Nova Scotia, 1750–1810." *Journal of the Royal Nova Scotia Historical Society* 13.23-VIII.

Wilderson III, Frank B. 2010. *Red, White & Black: Cinema and the Structure of Us Antagonisms.* Durham and London: Duke University Press.

Williams, Alex (director). 2015. *The Pass System.*

Williams, Roosevelt. 1971. "Reactions: The Myth of the White 'Backlash.'" In Dennis Forsythe, (ed.), *Let the Niggers Burn: The Sir George Williams University Affair and Its Caribbean Aftermath.* Montréal: Black Rose Press. 141–43.

Wilson, Deborah. January 16, 1989. "Police at Loggerheads with Black Activist Organization." *Globe and Mail*: A12.

Wilton, Katherine. July 27, 2016. "Suspect in Police Shootout Remains in Critical Condition." *Montreal Gazette.* <http://montrealgazette.com/news/suspect-in-police-shootout-remains-in-critical-condition>.

Windsor Star. January 29, 1990. "Crippled by Police, Woman Vows to Walk."

Winks, Robin W. 1997. *Blacks in Canada: A History.* Montreal & Kingston, London, Chicago: McGill-Queen's University Press.

Wolfe, Patrick. 2007. "Settler Colonialism and the Elimination of the Native." *Journal of Genocide Research* 8.4 387–409.

Wong, Alia. February 8, 2016. "How School Suspensions Push Black Students Behind." *Atlantic.* <theatlantic.com/education/archive/2016/02/how-school-suspensions-push-black-students-behind/460305/>.

Wood, Marcus. 2000. *Blind Memory: Visual Representations of Slavery in England and America, 1780–1865.* New York: Routledge.

Woods, Allan. April 25, 2016. "A First Nations Cry for Help Gets Little Government Attention: Star Investigation." *Toronto Star.* <thestar.com/news/canada/2016/04/25/a-first-nations-cry-for-help-gets-little-government-attention-star-investigation.html>.

———. January 23, 2017. "Quebec Woman Suing over Solitary Confinement 'Hell.'" *Toronto Star.* <thestar.com/news/canada/2017/01/23/quebec-woman-suing-over-solitary-confinement-hell.html>.

World Health Organization. 2005. *Violence Against Sex Workers and HIV Prevention.* Information Bulletin Series, Number 3. <who.int/gender/documents/sexworkers.pdf>.

Wortley, Scot. 2006. *Police Use of Force in Ontario: An Examination of Data from the Special*

Investigations Unit, Final Report. Toronto: African Canadian Legal Clinic.

Wortley, Scot, and Julian Tanner. 2003. "Data, Denials and Confusion: The Racial Profiling Debate in Toronto." *Canadian Journal of Criminalogy and Criminal Justice* 45.3: 367–90.

Wun, Connie. 2015. "Against Captivity: Black Girls and School Discipline Policies in the Afterlife of Slavery." *Educational Policy* 30.1: 171–96.

Wynter, Sylvia. 1995. "1492: A New World View." In Vera Lawrence Hyatt and Rex Nettleford (eds.), *Race, Discourse, and the Origin of the Americas: A New World View.* Washington: Smithsonian Institution Press. 5–57.

———. 2003. "Unsettling the Coloniality of Being/Power/Truth/Freedom: Towards the Human, after Man, It's Overrepresentation—an Argument." *New Centennial Review* (Fall). 257–337.

Yee, Shirley J. 1997. "Finding a Place: Mary Ann Shadd Cary and the Dilemmas of Black Migration to Canada, 1850–1870." *Frontiers: A Journal of Women Studies* 18.3: 1–16.

Yesufu, Adenike O. 2005. "The Gender Dimensions of the Immigrant Experience: The Case of African-Canadian Women in Edmonton." In Wisdom J. Tettey and Korbla P. Puplampu (eds.), *The African Diaspora in Canada: Negotiating Identity & Belonging.* Calgary: University of Calgary Press. 133–48.

Yuen, Jenny. July 23, 2013. "Deporting Mom to Jamaica Lacks 'Common Sense': Lawyer." *Toronto Sun.* <torontosun.com/2013/07/23/move-to-deport-jamaican-mom-lacks-common-sense-lawyer>.

Abbott v. Toronto Police Services Board [2009]. Human Rights Tribunal of Ontario 2009.

Baker v. Canada (Minister of Citizenship and Immigration) [1999] 2 S.C.R. 817.

Bedford v. Canada [2010] ONSC 4264.

Faster Removal of Foreign Criminals Act S.C. 2013, C. 16.

R v. Hamilton [2003] CanLII 2862 Ontario Superior Court.

R v. Hamilton [2004] CanLII 5549 Court of Appeal for Ontario.

R v. Reid [2016] ONSC 954.

Nassiah v. Peel (Regional Municipality) Services Board [2007] Human Rights Tribunal of Ontario.

INDEX